How to Do *Everything* with

Microsoft Office

Outlook® 2007

About the Author

Bill Mann is the author of more than a dozen books on personal technology, along with numerous articles for various technology magazines, including *Computing Unplugged*, where he is a contributing editor. In addition to his writing, Bill develops and leads online courses on Outlook 2003 and Outlook 2007. During the day, Bill works as an engineering manager at the fastest growing private company in New Hampshire. When not working, he spends his time with his daughter or his friends.

About the Technical Editor

Will Kelly is a freelance technical writer and consultant living and working in the Washington, DC area. He was the technical editor of over 30 computer books about web development and Microsoft Office products between 1994 and 2004. This is his second project with Bill Mann. His articles about Small to Medium Enterprise and mobile computing topics appear regularly in *Processor Magazine* and *PC Today Magazine*. He rarely misses spinning class and the gym (even on the night before a deadline).

How to Do *Everything* with

Microsoft® Office Outlook® 2007

Bill Mann

New York   Chicago   San Francisco   Lisbon
London   Madrid   Mexico City   Milan   New Delhi
San Juan   Seoul   Singapore   Sydney   Toronto

The McGraw·Hill Companies

McGraw-Hill books are available at special quantity discounts to use as premiums and sales promotions, or for use in corporate training programs. For more information, please write to the Director of Special Sales, Professional Publishing, McGraw-Hill, Two Penn Plaza, New York, NY 10121-2298. Or contact your local bookstore.

How to Do Everything with Microsoft® Office Outlook® 2007

1234567890 CUS CUS 019876

ISBN-13: 978-0-07-226338-1
ISBN-10:   0-07-226338-5

Sponsoring Editor	**Copy Editor**	**Illustration**
Megg Morin	Bart Reed	International Typesetting and Composition
Editorial Supervisor	**Proofreader**	
Patty Mon	Megha Ghai	**Art Director, Cover**
Project Manager	**Indexer**	Jeff Weeks
Arushi Chawla	Steve Ingle	**Cover Designer**
Acquisitions Coordinator	**Production Supervisor**	Pattie Lee
Carly Stapleton	George Anderson	**Cover Illustration**
Technical Editor	**Composition**	Tom Willis
Will Kelly	International Typesetting and Composition	

This book is dedicated to Jenn,
who is growing up to be someone very special.

Contents at a Glance

Contents

Acknowledgments

My thanks go out to the team at McGraw-Hill/Osborne who were always pleasant, helpful, and supportive through this crazy, crazy project. Megg, it has been a pleasure to work with you on every project we've done together.

Will, as always, you go above and beyond the call of tech-editing duty. Your insights and feedback from a very different part of the real world have made this a stronger book.

Arushi and Bart, you've been great.

Last but not least, a heartfelt thank you to my agent Margot, who does the deals and handles all the other stuff so I can concentrate on my writing.

Introduction

It seems that every new version of Microsoft Office brings significant changes to Microsoft Outlook. The pattern holds with the 2007 Microsoft Office system. Outlook 2007, officially Microsoft Office Outlook 2007, is significantly different from its predecessor, Outlook 2003.

Outlook has long been a powerful e-mail program and personal information manager. And Outlook 2007 is even better. Not only does it do even better on the tasks it has always done, it gains several new features and capabilities that make it an ever more valuable tool. Some of the big changes in Outlook 2007 include:

- The Ribbon, a replacement for menus and toolbars in windows and views where you are likely to create, read, or edit a lot of text.

- Instant Search, a web-style search engine that replaces the old Find feature.

- Attachment previewing, which lets you peek inside an attached document without having to fully open it.

- RSS integration. Blogs and newsfeeds are popular new ways to get and share information online, and RSS feeds are one of the main ways you can read them. Outlook 2007 has an RSS feed reader built right into it, allowing you to work with these new tools as if they were mail messages.

- Electronic business cards. Make your contact information stand out by creating an electronic business card that Outlook can display.

Those are just some of the new and changed features of Outlook. Together, all the changes make it easier and faster to work with your e-mail, contacts, calendar, notes, and all the rest of your Outlook data.

This book is meant to be a practical guide to the most commonly used, and most useful features of Outlook. It isn't a comprehensive encyclopedia of all things Outlook—there are 1000+ page books written for people who need that kind of information. *How to Do Everything with Microsoft Office Outlook 2007* is meant for regular folks who need to, or want to use Outlook in their day-to-day life. You'll learn to set up, use, and maintain Outlook 2007. You'll learn one good way to do each thing (there are often several ways) you need to do, and perhaps a keyboard shortcut that will let you do something with a few keystrokes instead of a lot of scrolling and clicking with the mouse.

Perhaps you're wondering what qualifies me to teach you this kind of thing. Well, I've been using Outlook since the beginning, and writing about it for years. I've written several Outlook-related articles over the years, along with *How to Do Everything with Microsoft Office Outlook 2003*, the predecessor to the book you hold in your hands now.

But most important, I've taught 2000+ students about Outlook through my introductory online courses in Outlook 2000, Outlook XP (also known as Outlook 2002), and Outlook 2003. By the time you read this, my Outlook 2007 course could be online as well. These courses have helped busy people like you learn about Outlook online, using course material I created, online testing tools, and online discussion areas where the students can ask me and each other Outlook-related questions.

Through these courses, I've learned a lot about how best to present the material, and which things give users the most problems. I used this information to help me design this book, including the topics and procedures that my students have had the most questions about. I think you'll find that your most common questions are answered between these pages too.

In support of this book and my courses, I've created the Living With Outlook website (www.living-with-outlook.com), where I write about the kinds of Outlook tips and tricks that normally don't make it into a book like this. It's also the place where I can get you the latest news and information about Outlook. In Chapter 5 of this book, you'll learn how to subscribe to an RSS feed by subscribing to the Living With Outlook feed, which will keep you informed whenever I add new information to the site. I think you'll find this a great resource.

Parts of the Book

In Part I, you'll get a more in-depth introduction to Outlook 2007, then set it up and do basic configuration so you can start putting Outlook to work for you.

In Part II, you'll learn how to take advantage of Outlook's communication capabilities. E-mail, RSS feeds, instant messaging integration, even a bit about newsgroups will show you how to get Outlook talking to the rest of the world.

The book's Special Project walks you through the steps needed to connect Outlook 2007 to a Gmail or Hotmail e-mail account.

TIP	*My Living With Outlook website provides information on connecting some other types of e-mail accounts to Outlook, including AOL and Yahoo! Mail.*

In Part III, we shift the focus to managing your personal information. From Outlook's Calendar, Tasks, Notes, and To-Do, to the Shortcuts pane and the Journal, when you finish this part of the book, you'll be able to use them all.

In Part IV, you'll learn about customizing and managing Outlook. You'll learn how to create regular Outlook folders, custom views, and Search Folders, along with how to customize the Outlook user interface to better suit your own working style. And you'll learn about the security features that help to protect Outlook from creeps who want to do it (and thereby you) harm.

In Part V, you'll go even further. You'll literally go further as we talk about ways to mobilize your Outlook data. Then you'll learn about integrating Outlook 2007 with other Office 2007 applications, as well as get a quick introduction to using Outlook with Microsoft Exchange Server 2007 and Windows SharePoint Services 3.0.

The appendixes cover a selection of particularly useful keyboard shortcuts, along with a set of maintenance activities you can do to keep Outlook running its best.

In short, there's a bunch of useful and interesting stuff in every part of this book.

Design Elements

As I hope you can already tell, I've tried to write this book in a casual, easy-to-read style for you. It's designed, to a large extent, so that each chapter stands alone and you can dig in where you want to learn about the specific topics that are most important to you. That said, you can certainly read the book cover-to-cover, and should definitely at least read the introduction to each chapter to get a feel for whether or not you want to read the rest of that chapter.

To make this book even more useful to you, I've included several specific design elements:

- ■ **How To sidebars**   How To sidebars provide step-by-step instructions on completing a specific task.

- ■ **Did You Know sidebars**   Did You Know sidebars contain extra information. They're usually background info such as historical notes or other interesting tidbits.

- ■ **Note icons** Note icons provide helpful information related to the topic at hand. Be sure to read any Notes you come across.

- ■ **Tip icons** Tip icons describe ways to make better use of a specific feature of Outlook, or provide keyboard shortcuts that can speed up whatever it is you are doing at the time.

- ■ **Caution icons** Caution icons flag issues you need to be aware of. You should definitely read these to avoid potential problems.

Now that we have all the preliminary stuff out of the way, it's time to dig into Outlook 2007. If you have any thoughts on the book, or about Outlook 2007 in general, I would love to hear from you. You can reach me by e-mail at Outlook2007@techforyou.com, or visit my website (http://www.living-with-outlook.com) and use the Feedback form.

Thank you, and enjoy *How to Do Everything with Microsoft Office Outlook 2007*.

Part I

Get Acquainted with Microsoft Office Outlook 2007

Chapter 1

Meet Microsoft Office Outlook 2007

How to...

- Navigate the New User Interface
- Use Other New Features and Capabilities
- Deal with What Isn't There Anymore
- Take Advantage of Some Common Keyboard Shortcuts
- Use the Help Systems

Microsoft Office Outlook 2007 (formerly known as Outlook 12) is part of the 2007 Microsoft Office system (a.k.a. Office 2007). Office 2007 is available in many different forms, and Outlook is part of all of those, except the least expensive two. In Office 2007, Outlook received the significant user interface redesign that the rest of the Office suite got, along with a number of unique changes meant to make it easier to use and better adapted to the ways we communicate and manage information today.

This chapter is a quick guide to many of the new and improved features of Outlook, as well as those features that have been removed in the new Outlook. To round out the chapter, you'll learn about the redesigned user interface and how to get help if you get stuck.

Navigate the New User Interface

The new Outlook user interface is a bit schizophrenic, but in a good way. Figure 1-1 shows the Outlook user interface in the Mail view. Except for the To-Do Bar running down the right side of the window (more on that in a bit), this looks pretty much the way Outlook 2003 would if you were running it in Windows Vista.

Now take a look at the New Message window in Figure 1-2. The menus and toolbars that used to be here have been replaced by the Ribbon. This change is meant to make it easier to find the mot commonly used options for creating or editing. Wherever you will be doing a lot of writing or editing of text, the Ribbon is there to make it easier and faster for you.

Do you see what I mean about the interface being schizophrenic? It's one style here, another style there. It can be a bit confusing at first, but it is a good thing in the end. The interface adapts itself to what you are doing. And as you will see later, the Ribbon also adapts itself to what you are doing. If you are someone who has memorized lots of keyboard shortcuts, or have the structure of the old-style menus

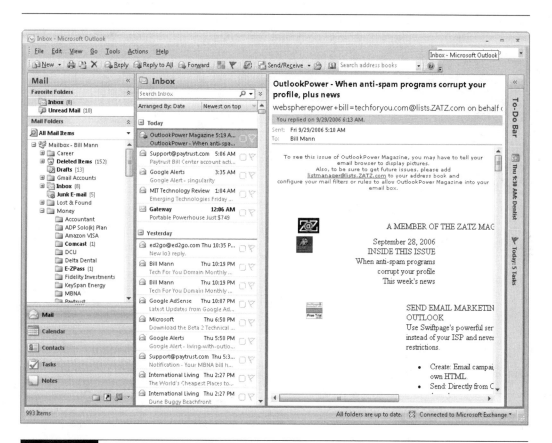

Inbox - Microsoft Outlook

FIGURE 1-1   The Outlook 2007 Mail view.

and toolbars fixed in your mind, you will have some relearning to do. If you aren't that proficient and efficient with Outlook, you will likely find that the redesigned user interface is an improvement.

Either way, you need to get used to the new user interface. Outlook 2007 doesn't give you the option to continue using the old style.

Getting Around and Switching Sections

While Chapter 4 goes into detail on navigating the Mail view specifically, we can use this view to get a quick overview of the user interface.

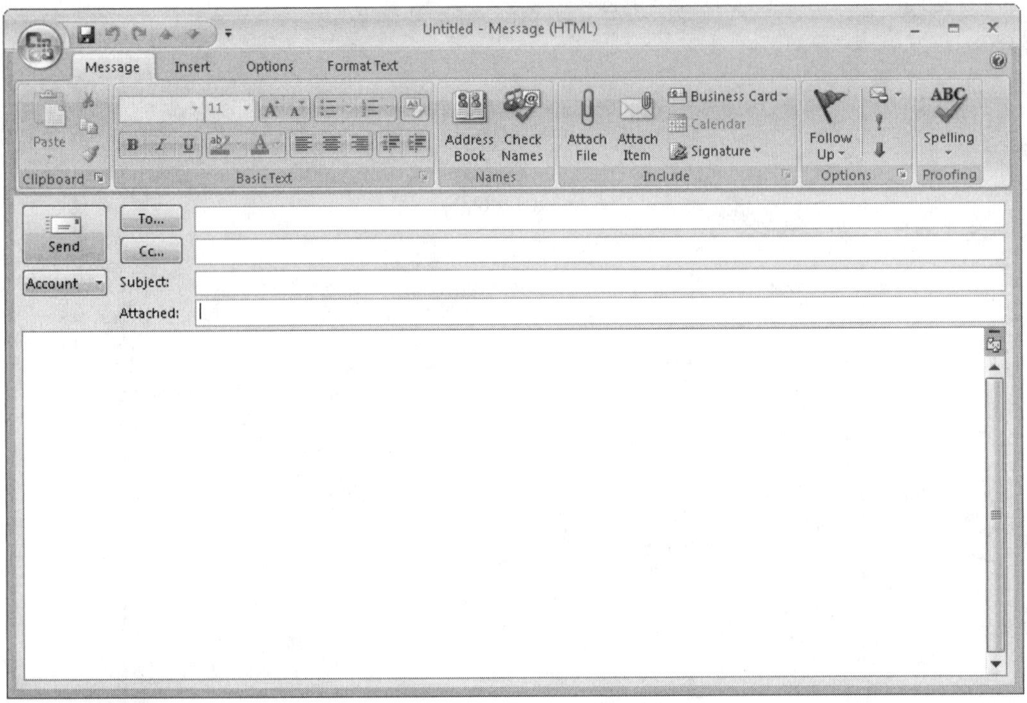

FIGURE 1-2 A New Message window showing the Ribbon user interface.

The bulk of the Outlook window is divided into two or more columns and remains unchanged from Outlook 2003. The leftmost column (shown in Figure 1-3) is the *Navigation pane.* The Navigation pane handles the functions of the Outlook bar and the Folder List you may have used in early versions of Outlook. In addition to these, the Navigation pane displays folders and other information relevant to a specific view.

The content and even the title of the Navigation pane automatically change to match the view you're working in. The main Outlook sections—Mail, Calendar, Contacts, Tasks, Notes, and Journal—each have their own highly customizable view. Changing between sections is as easy as clicking the large buttons at the bottom of the Navigation pane, selecting a destination from the Go menu, or using simple keyboard shortcuts.

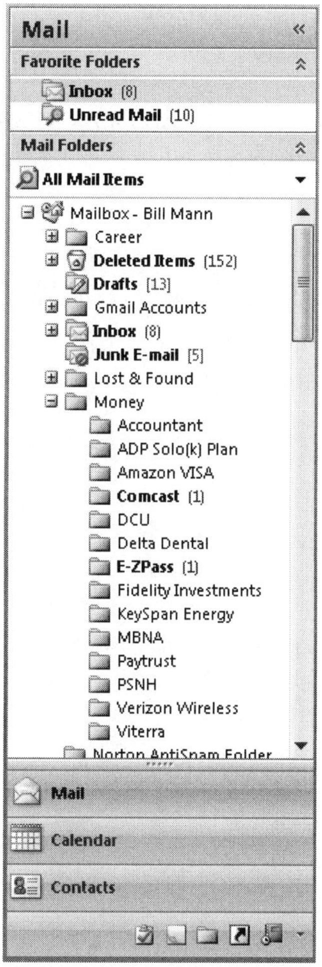

FIGURE 1-3   The Navigation pane lets you move around Outlook quickly.

Next comes a list of the messages that are in the e-mail folder selected in the Navigation pane. This pane works great for this particular Mail view, but doesn't appear in other views where it wouldn't make sense.

Further to the right you find the *Reading pane*. This is a vertically oriented area where you can read messages like you were reading a column of text from a newspaper or magazine, without having to open a message in a new window.

Finally comes the To-Do Bar, which is described in detail in Chapter 8. Each view has its own distinct look, but the goal is always the same: to let you make the best use possible of the information Outlook contains.

NOTE *Chapter 4 provides complete information on Mail view, the Reading pane, and other interface enhancements that make working with Outlook 2007 a superior experience.*

Use Other New Features and Capabilities

Aside from a new user interface, Outlook 2007 has numerous additional improvements and new features. The following sections discuss some of the major ones.

Instant Search (New)

Instant Search replaces the Search and Advanced Search features of previous versions of Outlook. Instant Search relies on indexing the contents of Outlook items and is extremely fast. It is so fast, in fact, that as you type the characters of the word or phrase you want to search for, Instant Search displays the items that contain those characters. Aside from being pretty cool, this is quite useful, since you can stop typing your search as soon as the item you are looking for appears. Compare this to the old approach of typing in your entire search word or phrase, clicking Find Now, and waiting to see what shows up. By default, Instant Search is always available in these views:

- Calendar
- Contacts
- Folder List
- Journal
- Mail
- Tasks

The Instant Search box integrates itself smoothly into each view. It looks like it belongs (see Figure 1-4), and it is that much quicker to do a search when the box is right there on the screen for you.

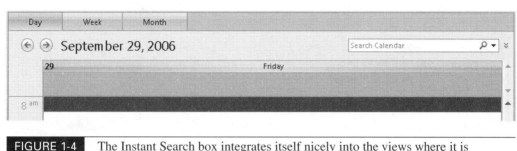

FIGURE 1-4   The Instant Search box integrates itself nicely into the views where it is available.

NOTE   *Chapter 13 covers Instant Search in detail.*

Attachment Previewing (New)

Outlook 2003 lets you preview messages without opening them. Outlook 2007 lets you preview attachments to those messages. Say that Sally sends you a message with an Excel spreadsheet and you don't want to do anything with it right now, beyond figuring out whether it is the one for the Johnson project or the one for the Smith project. With attachment previewing, you can take a quick look at the spreadsheet without having to open Excel and load the whole thing.

Right out of the box, Attachment Preview works with attached Microsoft Office documents. Despite a few little quirks you need to be aware of, Attachment Preview can definitely add some speed and convenience to your life with Outlook.

NOTE   *Chapter 3 provides more information on previewing attachments.*

Enhanced Calendar Capabilities (New)

The Calendar got a significant reworking in this release of Outlook. It is easier than ever to share calendar information with others and to work with multiple calendars simultaneously. Internet calendars are, not surprisingly, calendars published on the Internet. Outlook 2007 lets you view Internet calendars published by others, or publish your own Internet calendars. For even quicker results, you can publish Calendar Snapshots to the Microsoft Office Online website.

I like the ways you can view multiple calendars simultaneously. Side-by-side calendars are useful—overlaid calendars are even more so. If you keep separate

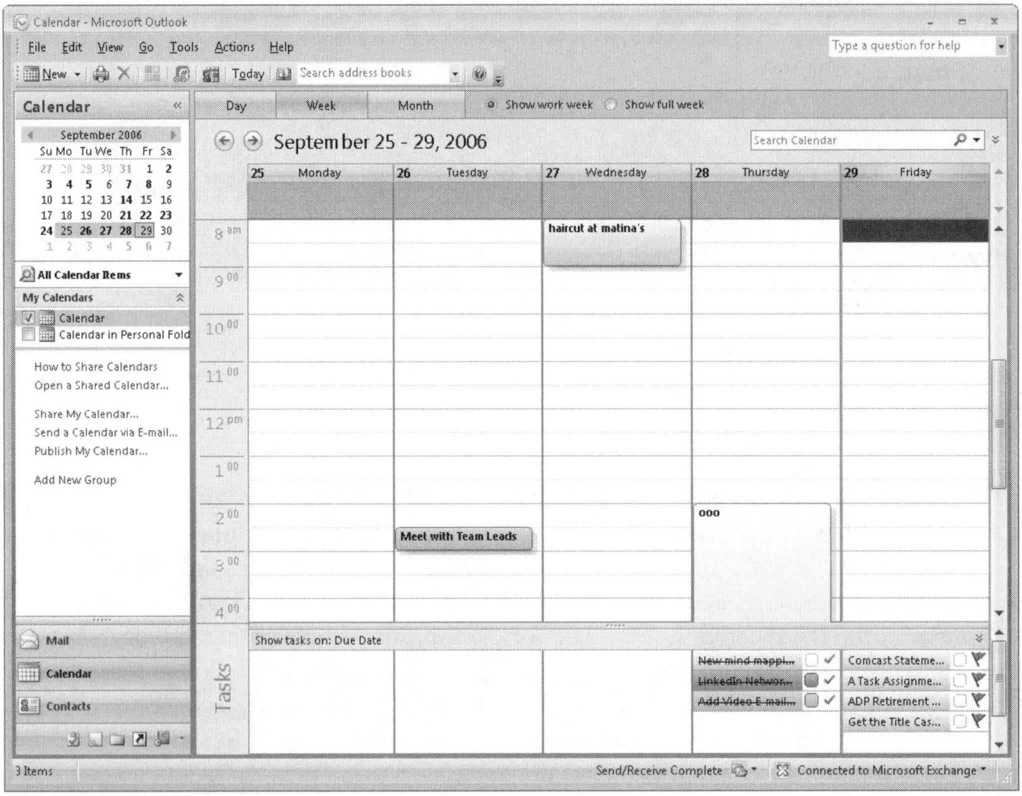

FIGURE 1-5   The Calendar got a lot of enhancements in Outlook 2007.

business and personal calendars, viewing them overlaid is so convenient. You can see your whole schedule in one spot instantly. Figure 1-5 shows some of the new features of the Calendar view, including my overlaid calendars.

Another useful addition to the Calendar is task integration. If you've ever blocked out a chunk of time on the Calendar to work on a particular task, you'll love this one. Tasks automatically appear below the Calendar on the day they are scheduled to be done. You can drag them from there right into the Calendar itself and block out the time to complete them in seconds.

NOTE   *Chapter 7 is dedicated to the Calendar.*

RSS Integration (New)

Once upon a time Usenet newsgroups were the "in" way to publish information on the Internet. Today, blogs and syndicated newsfeeds are the way to get the word out. The technology of choice for distributing this information is through RSS (Really Simple Syndication) feeds. Outlook 2007 has the ability to receive RSS feeds, and treats them as if they were just another form of e-mail. That means you can read them, flag them, color code them, and apply rules to them just like regular e-mail messages.

To make using RSS even easier, Outlook includes a directory of useful RSS feeds that you can subscribe to with only a few clicks.

NOTE   *Everything you need to know to make RSS feeds a part of your Outlook lifestyle appears in Chapter 5.*

Electronic Business Cards (New)

Outlook XP and 2003 have address cards. Outlook 2007 has electronic business cards. These are electronic versions of the classic business cards people have been handing out since, well, forever. They're a graphical way to present your contact information to someone, and can include logos, even photos. Figure 1-6 shows an example.

You can hand out electronic business cards as attachments to messages or place them in your e-mail signature. The Business Cards view replaces the Address Cards view of previous Outlook versions.

NOTE   *Chapter 6 has all the information you could want about electronic business cards.*

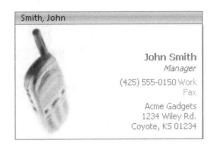

FIGURE 1-6   Electronic business cards can help you get noticed.

Outlook E-mail Postmarks (New)

Have you ever received any junk e-mail messages in Outlook? I thought so. Outlook E-mail Postmarks are an attempt by Microsoft to reduce the amount of junk that makes it into our Inbox. Outlook's junk e-mail filtering system can check messages for valid postmarks, and use that information to help decide whether a message is junk or something you might actually want.

> NOTE   *If you want to learn more about how Outlook E-mail Postmarks might cut some of your junk mail (or how you manage this unusual feature), turn to Chapter 14.*

The Trust Center (New)

The Outlook E-mail Postmarks you just read about are unusual not only in what they do, but in the fact that they are not controlled from the Trust Center, a one-stop control center for security and privacy-related features. From managing add-ins to warning you of suspicious activity by other programs, the Trust Center (shown in Figure 1-7) is the first place to look when you want to manage Outlook security and privacy.

> NOTE   *The Trust Center is featured in Chapter 14.*

Reworked Search Folders (Improved)

Search folders are virtual folders that address the problem of what to do with messages that pertain to more than one subject. One message can appear in many search folders without your having to move or copy it. Outlook 2003 came with four predefined search folders (For Follow Up, Important E-mail, Large E-mail, and Unread E-mail). In Outlook 2007, the changes to the way messages are flagged and color-coded mean some new options for search folders.

> NOTE   *Outlook 2007's improved ability to flag and categorize items (the color categories described next) has made this already valuable feature even more powerful. See Chapter 10 for the details.*

Color Categories (Improved)

In Outlook 2003, you could apply colors to things like Calendar appointments. The splashes of color made it a lot easier to pick out specific appointments in

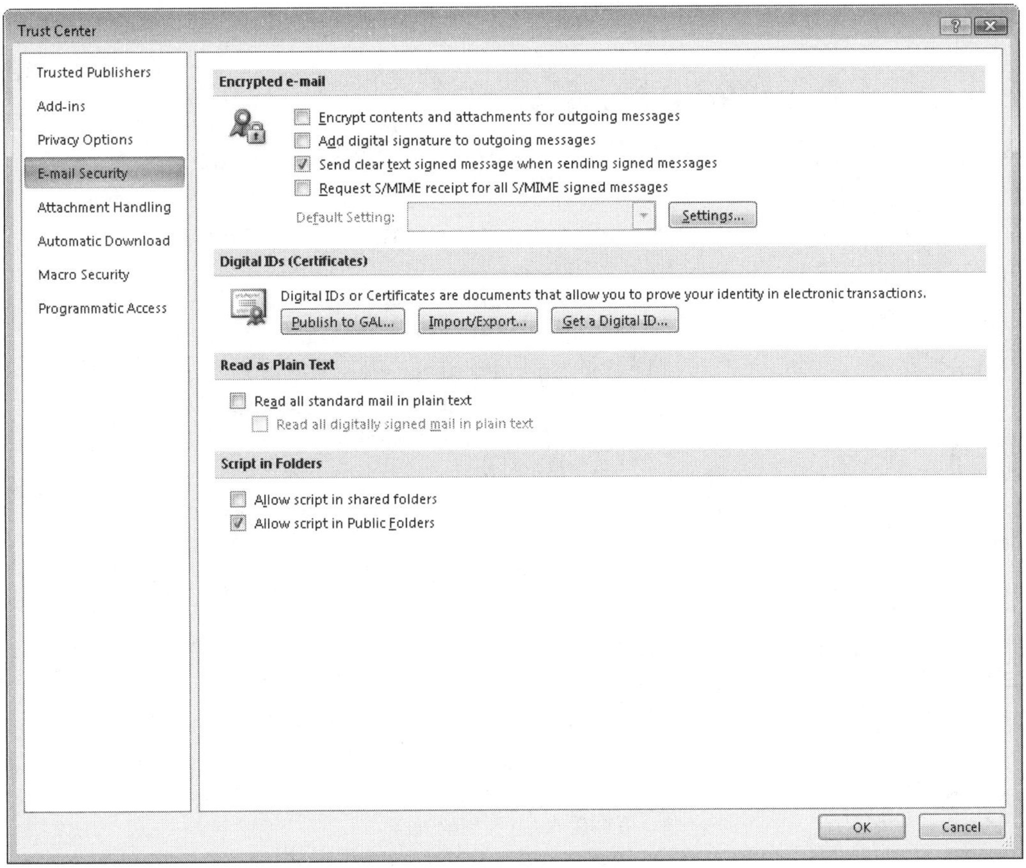

FIGURE 1-7   You manage most Outlook security features in the Trust Center.

your crowded days. Outlook 2007 color categories take this basic concept, and really run with it. Now you can apply color categories to any Outlook item. Assign a descriptive name to a color, then apply that color category to any related item. Going to Ireland in the Spring? Create a bright green color category named Eire, and apply it to every message, appointment, and task related to your trip. You'll always be able to keep track of anything to do with your big trip to the Emerald Isle.

Outlook 2007 rules and search folders understand color categories too. That means you can apply rules for handling all those trip-related items, or create a search folder that only shows stuff related to the trip.

NOTE *Chapter 4 is the place to go to learn how you can use color categories to track and manage your own special projects and plans.*

Enhanced SharePoint Services and Exchange Server Integration (Improved)

In the corporate world, Outlook is often hooked up to Windows SharePoint Services and a Microsoft Exchange Server. Outlook 2007 can integrate itself with them even more effectively than Outlook 2003 could.

When it comes to SharePoint Services, Outlook 2007 lets you work with shared calendars, contacts, and tasks whether you are connected or not. Any changes you make get synchronized to SharePoint Services the next time you are connected. Similarly, any updates that have taken place since you were last connected flow back to Outlook so you can stay up to date. Outlook 2007 also can store copies of documents from a SharePoint site in their own Outlook folders, letting you work with them on- or offline, then synchronize any changes the next time you are connected.

As with previous versions of Outlook, while many Outlook 2007 features work independently, others require a connection to a Microsoft Exchange Server. These are addressed in the relevant chapters. However, when Exchange 2007 and Outlook 2007 play together, you also get new or greatly enhanced features, such as unified messaging. Unified messaging means things like getting faxes and voice mails delivered to your Inbox.

NOTE *Chapter 17 looks specifically at ways Outlook 2007 interacts with SharePoint Services and Microsoft Exchange Server 2007.*

Enhanced Information Rights Management (IRM) (Improved)

Information Rights Management (IRM) is for when you are serious about getting control over your information. You can use IRM to enforce rules on who gets to see what information and what they can do with it. IRM technology is built into all Office 2007 products, including Outlook, where it controls things like whether you can forward a message you receive.

NOTE *I've put IRM-related information in Chapter 14. And the rules of this book say that anyone* can *read it.*

Deal with What Isn't There Anymore

If you've been using Outlook 2003, you will find that Outlook 2007 has a lot of new features, but no longer has some features you may have relied on in the past. Here I'm going to fill you in on features that are no longer supported in Outlook 2007, and ways you can work around their elimination.

No More Native Outlook E-Mail Editor

Previous versions of Outlook came with a built-in editor you could use for e-mail messages. No more. Now you *must* use Microsoft Office Word 2007 as your e-mail editor. Thoughtfully, Microsoft includes with Outlook 2007, some software that provides the basic Word 2007 capabilities on computers that have Outlook 2007 but not Word 2007. You can't use it to work on Word documents or anything like that. But you can use it to edit Outlook items with the same commands you would use in Word.

No More NetMeeting

Microsoft has discontinued support for NetMeeting, Microsoft Exchange Conferencing, and Microsoft Windows Media Services. What can you do if you relied on any of these services? Microsoft recommends switching to Office Live Meeting (see Figure 1-8).

Office Live Meeting has lots of capabilities. It also has a flexible pricing plan, with fixed monthly charges for five or ten seats, and a pay-per-use plan running $0.35 per minute per participant. Office Live Meeting, and Office Live as a whole, is still in beta at the time of this writing. If you are interested in Office Live Meeting, I suggest you go to the Office Live Meeting home page for the latest information. Visit http://office.microsoft.com/en-us/FX010909711033.aspx.

The End of the Personal Address Book

Outlook 2007 doesn't support the Personal Address Book. When you install Outlook 2007, it imports contacts from the Personal Address Book and stores them in the default Outlook Contacts folder, or a destination of your choice.

Okay, I exaggerated a bit. The Personal Address Book doesn't really go away when you install Outlook 2007. It's just that after importing contacts from the Personal Address Book, Outlook 2007 ignores it. Working around this shouldn't be a big deal, since your contacts get imported.

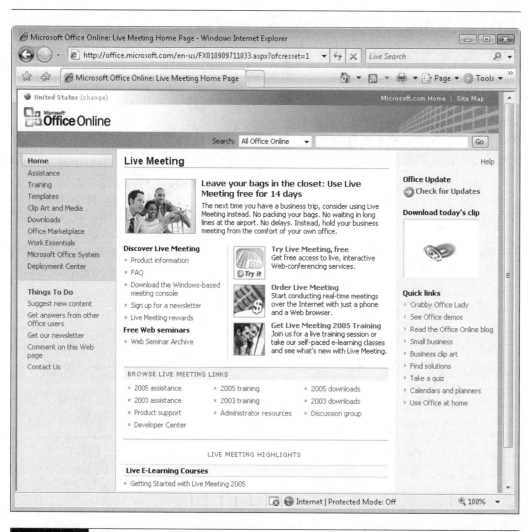

FIGURE 1-8 Microsoft Office Live Meeting replaces NetMeeting and similar services.

Farewell, Oh TaskPad

I found the TaskPad to be one of the more useful features of Outlook 2003. The TaskPad has bowed out of Outlook 2007, but this is actually a good thing. The TaskPad has been replaced by the To-Do Bar, which is even more useful. I don't think we'll miss the TaskPad at all.

For Follow Up Flags Are Permanently Lowered

For Follow Up flags were a way to keep track of messages that needed future attention. I used them a lot, but not very efficiently. Now they're gone, replaced by the task flags and color categories of Outlook 2007. In other words, they've been absorbed into a more general, flexible, and colorful way of keeping track of stuff. The big issue in working around this change is the question of what happens to all the messages you have flagged For Follow Up when it's time to upgrade to Outlook 2007.

The answer is that you need to put some work into the transition. Your existing For Follow Up items appear in an Outlook 2007 search folder called, appropriately enough, For Follow Up. So you don't lose them. But they don't really fit into the Outlook 2007 way of handling things either. You should evaluate each item in the For Follow Up folder, and assign them to the appropriate color category. Depending on how many items you had marked when you made the switch, this could take a while, but you only need to do it once. Besides, putting in the effort up front will mean that you don't have to deal with two different ways of tracking items within the same program.

All Signatures Get Created in One Place

In my Outlook 2003 classes, people frequently had problems with e-mail signatures. When you used Word as your e-mail editor, you created signatures with one tool. When you used the built-in editor, you created signatures a different way. Worse, signatures created with one editor weren't available for use with the other editor.

That problem has gone away in Outlook 2007. Since it only supports Word 2007 as its e-mail editor, you can only create Outlook 2007 e-mail signatures using Word 2007. This shouldn't be a problem for you, unless you've created signatures using the built-in editor from earlier versions of Outlook. In this case, you will have to re-create those signatures.

Detect and Repair Is Undetectable

The Detect and Repair feature that was part of Office 2003 is gone, replaced by Microsoft Office Diagnostics. I hope Outlook 2007 (or Office 2007 for that matter) never gets so broken that you need to use this feature. A few of my thousand-plus students have needed it, so it's good to know this feature is available.

NOTE   *See Appendix B for information on how to keep your copy of Outlook running its best, including how to use Microsoft Office Diagnostics if things go badly wrong.*

Various other (generally more minor) features and functions have been dropped from Outlook 2007. If you would like to see a complete list, you can search the Outlook help system for the word "discontinued." You'll see how to use the Outlook 2007 help systems at the end of this chapter, but first, let's talk about some common keyboard shortcuts that can make it faster and easier to do many things in Outlook 2007, including opening the help system so you can search for discontinued features and functions.

Take Advantage of Some Common Keyboard Shortcuts

Keyboard shortcuts provide an easy way to navigate the Outlook interface. Keyboard shortcuts are combinations of keystrokes that perform some function that would otherwise require a mouse click, a series of clicks, or even navigating menus or dialog boxes. Memorizing and using keyboard shortcuts can really speed things up when you work with Outlook 2007. You can enter a keyboard shortcut in a fraction of the time it takes to move the mouse and click something. You save even more time when you have to move your hand off the keyboard to reach the mouse. The seconds you save with keyboard shortcuts add up over the course of a day. It's a small improvement but a real one.

NOTE *If you learned the keyboard shortcuts in Outlook 2003, you are in luck. The new Outlook 2007 user interface brings with it new keyboard shortcuts, but still supports the old ones.*

Some keyboard shortcuts that you will find particularly useful when navigating the Outlook 2007 user interface are:

- The TAB key and arrow keys let you navigate a dialog box.

- CTRL-TAB moves through the tabbed pages of a dialog box.

- The ENTER key activates the command that the focus is on. You can tell which command has the focus because it will be highlighted, or its name will be surrounded by a box made of dotted lines.

- The SPACEBAR sets or clears the selected check box.

- SHIFT-F10 opens the shortcut menu related to the selected item. This is the same menu you get if you right-click the item.

- ALT-F4 closes the active window.

- F1 opens the Help window.

- CTRL-1 opens the Mail view.

- CTRL-2 opens the Calendar view.

- CTRL-3 opens the Contacts view.

- CTRL-4 opens the Tasks view.

- CTRL-5 opens the Notes view.

- CTRL-6 opens the Folder List in the Navigation pane.

- CTRL-7 opens the Shortcuts list in the Navigation pane.

One thing that will take getting used to is the way keyboard shortcuts work with the Ribbon. When the Ribbon is on the screen, you press and release the ALT key, followed by one or more additional keys to execute keyboard shortcuts. However, you can also just press the ALT key to see what are called *Key Tip badges*. These badges appear on the commands, and contain the keys you press (along with the ALT key) to execute the command. Figure 1-9 shows what this looks like.

When you are working in a dialog box that has a Ribbon with multiple tabbed pages, the first key after the ALT key selects the tabbed page in the Ribbon, and the remaining keys select the particular command on that page. One example is the command to center a paragraph while editing a message. To enter it, you press and release the ALT key, then you press and release the H key, the A key, and the C key.

NOTE   *You can find a much more extensive list of Outlook keyboard shortcuts in Appendix A, along with a detailed explanation of how Key Tips work. You will also find the keyboard shortcuts for specific actions listed where the action itself appears in the book.*

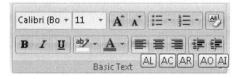

FIGURE 1-9   Key Tip badges help you learn the Ribbon keyboard shortcuts.

Use the Help System

While this book gives you the information you need to use Outlook 2007 as it originally shipped, programs like Outlook don't remain unchanged over their lives. Because Microsoft can modify Outlook through Service Packs and patches, the program will change over time, at least a little. Besides, the chances are decent that over the years if you use Outlook 2007, you will come up with a question or two that this book doesn't answer. So knowing how to use the Outlook help system will be important to you. Please take a few minutes to read this section of the chapter and familiarize yourself with the redesigned help system found in Outlook 2007 and other Microsoft Office Outlook 2007 products.

In Office 2007, Microsoft has combined the various older help systems into one unified system, displayed in the Help Viewer, and tied directly into Microsoft Office Online. The Help Viewer replaces the Help window, Office Assistants, and so on with the clean two-pane window shown in Figure 1-10. Clicking the Microsoft Office Outlook Help option in the Help menu takes you directly to the Help Viewer, as does pressing the F1 key.

The Type a Question for Help box that appears in the upper-right corner of the Outlook window takes you to the Help Viewer, where it displays a list of topics that match the question you typed.

Navigating the Help Viewer

The Help Viewer works a lot like your web browser. The toolbar has a set of browser-like buttons you can use to navigate as if the help system were a website. This makes sense, since the information in the help system comes mainly from the Office Online website. Outlook 2007 does come with a help system when you first install it, but it checks Office Online for the most current information and displays it.

The Help Viewer is a single location for all your Outlook help needs.

Most of the buttons in the toolbar will be clear to you if you've used a web browser, but a few merit short explanations:

- The Home button looks like a house, and takes you to the home page of the help system on Office Online.

- The Table of Contents button looks like a book. Click it to make the help system Table of Contents appear or disappear. When visible, the Table of Contents is a pane on the left side of the Help Viewer.

- The Keep on Top button looks like a push pin. When the pin appears as if it is pushed in, it makes the Help Viewer always appear on top of anything else on your Windows desktop. When not pushed in, the Help Viewer acts like any normal window and can be hidden beneath other open windows.

Below the toolbar is a Search box that you can use to search the Outlook help system as well as some additional resources. Click the down arrow in the Search button to see a list of places to search.

When it comes to navigating within the help pane itself, treat it as if you were navigating a website. Click links to follow them, use the arrows to navigate between panes you've visited, and click the Home button to return to the start of the help system. With this information, you should be all set to use the Outlook help system.

Welcome to Microsoft Office Outlook 2007

This chapter has given you a quick tour of what's new and cool in Outlook 2007. It also showed you how to deal with the absence of some of the stuff that was in Outlook 2003 but isn't in Outlook 2007. Next, we looked at some particularly useful keyboard shortcuts you can use with Outlook. Finally, you learned the basic information you need to use the new Outlook 2007 help system embodied in the Help Viewer.

It's almost time to really dig into specific aspects of Outlook 2007. But before you do, Chapter 2 helps you to be clear on the environment where you'll be using Outlook 2007, and shows you how to import information from an older version of Outlook if you've just upgraded to Office Outlook 2007.

Chapter 2

Get Ready to Dig In

How to...

- Understand Your Outlook Environment

- Avoid Upgrade Problems

- Install Outlook 2007

- Start Outlook for the First Time

- Set Up E-Mail Accounts

- Decide Where Outlook Stores Your Information

In this chapter you'll learn how to install and configure Outlook 2007. But before you do that, it's worth spending a few minutes thinking about the environment in which you will use Outlook. Outlook is still Outlook whether it is connected to a Microsoft Exchange server on a major corporate network or is running as a standalone e-mail program on your home computer. But some aspects of installing and using Outlook do vary depending on the environment. The first part of this chapter describes the major environments you might use Outlook in, and points out any issues you should be aware of.

It's also worth spending some time learning about potential snags that can cause problems when you upgrade to Outlook 2007 from an earlier version of Outlook. The next part of the chapter addresses some possible problem areas.

After all that, it's finally time to start working with Outlook itself. In the last part of this chapter, you'll install Outlook (if it isn't already installed on your system), go through product activation, and complete the basic configuration tasks. By the time you finish, Outlook should be up and running and you should be ready to send and receive e-mail.

Understand Your Outlook Environment

As I mentioned in the beginning of the chapter, some aspects of Outlook differ depending on the environment in which you use the program. While you can install Outlook and start using it without worrying about these differences, it can be useful to at least know about them, particularly if you are installing and maintaining Outlook yourself.

Outlook as a Standalone E-Mail Program

If you will be using Outlook at home, you will probably be using it as a standalone e-mail program. This means that Outlook will most likely connect directly to your

Internet Service Provider for access to your e-mail. It also means that all your Outlook data will be stored on your PC, instead of on a central server that's backed up by someone else. Finally, using Outlook as a standalone program means that you'll likely have to set up your own e-mail accounts; attend to your own online security concerns; and manage, archive, and maintain your own Outlook data.

> **NOTE** *When I refer to Outlook 2007 as a standalone e-mail program, I am only referring to the idea of not using Outlook with Microsoft Exchange. You may be using Outlook as part of Microsoft Office, or by itself, and I would still call it a standalone e-mail program if it isn't connected to Exchange.*

I wrote this book assuming that you are using Outlook as a standalone program. With the exception of a few sections that are specific to the use of Microsoft Exchange or SharePoint Services, everything in the book is relevant to you, and you should find Outlook working as described in these pages.

Outlook with Microsoft Exchange

If you will be using Outlook in a corporate setting, it will probably be connected to a Microsoft Exchange server on the corporate network, and perhaps to Windows SharePoint Services as well. In this environment, the Exchange server interacts with the outside world. Outlook works as a client of Exchange, interacting with the rest of the world through Exchange.

You need to be aware of several things when you are using Outlook as a client of Exchange. The first and most important is that you need to talk to your network administrator before upgrading to or installing Outlook 2007. This is very important! Very few network administrators are comfortable having users installing major applications such as Outlook without explicit permission and detailed instructions provided by the administrator.

Beyond this, there are several other things you should keep in mind. In most corporations today, by default, Exchange stores all your Outlook data on central servers, rather than on your computer. This is good in that your data will almost certainly be backed up for you. But it is bad in that if you lose the connection to Exchange (say the network fails), you won't be able to do much in Outlook.

However, if your network administrator authorizes you to use Cached Exchange Mode (more on this in a bit), Outlook maintains a continually updated copy of your data on your hard drive. In Cached Exchange Mode, Outlook becomes much less affected by the performance of the network. Within limits, you can work efficiently across slow or unreliable connections, and even work with your data while completely disconnected from the network (Outlook synchronizes everything for you the next time you have a connection).

The other important thing to know about using Outlook when connected to an Exchange server is that the network administrator can define policies that override your personal control of Outlook features. One example is a corporate retention policy, which limits how long you can store certain Outlook items.

Outlook with Windows SharePoint Services

Windows SharePoint Services allow you to connect Outlook to a shared team website like the one in Figure 2-1. When you link Outlook to a shared team site, you can synchronize contacts, events, and tasks with the site, share discussion lists, use Outlook as a library for SharePoint documents, and export some or all of your contacts to the team website.

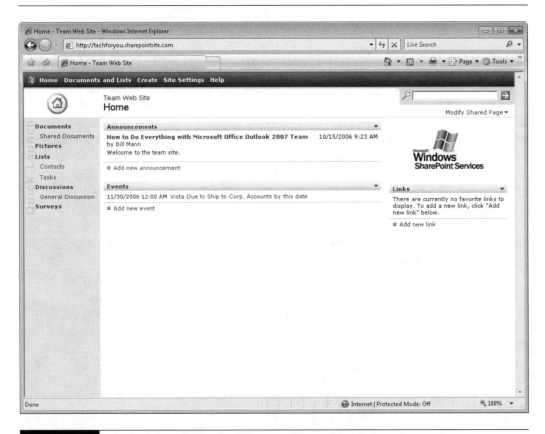

FIGURE 2-1   Outlook integrates with Windows SharePoint Services.

If you use Windows SharePoint Services to connect Outlook to a team website, you will probably do so in a corporate setting, likely as part of a project team.

> **TIP** *For more information on using Outlook with Windows SharePoint Services, see Chapter 17.*

Avoid Upgrade Problems

If you use an earlier version of Outlook right now and are preparing to upgrade to Outlook 2007, you should find that the upgrade goes smoothly in the majority of cases. However, there are a few situations where you might run into problems:

- Outlook 2007 does not coexist with earlier versions

- Outlook 2007 does not have its own editor

Outlook 2007 Does Not Coexist with Earlier Versions

Outlook 2007 cannot coexist with earlier versions of Outlook. This means that you can't keep a copy of Outlook 2003 (or any earlier version) on your computer when you install Outlook 2007. If you do not uninstall earlier versions of Outlook before you start Outlook 2007, you will be directed to do so before you can use Outlook 2007.

> **TIP** *If you must run Outlook 2003 or an older version on a computer for some reason, do not install Outlook 2007 on that computer.*

Outlook 2007 Does Not Have Its Own Editor

Previous versions of Outlook had a built-in editor that you could use instead of Microsoft Office Word for editing e-mail messages. This editor worked differently than Word, and had different capabilities. In particular, it had it's own way of doing e-mail signatures, and kept them separate from those created with Word as the editor. Outlook 2007 does not have its own e-mail editor. It either uses Microsoft Office Word 2007 (if that is installed) or an included subset of Word 2007 if Word is not installed on the computer. If you previously used Outlook's built-in editor, you will need to get used to using Word (or at least a subset of it) for editing your Outlook 2007 items.

Install Outlook 2007

At the time of this writing the Microsoft Office 2007 system is planned to be available in eight different suites. Four of them include Outlook 2007. These four suites contain Outlook 2007:

■ Microsoft Office Basic 2007

■ Microsoft Office Standard 2007

■ Microsoft Office Professional Plus 2007

■ Microsoft Office Enterprise 2007

If you have one of these Microsoft Office 2007 system suites installed, Outlook 2007 should already be installed on your computer.

If you have one of the other four Microsoft Office 2007 system suites installed, or do not have an Office 2007 suite installed on your computer, you will need to acquire and install Outlook 2007 separately.

Fortunately, if you're using Outlook 2007 at work, the IT department has probably already installed it for you. Either that or they will provide you with instructions on how to install it according to company policy.

If you have to install Outlook yourself, whether as a new installation or an upgrade, don't worry; it isn't very hard to do. All you really need to do is make sure that your product key (the long sequence of letters and numbers unique to each copy of Outlook) is handy and follow the instructions as they appear onscreen.

TIP   *If you are upgrading from a previous version of Outlook or from another e-mail program, Outlook will offer to upgrade from that program. As part of upgrading, Outlook will copy the e-mail messages, contacts, and other settings from your old e-mail program. I strongly recommend taking advantage of this option if it's offered.*

During installation, an Account Configuration dialog box may appear. In it, Outlook offers to help you connect to an e-mail server. You'll learn all about the process later in the chapter, so for now, decline this option and finish the installation.

Start Outlook

You can now start Outlook. Assuming this is the first time Outlook 2007 has been started on your computer, you'll see the Product Activation dialog box. Product activation is an attempt by Microsoft to eliminate, or at least reduce, software piracy. The idea behind it is simple. When you install a product that requires activation, the installation program examines the hardware in your computer and generates an activation ID. Assuming your PC is connected to the Internet, the product then checks your activation ID against a central database at Microsoft to be sure that your copy of Outlook has not already been activated on another computer.

If you don't activate Outlook right away, a reminder appears each time you start the program. You can only start Outlook 50 times without activating it. After that, Outlook only lets you view items, but not create new ones until you activate the product.

When you activate Outlook 2007, you can enter lots of personal information, but only your country or region is required. If your computer has an Internet connection, you can activate Outlook across the Internet. This takes a minute or two.

CAUTION

Don't be surprised if a message pops up on your screen warning you that a program is trying to connect to the Internet while you are activating Outlook. This is just your antivirus or anti-spyware program doing its job. If this happens, just click OK, click Yes, or click whichever button is needed to allow the Internet connection.

You use the Activation Wizard to activate Outlook 2007 across the Internet. If the Activation Wizard is not visible, closing Outlook and opening it again should bring the Activation Wizard into view. Follow these steps to activate Outlook:

1. Read the Microsoft Office Privacy Policy in the initial Activation Wizard screen, and then click Next to go to the Customer Information screen.

2. Select your country or region in the Country/Region list. All other information is optional. Click Next to continue.

3. Follow the onscreen instructions to complete the activation process.

The main Outlook window should now be visible. Which folder appears when you start Outlook is determined by settings Outlook 2007 inherited from your previous version or settings that the IT department entered. You can make Outlook open in whichever folder you want, including folders you define yourself, by following the procedures in Chapter 11.

Now that Outlook is installed and running, you might want to play around with it a bit and check out some of the features you learned about in Chapter 1. Go right ahead. After you're done playing, come back here to learn about setting up additional e-mail accounts.

Set Up E-Mail Accounts

If you upgraded to Outlook 2007 from an earlier version, your e-mail account should already be set up for you. Similarly, if someone from your IT department at work sets up Outlook for you, your work e-mail account is probably already set up. In such cases, you may be wondering why you need to be concerned with setting up an e-mail account. The answer: Because most people have more than one e-mail account. You might have a work account that's connected to the Microsoft Exchange server at the office, as well as a personal one running on an Internet service such as Yahoo! or Hotmail. Many people have multiple work accounts and personal accounts. I have at least a half-dozen for various purposes.

Most e-mail services provide their own interfaces to their e-mail system, meaning you have to check for e-mail in two, three, or more different places. But with a little work, you can set up Outlook to handle virtually any e-mail account on virtually any system. You can arrange for all of your e-mail to come to the Outlook Inbox. You can read your e-mail and write e-mail messages for all your e-mail accounts in Outlook.

Outlook's ability to easily handle multiple e-mail accounts can save you lots of time and effort, but you need to learn a few simple rules that govern how Outlook handles multiple accounts. For now, the goal is to get Outlook connected to these accounts. You'll learn how to work with multiple accounts in Chapter 4.

NOTE *Outlook 2007 works with e-mail servers using the following protocols: POP3, IMAP, and HTTP.*

Outlook 2007 includes Auto Account Setup. Feed Auto Account Setup your name, an existing e-mail address, and the password associated with that e-mail address. With that information Auto Account Setup attempts to connect to the server associated with that e-mail address and automatically configure Outlook for access to that account. While Auto Account Setup doesn't always succeed, when it does, it is a huge improvement over manually configuring an account. To see what I mean, check out the "Did You Know the Information Needed to Configure an Account Manually" box.

Did you know?

The Information Needed to Configure an Account Manually

If you must manually configure Outlook to connect to an existing e-mail account, you will need to have the following information:

- The type of the e-mail server you will be connecting to. Most of the time when you are working with accounts outside of work, you connect to a POP3 server.

- The name of the incoming mail server (the e-mail server that handles messages being sent to your account).

- The name of the outgoing mail server (the e-mail server that handles messages being sent from the account).

- The account's e-mail address. Outlook uses this to tell the server which e-mail account it wants to connect to.

- Your name. Whatever you enter in this field will appear in the From box of messages you send.

- The user name of the e-mail account Outlook will be connecting to. Usually, the user name is the first part of the e-mail address.

- The password for the e-mail account.

- Any special information that the ISP requires.

TIP   *This book's special project walks you through the entire process of acquiring a Hotmail or Gmail e-mail account and connecting Outlook 2007 to it.*

CAUTION   *At work, most e-mail administrators don't take kindly to the idea of employees connecting to additional e-mail accounts without permission. Assuming you get approval to go ahead, the administrator will likely set up the account for you or give you detailed instructions for setting it up.*

Did you know?

Providers Are Blocking Outlook Access?

Once upon a time (like 3 or 4 years ago) if you had an e-mail account at your Internet Service Provider, you could almost surely connect to it with Outlook. Today, things have changed. For whatever reason (to make it expensive for spammers, to recoup costs, or just because people were willing to put up with it) most Internet Service Providers have decided to block Outlook access to their free e-mail accounts. You can still use Outlook with your e-mail account, but to do so you must upgrade the account and pay a monthly or yearly fee. These fees are usually small, typically $20 per year for the cheapest, but they do exist.

The major exception to this trend is Google's Gmail accounts, which are free and still allow you to use Outlook with them.

The moral of the story is this: Before you try to connect Outlook to your e-mail account, visit the provider's website, or talk to their support people to find out if they do allow Outlook access to your e-mail and if they charge a fee for the privilege.

Set Up Exchange E-Mail Accounts

Microsoft Exchange is the corporate messaging server Outlook is designed to work with. Since it is part of the corporate messaging system, Exchange is not something you can mess around with by, for example, setting up Exchange e-mail accounts on your own. Not only is it a bad idea to set up an Exchange e-mail account without the administrator's guidance, but you need additional information to get the job done.

NOTE   *If you use a hosted Exchange mailbox for your personal e-mail, you will likely have more flexibility as to what you can do with your account. See Chapter 15 for more information on hosted Exchange mailboxes.*

TIP   *See Chapter 17 for more information on using Outlook with Exchange.*

Set Up E-Mail Accounts with Auto Account Setup

Unless you already know it won't work, setting up e-mail accounts with Auto Account Setup is clearly the way to go. Letting Outlook do all the work saves you time and reduces the chances of making a mistake.

Set Up an E-Mail Account with Auto Account Setup

For this procedure, we are assuming that the account you want to set up is one that supports Outlook access. Follow these steps to set up an e-mail account with Auto Account Setup:

1. In the main Outlook window, click Tools | Account Settings. This opens the Account Settings dialog box. Click the E-mail tab to see a view like Figure 2-2.

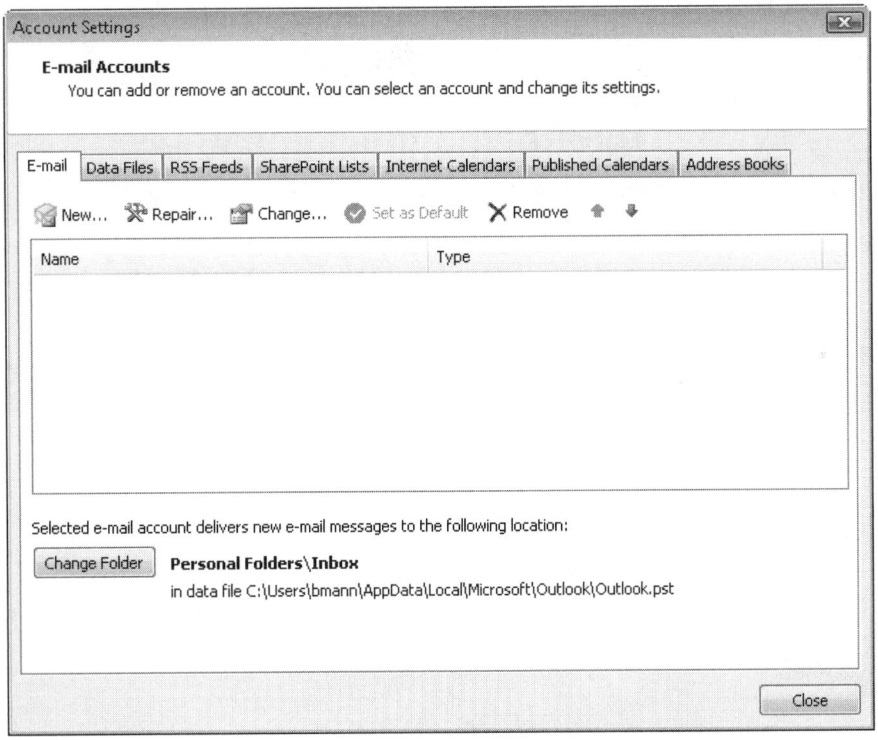

Account Settings

E-mail Accounts
You can add or remove an account. You can select an account and change its settings.

| E-mail | Data Files | RSS Feeds | SharePoint Lists | Internet Calendars | Published Calendars | Address Books |

New...   Repair...   Change...   Set as Default   X Remove   ↑   ↓

Name	Type

Selected e-mail account delivers new e-mail messages to the following location:

Change Folder   **Personal Folders\Inbox**
in data file C:\Users\bmann\AppData\Local\Microsoft\Outlook\Outlook.pst

Close

FIGURE 2-2   You launch the Auto Account Setup Wizard from here.

2. In the wizard's first screen, select Microsoft Exchange, POP3, IMAP, or HTTP and then click Next.

Add New E-mail Account	
Choose E-mail Service	

◉ **Microsoft Exchange, POP3, IMAP, or HTTP**
Connect to an e-mail account at your Internet service provider (ISP) or your organization's Microsoft Exchange server.

○ **Other**
Connect to a server type shown below.

> Fax Mail Transport
> Outlook Mobile Service
> Outlook Mobile Service (Text Messaging)

`< Back`   `Next >`   `Cancel`

3. In the Auto Account Setup screen that appears, enter Your Name (as you would like it to appear in messages), the E-mail Address of the account you want to set up, and the password.

Add New E-mail Account

Auto Account Setup
    Clicking Next will contact your e-mail server and configure your Internet service provider or Microsoft
    Exchange server account settings.

Your Name: [   ]
                    Example: Barbara Sankovic

E-mail Address: [   ]
                    Example: barbara@contoso.com

Password: [   ]
Retype Password: [   ]
                    Type the password your Internet service provider has given you.

☐ Manually configure server settings or additional server types

[< Back]   [Next >]   [Cancel]

4. Click Next, and the Auto Account Setup Wizard goes to work. If all goes well, you will see a Congratulations! message in the window and your account will be configured.

If Auto Account Setup can't successfully set up the account, the window displays information about the problem, and if possible, additional steps you can take to try to get a connection. Figure 2-3 shows an example of one such situation. Note that in this case, the wizard offers you the opportunity to try a different approach to get the connection.

If Auto Account Setup is unable to set up this account, you can either attempt to set up the account manually, or contact whatever organization provides the account for help. Oftentimes, all the information you need is available on the organization's website.

Specify E-Mail Connections

Not everyone has a full-time connection to the Internet. The type of connection you have affects how Outlook works with your Internet e-mail account. Which type of connection you have for a particular account may change, depending on circumstances. If you have a notebook computer for example, the machine may be

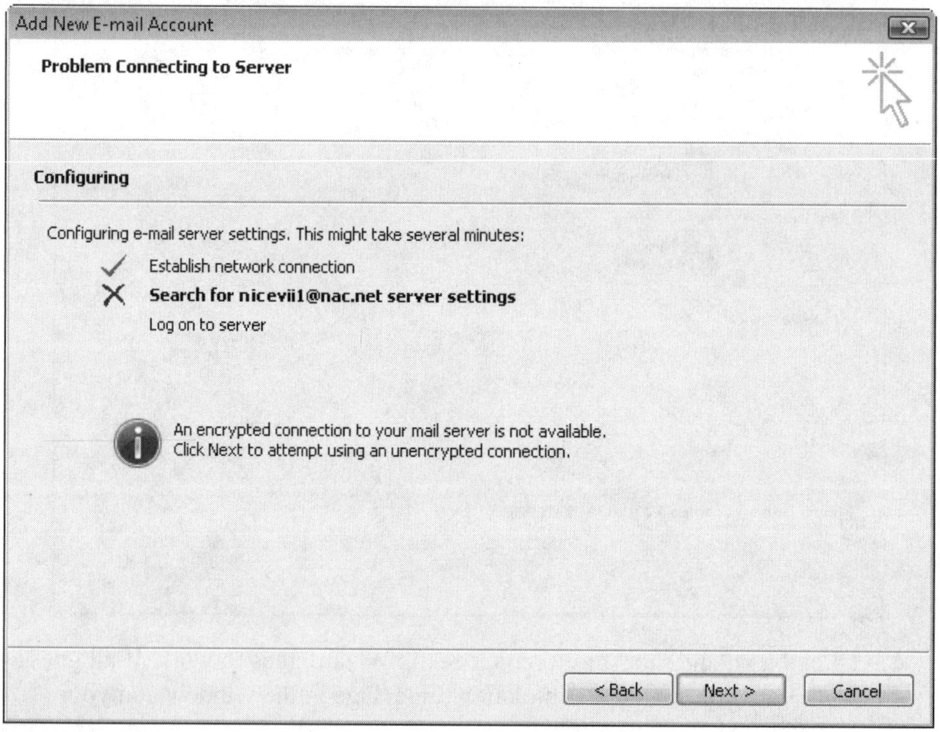

FIGURE 2-3   Auto Account Setup failed to connect, but hasn't given up yet.

connected full-time when you're in the office or near a wireless hotspot, but use a modem connection if not otherwise connected.

You can tell Outlook what kind of connection to use for each e-mail account in the Internet E-Mail Settings dialog box. Follow these steps to specify the connection for each account:

1. In the Outlook main window, choose Tools | Account Settings. This opens the Account Settings dialog box. Click the E-mail tab to see a view like Figure 2-2.

2. Select the account you want to work with, then click Change to open the Change E-mail Account dialog box shown here.

3. Click More Settings to open the Internet E-Mail Settings dialog box. The Connection tab has a collection of connection options.

4. Select the connection type that best describes the way you want this account to connect, and if you are using a modem, enter any modem-related information needed.

5. Click OK and then Next. You can now repeat the process for any other e-mail accounts that need it.

Decide Where Outlook Stores Your Information

Outlook stores your information in various locations, depending on how you or your network administrator configured Outlook. The location where your personal information is stored is called the *primary store*. In most cases, the primary store is a *Personal Folders file* on your hard drive. Personal Folders files are often called .pst files because .pst is the filename extension.

Most of the time, you can leave Personal Folders files in the default location selected by Outlook. But you can move Personal Folders files to new locations, as well as create additional files in the Outlook Data Files dialog box.

Why create additional files? While Personal Folders files can hold gigabytes of data, they can be difficult to manage when they get that large. Some people create new Personal Folders files every few months to simplify the task of backing up and maintaining the files.

Work with Your Personal Folders Files

To view information about your Outlook data files or create new files, follow these steps:

1. In the Outlook main window, click File | Data File Management to open the Account Settings dialog box to the Data Files tab, as shown in Figure 2-4.

2. Select the Data File you want to work with, then click Settings to open a Personal Folders dialog box like the one in Figure 2-5 for that data file.

3. Enter a new name in the Name field if you wish to rename this data file. Doing so from this dialog box ensures that Outlook will still be able to find and open the file afterward.

4. Click Change Password to open the Change Password dialog box if you want to assign a password to a data file, or change the existing password. If you do apply a password to the file, either set the Save the Password in Your Password List check box option, or be prepared to manually enter the password whenever Outlook tries to access this data file.

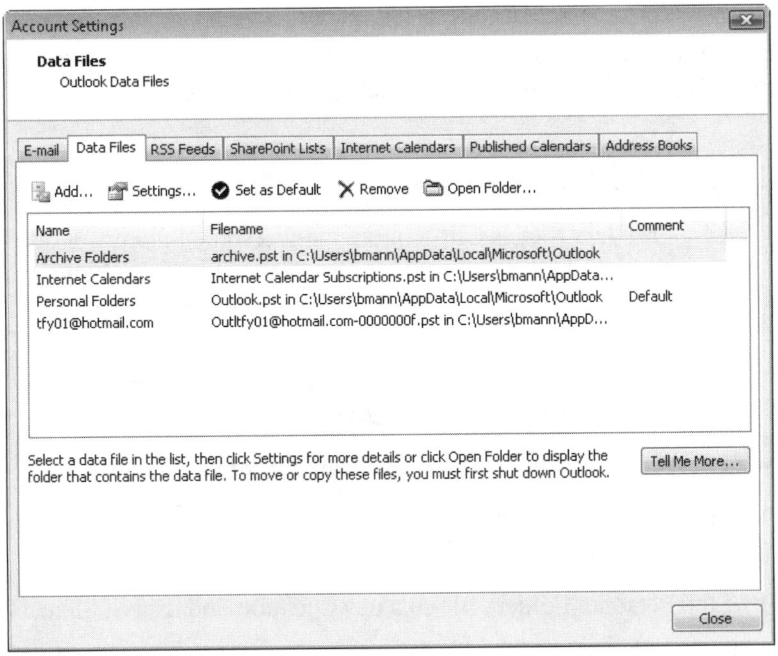

FIGURE 2-4   This is where you can manage Outlook's data files.

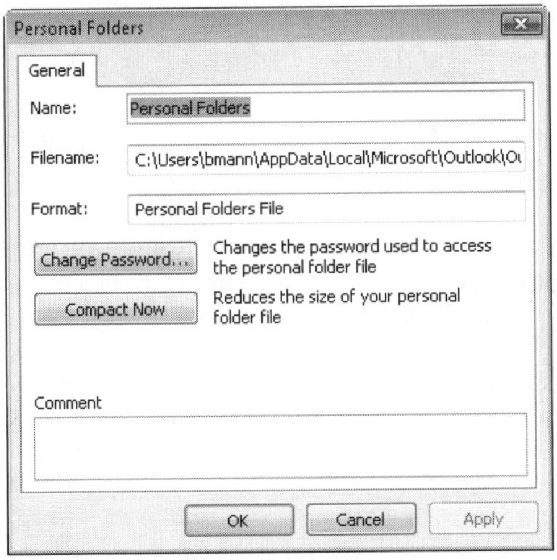

FIGURE 2-5   Use this dialog box to make the few changes you can make to a .PST file itself.

5. Click Compact Now if you want to reduce the size of the data file by compacting (or compressing) it. Doing so every once in a while not only reduces the amount of disk space the file takes up, it also makes using the file more efficient by removing dead space from the file.

Move Personal Folders Files

Moving Personal Folders files is a little more cumbersome than just working with them. To move a Personal Folders file, you start in the Data Files Management dialog box. Follow these steps to move a Personal Folders file:

1. In the Outlook main window, choose File | Data File Management to open the Outlook Data Files dialog box you already saw in Figure 2-4.

2. Select the file you want to move and then click Open Folder.

3. With the folder containing the Personal Folders file you want to move open, close Outlook.

4. Drag the Personal Folders file to a new location and drop it there.

5. Restart Outlook. You'll see a message stating that Outlook cannot find the Personal Folders file. Click OK to continue.

6. In the Create/Open Personal Folders File dialog box that appears (see Figure 2-6), navigate to the new location of the Personal Folders file, select the file, and click the Open button.

7. If Outlook displays a message saying that it is unable to display the folder, ignore the message and click one of the folders in the Navigation pane. Outlook should function normally again.

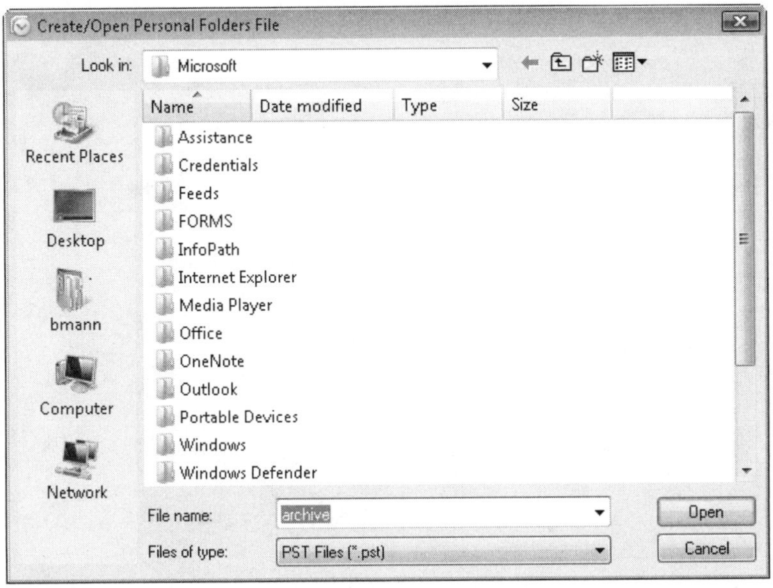

2

FIGURE 2-6   Use this dialog box to show Outlook where you moved the data file.

CAUTION   *This approach won't work for Hotmail accounts, since after you move the data file, Outlook just downloads another copy of the data from the Hotmail account.*

Now that Outlook 2007 is installed and ready to go on your computer, it is time to start working with it. And the natural place to start is with sending and receiving e-mail. So turn to Chapter 3, and let's get started.

Part II

Communicate with the World

Chapter 3

Send and Receive E-Mail

How to…

- ■ Navigate the Mail View
- ■ Compose and Send Messages
- ■ Receive and Reply to Messages
- ■ Format Messages
- ■ Handle Alerts and More

While Outlook 2007 has incredibly powerful personal information management features, and is becoming more and more of an electronic communication hub, its primary use for most people is still sending and receiving e-mail messages. This chapter focuses on exactly that. In it, you'll learn your way around Outlook's Mail view, as well as how to compose, send, receive, and reply to messages.

The chapter also covers topics that are related to the basics of sending and receiving e-mail messages. Desktop alerts, for example, let you know that new messages have arrived when Outlook is not open on your desktop. Outlook messages have lots of flexibility—they can be designated as urgent or sensitive, their delivery can be tracked, and you can even use them to vote on issues!

You'll even learn how to send Internet faxes here. Outlook works smoothly with fax service providers to give you a virtual fax machine. It's another step toward making Outlook your complete digital communications center.

Navigate the Mail View

There are reportedly over 200 million users of Outlook in the world. The vast majority of them spend most of their time in Mail view. Any changes that improve the usability of this view have the potential to save vast amounts of time and effort. In Outlook 2003, Microsoft made significant productivity-enhancing changes to Mail view. For Outlook 2007, the changes are smaller, evolutionary improvements. Figure 3-1 shows the basic Outlook 2007 Mail view.

A Three-Pane View for Better Usability

If you've jumped right over Outlook 2003 to Outlook 2007, you've probably noticed a number of changes, the most obvious being the Outlook bar that used to run down the left side of the Outlook window. It has been replaced by the *Navigation pane,* which combines the functions of the Outlook bar and the old

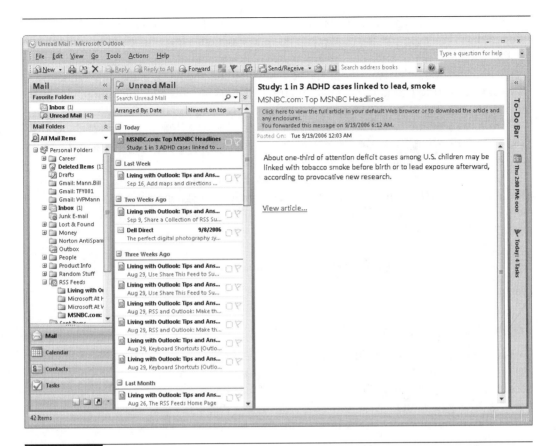

FIGURE 3-1   The Outlook 2007 Mail view sports incremental improvements over the Outlook 2003 Mail view.

Folder List. The four most commonly used Outlook views—Mail, Calendar, Contacts, and Tasks—appear as clickable bars at the bottom of the Navigation pane. Other Outlook views (Notes, Folder List, and Shortcuts) appear as small icons below these. At the top of the Navigation pane (at least while you are in Mail view) is Favorite Folders. It's a place to stash links to the folders you use most often, sort of a speed-dial for Outlook folders.

   To the right of the Navigation pane is the Inbox pane. By default, this pane provides a two-line presentation of messages as opposed to the one-line presentation in earlier versions of Outlook. This layout makes it easier to see key information in messages all at once without having to open or preview messages. Messages in the Inbox pane are typically grouped by date, but Outlook provides numerous ways to group messages in this pane (you'll learn about them in Chapter 4).

While we are calling this pane the Inbox pane, in reality it displays the contents of any folder. For example, if you were looking at Calendar view, this pane would contain Calendar items, and the Reading pane (which we'll talk about in a minute) would disappear completely. Perhaps the best way to think about this is that regardless of what you want to call it, the pane to the immediate right of the Navigation pane shows the contents of the folder you selected in the Navigation pane.

If you are viewing an e-mail folder in the Inbox pane, the Reading pane appears next to it on the right. This pane gives you lots of room for viewing messages, and with its vertical orientation, the pane is easy to read.

On the far right of the Mail view is a new addition to Outlook 2007, the To-Do Bar. You'll learn all you need to know about this helpful newcomer in Chapter 8. For now, all you need to know is that it appears on the right side of the Mail view and other Outlook 2007 views.

TIP   *You can reposition the panes and most other elements of Outlook. See Chapter 11 for details.*

Introducing the New Mail View

Now that you have an idea of the basic layout of Outlook views, let's talk about the Mail view in detail. The organization of the Mail view is actually quite sensible. Start in the Navigation pane on the left and select the folder containing the messages you want to view. The Inbox pane then displays those messages. Select one of the messages in the Inbox pane to read it in the Reading pane.

NOTE   *The name of the pane displaying messages changes to match the name of the folder you selected in the Navigation pane.*

You can also make a message appear in its own window instead of the Reading pane. To do this, double-click the message in the Inbox pane. You might want to view messages in windows, for example, if you need to deal with several messages in the Inbox. You may also find that some messages you receive do not display properly in the Reading pane. If a message looks weird, try opening it in its own window. You could go through the Inbox, open all the messages that need attention in their own windows, and handle them at your leisure. This is an approach that many people use. I used to do so myself.

While you can still use this approach, Outlook 2007 gives you much better ways to keep track of messages that need further attention or special handling of any sort.

> NOTE   *Chapter 4 will show you how to group, color code, flag, and otherwise tag messages for special attention.*

You now have the basic information you need to navigate Mail view. It's pretty straightforward if you follow the left-to-right progression I described earlier. Between here and the end of Chapter 4, we'll cover all the basics of working with your e-mail.

Compose and Send Messages

The tasks of composing and sending e-mail messages work much the same as they did in earlier versions of Outlook. If you're familiar with doing these tasks, are up to speed on the use of the spell-checker, and know the keyboard shortcuts for creating and sending messages, you might think you can skip ahead to the next section, *but don't!* Things are about to get interesting.

If you read Chapter 1, you know what I'm talking about. If not, well, keep reading.

While the main views of Outlook 2007 are recognizably descended from Outlook 2003, when it comes time to compose a message, things are very different. Here's where the Ribbon comes into play. As I described in Chapter 1, the Ribbon is a replacement for the menus and toolbars in Microsoft Office 2007 products. In Outlook 2007, the Ribbon makes an appearance wherever you are entering or editing lots of text. And there's no place in Outlook that fits the description better than in the New Message window you use to compose e-mail messages. Take a look at Figure 3-2 and you'll see what I mean.

Compose a New Message

The first step in composing a new message is to open a blank message window. If you're working in Mail view, you can do this by clicking the New button on the Outlook toolbar. You can also open a blank message window from other views by clicking the little down arrow next to the New button and choosing Mail Message on the drop-down menu.

> SHORTCUT   *Press CTRL-SHIFT-M to open a new message window no matter where you are in Outlook.*

The New Message window looks something like the one in Figure 3-2. As with most things in Outlook, the details depend on the options you selected and the

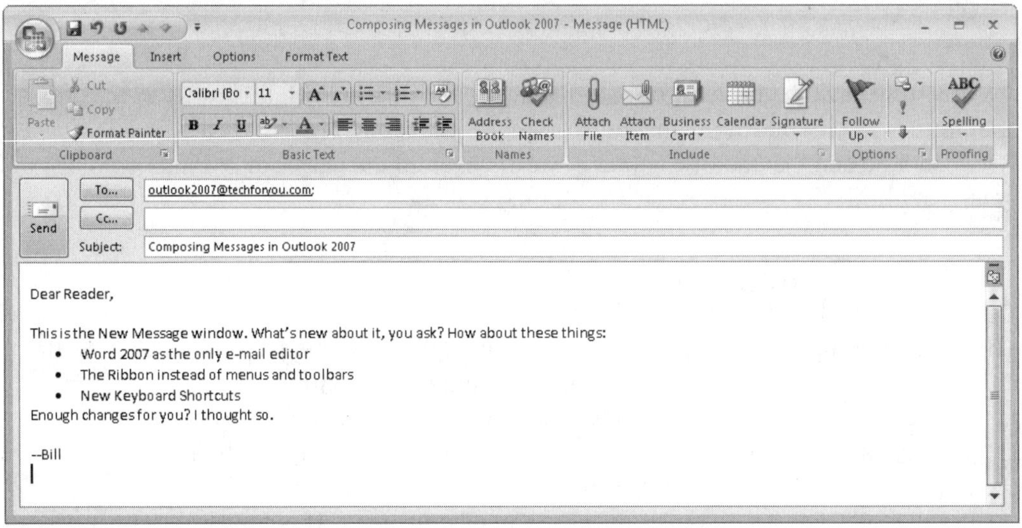

FIGURE 3-2 The New Message window has a very different look and feel now that the Ribbon is here.

ways you customized the user interface. But the default new message window should look very much like the one in the figure.

Starting from just below the Ribbon, you enter the e-mail address of the person to whom you are sending the message in the To field. Click the To button to see the Select Names: Contacts dialog box (shown in Figure 3-3), where you can choose from a list of contacts you can send the message to.

The CC field is for entering the address of anyone you want to receive a copy of the message. People whose addresses appear in the CC field typically are receiving a copy of the message for informational purposes only. You can use the same Select Names: Contacts dialog box to fill in the CC field.

Enter the subject of the message in the Subject field.

You enter the body of your message in the large empty field beneath the Subject field. Because HTML is the default format for messages in Outlook, and Word 2007 is your only e-mail editor, you can use different fonts for text, boldface or italicize text, include images, and enter hyperlinks to web pages. The Message tab of the Ribbon lets you handle all the basic activities involved in creating

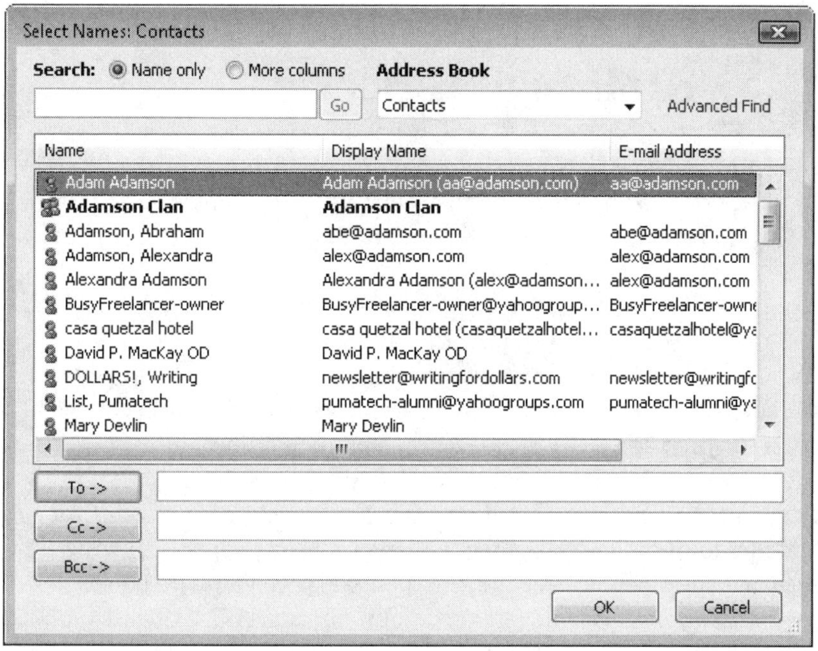

3

FIGURE 3-3   Use this dialog box to select contacts without having to type their addresses manually.

a message, including standard formatting. The Insert tab of the Ribbon lets you insert all kinds of things into your message, including file attachments. The Format Text tab includes the standard formatting from the Message tab, and adds pretty much any other formatting you might want to do.

When you're done entering text into the message body, I recommend checking your spelling using the spell-checker. Because Outlook 2007 uses Word 2007 as its editor, you get the full spelling- and grammar-checking power of Word applied to your messages. To do this, compose your message as you normally would, and then press F7 to launch the spell-checker. Using these capabilities will help you send cleaner, and likely better-received messages.

SHORTCUT   *You can also launch the spelling and grammar checker by using the ALT, H, S, S keyboard shortcut.*

Did you know?

Not Everyone Will Accept the HTML Mail Format

While Microsoft has made HTML the default format for mail messages in Outlook 2007, not everyone is going to accept this. Some organizations will ban HTML format and require users to work in Plain Text format for mail messages.

One reason for this is to conserve resources. Messages created in HTML format are much larger than the equivalent message created in Plain Text format. While the size of messages may not seem like a big issue to you as an individual user, when you run equipment that has to send and receive and store (often for years to satisfy regulatory requirements) millions of messages, reducing the average size of a message can become an issue.

A bigger issue is security. HTML messages can contain commands for your computer to run. That makes them a target for the people who write the viruses and spyware and other assorted junk that plague e-mail users everywhere these days. So some organizations will ban HTML messages as a way to reduce these risks.

Add a File Attachment to Your Message

E-mail messages can include *attachments* as well as the written material in the body of the message. Attachments are files that get carried along with an e-mail message to its destination. Using attachments, you can e-mail documents, pictures, music files, or any other kind of computer file. Attachments can be a great way to transfer files quickly and efficiently.

Unfortunately, attachments are also a great way to transmit viruses. Many people won't open messages with attachments and delete them automatically. Some companies block messages with attachments from ever even reaching their employees. And some e-mail programs, including Outlook, block certain kinds of attachments from reaching their recipients. Chapter 18 talks about this in more detail. For now, we'll concentrate on how to send attachments and leave the security ramifications for later.

3

How to ... Some Useful Keyboard Shortcuts for Formatting Messages

Here are some keyboard shortcuts that you'll find useful when formatting a message. Remember, to enter a shortcut for the Ribbon, you press and release the ALT key, then press and release each key in the shortcut until the command is activated.

- ALT, H, A, C centers the selected paragraph.

- ALT, H, A, L aligns the selected paragraph flush with the left margin.

- ALT, H, A, U turns the selected paragraphs into an unnumbered (bullet) list.

- ALT, H, A, N turns the selected paragraphs into a numbered list.

- ALT, H, F, F selects the Font list so you can change fonts. Press the DOWN ARROW key to open the list, then navigate it with the UP and DOWN ARROW keys. Press ENTER to select the new font.

- ALT, H, A, I indents the selected paragraph.

- ALT, H, A, O reduces the indentation of the selected paragraph.

- ALT, H, Y, S starts the spelling checker.

- ALT, H, A, F, F opens the Insert File dialog box so you can attach a file to the message.

- ALT, N, F opens the Insert Picture dialog box so you can insert a picture into the body of the message at the current location of the cursor.

For a more complete list of keyboard shortcuts, see Appendix A.

The easiest way to send an attachment with a message is simply to drop a file onto the message. When you do this, Outlook automatically includes the file as an attachment to the message. The following illustration shows a message with an attachment. The attachment is named "BillMann.jpg." It appears in the Attach field, a field that Outlook displays in a message header whenever you attach a file to a message.

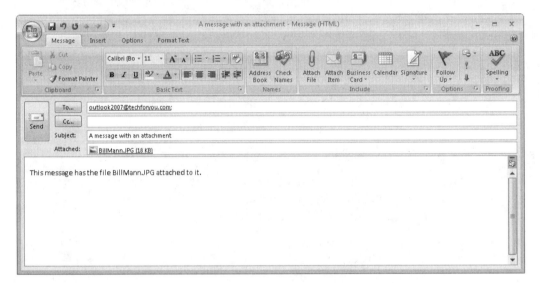

If you look closely at the file icon in the preceding illustration, you can tell that the attachment is an image file. Outlook displays the same kind of file type icon that Windows does.

If the file you want to send is a picture, you can embed it in the body of the message instead of attaching it to the message. To do this, you use the Illustrations commands on the Insert pane of the Ribbon. There you will find commands to insert pictures (graphic files or photos stored on your computer), clip art, diagrams, charts, and simple geometric shapes. The following illustration shows the same file, BillMann.jpg, added to the message as an illustration instead of an attachment.

SHORTCUT *You can use the ALT, N, P keyboard shortcut to open the Insert Picture dialog box, which you use to embed the picture in the body of the message.*

When you use the Illustrations commands, the image gets inserted into the body of the message as a picture, chart, or whatever. You have lots of options for specifying the placement of the illustration, the kinds of borders it has, and so on. If adding illustrations to your messages is interesting to you, I suggest you spend some time experimenting with all the possibilities.

Send Your Message

When you finish composing your message and are done running the spelling- and grammar-checker on it, you're ready to send it. Click the Send button on the Message tabbed page of the Ribbon, or use the ALT-S keyboard shortcut to send the message on its way. Since you will be sending so many messages over time, I strongly urge you to memorize and start using the ALT-S keyboard shortcut to send all your messages.

Outlook doesn't immediately send messages to their recipients. Messages you send go first into the Outbox. After a message arrives there, Outlook may send it on its way immediately or wait until certain conditions are met. This is controlled by the *Send/Receive groups* settings, a topic covered in Chapter 4 in the section titled "Manage Send/Receive Groups."

Eventually, however, Outlook does send the messages in the Outbox to their recipients. As messages are sent, Outlook's default behavior is to remove each message from the Outbox and put a copy of it in the Sent Items folder.

> TIP
> *If you ever want to look at the contents of a message you sent some time ago, and you didn't manually save a copy of it, check the Sent Items folder. It may still be there. You can find the Sent Items folder in the list of folders that appears in the Navigation pane in Mail view.*

Enhance Your E-Mail with Signatures

When you write a letter, you surely sign it. When you write an e-mail message, you should sign that as well. If your e-mail message is business-related, you may well have to include all sorts of information in the signature—not just your contact information, but company information and legal disclaimers, too. I've seen signatures that contain more words than the body of the message does.

Manually creating a long signature every time you send an e-mail message would be crazy. It would take too much work. Outlook's Signature feature lets you create one or more signatures, manually insert them into messages, or have one automatically appear at the end of every message you send. A signature can include your electronic business card.

> TIP
> *Creating and using electronic business cards is covered in Chapter 6.*

Create a Signature

In some ways, creating a signature is the easy part. Figuring out what information it should contain, and when to use each particular signature, can be difficult. Let's get the easy part out of the way and can concentrate on the hard part later.

Follow these steps to create a signature:

1. Open a new mail message window. Click the Signatures icon in the Includes section of the Message tabbed page of the Ribbon (or just use the ALT, H, G, S keyboard shortcut) to open the Signatures and Stationery dialog box shown in Figure 3-4.

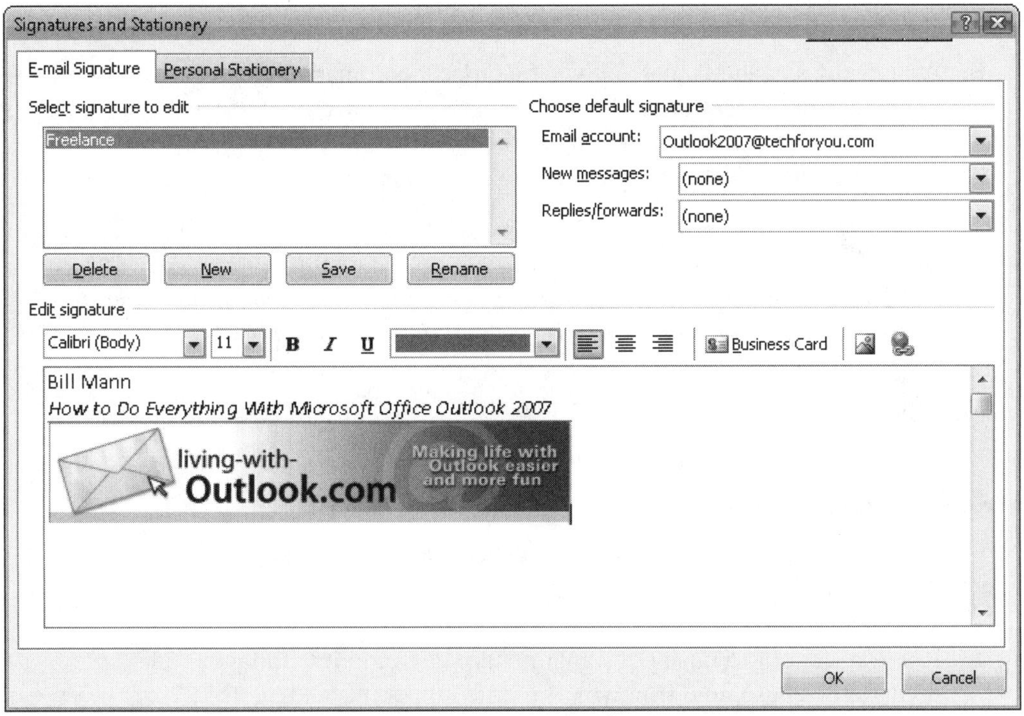

FIGURE 3-4 Signatures and Stationery is where you create and manage your signatures.

2. Click New to create a new signature, or click the name of the signature in the Select signature to edit box to edit an existing signature (I'm editing an existing signature in Figure 3-4).

3. If you are creating a new signature, enter a name for it in the New Signature box that appears.

4. Create your signature in the box at the bottom of the Signatures and Stationery dialog box, exactly as you would like it to appear in your messages. You can paste text into this window if, for example, your company has some standard text you're required to include in all messages. As you can see in Figure 3-4, you can change fonts and colors, add images, insert hyperlinks, and insert a copy of your electronic business card.

5. When you're happy with the signature, click Save. You can create more signatures or edit existing ones by repeating steps 2 through 5.

6. Assign any signatures that you want to appear automatically. In the Choose default signature section of the dialog box, select the e-mail account that will have the automatic signature. In the New messages and Replies/Forwards lists, select the signature you want to appear.

NOTE *In general, I suggest that you not add a signature when you are replying to or forwarding a message. However, the rules and policies of your organization always supersede such suggestions, so you may want to check to see if there is a formal policy regarding e-mail signatures.*

7. When you're done working with signatures, click OK to return to the New Message window you opened in step 1.

Tips for Creating Signatures

Now that you know how to create signatures, here are some guidelines for creating practical and useful ones:

- If you're creating a business signature, don't overdo it with fancy fonts or an outrageous quote from your favorite rapper. Instead, include your contact information and any other text required by your employer.

- If you're creating a signature for personal use, you can be a little more creative in the formatting and content. Just remember that e-mail messages tend to stick around for a while and are often forwarded to other people. Try not to include anything you will regret later.

- Consider the format of the messages that your signatures will be a part of. While by default your messages are in HTML format, if you are corresponding with someone using plain text format, that great signature you created may look very different to this recipient.

TIP *It can make sense to preview a signature by sending yourself a message that includes the signature to see what it looks like.*

Manually Inserting Signatures

You may want to manually control which messages get which signature. Once you have your signatures created, this is really easy to do:

1. In the message window, click the Signature icon in the Includes section of the Messages tabbed page of the Ribbon (or use the ALT, H, G keyboard shortcut) to see a list of available signatures.

2. Select the signature you want to use in this message. I told you it was really easy!

Once you start using Outlook's Signature feature, you'll wonder how you ever got along without it.

Receive and Reply to Messages

Whenever Outlook is online, it checks all of your e-mail accounts at regular intervals for new messages. When it finds new messages, Outlook puts a copy of them in the Inbox. They then appear in the Inbox pane.

NOTE *New messages can also appear in the Unread Mail folder, as well as get moved into various folders based on rules you create. But those are topics for Chapters 10 and 4, respectively. For now, we're concerned with messages in the Inbox.*

Things to Note when Reading Messages

Earlier in the chapter, you learned how to read messages (by clicking or double-clicking them in the Inbox pane). In general, but not always, messages look the same to you as they did to the person who created them. As part of Microsoft's efforts to protect you from e-mail–borne viruses and other nastiness, Outlook doesn't display certain kinds of content. Chapter 14 covers all the details, so for now just be aware that Outlook may block certain images or e-mail attachments.

If a message you receive contains an attachment, the attachment appears as a paperclip in the Inbox, and as an icon in the message window or Preview pane. Double-click the attachment icon to open it. Right-click the attachment icon, then click Save As in the shortcut menu that appears to save the attachment as a file on your hard drive.

Preview Attachments

Previous versions of Outlook allowed you to see the contents of a message in the Preview or Reading pane without opening the message in a separate window. In Outlook 2007, that philosophy has been extended with the Attachment Preview capability, which allows you to preview message attachments in the Reading pane. By this, I don't mean the ability to see illustrations in the body of messages, which we talked about a few pages ago. I mean the ability to see what's in an attached file, such as a Word document or Excel spreadsheet, without launching Word or Excel and opening the attached file in that program.

Here's how it works: When you are viewing a message that has an attachment, whether in the Reading pane or in its own message window, the Attachment Preview feature looks at the file extension of the attachment and checks to see if Outlook has a viewer for that kind of file. If it does, you can preview the attached file right in the Reading pane or message window.

Why is this good? Primarily because previewing within Outlook is faster and more convenient than launching another application and opening the file in it.

It also feels more intuitive. You want to see what's in the attachment? Just peek inside and give yourself an idea what it is without a lot of fuss. Here's what the header of a message with an attachment looks like:

Preview this Attachment

Bill Mann [bill@techforyou.com]

Sent: Tue 9/19/2006 6:36 AM

To: Bill Mann

✉ Message | 📄 Lookout world.doc (30 KB)

Each item that you can view has its own icon. In this case, there are two: one for the message, and one for the attached file. If there were more attachments, there would be more icons. By default, you start out seeing the message.

To view the attachment, click its icon. Initially, Outlook displays a warning message and makes you click a button to see the preview. Clear the check box in the warning message to keep this from happening in the future.

CAUTION *While active content such as scripts, macros, and ActiveX controls is removed from previews, Microsoft still recommends that you only preview attachments that you have received from trusted sources.*

Once you get past all that, the attachment preview appears in the Reading pane or message window. Right out of the box, Attachment Preview includes viewers for the following kinds of files:

- Outlook 2007 items (Message, Contacts, Notes, and so on)
- Word 2007 documents
- Excel 2007 worksheets

- PowerPoint 2007 presentations

- Visio 2007 drawings

- Common image and text formats

> NOTE   *If the Attachment Preview capability becomes popular, I expect that other companies will create viewers for their own file formats that we'll be able to download and add on to Outlook 2007.*

You do need to remember that what you are seeing is a preview of the attached file. You are not opening the document in Word or Excel or whatever program you would normally use to work with it. This has a couple of ramifications. First, you can't edit the file in any way. You are only viewing the content. Second, the content that you see in the preview may not be the most current content for the file. So if you want to be able to say, "Yep, that looks like the Johnson report to me. I'll deal with it after lunch." A preview is a quick-and-easy way to go. If you want to do something serious with an attachment or the information it contains, you'll need to open it and work with it the old-fashioned way.

Reply to a Message or Forward It

You'll often want to respond to an e-mail message by replying to it or forwarding it to someone else. You can reply to or forward a message that appears in the Reading pane, in its own separate window, or even one in the Inbox pane that you haven't done anything with yet. But first you need to figure out which kind of response you want to make. You can reply to the sender of the message, reply to the sender and everyone else who received the message, or forward the message. Here are some guidelines to follow:

- If you only want to communicate with the person who sent the message, you want to use Reply.

- If you want to communicate with everyone who received the message as well as the person who sent it, you want to use Reply to All.

- If you want to pass the message along to someone who wasn't originally included, you want to use Forward.

- If you want to reply to people who received the original message as well as pass it along to others, you have to choose. Typically, the easiest thing to do is start out with a Reply to All, then add new people and delete any of the original recipients who you don't want to send this message to.

How you tell Outlook which of these you want to do depends on where the message is. There are three possibilities here:

■ If you are working with a message that's in the Inbox pane and not yet visible in the Reading pane, you need to right-click the message and then select the option you want in the shortcut menu that appears.

■ If you're responding to a message that's visible in the Reading pane, the buttons you need are on Outlook's toolbar.

■ If you're responding to a message that appears in its own window, you need to use the Ribbon. In this case, the three commands you want all appear in the Respond section of the Message tabbed page.

SHORTCUT   *Actually, this is one place where you can still use the keyboard shortcuts from earlier versions of Outlook. You can use these old-style keyboard shortcuts to respond to the active message (the one selected in the Inbox pane or open in the active window):* CTRL-R *for Reply,* CTRL-SHIFT-R *for Reply to All, and* CTRL-F *for Forward.*

When you respond to a message, Outlook opens a new window like the one shown next for your response. In the message shown here, I selected Reply, so Outlook automatically entered the letters RE: (for "reply") at the start of the message subject line, and addressed the message to the person who sent it originally.

In addition, Outlook included the body of the original message at the bottom of the message window and placed the cursor at the top of the window. Including the original message provides some context for my reply. Now I can easily address the relevant parts of the original message in my response.

TIP

It is considerate to include only the relevant parts of the message you're responding to in a reply. This is particularly the case when you're responding to a lengthy message.

Another thing to notice here is that the attachment described in the message doesn't appear in the reply message. Why? This is a nice little feature. Since I am replying to someone who already has the attachment (they sent it to me, after all), Outlook is smart enough not to send them another copy of it. On the other hand, if I were forwarding the message, Outlook *would* include the attachment since the person I'm forwarding it to might not have the attached file.

Format Messages

Quick! What's this section about? What does the title "Format Messages" mean to you? If you are an Outlook veteran, you are probably thinking we're going to talk about whether to compose messages in plain text, Rich Text, or HTML format. If you are newer to Outlook, you are probably thinking that we're going to talk about how to lay out words and illustrations in the body of a message.

Whichever you were thinking, you're right. We need to talk about both of these, and they turn out to be intertwined, so we might as well talk about them together. Ready?

Three Message Formats

With Outlook 2007 using Word 2007 as its editor, you have access to Word's message-formatting capabilities in your messages. While you can't do everything in a message that you can do in a Word document, you can do almost everything. This includes using document templates to format your messages just so.

However, even with Word 2007 as the editor, what you can do to format the content of a message depends on the *message format* you use. The message format determines what kind of information can be contained in a message and how the file itself is constructed. I touched on this briefly in an earlier section when I mentioned that a signature in a plain text message could look different from the same signature in an HTML message. Let's start at the beginning....

Outlook can handle three message formats: plain text, RTF, and HTML. There's a lot of history behind all this, and most of it doesn't matter to us. What does matter to us is that there are people out in the world using each of these formats for their e-mail, and each format has different capabilities. The default message format in Outlook 2007 is HTML. HTML is the basic format of web pages. It has lots of options for formatting the content of messages.

RTF is a format that is used primarily by Microsoft. Like HTML, it has lots of options for formatting the content of messages. Some companies require all messages to be created in RTF format. When you use RTF to send a message to an Internet address (basically any recipient who isn't using Outlook and Microsoft Exchange server), Outlook automatically translates the message to HTML format so it is received properly.

Plain text format is what it sounds like. The plain text message format gives you virtually no capabilities for formatting the content of messages. No fancy lists, no embedded illustrations, no bold or italics, nothing.

Given that HTML is the default message format for Outlook 2007 and it lets you format the content of your messages nicely and is widely supported, it would seem that choosing the message format would be simple. And it usually is. But not always. See the How to "Which E-Mail Format to Use, and How to Switch?" box for more information.

Set Outlook's Default Message Format

To set Outlook's default message format, it's back to our old friend the Mail Format tab:

1. In the main Outlook window, choose Tools | Options to open the Options dialog box.

2. In the Message Format section of the Mail Format tab, select the format you want to use from the Compose in This Message Format list.

3. Click OK.

NOTE   *From this point on, new message windows that you open will open in the default format you chose. Message windows that you opened in a different format before changing the default format retain their original format.*

How to ...   **Which E-Mail Format to Use, and How to Switch?**

As we've seen, in most cases HTML is clearly the message format to use. Hopefully, the people you communicate with will be using HTML as well, and you won't have to worry about this. Here are some circumstances where you may want to use a different message format:

■ You are replying to a message that didn't use HTML format. In this case you will probably want to reply using the same format as the message to which you're replying. That's because you know the recipient will be able to read it.

■ Newsgroup programs (you'll learn about these in Chapter 5) typically don't understand HTML format. Before sending messages to a newsgroup, you should check the group's frequently asked questions (FAQ) file to find out which format to use. If you're still unsure what format to use, start with plain text. That's sure to work.

■ When you're sending a message to someone and you don't know what formats their software works with, consider sending your message in plain text format. Better yet, check with them or read their FAQ files to see what message formats they support, then use one of those.

■ If your company has set a standard format for e-mail, then, of course, use that.

Set the Format of a Single Message

To change the format for just the message you are working on, go to the Format group of the Options tabbed page of the Ribbon and click the format you want to use.

Format the Contents of Messages

Now that you know about the different message formats, we can talk about formatting the contents of your messages. We won't go into the aesthetics, but will talk about the mechanics of it all.

The simplest case is if your message is in plain text format. All you can really do with it is type. You don't have any of the nice formatting tools the other message formats have, so all you have to work with is numbers, letters, and the other symbols you see on the keyboard. You'll have to show your style in your words because that's all you've got.

If you are using RTF or HTML, you have far more formatting options than we have room to talk about. You'll have to experiment with the possibilities to find the ones that work best for you. I do have three options I want to mention. They are Automatic Formatting, Templates, and the Mini toolbar.

Automatic Formatting

Microsoft Word has long had automatic formatting features. Since Word is now the editor for Outlook, these automatic formatting features are applied to Outlook. To see and change what automatic formatting features are in effect, follow these instructions:

1. In the main Outlook window, choose Tools | Options to open the Options dialog box.

2. In the Editor Options section of the Mail Format tab, click Editor Options.

3. In the Editor Options dialog box, click Proofing, then on the Proofing page, click AutoCorrect Options to see the AutoCorrect dialog box shown in Figure 3-5.

Templates

Microsoft Word allows you to create and more importantly download predesigned document templates, and you can now use those templates in the Outlook 2007 messages you create. You can also download Outlook-specific topics from the Microsoft Office Online website.

Using a Word template is a bit of an ad hoc process. What you want to do is open the template in Word 2007, then cut and paste it into the Outlook message you are working on. Once you have it in your message, you can customize it for your needs.

I think a better source of templates you can use in Outlook 2007 is the Microsoft Office Online website. You can get there by going to the Outlook main window and clicking Help | Microsoft Office Online. This site has a ton of useful stuff for Outlook and all the rest of the Office 2007 products. For right now though,

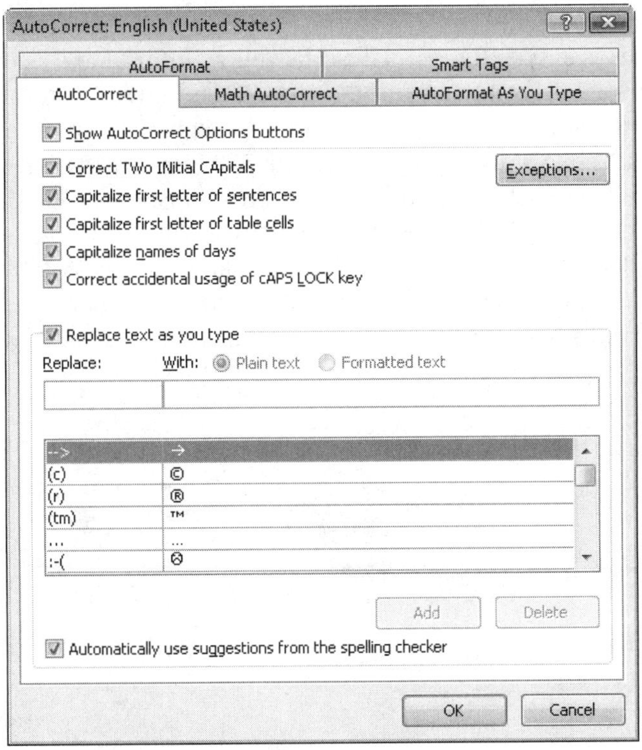

FIGURE 3-5   Come here to view and manage the automatic corrections that are made to your messages.

we're hunting down templates. So click the Templates tab on the Microsoft Office Online home page.

Microsoft and the users of Office 2007 have created a massive collection of templates that are available for free download here. This includes dozens of Outlook 2007 templates. You can find them by browsing through the collections, or by doing a search on Outlook.

Once you find an Outlook 2007 template you want, you can download it. Or more likely you can attempt to download it. To download templates here, you need to install the Microsoft Office Template and Media Control ActiveX Control. This control comes from Microsoft, and ActiveX was created by Microsoft. Nonetheless, because it has been used so frequently to get viruses and other nasty stuff onto computers, Microsoft has decided that ActiveX controls are dangerous and block you from downloading them by default. If you have your web browser configured with its default settings, it will likely object when you try to download your first template.

Happily, this is easy to remedy. Click the yellow InfoBar and select Run the ActiveX Control. Your computer will then install the ActiveX control. From there, follow the instructions that appear on the screen to complete the process.

The nice thing about downloading Outlook 2007 templates from this site is the way they run automatically. For example, I downloaded the Golden Design Electronic Business Card template. When the download was complete, and the template installed, Outlook started up a New Contact window, with the Golden Design template loaded, and a set of dummy data loaded so I can see what the new contact will look like when I fill it in with real data. Here's what I saw:

I suggest that you visit Microsoft Office Online's Template pages whenever you want to give an Outlook item a little character.

Mini Toolbar

The first time I saw the Mini toolbar, I thought it was some kind of glitch. Instead, it is a helpful little formatting feature.

When you select text in the body of a message or task, you will notice what looks like a ghost of a toolbar. That's the Mini toolbar. It gives you a quick way to work with fonts and other basic formatting features. To use it, rest the mouse pointer on it. The Mini toolbar becomes solid, and you can use it like any other toolbar. The Mini toolbar disappears but remains available as long as the text is selected.

Handle Alerts and More

A *desktop alert* is a message that appears on your desktop to alert you to the arrival of certain Outlook items. The alerts appear when Outlook is minimized. They allow you to see what item has arrived, as well as perform certain actions on items, all without opening the Outlook Inbox.

The following list describes the types of items that can generate desktop alerts and how Outlook displays them:

- **E-mail messages**   An e-mail message alert displays the name of the sender, the subject of the message, and the first two lines of the message. If the message is encrypted or digitally signed, the alert will not display the contents. In that case, you'll have to open the message to see what it says.

- **Meeting requests**   A meeting request alert displays the name of the sender, the subject of the meeting, its date and time, and its location.

- **Task requests**   A task request displays the name of the sender, the subject, and the start date of the task to be assigned.

When it receives items from the Exchange server or from Internet e-mail and the items are destined for the default Inbox, Outlook automatically generates desktop alerts. However, Outlook doesn't automatically generate alerts for items bound for a location other than the default Inbox, nor does it automatically generate alerts for messages that come in through an IMAP or HTTP account. If you want Outlook to generate desktop alerts for these types of items, you need to create rules to do so (Chapter 5 shows you how).

Work with Desktop Alerts

When a desktop alert appears, you can do several things with it. First, you can read it to see what kind of item has arrived. Alerts are designed so you can make a decision as to what to do about them at a glance. That's why they appear for a few seconds only. If you want the alert to remain visible longer, just hover the cursor over it. As long as the cursor is pointing to the alert, it will remain on the screen.

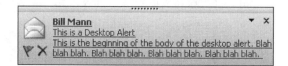

To work with the item that triggered the alert without opening the Outlook Inbox, you just click the down arrow to open the alert's Options list. The list contains a set of options appropriate for the type of alert you are dealing with. You can choose to open the item, flag it, mark it as read, disable future alerts for this type of item, or change desktop alert settings.

> NOTE
>
> *Desktop alerts don't appear for messages that don't get stored in the default Outlook Inbox. If you choose to use rules to sort messages into folders when they arrive (topics you'll learn about in Chapter 4), you'll want to include desktop notifications in those rules.*

Customize Your Desktop Alerts

You customize desktop alerts with the Desktop Alert Settings dialog box. You can reach this dialog box from the menu of an open alert or from the Outlook window. Follow these steps to open the Desktop Alerts Settings dialog box and customize your desktop alerts:

1. On the Outlook menu bar, click Tools | Options | E-Mail Options | Advanced E-Mail Options | Desktop Alert Settings. This opens the Desktop Alert Settings dialog box.

2. Adjust the Duration and Transparency settings to meet your needs. The higher the transparency, the more alerts will blend into the background.

3. To see the results of your changes, click the Preview button to display a dummy alert with the settings you selected.

Send and Receive Internet Faxes

Outlook 2007 (and other Microsoft Office System applications) can send faxes using Internet-based fax service providers. These service providers offer additional capabilities beyond those provided by the fax modem software that you may have on your PC. Additional capabilities may include sending faxes to multiple recipients at once, attaching multiple documents to a fax, and composing and sending faxes while your computer is offline (stored in the Outbox and sent the next time Outlook is connected).

Sign Up with a Fax Service Provider

The first time you try to send a fax, Outlook offers you the option to sign up with a fax service provider. Here's how to sign up with a fax service provider:

1. In the main Outlook window, click File | New | Internet Fax. Assuming this is the first time anyone has tried to send an Internet fax on your computer, Outlook pops up the message box prompting you to sign up with a fax service provider.

2. Click OK. Outlook opens an Internet Explorer window like the one in Figure 3-6. It offers information about approved fax service providers.

3. Follow the instructions provided by the fax service provider to finish setting up the service.

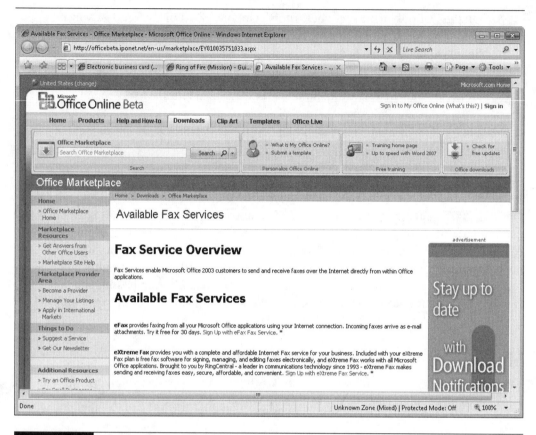

FIGURE 3-6 Select a fax service provider from among the ones on this page.

Send an Internet Fax

After you've signed up with a fax service provider, you're ready to send Internet faxes. In Outlook, a fax is treated very much like an e-mail message, although you are required to fill in some additional fields. Here's how to send a fax:

1. In the main Outlook window, choose File | New | Internet Fax. Assuming you've successfully set up an account with a fax service provider, Outlook opens a fax message window. This window looks very much like any e-mail message window, with a few extra fields.

SHORTCUT *You can jump directly to a new fax window by pressing* CTRL-SHIFT-X.

3

2. Fill in the Fax Recipient, Fax Number, and Subject fields. The Fax Service pane on the right side of the window provides a set of options that you can apply to your fax.

3. If you wish to have a cover sheet on your fax, make sure that the Use Cover Sheet check box in the Fax Service pane is selected, and fill in the cover sheet fields that appear in the body of the message.

4. If you're attaching documents to the fax, include them in the Attach field in the heading of the message.

5. Click the Send button to transmit the fax.

Receive an Internet Fax

Receiving a fax is incredibly easy. When someone sends a fax to your fax service provider fax number, the service accepts the fax and converts it into an e-mail message. It then sends that message to your Inbox, where it is treated just like any other e-mail message.

The body of the message corresponds to the cover sheet. Any attached documents arrive as attached .tif files (a type of image file) in the Attachments line. Windows and Outlook 2007 both know how to display .tif files, so you can preview the faxed information or open it by double-clicking the attached .tif files.

Chapter 4

Manage Your E-Mail

How to…

- Work with Multiple E-Mail Accounts
- Manage Send/Receive Groups
- Group Messages
- Create Folders to Store Messages
- Automate Mail Handling
- Work with Some Additional E-Mail Features

Among other things, Chapter 2 helped you get Outlook connected to your e-mail account or accounts. Chapter 3 got you started on sending and receiving e-mail messages. This chapter takes you the next step. For many people, the biggest problem with e-mail is how to manage it all. I recently worked with a person who had over *2000* unread messages from who knows how many different accounts, all sitting in her Outlook Inbox. How she keeps track of what she needs to do is beyond me, but she certainly could use some help in managing that mess!

First, we're going to talk about how to work with multiple e-mail accounts. Making sure that you don't accidentally mix messages from various accounts is the first step in managing your mail.

Next, we'll look at Send/Receive groups. One of the benefits of having multiple e-mail accounts is that you can check them on different schedules. Send/Receive groups make this possible.

Speaking of groups, the next topic of discussion is grouping messages. One of the simplest things my friend with the overflowing Inbox could do to start getting control of her mess is to let Outlook group the messages for her. She would at least have a better idea of what's happening, and so will you when you learn to group messages.

The next big topic is automating the way you work with your e-mail by applying rules to sort and filter it. But first, we take a quick look at creating folders in Outlook. After all, what good are rules for sorting your messages into different piles if you don't have anyplace to put the piles once you sort them?

Finally, we wrap up the chapter with a few helpful e-mail features that don't fit neatly into any other section. While we'll talk about e-mail intermittently in the rest of the book, once you finish this chapter, you'll be ready and able to handle most anything you need to do with e-mail in Outlook 2007.

Work with Multiple E-Mail Accounts

Chapter 2 and my Living With Outlook website (http://www.living-with-outlook
.com) show you how to configure Outlook to connect to multiple types of e-mail
accounts on multiple servers. After you set up these accounts, Outlook automatically
receives messages directed to them. But if you're not careful, things can quickly get
complicated. For example, you don't want to get your personal e-mail mixed up with
your work e-mail. And it would certainly be helpful to control which e-mail account
Outlook uses to send or reply to a message.

4

The engineers that designed Outlook had these kinds of situations in mind.
Outlook can send messages using any of your e-mail accounts, and it automatically
keeps track of which messages are associated with which accounts. This means
you can use Outlook for all your e-mail needs and still avoid embarrassing
situations such as sending personal messages to business associates or forwarding
confidential corporate messages to friends.

NOTE *While you can manage all your separate e-mail accounts manually,
Chapter 5 shows you how to create rules that automatically process
incoming messages based on which accounts they came from. For now,
we'll concentrate on the things you can do manually.*

Send Messages with Multiple Accounts

One of the most important aspects of handling multiple e-mail accounts with a
single program is being able to select the account that the program uses to send
a message. If a message is going to a friend, you probably want to use one of your
personal accounts; if you're writing to your boss, you likely want to use your
company e-mail account.

Outlook applies these commonsense rules to determine which account to use
when writing a message:

- If you're replying to a message, Outlook assumes you want to reply using
  the same account to which the original message was sent.

- If you're creating a message from scratch, Outlook assumes you want to
  use your default account. Unless you've changed it, your default account
  is the first e-mail account you set up with Outlook on your computer. (See
  the "How to Change Your Default E-Mail Account" box to find out which
  account is your default account and change it, if necessary.)

How to ... Change Your Default E-Mail Account

To find out which e-mail account is your default e-mail account and change it if necessary, follow these steps:

1. On the Outlook main menu, click Tools | Account Settings to open the E-Mail Accounts dialog box.

2. On the E-mail tabbed page, look at the list of e-mail accounts. All your available e-mail accounts appear in this list. Your default account will have the text "(send from this account by default)" in its Type field.

3. If you want to change the default account, select the account you want to be the new default account and click the Set As Default button.

4. Click Close when you're done.

What if you don't want to use the default account to send a message? Changing the e-mail account Outlook uses to send a specific message is even easier than changing the default account. Before you send the message, click the Account button (below the Send button) in the Message window. This opens a menu of available e-mail accounts. A check mark appears to the left of the one Outlook is planning to use to send the message. Click the name of the account you want Outlook to use, or press the corresponding number on the keyboard. Outlook uses the account you selected when it sends the message.

Receive Messages from Multiple Accounts

Normally, Outlook checks each of your e-mail accounts one after the other. If you have a broadband (high-speed, always-on) Internet connection, you probably don't need to worry about how long it takes for Outlook to check all your e-mail accounts or how frequently it checks them. But there are two particular situations when you do care: when you have dial-up access and when you are mobile.

With a dial-up connection, the issue is time. If Outlook spends 5 minutes online checking a bunch of e-mail accounts, your phone line will be tied up for that whole time. Plus, while Outlook is chugging away doing that, you can't do anything else with Outlook.

If you are mobile, we're talking time and money and power. If you're sitting in the conference room with the big boss and you're running Outlook on your laptop, you've probably got a Wi-Fi connection and a power outlet nearby, so life is good. But in other situations, any or all of the above could come into play. Here are some scenarios to ponder:

- You're hanging out at your local coffee shop using a T-Mobile hotspot to connect. You are probably paying by the hour, so time spent waiting for Outlook to check your more obscure e-mail accounts is wasted money.

- It's a beautiful day, and you're sitting in the park taking advantage of your super-deluxe mobile broadband account. It isn't costing you any extra money for Outlook to check your messages (you are paying for unlimited access after all), but man, it sure sucks up battery power when that wireless modem is active. The less time it takes to check your mail, the longer you can hang in the park before your battery dies.

- You don't have one of those all-you-can-eat mobile broadband accounts. Instead, you have one of those phones that doubles as a wireless modem. It works great, but when Outlook checks your mail, it takes a long time, burns up your phone's battery, uses up minutes, uses up another chunk of that 5 megabytes per month download limit on your account, and keeps your significant other from getting through on the phone. Time, money, power, and romance all going down the drain so Outlook can check that one old e-mail account you haven't used in months.

Now that you've seen the true costs, if you are a dial-up or mobile user, you might want to manage Outlook's schedule for checking your accounts. And if you get distracted by every new message that arrives, you might want to limit how often Outlook checks for new mail, even if—particularly if—you have a high-speed, always-on connection.

Outlook uses *Send/Receive groups* to determine when accounts get checked for new mail. Send/Receive groups are collections of accounts and folders that you can apply tasks to on a schedule you define. For example, you might define a Send/Receive group that automatically sends and receives messages every 3 minutes when your computer is online, but doesn't try to send or receive messages at all when your computer is offline.

One thing to remember is that an account can be in more than one Send/Receive group. This actually makes a lot of sense, since it allows you much greater flexibility when you're trying to manage your accounts. If you're just working with a desktop PC that has a broadband Internet connection, you'll do just fine with a single Send/Receive group using the default options.

But if you're working with a notebook or a Tablet PC that is sometimes online and sometimes off, that sometimes uses a dial-up connection, sometimes connects through your mobile phone, and sometimes uses broadband, you will probably be better off with a few different groups that you can use in different situations. The following sections show you how to define and manage groups, including how to tell your computer whether it is online or offline.

Manage Send/Receive Groups

Outlook automatically creates a Send/Receive group named All Accounts, which, not surprisingly, contains all your accounts. The All Accounts group holds one set of default settings for when your computer is online and another for when it is offline. You can adjust these settings using the Send/Receive Groups dialog box shown in Figure 4-1. (The figure shows only the default All Accounts group, which is all most people, including me, normally need).

Follow these steps to manage the All Accounts group or any other Send/Receive groups you create:

1. On the Outlook menu bar, click Tools | Send/Receive | Send/Receive Settings | Define Send/Receive Groups. This opens the Send/Receive Groups dialog box.

SHORTCUT *You can also press CTRL-ALT-S to open the Send/Receive Groups dialog box.*

2. Select the Send/Receive group you want to work on.

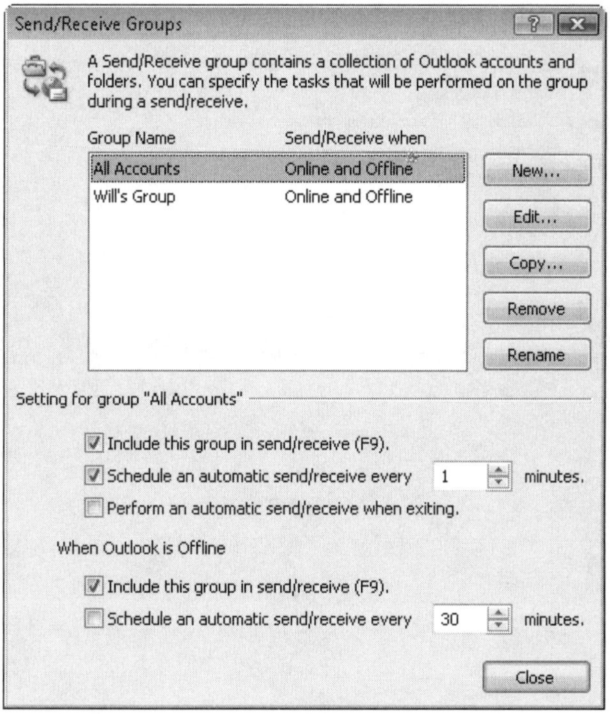

FIGURE 4-1   Control how Outlook checks your mail with the Send/Receive Groups dialog box.

3. If you want to control when Outlook sends and receives messages in this group, use the Setting For Group section at the bottom of this dialog box. As Figure 4-1 shows, you can separately control how frequently Outlook sends and receives message depending on whether it is online or offline.

4. If you want to change the accounts that are included in a group or specify the tasks that will occur for a group, click the Edit button. This opens another dialog box, as shown in Figure 4-2. This dialog box works a little differently than the typical Windows dialog box. See the "How to Edit Send/Receive Group Settings" box for more information.

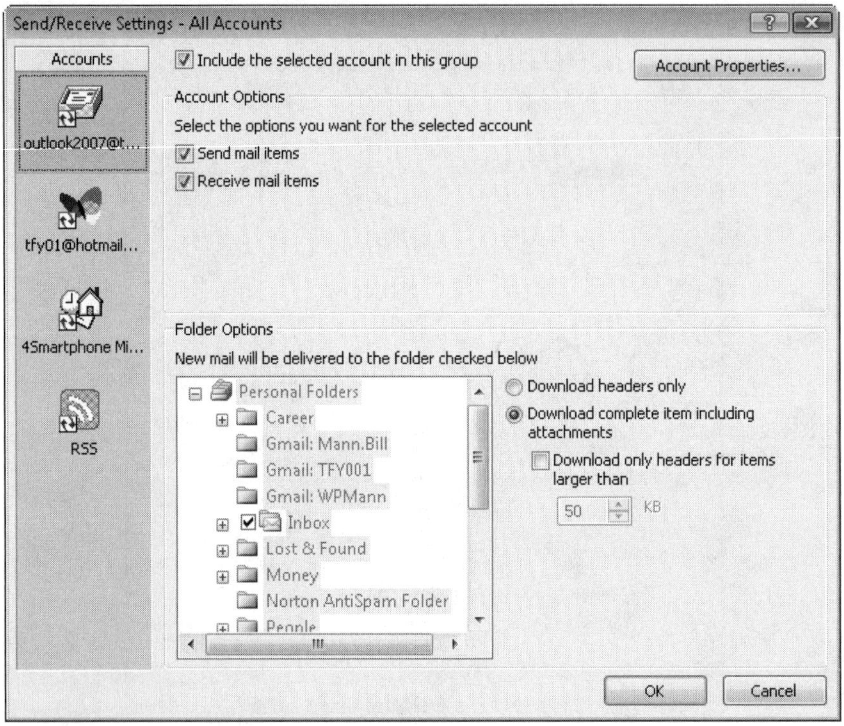

FIGURE 4-2 Use this unusual-looking dialog box to control the settings for a Send/Receive group.

Keep in mind that any settings you change in this dialog box only apply when this Send/Receive group is active. One account can appear in multiple Send/Receive groups and can have different options set in each group without any conflicts.

Define a New Send/Receive Group

The process for defining a new Send/Receive group starts in the Send/Receive Groups dialog box:

1. On the Outlook menu bar, click Tools | Send/Receive | Send/Receive Settings | Define Send/Receive Groups (or press CTRL-ALT-S). This opens the Send/Receive Groups dialog box (refer to Figure 4-1).

4

How to ...   **Edit Send/Receive Group Settings**

You edit the options for accounts and folders in a particular Send/Receive group by using the dialog box shown in Figure 4-3. The Accounts list on the left side of the dialog box shows all of your defined accounts, including Internet Calendars and RSS feeds, two types that are new in Outlook 2007. The options in the rest of the dialog box pertain specifically to an account within this Send/Receive group. To edit the account options, select the account you want to work with in the Accounts list and make any necessary changes in the rest of the dialog box.

You can remove an account from a Send/Receive group by clearing the Include the Selected Account in This Group check box.

The specific options that appear in the Account Options and Folder Options sections of the dialog box vary, depending on the type of e-mail account you've selected in the Accounts list. In most cases, you'll do best if you just leave all the default values.

If you're unsure which icons in the Accounts list represent which e-mail accounts (perhaps you didn't use descriptive names for your accounts), select the account in question and then click the Accounts Properties button. This opens an Internet E-Mail Settings dialog box with all the settings for the selected account.

2. Click the New button to open the Send/Receive Group Name dialog box:

3. Enter the name of the new group and click OK. A Send/Receive Settings dialog box appears for the new group. It will look like the one in Figure 4-3, with your specific e-mail accounts appearing in the Accounts column on the left. The new

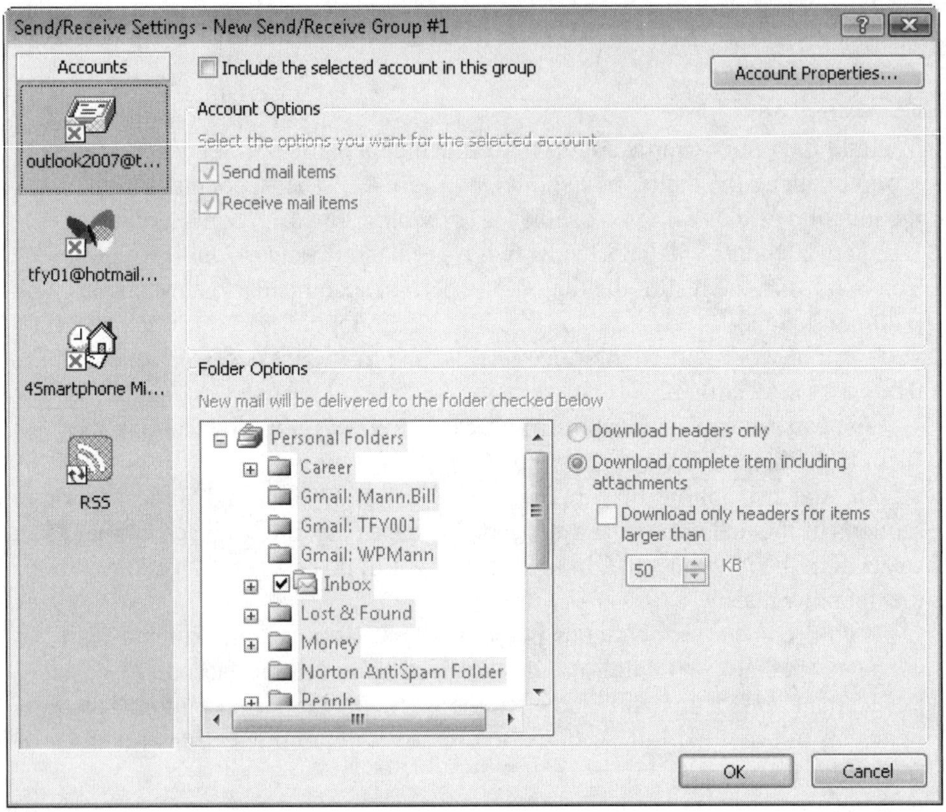

FIGURE 4-3 Use this dialog box to set up Send/Receive groups.

group starts out with no accounts in it, as indicated by the little red *X* in the icons for each e-mail account in the Accounts list.

4. Select an account you want to include in the group and then set the Include the Selected Account in This Group check box.

5. Before adding the next account, look in the Folder Options section of the dialog box to ensure that the appropriate folders are selected.

6. When you're done configuring accounts, click OK. Your new Send/Receive group appears in the group list at the top of the Send/Receive Groups dialog box.

7. Check the online and offline settings for the new group at the bottom of the dialog box, and click the Close button to put the changes into effect.

In addition to the settings you control using the Send/Receive Groups dialog box, Outlook automatically takes certain actions when it is online. For Exchange, IMAP, and HTTP (such as Hotmail) e-mail accounts, Outlook sends and receives messages immediately. For POP3 accounts, it sends messages immediately only if you select the Send Immediately When Connected check box on the Mail Setup tab of the Outlook Options dialog box, as shown in Figure 4-4. To reach this tab, choose Tools | Options and select the Mail Setup tab. The Send Immediately When Connected check box is in the Send/Receive section of the dialog box.

4

| **FIGURE 4-4** | Tell Outlook to send POP3 messages immediately in this dialog box. |

Tell Outlook Whether It Is Online or Offline

The idea that you need to tell Outlook whether it is online or not seems very strange at first. But it really makes sense, particularly if you are a mobile worker. You may want to work in Outlook without having a live connection to the nearest Wi-Fi access point or burning connect time and battery power to link to a wide-area connection while reading that long, convoluted message from the boss.

Or consider the situation of someone who uses a dial-up modem to connect to the Internet. What state is their computer in when the modem is connected to the phone line but it hasn't yet dialed out to their ISP? Their computer is offline, despite being physically connected to the wires and networks that lead to their ISP.

What if your computer is connected to the Internet, say, through a cable modem or other broadband connection, but you don't want to send and receive messages right now? Technically, your computer is online because it is connected to the Internet through your ISP, but you want it to behave as if it isn't online and can't send or receive messages.

And what if you're using a dial-up connection on a trip? Connecting to your ISP from a hotel room will usually entail long-distance charges plus all sorts of surcharges for the calls you make. In this situation, do you want Outlook making calls every 5 or 10 minutes to check for e-mail?

So "online" and "offline" turn out to be concepts that are a little more subjective than they appear at first glance. Add to this the potential technical difficulties of figuring out whether a computer is physically connected or not, and it makes sense for online or offline to be something that the user, not the computer, controls.

Now that you know why the online-offline issue has come up, you're probably wondering how you tell Outlook whether it's online or offline. It's quite easy. In the main Outlook window choose File | Work Offline or File | Work Online. If Outlook is offline, there is a check mark next to the Work Offline menu option. If Outlook is online, there is no check mark. Each time you select the Work Offline option, it switches state between online and offline.

Group Messages

If you only get a few e-mail messages a day, you might not have to worry about grouping or sorting them. You can just scan the Inbox until you find the message you are interested in. For most Outlook users, however, that approach is totally inadequate. According to one study, the average e-mail user gets many thousands of messages a year. Heck, lots of people get 50, 100, or even more messages a day.

Anybody who gets that many messages can surely use help in sorting and grouping them.

Outlook 2007 helps you out by giving you lots of ways to group messages. By default, Outlook automatically arranges messages in the Inbox pane by date. All the messages that arrive today are part of one group, and all those that arrived yesterday are part of another. Continuing that pattern for every message you receive would help somewhat, but the simple-minded approach would quickly lose value. Having a separate group for today, yesterday, and the day before is helpful. Having separate groups for three weeks ago last Wednesday and three weeks ago last Thursday isn't so helpful.

Outlook employs commonsense rules for grouping messages more like you or I would. After a week has passed, Outlook places the previous week's messages in one group, messages from the week before that in another, the previous month's messages in a third, and so on. Outlook's intelligent grouping system groups messages the way human beings would do it.

Groups Can Act Like Outlook Items?

Message groups are more than just abstract concepts. You can treat each group as if it were an Outlook item. You can open and close groups, mark all the messages within groups as read or unread, and even delete an entire group at once. Here are some tips to keep in mind:

- To open or close a group, double-click its name in the Inbox pane or folder.

- To move a group, select the group's name and drag it to the destination. The mouse pointer changes shape to let you know whether you can drop the group in any given location.

- To perform other actions on a group, right-click the group's name and select the action on the shortcut menu.

Select a Grouping Method

Outlook 2007 offers 13 predefined ways to group messages, as well as a way to create your own custom groupings. You select a grouping method by clicking the Arranged By bar at the top of the Inbox pane. This opens the Arranged By menu:

Click a grouping method to select it. A check mark is visible next to the current method. Control whether Outlook groups messages at all by clicking the Show in Groups option in this menu.

Group Messages by Conversation

One grouping method that has the potential to change the way you work with Outlook is called Arrange by Conversation. This arrangement is explicitly designed to help you read e-mail messages that are part of a *conversation*, an ongoing thread of messages related to a particular topic.

When you tell Outlook to arrange messages by conversation, it creates groups in the Inbox pane that consist of all the messages in a particular thread. Each thread consists of an initial message, along with all the preceding replies by all parties to the conversation. Outlook indents messages to indicate who replied to whom during a conversation.

4

> **TIP**   *When arranging messages by conversation, Outlook treats each message as if it were part of a conversation, even if it has no replies.*

When you look at the Inbox pane while Outlook 2007 is grouping messages by conversation, you typically just see the most recent message in the conversation. If there are replies that go with a particular message and aren't visible, the message subject in the Inbox pane has a tiny button with a down arrow. Click the down arrow to see the rest of the messages in the conversation. Similarly, if all the messages of a conversation are visible, Outlook displays a tiny button with an up arrow next to the subject of the conversation. Click that to hide the messages. The following illustration shows a portion of the Inbox pane with Arrange by Conversation selected.

Outlook does something to make the conversation arrangement even more useful. When a new message arrives in a conversation, Outlook automatically moves that conversation to the top of the Inbox pane.

NOTE *Moving the newest conversation to the top of the Inbox pane is the default behavior. If you prefer to work the other way around and place the newest message at the bottom, click the Newest on Top bar in the upper-right corner of the Inbox pane to switch it to Oldest on Top.*

Because all the messages in a conversation have the same subject, Outlook only displays the subject once. This way, Outlook can fit far more messages in the given space.

If you conduct discussions by e-mail, you'll find the Arrange by Conversation option incredibly useful. I encourage you to give it a try.

Create Folders to Store Messages

In the next section we're going to talk about automating the handling of your messages. One of the most common tasks to automate is sorting messages. Before you can sort them effectively, you need to have places to put them. So we need to talk about folders first.

Outlook comes with a set of folders, and you can add more. You can see the set of mail folders in the Navigation pane under the Mail Folders heading. You can see *all* your Outlook folder if you open the Folder List. To see the Folder List, click Go | Folder List. The Folder List appears in the Navigation pane under the heading All Folders.

The preceding illustration includes a lot of folders that don't come with Outlook. I added them to help me keep organized. You may have noticed that some of the folders, such as Inbox, have numbers in brackets to the right of their names. The numbers reflect the number of unread messages in those folders.

You may also have noticed that the Career folder has subfolders underneath it. Outlook folders typically appear under the Personal Folders file that you can see at the top of the All Folders list. You can organize folders in Outlook just as you would in Windows Explorer.

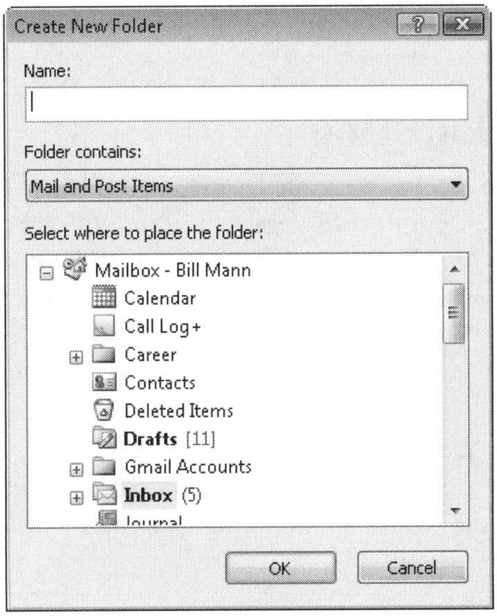

FIGURE 4-5   Creating a new folder in Outlook requires you to consider a few options.

So how do you add your own folders to Outlook? Click File | New Folder to open the Create New Folder dialog box. Figure 4-5 shows this small, but information-packed dialog box.

Enter the folder's name in the Name box. Give it a short, yet descriptive name so you can know what's in the folder at a glance.

The Folder Contains list lets you specify the kind of Outlook items you will store in the folder. You will learn more about the different types of items throughout the book. For now, know that Outlook will offer you an option that is appropriate for the view you are in now. For example, I created Figure 4-5 while Outlook was in a Mail view, so the Create New Folder dialog box assumes I will want to store mail in this folder.

All of your existing folders appear in the Select Where to Place the Folder list. Your new folder will become a subfolder of whichever existing folder you select in this list. When you click OK, the new folder is created and placed in the location you selected. If there is more than one folder in that location, Outlook displays them alphabetically in the Folder List and any other lists that show your folders.

This is really all you need to know about folders right now.

SHORTCUT *If you want to get the Folder List out of the Navigation pane, click Go, followed by the name of whichever folder you do want to see.*

Automate Mail Handling

Being able to send and receive messages using multiple e-mail accounts is one of Outlook's strengths, but bringing all your e-mail into the Inbox exacerbates the problem of handling it all. You don't want to worry about mixing up personal and business e-mail, and you certainly don't want to spend even more time sorting and arranging messages. To help you handle all that e-mail, Outlook lets you automate much of your message handling through the use of rules and the Rules Wizard.

NOTE *Another important way to use rules is in the seemingly endless battle against junk e-mail, commonly known as* spam. *Chapter 14 covers security issues when using Outlook, including techniques you can use to protect yourself against spam.*

If e-mail is a regular part of your personal and work life, you probably get dozens, even hundreds of messages each day. Even if you have a great organizational system set up, manually sorting so many messages into the right places can take up much of your day. Instead of wasting time manually sorting messages, you can set up rules that deal with the most common messages you receive, and let Outlook do most of the sorting and filing for you.

TIP *Rules are especially useful when combined with search folders. The combination lets you store each message in a single folder, yet still have access to it in multiple places. Chapter 10 is dedicated to the powerful search folders feature.*

Here are some examples of what rules can do:

- Move or copy messages to an Outlook folder
- Flag messages for follow-up
- Delete messages or entire conversations
- Display a message or play a sound when a message arrives
- Send an alert to a mobile device

One common use of rules is to automatically sort incoming messages. You can create rules that sort all messages from friends into a Personal folder or organize work-related messages by project. Suppose you sometimes get urgent messages from your boss, complete with all sorts of dire consequences if you don't respond quickly. You could create a rule that causes Outlook to alert you whenever a message from your boss arrives. A set of well-thought-out rules can definitely make your life easier.

Ways to Create a Rule

Outlook gives you two ways to create a rule. For simple rules that require the most common actions, the Create Rule dialog box is the way to go. For anything beyond the simplest rules, you'll want to enlist the help of the Rules Wizard.

Use the Create Rule Dialog Box

The simplest way to create a rule is to right-click the name of a message in the Inbox pane and select Create Rule on the shortcut menu. This opens the Create Rule dialog box. The Create Rule dialog box (shown in Figure 4-6) is the best place to create simple message-handling rules.

> **TIP** *The first time you do this, Outlook pops up an information box that tells you messages from HTTP accounts can't be manipulated with rules. When the box appears, read it, then set the Please Do Not Show Me This Dialog Again check box to keep it from reappearing.*

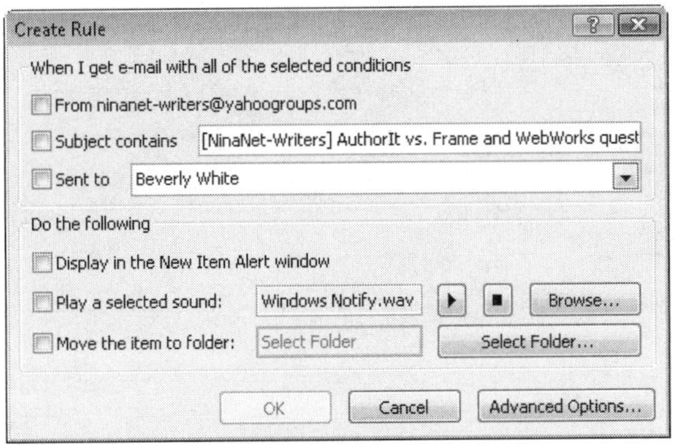

FIGURE 4-6   This dialog box makes it easy to create basic rules.

To start with, Outlook uses information from the message you selected to fill in the dialog box. The From, Subject, and Sent To check boxes all contain information taken from the message you selected when you opened the Create Rule dialog box.

Those first three check boxes are conditions that you can use to trigger the new rule you are creating. In Figure 4-6, I could, simply by selecting the appropriate check boxes, create a rule that is triggered whenever a message arrives from Bill Mann that is addressed to me only. If you select more than one condition in the Create Rule dialog box, all of them must be satisfied before the rule is triggered. (Yes, I often send e-mail to myself!)

The Do the Following section of the dialog box is where you specify what happens when the rule is triggered. By choosing the appropriate check boxes, you can have Outlook:

- Display the item (a message in this case) in the New Item Alert window

- Play a sound

- Move the item to a folder

As with the Conditions section of the dialog box, you can select more than one action and all of them will occur when the rule is triggered.

After you create the rule, click OK to exit the Create Rule dialog box. If you successfully created a new rule, a Success message box like the one in the following illustration appears. This message box lets you apply your new rule to all the messages in the Inbox right now. Select the check box if you want Outlook to apply the new rule to all the messages in the Inbox as well as future messages.

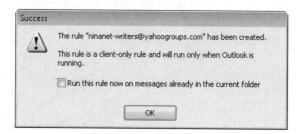

Use the Rules Wizard

The Create Rule dialog box is great for simple rules. But if you need to create more complex rules, rules triggered by conditions other than those in the Create Rule dialog box, or rules that perform other than the most common actions, the Rules Wizard is the way to go. It gives you access to the full power of Outlook's rules.

To activate the Rules Wizard, click Tools | Rules and Alerts in the Outlook main menu. This opens the Rules and Alerts dialog box. Select the E-Mail Rules tab if it isn't already visible. Using this tab, you have complete control over the rules that Outlook uses. Return here if you want to change, copy, delete, or disable a rule.

To activate the Rules Wizard, click New Rule. This launches the Rules Wizard shown in Figure 4-7.

The Rules Wizard helps you get started by providing a collection of rule templates. These templates are organized into two broad categories: Stay Organized and Stay Up to Date. When you have more experience with rules, you can dispense with the templates altogether, but when you're starting out, the templates are definitely the way to go.

TIP

If you want the most flexibility in creating Outlook rules, start the Rules Wizard, and then select one of the options under Start from a Blank Rule. This gives you access to all of Outlook's options and conditions for creating rules.

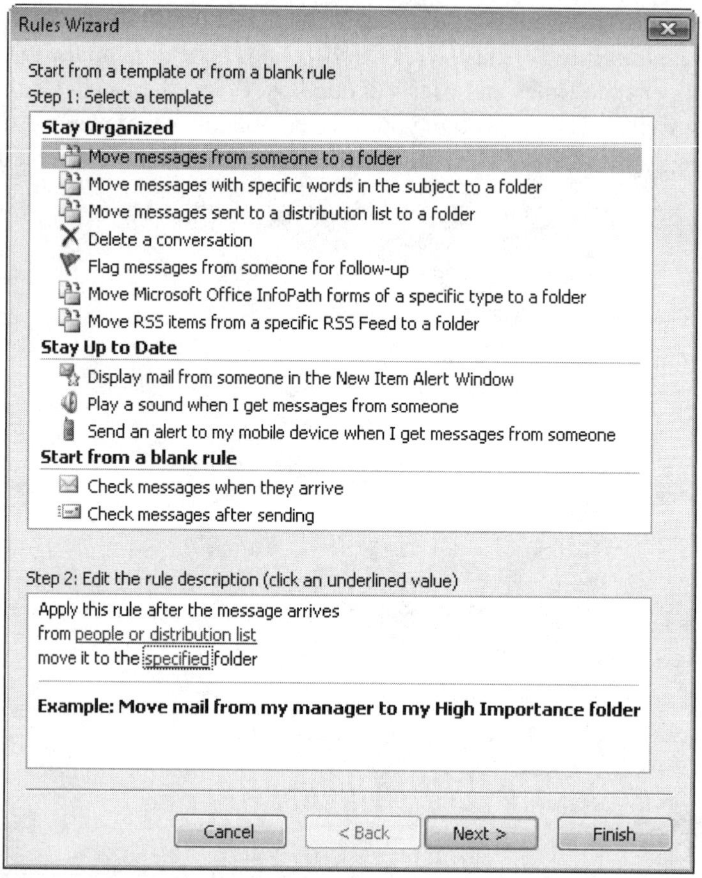

FIGURE 4-7 This is the first screen of the Rules Wizard.

Using a template is a multistep process. In Step 1, you select a template from the list of available templates. The rule description for the template you selected appears in the wizard's Step 2 box.

If you look at the Step 2 box shown in Figure 4-7, you can see underlined values in the rule description. You customize the rule by selecting specific values for these placeholders. When you click an underlying value, the Rules Wizard displays a dialog box that helps you fill in that value. Once you replace the placeholders with specific values in the rule, click Next to continue.

Work your way through the wizard's screens to complete and customize the rule, as well as indicate any necessary exceptions to the rule. In its last screen, the wizard lets you name the rule, turn it on, and review it before putting it into effect. Finally, you have the option to apply the rule to all the messages currently in the Inbox. When you're done selecting these options, click Finish, and you're done.

Some Rules Tips

Outlook's rules are very powerful and flexible. While you can use them in the most straightforward manner—create a specific rule for each message, for example, and let the rules run all the time—you can get more out of Outlook rules if you know some simple tips. Here are two good ones:

- Combine rules if you can
- Carefully consider the order of your rules

Combine Rules If You Can

Whenever possible, combine rules. It's easy to end up with redundant or nearly identical rules, particularly when you use the Create Rule dialog box to create rules. The more rules Outlook has to process, the longer it takes to process them. A large collection of rules can have a noticeable impact on Outlook's performance. Also, rules that are similar to one another can make it hard to update your rules list, because you have to update all the related rules instead of a single rule.

The answer to the problem of too many rules is to combine rules whenever possible. Suppose you have a rule that moves all messages from my friend AA (Adam Arnold) Adamson to the Stuff to Keep folder, and you decide to do the same with messages from his sister Alex. You could easily use the Create Rule dialog box to create a separate rule that moves messages from Alex to the Stuff to Keep folder. However, what happens if you decide to start putting messages from AA and Alex and the rest of their siblings into an Adamson clan folder? You have to remember to change two rules.

A better approach would be to add Alex to the existing rule that already handles messages from AA. As shown in Figure 4-8, you can modify any existing rule by opening the Rules and Alerts dialog box and directly editing the rule description in the Rule Description window. You can also double-click the name of a rule to open the Rules Wizard and directly edit the rule there. And you can make certain changes by clicking Change Rule and choosing a change from the menu that appears.

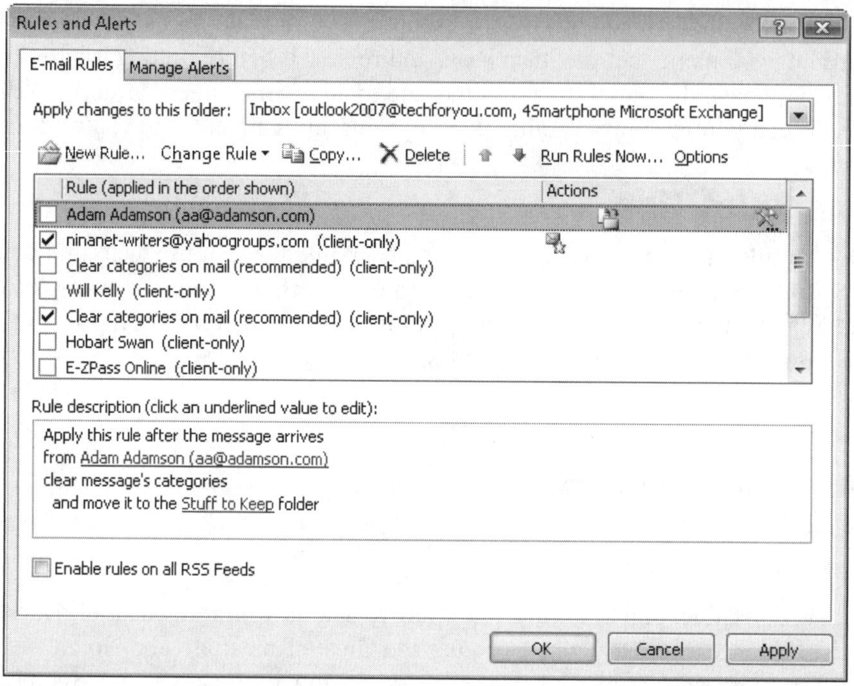

FIGURE 4-8   If you select a rule, you can modify it in the Rule description box.

Carefully Consider the Order of Your Rules

Outlook executes rules in the order in which they appear in the Rules and Alerts dialog box. You can take advantage of this fact along with the Stop Processing More Rules action to speed the processing of rules and deal with special situations.

Moving messages that meet certain conditions into folders is a common use for rules. If you create a rule that moves messages from Joe into the Buddies folder, and that's the only (or last) thing you want to happen when a message from Joe arrives, you can add the Stop Processing More Rules action to the rule that moves Joe's messages. This way, Outlook doesn't need to check any of the following rules for messages from Joe, and it can start processing the next message sooner.

Work with Some Additional E-Mail Features

This section of the chapter provides a home for three e-mail–related features that don't fit anywhere else: Flagging, AutoComplete, and Info Tags. All three are examples of the kind of small changes that Microsoft has made to Outlook 2003 to increase your productivity. Here are the main advantages of each feature:

■ Flagging turns a message that you want to follow-up into a task with a reminder in only a few clicks.

■ AutoComplete saves you from having to type long e-mail addresses.

■ Info Tags give you access to key information about a message without having to open it.

Keep Track of Messages You Must Act on with Flagging

According to Microsoft, research shows that people do one of three things with their messages: They respond to them immediately, discard them immediately, or plan to deal with them later when they have the time to reply or access to the information they need.

Where people get in trouble is option three, the "plan to deal with them later" bit. One way to deal with the problem is to open each message that needs attention in its own window and address the messages when you have the opportunity. But there are some real problems with this short-term approach. Leaving windows open on the desktop is only practical if you're never going to turn off your computer. Plus, having 5, 10, 15 or more message windows open on the desktop is awkward.

People come up with many ways to tackle this issue, including establishing a separate "To Do" folder or leaving messages unread so that they're more visible in the Inbox, but none of these techniques works especially well.

To help you track messages, Outlook 2003 introduced Quick Flags. Quick Flags are flags that appear on the right side of each message in the Inbox pane. By choosing a Quick Flag for a particular message, you could, with a minimum amount of effort, signify that a message needed attention in the future.

Outlook 2007 takes the concept further. Instead of a set of colored flags that merely grab your attention, flagging marks a message as something that needs to be taken care of, and creates a task, with a due date, for dealing with that message. I like this feature a lot.

4

FIGURE 4-9   A message flagged for follow up.

If you look at a message in the Inbox or Unread Mail pane, or any other list or mail messages, you will see that they have a dim flag to the right of them. If you click the flag, it turns red to signify that you need to follow up on the message. Click it again, and it turns into a check mark so you know you've completed whatever action was needed.

Now view a flagged message in the Reading pane or an open window, and you will see when the message was flagged, and when you are due to have acted on it in the message's Info Bar. Figure 4-9 shows what this looks like.

CAUTION   *Messages you imported from Outlook 2003 that already were flagged do not show the dates. They just say, "Follow up."*

So far, this isn't much different from what we had in Outlook 2003. Now right-click one of those ghostly flags. A shortcut menu appears with a bunch of interesting options. With one or a few clicks, you can set the follow-up date to any of five predefined options or a custom one. You can add a reminder to the task, mark it complete, or simply clear the flag (assuming it is already set). The Set Quick Click option lets you change which flag is added when you left-click on the flag icon.

Work Faster with Outlook's Improved AutoComplete

AutoComplete helps you work faster by suggesting entries you have used before when you are filling in certain fields. For example, if you have typed the address "john.smith@techforyou.com" into the To field of a message before, and you have just typed the letter *j* in the To field of a new message, Outlook may suggest that you are typing john.smith@techforyou.com. The idea is that you can select the suggestion, rather than typing the entire address.

As you type, Outlook displays a list of suggestions. If the list of suggestions that AutoComplete offers contains only one entry, or the entry you are typing is highlighted in the list, you can immediately press ENTER to insert that entry in the field without typing the rest of it.

AutoComplete offers suggestions as soon as you type the first letter of an entry. As you continue to type, the list of suggestions shrinks as the number of possibilities narrows. In many cases, you need to type only one or two characters and press ENTER.

AutoComplete displays the most frequently used entries first, thereby adapting its suggestions to match your changing needs and reducing the number of characters you have to type.

Figure 4-10 shows AutoComplete in action. For the figure, I typed the letter *o* into the To field, and AutoComplete opened a screen tip containing a list of e-mail

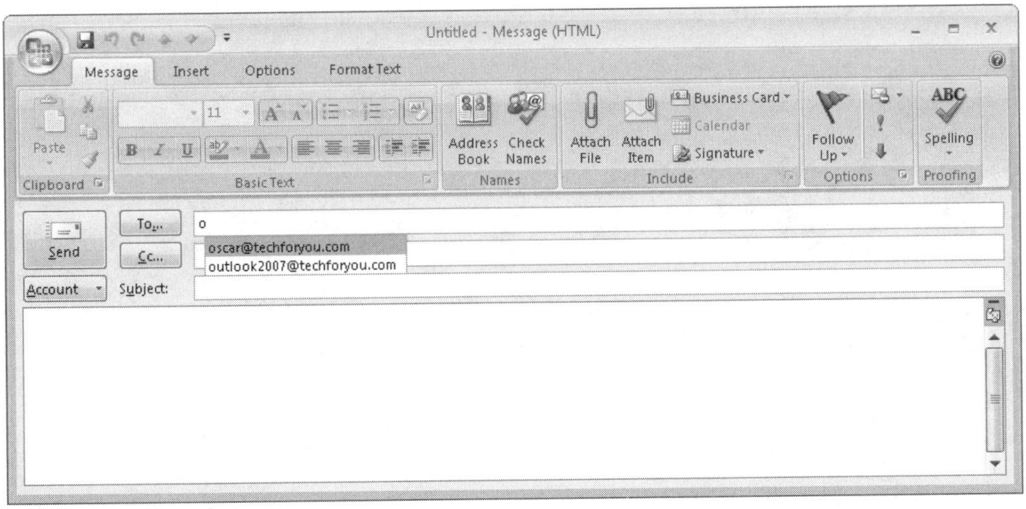

4

FIGURE 4-10   AutoComplete suggests names and addresses to save you typing.

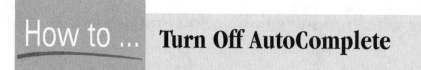

How to ... Turn Off AutoComplete

Not everyone likes AutoComplete or finds it helpful. If you are one of those people, you can turn off the feature altogether by following these steps:

1. In the main Outlook menu, click Tools | Options to open the Options dialog box.

2. On the Preferences tab, click E-Mail Options to open the E-Mail Options dialog box.

3. Click Advanced E-Mail Options to open the Advanced E-Mail Options dialog box shown here.

Advanced E-mail Options	? ✕

Save messages

AutoSave items in: [Drafts ▼]

☑ AutoSave items every: [3] minutes

☐ In folders other than the Inbox, save replies with original message

☑ Save forwarded messages

When new items arrive in my Inbox

☑ Play a sound

☑ Briefly change the mouse cursor

☑ Show an envelope icon in the notification area

☑ Display a New Mail Desktop Alert (default Inbox only)

[Desktop Alert Settings...]

When sending a message

Set importance: [Normal ▼]

Set sensitivity: [Normal ▼]

☐ Messages expire after: [   ] days

☑ Allow comma as address separator

☑ Automatic name checking

☑ Delete meeting request from Inbox when responding

☑ Suggest names while completing To, Cc, and Bcc fields

☑ Press CTRL+ENTER to send messages

[OK] [Cancel]

4. Clear the Suggest Names While Completing To, Cc, and Bcc Fields check box in the When Sending a Message section of the dialog box.

addresses I've used before that start with the letter *o*. The addresses in the list are arranged by frequency of use, with the one I use most frequently highlighted at the top of the list.

If the highlighted address is the one you want to enter, all you need to do is press ENTER and AutoComplete enters it in the To field. If the highlighted address isn't the address you want to enter, you can manually select a different address from the list or keep typing. Eventually, the address you want to use will either be highlighted in the AutoComplete list or you will have typed the entire address manually. Every time you type an address manually, AutoComplete adds it to its own list of addresses to offer next time around.

What if AutoComplete offers a bunch of addresses that you don't want anymore? You can delete addresses from the AutoComplete menu easily. When you see an AutoComplete menu with an address that you don't want, press the UP or DOWN ARROW key to select the address and press DELETE. Doing so removes the address from the set that AutoComplete offers.

TIP   *The Calendar has its own form of AutoComplete that you'll learn about in Chapter 7.*

Scan Your Inbox with Message Info Tags

While the Inbox pane makes a good bit of information about each message visible, the information you can see isn't always enough. For that reason, Info Tags provide additional information when you hover the mouse pointer over a message.

The information that appears in an Info Tag depends on what information is visible in the Inbox pane. For example, if the sender and subject of a particular message are completely visible but the date and message size are not, the Info Tag shows only the date and size of the message. I suggest you play with Info Tags a bit to see the kinds of information available for different messages.

Chapter 5

Take Advantage of RSS Feeds, Instant Messaging, and Newsgroups

How to...

- Learn about RSS
- Use RSS Feeds with Outlook
- Learn about Instant Messaging
- Use Instant Messaging with Outlook
- Learn about Newsgroups
- Use Newsgroups with Outlook

The Internet is primarily a means of communication. And we humans love to communicate. That's why e-mail became so popular so fast. But e-mail isn't the only way to communicate online. Outlook 2007 supports three additional ways of communicating online that you can learn about here. Two of them, instant messaging and newsgroups, have been around for a while (in fact, newsgroups predate the World Wide Web). Outlook 2007 supports them through integration with instant messaging programs such as Windows Live Messenger and newsreaders such as Outlook Express. In this chapter you'll learn how to make Outlook and these programs play together to expand your communication options.

The third additional way to communicate (receive information, to be more exact) with Outlook 2007 is through RSS feeds. These are pretty new, and becoming very popular for reasons you'll discover shortly. Outlook 2007 has support for RSS feeds built right in, making them as easy to work with as e-mail.

This chapter divides into three sections, one for each of these major topics. By the end of it, you'll be ready to use them all to expand the ways you communicate with the world.

Learn About RSS

RSS stands for *Really Simple Syndication*. RSS is yet another way to publish information across the Internet. You can subscribe to RSS feeds, and receive information when it is published, rather than having to go look for it yourself. RSS feeds deliver the latest news and information right to your computer.

Even better, RSS readers, also known as *aggregators,* are programs that can gather all the content you receive from your RSS feeds in one location. Sound familiar?

RSS Is a Collection of Standards?

The RSS feeds we use on the Internet today can be composed of any of several standard types of content. Just as mail readers (such as Outlook) can automatically handle different forms of e-mail, RSS readers (such as Outlook) can automatically handle different forms of content feeds. Since Outlook supports all the standard feeds, you don't normally have to worry about the details.

5

Just as RSS readers gather information from multiple sources and aggregate it in one place to make it easier to work with, so does Outlook gather e-mail messages from multiple sources and aggregate them in one place to make them easier to work with.

Given this (and the fact that we are talking about RSS in this book), you won't be surprised to learn that Outlook 2007 can function as an RSS reader. Outlook 2007 lets you subscribe to RSS feeds, read items posted to those feeds, and manipulate the items almost as if they were e-mail messages. You can even forward and categorize them.

Use RSS Feeds with Outlook

To use RSS feeds with Outlook, you must subscribe to those feeds. Once you do, Outlook will create an RSS Feeds folder, containing a subfolder for each feed. Once these folders are created, they act very much like other Outlook message folders such as the Inbox.

But before you can do anything, you need to find RSS feeds you can subscribe to.

Finding RSS Feeds

Here are some ways to find RSS feeds you can subscribe to:

- Use the Outlook RSS Feeds home page
- Stumble across them while browsing the Web
- Have someone share a feed with you

Use the Outlook RSS Feeds Home Page

If you are just learning about RSS feeds (as opposed to trying to figure out how to use one you have already found or that someone has shared with you), the Outlook RSS Feeds home page is a good place to start. You can find an assortment of feeds from Microsoft and selected partners that Microsoft thinks you will find interesting. If nothing else, you can pick up some good general news feeds and start getting comfortable with the RSS way of life.

To reach the Outlook RSS Feeds home page, look for the RSS Feeds folder in the Outlook 2007 Mail Folders list. Click that, and Outlook opens a page (right within the Mail view) that looks something like this:

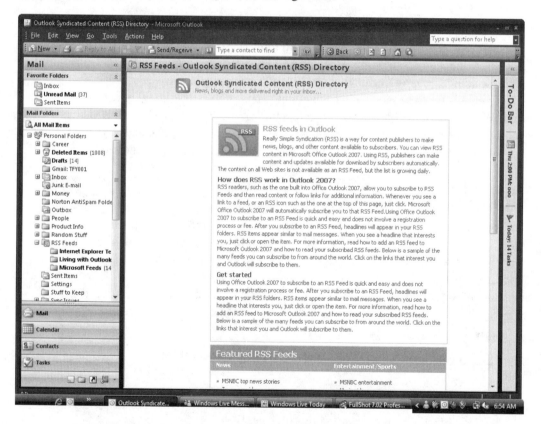

Scroll through the page and look for an interesting feed. Click the link and follow the directions that appear onscreen to add that feed to Outlook (I walk you through the full process of adding and configuring an RSS feed later in this chapter).

An important thing to note here is that, despite Microsoft having selected these feeds as good resources for you, Outlook may balk at you actually using them.

When you click on one of the feeds (Crabby Office Lady, for example), Outlook notices that the feed contains hyperlinks (links to web pages or other Internet resources) and flags the feed as potentially dangerous. So instead of seeing instructions on configuring the RSS feed, you may see this security notice:

Your best bet is to ignore this warning and click Yes to continue. While it is true that hyperlinks are potentially dangerous, they are also the basic means of navigation on the Internet and avoiding any feed with a hyperlink in it would leave you with nothing. In fact, as of the summer of 2006, 100% of the feeds that Microsoft recommends trigger this warning. The warning is pointless.

Did you know?

RSS Protects Your Privacy?

Whenever you do anything on the Internet, some information about you (about your Internet connection, actually) is available to the computer at the other end of the connection. Beyond that, when you do things such as subscribe to an e-mail newsletter, you must provide additional information. Typically, you will have to enter your e-mail address, along with some personal information about yourself, such as your name.

When you subscribe to an RSS feed, you don't need to provide any of that additional information. Your RSS reader requests information from the computer that publishes the information, providing only enough information for the other computer to reply. No e-mail address. No name. No ridiculous marketing surveys to fill out. This is about as private as you can get on the Net.

Stumble Across RSS Feeds on the Web

In your travels on the World Wide Web, you will sometimes come across a site that provides an RSS feed. Such a site will usually display a bright orange button with the letters *RSS* in it. Here's an example from my Living with Outlook website:

Notice the RSS button on the left side. It indicates that the site provides an RSS feed. Clicking that button will start you on the road to subscribing to the feed. Exactly what you have to do will vary somewhat from site to site. Sometimes you will need to left-click, sometimes right-click. Sometimes you will get a page that describes RSS and what you need to do to subscribe to this feed, or a list of all the feeds available at the site. Sometimes you will just get a link you can manually paste into Outlook (I'll show you how that works shortly). The thing to remember is that the RSS button means there is one or more feeds you can subscribe to that are associated with this site.

Have Someone Share an RSS Feed with You

One of the fun and useful characteristics of RSS feeds is how easy they are to share with friends, family, and coworkers. All you need to do is get the other person a copy of the link to the feed, and they can subscribe in seconds.

Outlook 2007 supports sharing feeds by automating the process of e-mailing one or more feeds to someone. You'll see how it is done in the next section.

Subscribing to RSS Feeds

Now it's time. In this section, you'll subscribe to one or more RSS feeds. Regardless of what else you do, I strongly urge you to try subscribing by pasting a link. There are two reasons for this. One, as RSS becomes ever more common, I think this will be the most common way to subscribe to feeds. Two, by working through the procedure in this section, you will subscribe to the Living with Outlook RSS feed. I use this feed to provide information that didn't fit into this book, or that has changed since publication, as well as reports and reviews on products and tools that support Outlook. Subscribing to this RSS feed lets me continue to give you the information you need to get the most out of Outlook, long after you've finished reading this book.

Subscribing by Pasting a Link

Let's start this off by subscribing to an RSS feed—specifically, the Living with Outlook RSS feed. This will show you not only how to subscribe to a feed you happen to run across on the Web, but provide you with Outlook-related news as I write about it. Start by pointing your web browser to http://www.living-with-outlook.com and finding the RSS button (near the top of the page on the left side). Now follow these steps:

5

1. Left-click the RSS button. On this site, left-clicking the button displays a message telling you that you need to right-click the button, then copy the shortcut and paste it into your RSS reader (Outlook 2007 in our case). If I had created multiple feeds, left-clicking would have displayed a page listing links to those feeds. You would have right-clicked those links to copy and paste them into the RSS reader.

2. In the Outlook Navigation pane, under Mail Folders, right-click the RSS Feeds folder. In the shortcut menu that appears, click Add a New RSS Feed.

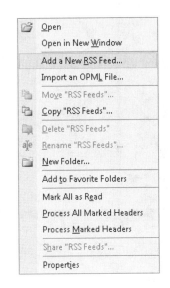

3. Paste the shortcut from step 1 (http://www.living-with-outlook.com/outlook-rss.xml) into the New RSS Feed dialog box that appears, then click Add. This opens another dialog box that asks, "add this RSS feed to Outlook?"

4. Click Yes to add this feed to Outlook 2007 with its default values, or click Advanced to customize things. I suggest you stick with the defaults, which will work fine for you in the vast majority of cases.

5. After a moment or two of buzzing and whirring, Outlook adds the feed to the RSS Feeds folder, and downloads any available articles. The result will look something like Figure 5-1. That's it. You are now subscribed.

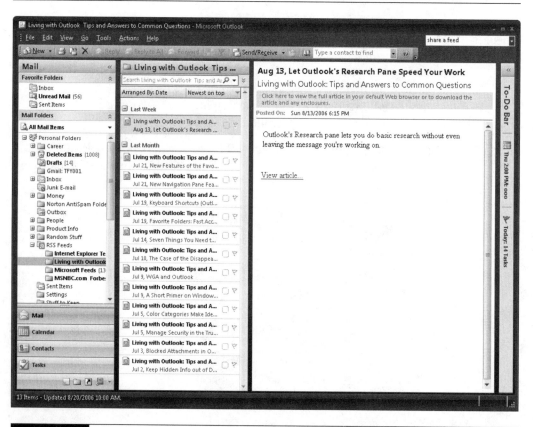

 FIGURE 5-1　Outlook has just finished subscribing to the Living with Outlook feed.

Subscribing Through the Outlook RSS Feed Home Page

Subscribing to RSS feeds through the Outlook RSS Feeds home page is really easy. Follow these steps and you'll have one of these feeds in no time:

1. Click the RSS Feeds folder to open the RSS Feeds home page.

2. Find a feed you want to subscribe to and left-click its name.

3. The security notice described earlier appears. Click Yes to continue despite the warning. This opens the dialog box that asks, "add this RSS feed to Outlook?"

4. Click Yes to add the feed. Outlook downloads the feed and adds it to the RSS Feeds folder, and you are done.

Subscribing to a Link Someone Shared with You

People can e-mail you links to RSS feeds in two ways. If they are using Outlook 2007, they can use the special automated approach that Outlook offers. People can also send you a link in a message without using Outlook's special features for doing so. In this second case, all you need to do is copy the link out of the message, and follow steps 2–5 of the procedure for subscribing by pasting a link.

Here we talk about how to subscribe to the RSS feed that someone sent you using Outlook 2007's Share This Feed capability. Here's what you need to do if want to subscribe to a feed you have received as an RSS Feed e-mail like the one in Figure 5-2.

Click Add This RSS Subscription in the Reading pane, or open the message and click Add This RSS Subscription in the Ribbon. Outlook 2007 adds the feed.

Things can't get any simpler than this!

FIGURE 5-2   Using Outlook 2007's Share This Feed feature to mail a feed to someone is quick and easy.

Subscribing to a Set of Links Someone Shared with You

Not only can people e-mail you links individually, they can share entire collections of links with you at once. This process is slightly more complicated, but faster if there are a lot of feeds to share. Here's what you need to do if want to subscribe to one or more feeds in a collection you have received in an e-mail like the one in Figure 5-3:

1. Double-click the attachment file in the message. Outlook may display an Opening Mail Attachment warning dialog box.

2. Click Save to store the attachment file on your hard drive. Make sure to remember the full filename and choose a location you can find again, since you will have to tell Outlook where the file is located in a moment.

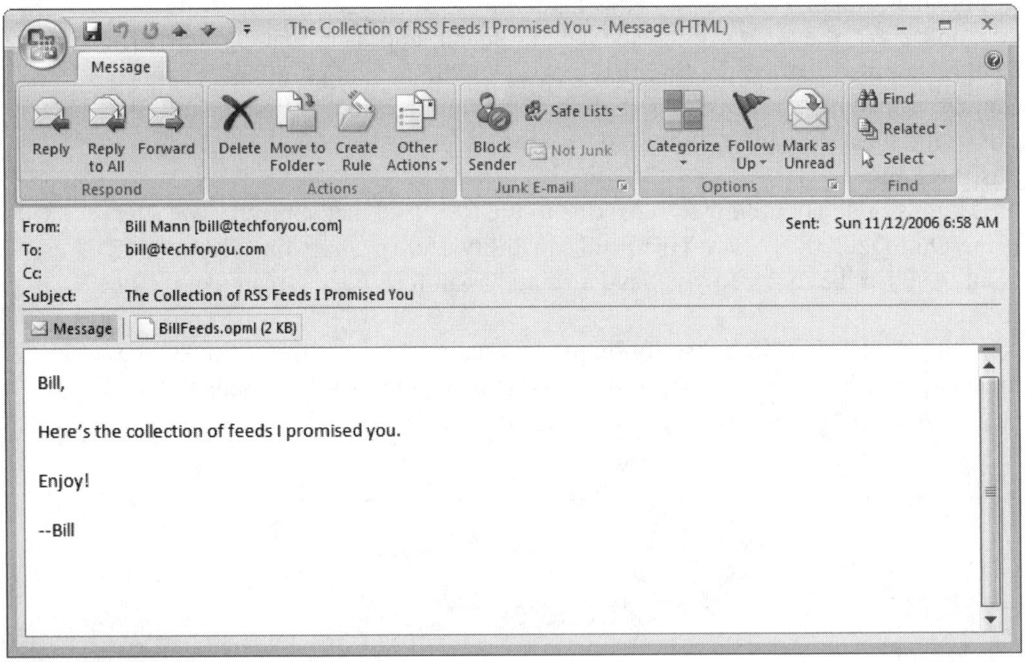

FIGURE 5-3   The file attached to this message contains links to a collection of RSS feeds.

3. In the main Outlook window, click File, then Import and Export to launch the Import and Export Wizard.

4. In the Choose an Action to Perform list that appears, select Import RSS Feeds from an OPML file and then click Next.

5. In the Import an OPML File screen, enter the path to the collection file from step 2, or click Browse to navigate to the location of the file.

NOTE   *If you browse to the file, the navigation dialog box will by default only show files that have an ".opml" file extension. To see files with other extensions, you will need to select All Files in the file type list at the bottom of the dialog box.*

5

6. Click Next. A screen appears with a list of all the feeds included in the collection.

7. Select the feeds you want to add to Outlook, then click Next.

8. Outlook subscribes to the RSS feeds you selected, then displays a screen that lists the feeds that were successfully added.

9. Click Finish to complete the process. After Outlook downloads any current articles, your new feeds are available in the RSS Feeds folder.

Working with RSS Feeds

Now that you are subscribed to one or more feeds, it's time to put them to use. Figure 5-1 shows the Living with Outlook feed. The view looks a lot like an e-mail view, and it acts like one too. The articles appear in a list just like e-mail messages do, with the selected one appearing in the Reading pane. You can search the feed using Instant Search, and sort the messages in the feed the same way you would e-mail messages. You can categorize them, forward them, mark them as read or unread, apply rules to them, move them to folders—virtually anything you can do to an e-mail message except reply to them.

> NOTE *There is a difference between forwarding and sharing. When you forward an RSS article, you send a copy of that article to someone. When you share, you are giving someone the ability to quickly subscribe to the RSS feed, rather than to read a particular article from that feed.*

There are, however, differences between RSS articles and e-mail messages. As mentioned so far, you can't reply to articles, and you can share them with others. Beyond that, when you select an article, it appears in the Reading pane as you would expect (see Figure 5-4). At the top of the message you see the title of the article and where it comes from. Below that, the Info Bar gives you some options.

Click the Info Bar to select whether to view the full article in your web browser or to download all content related to that article. RSS feeds often deliver only a small part of the entire article. The idea is that this gives you enough information to decide whether you want to read the full thing or not.

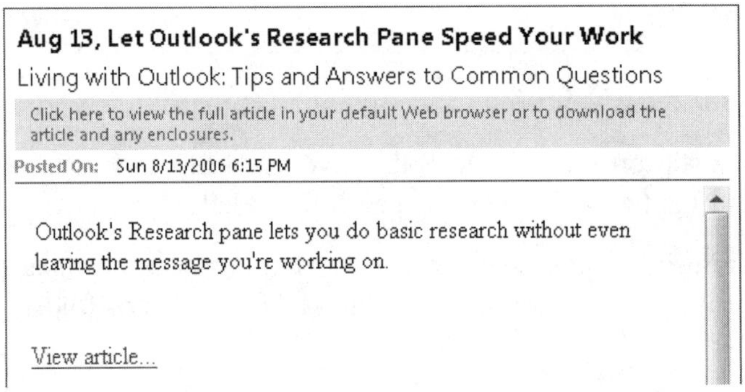

Aug 13, Let Outlook's Research Pane Speed Your Work

Living with Outlook: Tips and Answers to Common Questions

Click here to view the full article in your default Web browser or to download the article and any enclosures.

Posted On: Sun 8/13/2006 6:15 PM

Outlook's Research pane lets you do basic research without even leaving the message you're working on.

View article...

FIGURE 5-4   An RSS article looks similar, but not identical to, an e-mail message.

If you decide to view the whole article in your browser, selecting that option launches your browser and loads the article. If you don't want to read the whole article, you've only spent a few seconds to determine this.

Sharing RSS Feeds One by One

Earlier in the chapter we talked about what to do if someone uses Outlook's Share This Feed feature to share an RSS feed with you. It will only take a moment to learn how to use this feature yourself and share the feeds you like best with other Outlook 2007 users. Follow these steps to share an RSS feed:

1. Select an article in the feed you want to share. To share the feed, you must select an article in the feed, rather than the feed folder in the Navigation pane.

2. Right-click the article and select Share This Feed in the menu that appears. This opens a specialized e-mail message designed for sharing feeds.

3. In the To field, add the name of the person or persons you want to share this feed with.

4. Click Send in the Ribbon to send the message and share the feed.

Sharing Collections of RSS Feeds

You've seen how to import a collection of RSS feeds that someone e-mails to you. Now let's see how you can create your own collection to send to someone else. Follow these steps to share a collection of RSS feeds:

1. In any Outlook view, click File, then Import and Export. This launches the Import and Export Wizard.

2. Select the Export RSS Subscriptions to an OPML file option, then click Next. This opens the Export to an OPML file screen in Figure 5-5.

3. Select the RSS feeds you want to add to the collection, then click Next.

4. In the screen that appears, enter a name and location for the collection file you are about to create. You can use the Browse button to navigate to a specific location where you will store the file. I suggest that you put the file someplace it is easy to find, such as your My Documents folder or even the Windows Desktop. Also, I suggest that you give the file an

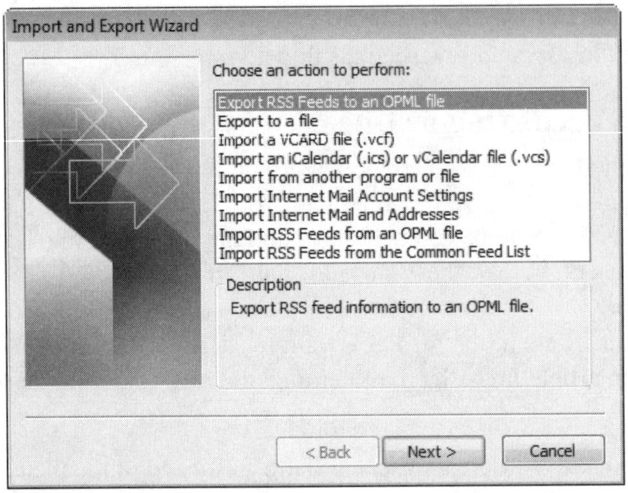

FIGURE 5-5   You can export any of your RSS feeds as a collection using this dialog box.

".opml" extension to make it easier for the recipient to find. If you wanted to name the file "MyCollection," for example, in this step you would enter a filename of MyCollection.opml to make it easier for the recipient to find the file. Remember this location, as you will have to attach this file to a message later.

5. Write an e-mail message to the person (or persons) you want to share the collection with.

6. Attach the collection file you created earlier to this message and send it along.

7. That will do it. The recipient will get the collection file, and by following the procedure we discussed earlier in the chapter, will be able to import any or all of the feeds in the collection.

Learn About Instant Messaging

Us humans prefer to communicate face to face, in real time. Conversations by e-mail are good; conversations with instant feedback are even better. That's where *instant messaging* (IM) comes in. With instant messaging, you can communicate with other people in real time, using the Internet to connect you whether you're in the next office or thousands of miles apart. Figure 5-4 shows part of an IM conversation.

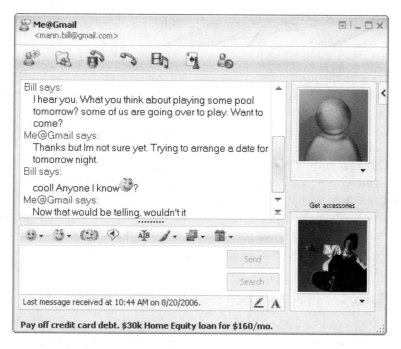

Note the informal tone of the messages and the occasional typo. Exchanging instant messages is more like chatting with a friend than publishing a formal document.

Not long ago, instant messaging was primarily a tool for socializing, as anyone with a teenage child can attest. But adults have quickly caught on, and now instant messaging is an important business tool. Project teams often use instant messaging in place of the telephone as a quicker, less intrusive way to ask questions and exchange information. I once managed a team of writers scattered across five locations in four states. Instant messaging was our primary means of regular day-to-day communication, and it worked out great.

Instant messaging is truly a powerful tool, and an important part of modern electronic communication. Recognizing this, Microsoft has integrated some instant messaging capabilities within Outlook. This chapter explains how to set up and use Windows Messenger, and how it works with Outlook.

Instant messaging systems work differently than e-mail systems or newsgroups (newsgroups are covered later in this chapter). Instant messaging systems are *client/server* systems. In an instant messaging system, the client program runs on your PC. The client program communicates with a server program running on one or more central computers.

When you log on with the client program on your PC, it begins exchanging information with the server. This information includes, among other things, a list of all your instant messenger contacts. The server program checks to see which of your contacts are online, and passes information back to the client program so you can see who is available right now.

Knowledge of who is online right now, known as *presence*, is one of the key distinguishing features of instant messaging programs. When you send e-mail to someone, you have no idea whether the other person is online and likely to receive your message soon. With instant messaging programs, you know that the person you want to talk to is available right now (or at least that the person's instant messaging client is online). Outlook takes advantage of presence to help you communicate with your contacts in the most efficient way.

Use Windows Live Messenger with Outlook

Windows Messenger was the included instant messaging program for Windows XP. Windows Vista does not include an instant messaging program. To use instant messaging with Outlook 2007 on a Vista machine, you must download an instant messaging client that works with one of the instant messaging services supported by Outlook 2007. That means you must use one of these services if you want to integrate instant messaging with Outlook:

- **Microsoft Windows Live Messenger**   This instant messaging service is part of Windows Live Services, a new set of services that "brings your online world together." At the time of this writing, Windows Live is still under development. Even so, Microsoft is encouraging people to use Windows Live Messenger, rather than Microsoft MSN Messenger. Since going to the MSN Messenger website now redirects you to Windows Live Messenger, we'll go with the flow and use Windows Live Messenger in this chapter.

- **Microsoft Office Communicator**   This is meant to be the instant messaging system for corporations that will host their own service on Microsoft Office Live Communications Server 2005. While this is a capable system, it isn't appropriate for us to work with as individuals. If your company standardized on this service, your IT department will handle the setup and configuration, and provide you with instructions for how to use it.

- **Microsoft MSN Messenger**   This service is one of the most popular in the world, and has been in service for years. Microsoft is pushing people to move to Windows Live Messenger as the replacement for MSN Messenger.

- **Microsoft Windows Messenger**   This is the instant messaging system that comes installed on Windows XP computers. It will be eclipsed by the services listed here, and we won't concern ourselves with it further.

> **NOTE**   *To simplify life, we will download Windows Live Messenger and use it with Outlook 2007, whether you are working on Windows Vista or Windows XP.*

Download and Install Windows Live Messenger

The process of downloading and installing Windows Live Messenger is, for the most part, straightforward. To begin, you need to get to the Windows Live Messenger page at the Windows Live Services website. In your web browser, go to http://get.live.com/ messenger/overview. The page should look similar to the one shown in Figure 5-6.

Did you know?

Many Companies Ban or Control IM?

Instant messaging originally found its way into the workplace through individual users, but corporations have increasingly seized control of IM use in the office. Just as they have telephone and Internet policies, many companies now have IM policies.

While IM programs use up relatively few computer and network resources, consumer-grade services are not secure and pose real security risks. One way that companies address the security issue is with IM policies. Don't install Windows Live Messenger or any other IM program on a business PC before consulting your company's IM policy, if it exists.

FIGURE 5-6 Download Windows Live Messenger from the Windows Live Services website.

CAUTION *The exact look of the Windows Live Messenger page is sure to change over time. And since Windows Live Services is itself still under development, the URL (web address) itself may even change. If you can't find the page using the URL listed here, you can always use Google or MSN Search to find the page, then continue from there.*

Somewhere on the page, you will find a button or link that reads Get It Free, Download Messenger, or something similar. Click that to start downloading. When your browser gives you the choice to run the file or save it, you can go ahead and run it.

Eventually, the Install Windows Live Messenger Wizard will appear on your screen. Follow the instructions in each screen to complete the installation process. When you come to the Choose Additional Features and Settings screen shown here, you can accept the defaults or any combination you want—for the purposes of Outlook instant messaging, none of them matters either way.

CAUTION   *As you install and configure Windows Live Messenger, you may see a Windows Security Alert dialog box telling you that Windows Firewall has blocked some of the features of Windows Live Messenger. Since we know what program we're installing and know that it is safe, click Unblock to give Windows Live Messenger its full capabilities.*

FIGURE 5-7   The Windows Live Messenger sign-on screen requires a Windows Live ID.

Eventually, Windows Live Messenger will appear. It should look very similar to what's shown in Figure 5-7. To use Windows Live Messenger, you need to have a Windows Live ID. If you have a Hotmail account, an MSN Messenger account, or you signed up for any of the incarnations of Microsoft's Passport service, you already have a Windows Live ID. If you don't, skip ahead to the section "Get a Windows Live ID" and complete that process before continuing.

After you've successfully created your Windows Live ID, you're ready to sign in. Consider selecting the Sign Me in Automatically check box so you don't have to log in to the service every time you start Windows Live Messenger. You'll need to have Windows Live Messenger running whenever you want to use instant messaging with Outlook.

Get a Windows Live ID

Before you can sign in with Windows Live Messenger, you must have a Windows Live ID. If you have a Hotmail, MSN Messenger, or .NET Passport account, those double as Windows Live IDs, and you don't need to do anything more. Go sign in to Windows Live Messenger!

If you don't have a Windows Live ID, the recommended way to get one is to create a new Hotmail account. And to do that, you need to go to the Microsoft Passport Network sign-in page at http://login.live.com/ and click the link Sign up for an account.

CAUTION   *With Microsoft .NET Passport transitioning into Microsoft Live, things are a bit confusing when it comes to setting up accounts. You will likely find that things work a bit differently when you are ready to create your own account, but the basics should remain the same.*

If you have an e-mail address, you can use that as the basis for your Windows Live ID account. If not, the sign-up page will give you the option to create a new Hotmail e-mail account and use that as your Windows Live ID. Follow the steps that appear on the screen to complete process.

NOTE   *Be sure to give the wizard a valid e-mail address. The address you enter will receive a confirmation message that you must reply to before you can use your Windows Live ID account.*

After you finish answering the wizard's questions, you'll be ready to start using Windows Messenger.

Enable Instant Messaging in Outlook

To use the integrated instant messaging capabilities of Outlook, you must first enable them. Enabling instant messaging in Outlook means activating the Person Names Smart Tags. Smart Tag icons look like the silhouette of a person's head and shoulders. Clicking them causes Outlook to display context-sensitive menus and options.

Follow these steps to enable instant messaging in Outlook:

1. Restart Outlook so it can detect that you have installed Windows Live Messenger.

2. In the main Outlook window, click Tools | Options. You see the Options dialog box.

3. In the Person Names section of the Other tab, select the Display online status next to a person name check box, as shown in Figure 5-8.

4. Click OK when done.

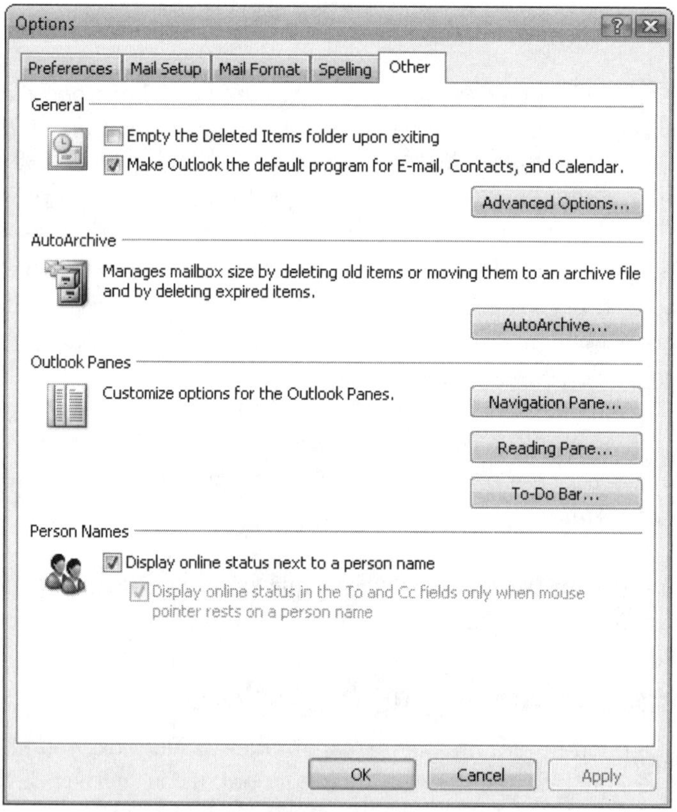

  FIGURE 5-8   Enable the display of online status in Outlook.

Add Instant Messaging Contacts

Contacts are the key to using Windows Live Messenger. The program tracks your contacts so you know who is online. It uses contacts to know which instant messages to accept, which to block, and when to ask you what to do with incoming messages. And it lets you communicate with your contacts with only a few clicks of the mouse. So how do you add contacts to Windows Live Messenger?

To add contacts manually, click Add a Contact. This button appears in the Windows Live Messenger window as a little green silhouette with a plus sign in a circle on its right side. This opens the Windows Live Contacts – Add a Contact dialog box shown in Figure 5-9, which walks you through the process of adding

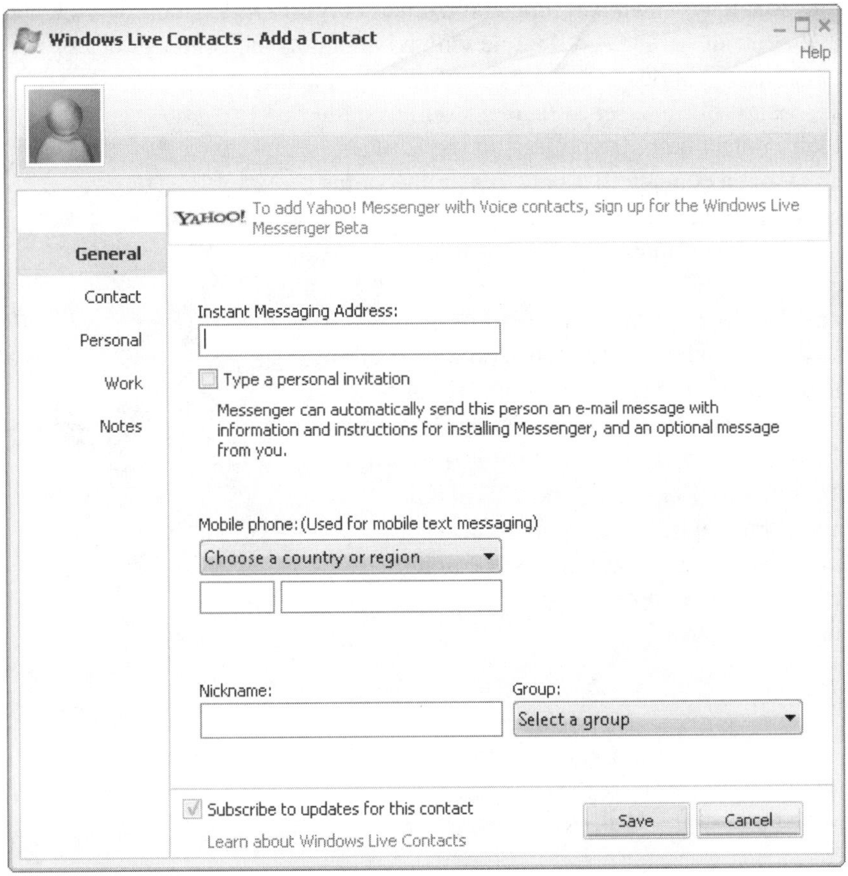

FIGURE 5-9   Add new instant messaging contacts here.

a contact. You can manually enter the person's Windows Live Messenger sign-in name or their e-mail address, or you can search for that person in the central Windows Messenger Service user database.

When you add a contact this way, that contact gets notified that you want to add them to your list of contacts. They have the option to block you from seeing their online status, so unless and until they allow you to do so, you cannot see their online status even if you successfully add them to your instant messaging contacts.

Know when Someone Is Online

Now that we've enabled the display of online status, and added the people we're concerned with to the instant messaging contacts list, what does the online status display look like? The display looks like one of three little circles. A green circle indicates that the contact is online and available. A dim reddish circle indicates that the contact is not online. A red circle with a bar across the center indicates that the person is online but busy, and doesn't want to be disturbed.

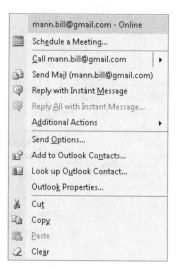

The easiest place to see someone's online status is in their contact item. If you look at the E-mail field in an open contact, that person's online status appears as a circle to the left of their e-mail address. Figure 5-10 shows an online contact in an open contact item.

Another place to see someone's online status is in a message. If you hover the mouse pointer over an e-mail address in a message, a circle will appear to the left of that address to indicate the online status.

The last place to see this status (at least while you are in Outlook) is in the shortcut menu that appears when you right-click an e-mail address in a message. In this case, you won't see colored circles. Instead, you will see a heading in the shortcut menu that includes the word Online or Offline.

FIGURE 5-10   This contact is online and available. The green circle tells you so.

Send and Receive Instant Messages

After Windows Live Messenger is set up and running properly, all you need to do is sign in, and you will be ready to receive messages. It will receive messages automatically if the person sending the message is on your Windows Live Messenger contacts list.

> **TIP**   *Standards for etiquette in corporate phone conversations and e-mail messages have been around for some time. Instant messaging etiquette is still evolving (heck, telephone etiquette is still evolving, and those things have been in the office forever), but there are some basic guidelines you can follow. Instant Messaging Planet has a helpful article about IM etiquette here: http://www.instantmessagingplanet.com/enterprise/article.php/1379121*

When someone sends you an instant message, Windows Live Messenger pops up a small box in the corner of your screen. That box stays there for a few seconds and then disappears. If you click the box, a Conversation window connecting you to the sender appears. If you don't click the little box in time, you don't lose the conversation—it's still available on the task bar.

Sending messages is slightly different, as you can do so directly from Windows Messenger or from Outlook. The following two sections explain how you do it in each case.

Sending Messages from Windows Live Messenger

To send an instant message to someone when you're working directly with Windows Live Messenger, find that person's name or e-mail address in the Windows Live Messenger main window. If the person is online, double-click his or her name or e-mail address to open a new instant messenger window. If the person is offline, you can send an e-mail instead.

Send Messages from Within Outlook

When you're working in Outlook, you can send an instant message to anyone whose status is other than offline. Right-click a person's e-mail address in the To, From, or CC field of an e-mail message, or the e-mail address field in a contact to get a list of options that includes sending an instant message.

Set Your Windows Live Messenger Status

Remember that the Windows Live Messenger Service knows when you're online and when you're not, and passes this information along to other users. When people see that you're online, they assume that you're available and willing to accept instant messages. Suppose you don't want others to contact you but also don't want to shut down Windows Live Messenger? It would be a pain to shut down your instant messaging service every time you want to concentrate on your work and not exchange messages with other people. A better approach is to let people know your situation by setting your instant messaging status.

To set your status, click your name at the top of the main Windows Live Messenger window. This opens the menu shown here. The menu contains more than a half-dozen status settings that you can use to keep others informed of your situation.

As of this writing, Windows Live Messenger offers seven options for describing your online status: Online, Busy, Be Right Back, Away, In a Call, Out to Lunch, and Appear Offline. By setting the right status at all times, you can better control the way people interact with you through Windows Live Messenger.

You now have all the information you need to use Windows Live Messenger as Outlook's instant messaging tool. But don't stop there. As you've seen, Windows Live Messenger can do far more than just exchange instant messages. I strongly suggest you experiment with some of its other features. They can really enhance your online communications.

Learn About Newsgroups

While e-mail is the most popular way to communicate on the Internet today, some older, more public means of communicating also exist. Many millions of people around the world use newsgroups to share information and discuss literally tens of thousands of topics in open conversations that virtually anyone can join. Newsgroups are an exciting and useful means of communication.

However, the importance of newsgroups is declining. Like Outlook 2003, Outlook 2007 doesn't directly work with newsgroups. Instead, it relies on another program to send and receive newsgroup messages. But here's the rub. Windows XP includes Outlook Express, a combined e-mail and newsgroup program that you could use with Outlook. Outlook Express is no longer included with Windows Vista. Among other things, this reflects the declining popularity of newsgroups. If you are running Windows XP, you can still use Outlook Express as a newsreader.

CAUTION   *As of this writing, there isn't a third-party newsreader for Outlook 2007 that I can recommend. Check the Living With Outlook website (http://www .living-with-outlook.com) and watch the RSS newsfeed you set up earlier for recommendations.*

5

This part of the chapter explains newsgroups and talks a bit about you how to use Outlook Express as Outlook's newsreader if you are running Office 2007 on Windows XP.

A *newsgroup* is the Internet equivalent of a bulletin board. Subscribers to a newsgroup can post messages to the group, and these messages can be viewed by other subscribers. People can respond to messages they see posted, and others can respond to their responses, and so on, creating what are known as *discussion threads.*

Newsgroups have been around a long time. Usenet, a network of *news servers* (computers that host newsgroups) that hosts most of the newsgroups in the world, is more than 20 years old. Google, the Internet search site at www.google.com, maintains an archive containing the last 20 years' worth of Usenet newsgroup messages. This archive contains over 700 million messages.

In addition to the vast array of public newsgroups, an unknown number of private newsgroups are available on corporate news servers. These newsgroups usually have restricted memberships and deal, not surprisingly, with issues of importance to the company or organization that hosts them.

Most newsgroups are unmoderated. That means no one is responsible for controlling the messages that appear in the newsgroup. While not having a moderator saves someone a lot of work, particularly on busy newsgroups, it does have some serious drawbacks. Unmoderated newsgroups often contain many messages unrelated to the subject of the newsgroup, junk e-mail, sales come-ons, and even obscenities and pornography. Despite these drawbacks, unmoderated newsgroups are by far the most common type of newsgroup.

Moderated newsgroups, on the other hand, are owned or managed by someone. A moderator determines whether incoming messages are allowed to appear on the newsgroup, and tries to keep the focus on the topics at hand. Moderated newsgroups are better at staying on track but depend heavily upon the efforts of the moderator or moderators.

Some newsgroups are open to anyone at all, but others limit membership to employees of a certain company, members of a particular group or organization, or another qualification established by the moderator.

> **NOTE** *One of the nicest things about newsgroups is that you don't have to pay to join them. Membership in the vast majority of newsgroups is completely free of charge (not counting whatever it costs to connect to the Internet in the first place) and open to anyone with a newsreader and access to a news server.*

You use a *newsreader* to view the messages in newsgroups. Newsreaders display a list of the newsgroups available on a particular news server, and allow you to download and read messages from newsgroups, as well as compose your own messages that the newsreader posts to newsgroups.

> **CAUTION** *The people who send junk e-mail (spam) also haunt newsgroups. Chapter 14 contains information you can use to protect yourself from newsgroup and e-mail spammers.*

Use Outlook Express as Outlook's Newsreader

Outlook Express is a free e-mail client and newsreader that Microsoft includes with Windows XP. It can manage multiple e-mail and newsgroup accounts for you under a single user identity, as well as manage multiple identities. Outlook 2007 is a much more capable e-mail program than Outlook Express, so we won't spend any time on the e-mailing aspect of Outlook Express. Instead, we'll concentrate on using Outlook Express as a newsreader. Unless you install and configure your own newsreader, Outlook assumes that you want to use Outlook Express as your newsreader.

Configure Outlook to Use Outlook Express on Windows XP

Before you can use Outlook Express as your newsgroup newsreader, you need to add Outlook Express to the Outlook Go menu. You only have to do this procedure once to be able to open Outlook Express as your newsreader directly from the Go menu. Follow these steps:

1. In the main Outlook window, find the Standard toolbar. While the exact contents of this bar vary, it normally contains the Print, Send/Receive, and Find commands, among others.

2. Click the Toolbar Options arrow on the right side of the Standard toolbar. The Toolbar Options arrow on the end of the Standard toolbar lets you add a newsreader to the Go menu.

3. In the menu that appears, click Add or Remove Buttons and then click Customize.

4. In the Customize dialog box, select the Commands tab.

5. In the Categories list, select Go. This allows you to alter the commands that are visible on the Go menu.

6. In the Commands list, select News.

7. Without releasing the mouse button, drag News to the Go menu on the Standard toolbar. After a moment, the Go menu appears.

8. Drag News to the position in the Go menu where you want it, and then release the mouse button. This assigns News to that position in the Go menu, as the illustration shows. You can place the News option anywhere on the Go menu that makes sense to you.

Now that you've configured Outlook to start Outlook Express as its newsreader, all you need to do is open the Go menu and choose News to start Outlook Express.

Meet Outlook Express

When you choose Go | News to activate Outlook Express as Outlook's newsreader, Outlook Express opens in newsreader mode, as shown in Figure 5-11. The pane on the left side of the screen is the Folders list, which shows all of Outlook Express's folders. The e-mail–related folders in the Local Folders section of the list are of little interest when using Outlook Express as a newsreader. What's important is the list of newsgroups that appears under your news server in this list.

NOTE   *If you've never used Outlook Express before, you will have to configure it to connect to the Internet and to the service that will provide your NNTP news. Your ISP can provide the appropriate information for accomplishing this. Once you have the information, follow the steps listed here to get connected to the news server.*

You probably don't have any news servers or newsgroups listed when you first start Outlook Express. In Figure 5-11, you can see the news server I use: news.comcast.net.

The large pane on the right side of the figure is the View pane. This pane is where basic information about the message appears (the subject, who sent it and when, and similar information), as well as the complete text of messages you are reading. The exact information you see in the View pane depends on what you're doing at the moment.

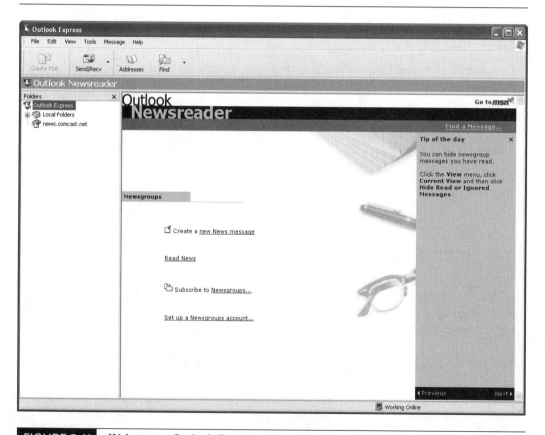

FIGURE 5-11 Welcome to Outlook Express Newsreader view.

Set Up a Newsgroup Account

Configuring Outlook Express to work with a news server is very similar to configuring Outlook to work with a mail server. You need to know the name of the news server before you start. Your ISP (for public news servers) or network administrator (for corporate news servers) can give the name of the news server to you.

Once you know the name of your news server, follow these steps to set up the account:

1. Start Outlook Express by clicking Go | News from the Outlook main window.

2. In the Outlook Express main window, click Tools | Accounts to open the Internet Accounts dialog box.

3. On the News tab, click Add and choose News to start the Internet Connection Wizard. It will guide you through the process of entering the name of your news server and setting up the account.

View a List of the Available Newsgroups

After you finish setting up a new server account, Outlook Express gives you the option to download a list of the newsgroups available on your news server. Downloading the list can take a while, as most news servers carry quite a few newsgroups. For example, the news server I use supports in excess of 36,000 newsgroups.

After Outlook Express finishes downloading the list of available newsgroups, you can start looking for some to join. To do this, click Newsgroups in the Outlook Express View pane. Doing so opens the Newsgroup Subscriptions dialog box, shown here:

As you learned earlier, your news server probably has thousands or even tens of thousands of available newsgroups. With so many newsgroups to choose from, how can you figure out which ones to subscribe to? Here are three ways to tackle the problem:

■ Know which newsgroup you want to subscribe to before you start. You may have been referred to a particular newsgroup by a friend or coworker, or perhaps by a directive from the IT department at work. In this case, your task is easy. Enter the name of the newsgroup in the Display Newsgroups Which Contain box of the Newsgroup Subscriptions dialog box. Assuming your news server carries the newsgroup, its name will appear in the list. Select the newsgroup and then click Subscribe.

■ If you don't have a particular newsgroup in mind, but are interested in a particular subject, the Display Newsgroups Which Contain box can be very helpful. Enter a word describing the subject you're interested in to see a list of each newsgroups on the news server whose name contains the word you entered. Enter "fishing" for example, and Outlook Express will list every available newsgroup on the news server that has the word "fishing" in its name.

TIP

You can increase your chances of finding a newsgroup that covers your subject by selecting the Also Search Descriptions check box. Some newsgroups publish a description that explains the purpose of the newsgroup. This description may include the name of the subject you're interested in, even if the newsgroup's name doesn't.

■ As an Outlook user, you might find Microsoft's Outlook, Office, and Windows newsgroups to be of use. Try entering the words "Microsoft" and "Outlook." Doing so returns dozens of newsgroups that cover Microsoft Outlook (and Outlook Express). Other searches containing the word "Microsoft" and the name of the application or operating system you're interested in will return similar results.

5

TIP

If your news server doesn't carry the newsgroup you're looking for, try using a different news server. One place to find publicly available news servers is newszbot.com (http://www.newzbot.com/serverlist.php).

Subscribe to a Newsgroup

You can read newsgroup messages without subscribing to a newsgroup. You can even post messages to a newsgroup without subscribing. So why subscribe?

When you subscribe to a newsgroup, your newsreader includes that newsgroup in a list that appears each time you start the newsreader. This gives you access to the newsgroup with as little as one click of the mouse, instead of requiring you to search for the newsgroup each time you want to view it.

To subscribe to a newsgroup, follow these steps:

1. Click Tools | Newsgroups to open the Newsgroup Subscriptions dialog box if it isn't already open.

TIP

You can also open the Newsgroup Subscriptions dialog box by pressing CTRL-W.

2. Find and select the newsgroup you want to subscribe to in the Newsgroup Subscriptions dialog box.

3. Click Subscribe or double-click the newsgroup's name.

When you subscribe to a newsgroup, an icon—it looks like a manila folder with a piece of paper tacked to it—appears to the left of the newsgroup's name in the Newsgroup list. When you finish selecting newsgroups to subscribe to, click OK to exit the Newsgroup Subscriptions dialog box. The newsgroup you subscribed to appears in the Outlook Newsreader Folders list.

Read Newsgroup Messages

After you subscribe to some newsgroups, you're almost ready to start reading messages. First you need to download the message headers from the newsgroup that you want to read. If you're only interested in working with a single newsgroup right now, just click that newsgroup's name in the Folders list. Outlook Express automatically downloads the headers for that newsgroup. Downloading message headers this way is called "synchronizing with the newsgroup." Newsgroup message headers contain information such as the subject of the message, who sent it, when it was sent, and its size.

Another approach is to download all the headers for all the newsgroups you subscribe to on this news server. To do this, click Tools | Synchronize All.

Similar to downloading the list of available newsgroups, downloading the headers of all the messages in one or more newsgroups can take a while. The Microsoft.public.windows.vista.general group alone contains over 35,000 messages, including about 35,000 messages that I haven't read yet! I know how many messages I haven't read because the number of unread messages appears to the right of each newsgroup name in the Folders list.

5

CAUTION *If you're not careful, newsgroups can become a major time sink. If you subscribe to busy newsgroups, you're likely to see tens, hundreds, and maybe even thousands of unread messages every time you open your newsreader. You could spend vast amounts of time reading and replying to messages, and not get any of your real work done. To avoid wasting too much time, try just skimming the subject names of the messages you haven't read yet, and only select messages that really interest you.*

To start reading messages in a particular newsgroup, click the name of the newsgroup in the Folders list. Outlook Express displays the headers of messages from that newsgroup in the View pane. Click a message in the View pane to make its contents appear in the Preview pane. Double-click a message in the View pane to make the message appear in its own window.

NOTE *If the newsgroup contains no unread messages, the name of that newsgroup in the Folders list is in normal type. If the newsgroup does contain unread messages, its name appears in boldface in the Folders list.*

Reply to Newsgroup Messages

You'll eventually want to reply to a message you read in a newsgroup. Doing so is very much like replying to an e-mail message, except for the fact that you're using Outlook Express instead of Outlook and you're replying to a newsgroup instead of an individual. Follow these steps to compose and post a reply to a newsgroup message:

1. Decide what kind of reply you want to make. No, I don't mean deciding whether to be sarcastic or funny; I mean deciding whether you want to reply directly to the person who sent the message or to the newsgroup as a whole.

2. Click Reply or Reply Group.

3. Type your reply in the message window. Note that Outlook Express automatically includes the contents of the message you're replying to.

4. Click Send to post a message to the newsgroup or send it to the individual recipient.

Compose and Post New Newsgroup Messages

Composing and posting new newsgroup messages is almost the same as replying to a newsgroup message. Select the newsgroup you want to post to in the Folders list, and then click New Post in the toolbar.

Outlook Express opens a New Message window that you can use to compose your message. Outlook Express fills in the address of the destination newsgroup for you, but, of course, you must type in the subject and body of the message yourself. Click Send when you're ready to post your message to the newsgroup.

What's Next

Now that you know how to use RSS feeds, instant messaging, and newsreaders with Outlook 2007, you are ready for a full range of communication. But there's another side to Outlook. That's the personal information management side. You have loads of things to do, and vast amounts of information to keep track of. Outlook can help. Part III of this book will show you how.

Part III

Manage Your Personal Information

Chapter 6

Work with Contacts

How to...

- Navigate the Contacts View
- Add Contacts
- Work with Contacts
- Manage Your Contacts
- Create and Use Distribution Lists

Outlook's Contacts folder is your storage center for information about people and organizations. The information you can store for each contact is quite extensive, including three e-mail addresses, an IM name, multiple phone numbers, a postal address, employer and title information, as well as personal information such as a spouse's name information and even a photo of the contact. New to Outlook

2007 is the ability to create, share, and display digital business cards.

In this chapter, you'll learn what you need to know to use Outlook 2007 contacts effectively. From navigating the Contacts view, to adding, using, and managing your contacts, this chapter shows you all the key information.

Navigate the Contacts View

Like Outlook's Mail view, the Contacts view is designed to use screen space efficiently. Figure 6-1 shows the default Business Cards view of the Contacts folder.

As you can see in the figure, Contacts is typically divided into three sections: the Contacts navigation pane on the left, the Contacts view in the center, and the To-Do Bar on the right. The Contacts pane has the following sections, starting from the top:

- **All Contact Items**   Controls which data files Outlook should look in for contacts to display. By default, all the available options (such as your personal folders file, Internet calendars you subscribe to, your Hotmail account) are selected. You click the down arrow to change which files are selected.

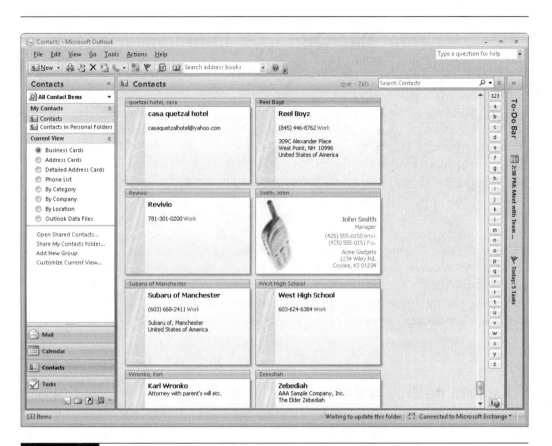

FIGURE 6-1   The Contacts folder showing the Business Cards view.

■ **My Contacts**   Gives you access to all your contacts, whether local to your PC, on a SharePoint Services server, or shared by another Outlook user.

■ **Current View**   Lets you switch between different Contact views easily.

■ **Links**   An untitled section that contains links to Contacts view features such as adding a new group of contacts and customizing the current view.

NOTE   *The exact links that appear in this section vary, depending on whether Outlook is connected to Exchange, connected to SharePoint, or is being used standalone.*

■ **Buttons**   The buttons on the bottom of the pane work just as they do in Mail view. For example, click the Mail button to go to the Mail folder.

Did you know?

You Can Optimize Contacts for Frequent Use?

If you use Contacts frequently, there are a couple of things you can do to optimize your experience. First, you can open Contacts in its own window, so it can be available at a click, without having to switch Outlook view. You can make this happen by right-clicking the Contacts button at the bottom of the Navigation pane in any view. A shortcut menu appears with the option to open the view in a new window. Click that and you will find two Outlook windows on the screen, the one you started with and one showing Contacts.

The second step comes into play when you create a new window for Contacts. Since you want this window to be available all the time, you probably don't need the Navigation pane anymore (you can move between views using the other open Outlook window). In the Contacts window, select the view you want to use, then click View, Navigation Pane, Off. This will give you significantly more space in the window for contacts.

Elements of the Contacts View

After using Mail view, Contacts view should look pretty familiar to you. There are, however, enough differences between Mail and Contacts view to make it worth spending a minute or two going over them.

Contacts appear in the large View pane. How they appear is controlled by which option you select in the Current View section of the Contacts pane. Try selecting a few options to see how they affect the appearance of the contacts in the View pane.

The View pane has features designed to make it easier to handle large numbers of contacts. In Business Card and Address Card views, next to the Search box on the upper-right side of the View pane, is an entry that—similar to a paper dictionary or encyclopedia—shows you the range of entries visible right now. Here, for example, the cards that are visible begin with characters between que and Zeb.

| 📇 Contacts | que - Zeb | Search Contacts | 🔎 ▾ ≫ |

Also in Business Card and Address Card views, Outlook displays a list of buttons down the right side of the View pane (see Figure 6-1). Use these buttons to jump to a specific section of your contact list. Click the K button to immediately jump to the first address card beginning with the letter *K*, and so on.

In the Phone List, By Category, By Company, By Location, By Follow-Up Flag, and Outlook Data Files views, your contacts appear in a table very similar to a spreadsheet. And they behave like a spreadsheet, too. For example, you can scroll through your contacts or sort them by field. At the same time, they work a lot like Mail view's Grouped by Conversation feature. They are grouped according to the View you selected. You can collapse or expand the groups and treat them as if they were single objects.

6

TIP *The By Company view can be particularly useful at work because it groups all people from the same company together. If you frequently deal with multiple contacts from the same company, this view can really help you stay organized.*

Each icon on the My Contact section of the Contacts pane represents a different source of contacts. Click an icon to view contacts from that source.

The Contacts view normally runs with the Reading pane turned off to leave the maximum amount of room possible for contacts in the View pane. To see information for a contact, double-click it so it opens in its own window.

Now you should be ready to start working with your contacts. The first step is to add some if you don't already have them.

Add Contacts

There are a few ways to add new contacts. You can create contacts in at least five ways:

- From scratch

- From information in an e-mail message

- By importing electronic business cards

- By scanning physical business cards with an appropriate card scanner

- By synchronization with a PDA (Personal Digital Assistant) or other remote device (more information on this in Chapter 15)

Let's first take a look at creating a new contact from scratch.

Create a New Contact from Scratch

To create a new contact from scratch, you open a new Contact dialog box and manually enter the information. Follow these steps:

1. From anywhere in Outlook, click File | New | Contact to open a blank Contact dialog box like the one shown in Figure 6-2.

TIP *You can also open a new Contact dialog box from any view other than a Contacts view by pressing CTRL-SHIFT-C.*

2. Be sure that the Contact dialog box has the Contact tab selected on the Ribbon, along with General selected in the Show section. Enter the name of the contact in the field next to the Full Name button. Outlook automatically

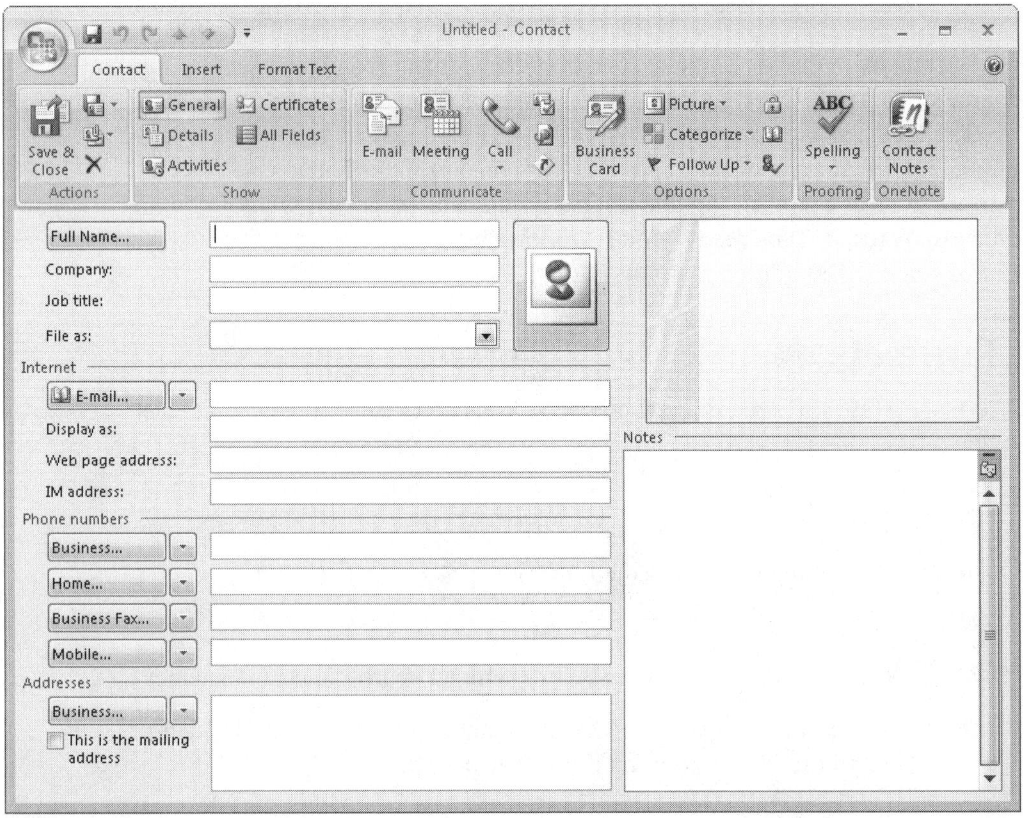

FIGURE 6-2 Create a new contact with this dialog box.

Did you know?

How to Check a Full Name

Checking a name is one specific example of checking the detailed information Outlook has stored in a particular field. To check a full name, click the Full Name button to the left of the name field after you've entered the name. This opens a small dialog box that displays all the detailed information that Outlook has stored for the name you entered, including the title (Dr., Miss); the first, middle, and last names; and any suffix (Jr., III).

6

Check Full Name
Name details
Title:
First:
Middle:
Last:
Suffix:
☑ Show this again when name is incomplete or unclear
OK   Cancel

If any of this information is incorrect or incomplete, you can correct it or add it here. Note that this dialog box will automatically appear when Outlook believes the name information is incomplete or unclear.

breaks the name into its constituent parts and stores each part in its own field. You can confirm that Outlook parsed the name correctly with the Check Full Name dialog box. See the "How to Check a Full Name" box for details.

NOTE *With the Contact dialog box open, you can always navigate back to General on the Contact tab using the keyboard shortcut ALT, H, C.*

3. Enter the rest of the information you want to include for the contact. The most basic information goes on the General page. Information such as the contact's boss's name or birthday goes on the Details page.

Did you know?

Mandatory Phone and Modem Information

The first time you enter a phone number into a contact, or even click one of the phone number buttons, then change your mind, Outlook forces you to enter some information that may or may not be at all relevant to you. Specifically, Outlook requires you to fill in some information in multiple dialog boxes. First, you are required to fill in some information about the phone system at your current location.

In this dialog box, the only thing you absolutely must enter is an area code. If you do not enter a valid area code, you cannot exit this dialog box, period. Once you do enter a valid area code, you may need to fill in additional information in additional dialog boxes.

Finally, and this will occur every time you enter a new phone number, you will see the Check Phone Number dialog box. Enter the phone number into the relevant fields of this dialog box so Outlook can check it before adding it to the contact. If you don't actually want to add a phone number at this stage of the process, you can cancel to abort the whole thing.

When you're entering information for a contact, here are some things to keep in mind:

- To tell Outlook how to file a contact, choose an option from the File As list on the General page. When you open this list, Outlook displays a number of options for filing the contact. Which options appear depends on what information you entered into the Contact dialog box fields.

- You can customize many of the fields on the General page. For example, if you look in the Phone Numbers section of the page, the first option is Business, but if you click the down arrow next to the Business button, you'll see an entire list of possible names for that field on the card.

  Here's what's going on: Outlook supports many more phone number fields than are visible on the General tab. By clicking the down arrow, you can change which field appears in that location. This not only allows you to control which fields appear on the General tab, it also allows you to enter information into fields that are not otherwise visible.

■ When a field name appears as a button (Full Name or Business, for example), you can click that button to see more detailed information that Outlook may have about the information in that field. The "How to Check a Full Name" box shows one example of the type of Check dialog box that appears.

■ If you entered more than one address for a contact in the Addresses section (by using the down-arrow button described previously), you can designate one address as the primary address by selecting the This Is the Mailing Address check box when the appropriate address is visible.

Create a New Contact from an E-Mail Message

If you've been exchanging e-mail with someone and you want to create a contact for your correspondent, you can save some time by automatically entering information into a new Contact dialog box. Here's how to do it:

1. In the Mail view, open a message that contains the person's name or e-mail address in the To, From, or Cc fields.

2. Right-click the person's name or e-mail address.

3. In the shortcut menu, click Add to Outlook Contacts. This opens a new Contact dialog box containing whatever information Outlook gleaned about that person from the e-mail message.

4. Add any additional information to the dialog box and save the contact.

Import an Electronic Business Card

As Outlook 2007 becomes more widely used, it will be ever more likely that you will see messages that include electronic business cards, either as attachments or as part of the signature of the message. Happily, importing the information from an electronic business card is easy, and greatly speeds up the process of creating a new contact.

When someone sends you a message with an attached electronic business card, it will look something like Figure 6-3. In this example, the electronic business card is the entire signature, although as you know from Chapter 3, a signature can contain lots of other information too. The electronic business card appears in two places in the message: as an image in the signature, and as a .VCF file attached to

Dear Sir,

Please review the attached blah, blah, blah...

Yours truly,

John Smith
Manager
(425) 555-0150 Work
(425) 555-0151 Fax
Acme Gadgets
1234 Wiley Rd.
Coyote, KS 01234

FIGURE 6-3   A message with a business card as the signature.

the message. Displaying the card as an attachment as well as part of the signature allows recipients who don't use Outlook 2007 to view the information in the card as well (assuming their e-mail program understands .VCF files).

To add the information from an electronic business card into your Contacts, right-click the card. Outlook displays the option Add to Outlook Contacts. Click that, and a new Contact dialog box appears with all the information from the card inserted into the appropriate locations. Add any additional information you wish, then click Save & Close to add the new contact.

Use a Business Card Scanner

If you receive lots of paper business cards, you may want to invest in a business card scanner. You insert a business card into one of these small devices, and it scans the card. Using optical character recognition (OCR) software, it reads the contact information on the card, and converts it to a form that can be imported into various contact management programs, including Outlook.

Include Pictures in Contacts

Including a picture in a contact is really a great idea when you think about it. The ability to match a face to the contact information you have can only help your relationship with that contact. Figure 6-4 shows a new Contact dialog box containing a photo of yours truly.

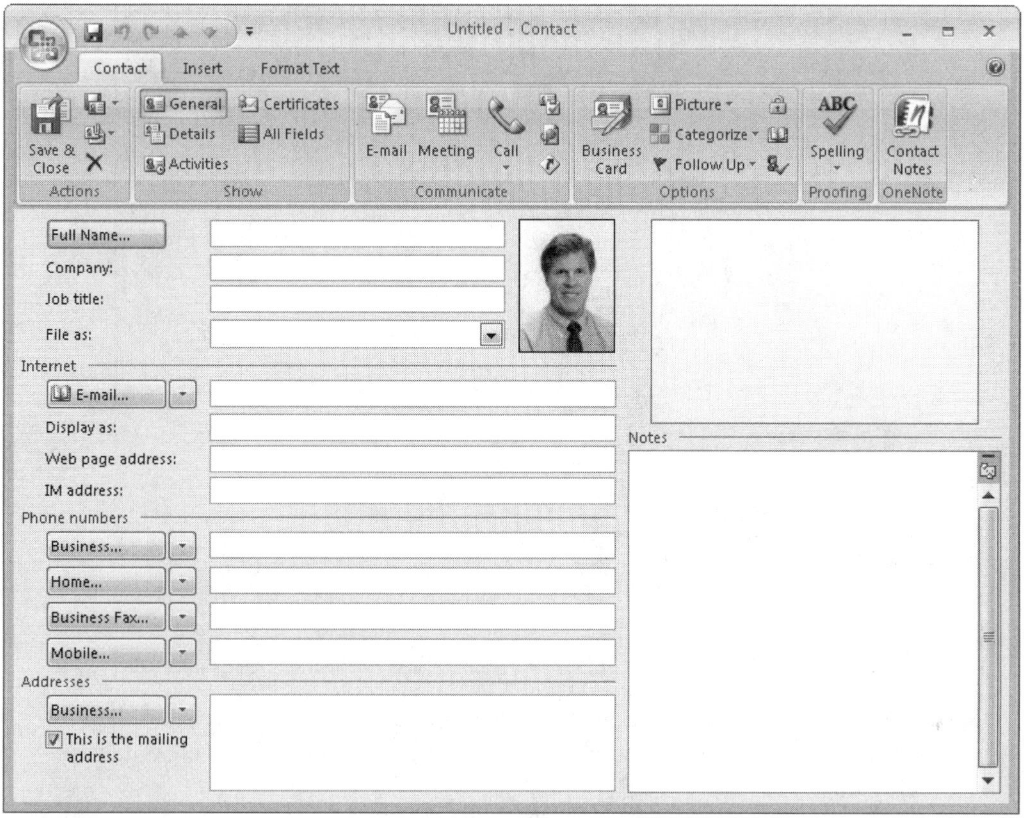

FIGURE 6-4 Adding a picture to a contact connects face and information.

Assuming you already have a picture of the person in question (anything from a camera-phone photo up to a photo from a high-end digital camera will do), adding that picture to the person's Contact dialog box is a simple process:

1. Open the person's Contact dialog box.

2. Click the Picture box (it appears to the right of the Full Name field. This opens a Find dialog box that you can use to locate the picture on your system or anywhere on a network.

3. Locate the picture you want to use and double-click it. Outlook copies the picture, resizes it to fit the contact picture space, and adds it to the Contact dialog box.

4. Save the contact and you are done.

Changing or removing a picture is even easier. Open the contact, right-click the picture, and select what you want to do in the shortcut menu that appears.

Work with Contacts

While you can use contacts simply as storage areas for information about users and organizations, they can be more than that. With a contact selected, it only takes a few clicks of the mouse to address a meeting request, send an e-mail message, or create a task associated with that contact. You can link Outlook items or Office documents to a contact, making it easy to keep track of activities related to the contact. If you've added the contact's street address, Outlook (with some help from Windows Live Local) will show you a map and give you directions to the contact's location.

The next several sections walk you through some of the most useful things you can do with contacts.

Create Outlook Items Related to the Contact

You can have Outlook create a variety of items related to a contact and automatically fill in the relevant information about the contact. To do this, right-click the contact in any one of the contact views. A shortcut menu appears. Click Create to open a submenu showing the kinds of items Outlook can create.

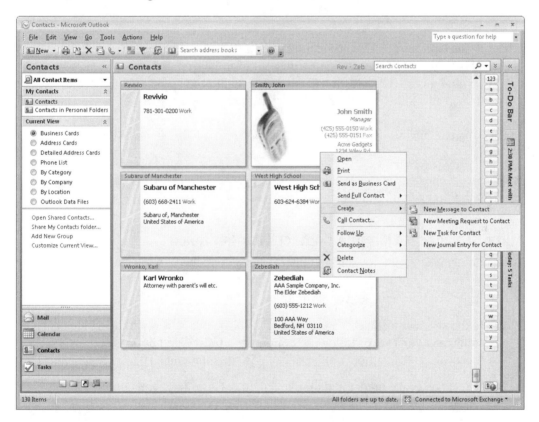

Select any of the options in this submenu (New Message to Contact, for example) and Outlook opens a new window for that type of item with the contact's address information already filled in. Another way to get the same result is to select the contact, click Actions, and select the option from the Create submenu of the Action menu.

Flag Contacts for Follow Up

Do you remember when we talked about flagging messages in Chapter 4? (See "Keep Track of Messages You Must Act on with Flagging" in Chapter 4 for details.) You have the same flagging capabilities for contacts. That means you can flag contacts for follow up, thereby creating a task and assigning a reminder if you wish. Here are the steps you need to take to flag contacts.

Add or Change a Flag to a Contact That Is Open

To add or change a flag for a contact that is already open, follow these steps:

1. In the Options group of the Contact tab of the Ribbon, click Follow Up. This opens a Follow Up menu with a set of follow-up options. If a follow-up option is already set for this contact, that option will be selected in the menu and visible in the contact's InfoBar below the Ribbon.

TIP   *You can also use the ALT, H, W keyboard shortcut to open this menu.*

2. Select one of the predefined options, or click Custom (if you don't want a reminder) or Add Reminder to create your own option.

Add or Change a Flag to a Contact That Is Closed

To add or change a flag for a contact that you haven't opened, follow these steps:

1. Right-click the contact you wish to flag.

2. In the shortcut menu that appears, click Follow Up. This opens up a submenu with a set of follow-up options. If a follow-up option is set for this contact, that option will be selected in the submenu.

3. Select one of the predefined options, or click Custom (if you don't want a reminder) or Add Reminder to create your own option.

Categorize Contacts

Applying categories to contacts can be a powerful organizational tool. Consistently applying the same category to all items related to a specific project makes it easier to track them. As you will see in Chapter 13, Outlook 2007's Instant Search capability makes it possible to instantly find every Outlook item of a particular category at once, whether it is a message, a contact, an appointment, whatever.

You can categorize contacts using almost the same steps that you use to flag them. While the contacts don't display their category colors in the contact views, they are visible when you open a contact, and you can still use them for sorting your contacts. This happens automatically in By Category view. In other tabular views, such as Phone List and By Company, you can display the Category field and use it to sort contacts. So let's see how to apply categories to your contacts.

Set the Category for a Contact That Is Open

To set the category for a contact that is already open, follow these steps:

1. In the Options group of the Contact tab of the Ribbon, click Categorize. This opens a menu with a set of Category options. If a category is already set for this contact, that category will be selected in the menu and visible below the Ribbon.

   TIP   *You can also use the ALT, H, G keyboard shortcut to open this menu.*

2. Select one or more of the existing categories (remember that any item can belong to more than one category), or click Clear All Categories to clear them. Click All Categories if you want to modify the categories before applying them.

Set the Category for a Contact That Is Closed

To set the category for a contact that you haven't opened, follow these steps:

1. Right-click the contact you wish to categorize.

2. In the shortcut menu that appears, click Categorize. This opens up a submenu with a set of category options. If one or more categories are already set for this contact, those categories will be selected in the submenu.

3. Select one or more of the existing categories (remember that any item can belong to more than one category), or click Clear All Categories to clear them. Click All Categories if you want to modify the categories before applying them.

Dial Contact Phone Numbers

If your PC has a dial-up modem installed and connected to the phone system, you don't even have to dial a contact's phone number yourself. You can have Outlook do it for you.

To have Outlook dial a contact's phone number, open the contact and then click Actions | Call Contact. This opens a new menu containing all of the Contact phone numbers that Outlook has, along with other options such as Redial and Speed Dial. Click a phone number or menu option and let Outlook do the rest.

Use vCards with Contacts

While electronic business cards are the new way to send and receive contact information using Outlook 2007, they're not the only way. You can also use a vCard, which is the way Outlook users transferred contact information before electronic business cards (and the way most programs still do it). The vCard standard is widely recognized by e-mail programs and contact managers, including Outlook. Outlook allows you to create and read vCards from contacts, as well as e-mail vCards to others or make a vCard part of your e-mail signature.

NOTE *Some firewalls remove vCards from messages as a security measure.*

Send Contacts as vCards

Follow these steps to send one or more contacts as vCards:

1. In any of the contact views, select the contact or contacts you want to send as vCards. (Hold down the CTRL key when clicking contacts to select multiple contacts.)

2. Right-click one of the contacts. In the shortcut menu that appears, click Send Full Contact.

3. In the submenu that appears, select In Internet Format (vCard). Outlook opens a new Message window with the selected contacts attached as vCards.

Import Contacts Sent to You as vCards

From time to time, you might receive vCards attached to e-mail messages. You can easily convert a vCard into an Outlook contact by double-clicking the vCard attachment. Outlook opens the attachment as a new contact. Click Save to save the information.

Include Electronic Business Cards in Signatures

Back in Chapter 3, we talked about how to add a signature to an e-mail message. Now that you know about electronic business cards, you are ready to learn how to add them to your signatures. But first, let's review the steps for creating a signature in the first place:

In the Options dialog box, go to the Mail Format tab, then click Signatures to open the Create Signature dialog box. Click New to create a new signature, or select the signature you want to edit, then work in the Edit Signature box at the bottom of the dialog box. Remember that you can have multiple signatures, so you can create ones for work, ones for play, ones with attached electronic business cards, ones without, and use whichever is appropriate for the message you're writing right now.

FIGURE 6-5 Use this dialog box to insert an electronic business card.

After all this buildup, adding the electronic business card is easy. All you need to do is position the cursor at the point in Edit Signature where you want to insert the business card, then click the Business Card button. This opens the Insert Business Card dialog box shown in Figure 6-5.

In the Filed As list, select the contact whose electronic business card you want to insert, then click OK to insert it. A picture of the selected card appears in the Business Card Preview area at the bottom of the dialog box, as shown in the figure. Clicking OK returns you to the Signatures and Stationery dialog box, where you can see the signature and do any additional editing that is needed.

Get a Map

If you are working with a contact that has a street address, Outlook can show you a map, and even give you directions. Or more accurately, Outlook can work with Windows Live Local to give you this information (an active Internet connection is necessary to connect to Windows Live Local). Follow these steps to get directions to the address contained in a contact:

1. Open the contact containing the address.

2. Make sure the address you want to map is visible in the Addresses section of the Contact window.

3. Click Map in the Communicate group of the Contact tab of the Ribbon. Map is located in the lower-right corner of the group, and looks like a yellow traffic sign with a "right turn" arrow.

TIP *You can also use the* ALT, H, F *keyboard shortcut to get a map.*

4. After a moment or two, your web browser will open a new window containing a Windows Live Local map of the address like the one shown here.

6

I strongly suggest you give this a try with some of your own contacts. Windows Live Local has all sorts of cool capabilities (directions, aerial views, the ability to save notes about the location) that could definitely come in handy.

Manage Your Contacts

There is one troublesome thing about contacts: they accumulate. Unlike e-mail messages, tasks, or appointments, you naturally tend to hang onto contacts. Some people accumulate hundreds, even thousands. Long before you get into the thousands, contacts can become cumbersome to deal with. That's why you need to learn some techniques for managing them. Aside from a general suggestion that you delete old contacts that you are sure you don't need anymore, I have two techniques to help you manage your contacts.

Find a Contact

When you have lots of contacts, the most difficult management task may just be finding the right one. Fortunately, the Contacts view menu makes it easy to search contacts without having to scan through all of them.

To search for a particular contact, type any information you can remember about the contact into the Search Contacts box. You can find this box directly above the Contacts view pane. When you press ENTER, Outlook opens the contact if only one contact matches your search, or displays all the matching contacts if more than one contact is found.

When searching for contacts, you can enter a full name, a partial name, an e-mail alias, a display name, or a company name. Searches with only a limited amount of information may return a large number of possibilities, but you're sure to find the contact you're looking for.

Deal with Duplicate Contacts

One final headache when managing contacts is dealing with duplicates. Sooner or later, virtually everyone ends up with one or more duplicate contacts. Finding that you have duplicates is easy, however, because Outlook tells you when you have them. The more difficult task is figuring out what to do about it.

Duplicate contacts can occur for various reasons, including synchronization with a PDA. Even if you have never seen this problem before, if you plan to go mobile someday, you will probably run into it eventually. Knowing how to use this dialog box will eventually come in handy.

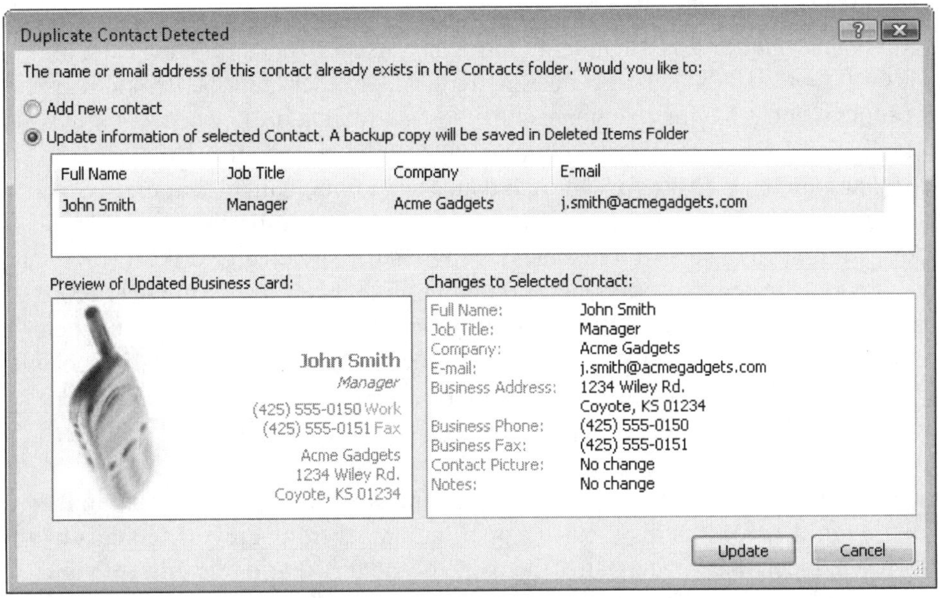

Duplicate Contact Detected

The name or email address of this contact already exists in the Contacts folder. Would you like to:

○ Add new contact
◉ Update information of selected Contact. A backup copy will be saved in Deleted Items Folder

Full Name	Job Title	Company	E-mail
John Smith	Manager	Acme Gadgets	j.smith@acmegadgets.com

Preview of Updated Business Card:

John Smith
Manager
(425) 555-0150 Work
(425) 555-0151 Fax
Acme Gadgets
1234 Wiley Rd.
Coyote, KS 01234

Changes to Selected Contact:

Full Name:	John Smith
Job Title:	Manager
Company:	Acme Gadgets
E-mail:	j.smith@acmegadgets.com
Business Address:	1234 Wiley Rd.
	Coyote, KS 01234
Business Phone:	(425) 555-0150
Business Fax:	(425) 555-0151
Contact Picture:	No change
Notes:	No change

[Update]   [Cancel]

FIGURE 6-6   This dialog box make it much easier to deal with duplicate contacts.

When you try to save a duplicate contact, Outlook displays the Duplicate Contact Detected dialog box shown in Figure 6-6. Now you have to make a decision. You can either add the new contact anyway, or update the existing contact with any new information from the new contact.

If there is a valid reason to have two contacts with the same name, you can select the Add New Contact option and click Update. But before you do, consider coming up with a way to distinguish between the two contacts (perhaps include the middle initial for one). Doing so will make it easier for you to tell them apart when you look in the contact list later, and prevent any further confusion about duplicate entries.

If you would like to update the existing contact with information from the new contact, select Update Information of Selected Contact and click Update. While Outlook can automatically transfer basic information from the new contact to the existing one, it is possible that some information will not get copied. This is the reason why it's best for you to deal with duplicate contacts as soon as possible. Doing so reduces the chance of losing information that you've entered into the duplicate contact.

Create and Use Distribution Lists

Outlook *distribution lists* are nothing more than lists of contacts. They exist to make it easy to send a message, meeting request, or other Outlook item to a group of people without having to enter each person's e-mail address whenever you want to send a message. Here's an example of one way to use a distribution list.

I maintain the website for the Irish dance school my daughter attends. Since the site doesn't change often, we offer people the opportunity to sign up for a notification list that sends them a message when the site changes. While there are lots of sophisticated ways to handle something like this, I use a simple Outlook distribution list. Whenever someone wants to join the notification list, I add them to an Outlook distribution list that I maintain for the school. When I make a change to the site, I simply address the notification message to the e-mail list and send it. Outlook handles the details of sending the message to each individual contact on the list. It's simple and effective.

Outlook stores distribution lists in the Contacts folder. When working in the Contacts folder, you can distinguish a distribution list from a regular contact by the two-headed icon that appears after the name of the distribution list in card views, the subheading "group" in Business Cards view, or by the way the name of the distribution list appears in bold in other views.

If you open a distribution list, Outlook displays a list of all the members of the list. The Ribbon includes all the options you could want for working with a distribution list (see Figure 6-7), including the ability to select specific members to communicate with, add or remove members, or update the list.

Create and Update Distribution Lists

The process for creating a distribution list is straightforward. Follow these steps:

1. In the Outlook window, click File | New. In the menu that appears, click Distribution List to open the new distribution list dialog box.

TIP   *You can also open a new distribution list dialog box with the CTRL-SHIFT-L keyboard shortcut.*

2. Enter a name for the new distribution list in the Name box.

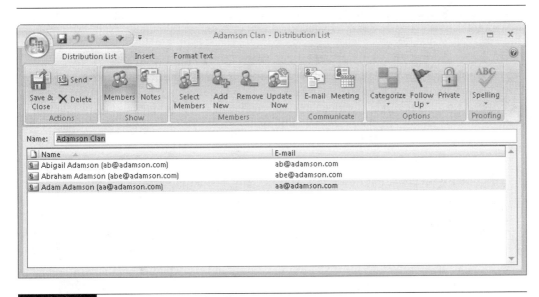

FIGURE 6-7   A sample distribution list.

3. Click Select Members in the Members group of the Distribution List tab of the Ribbon to open the Select Members dialog box.

4. In the Search area, select whether you want to search just the Name field or All Fields.

5. In the Address Book list, select the location containing the addresses you want to add to your new list. The available contacts appear in the main window of the dialog box.

6. To search for a specific contact, enter some of the information about the contact in the box below the Search options.

7. Select the contact or contacts you want to add to the distribution list, then click Members at the bottom of the dialog box to add the selected contacts to the list.

8. Repeat the process for any additional contacts you want to add to the distribution list.

9. Click OK to return to the distribution list dialog box. The names that you added should now appear in the list.

10. Click Save & Close to save your new distribution list.

Move a Distribution List Someone Sent You into Contacts

If someone e-mails you a distribution list, you can easily add it to your Contacts folder. Just open the message containing the distribution list and then drag the list into the Contacts folder.

Update the Addresses in a Distribution List

If you have changed the e-mail addresses of any of the contacts included in a distribution list, you'll need to update the list before using it again. To do this, find the distribution list in your Contacts folder. Double-click the list to open it, then click Update Now. Click Save & Close to save the changes.

Modify a Distribution List

Once you've created the distribution list, you can also modify it. To do so, find the distribution list in your Contacts folder. Double-click the list to open it, then use the Select Members, Add New, and Remove buttons to make any changes necessary.

Use a Distribution List

In general, you use a distribution list the same way you use any regular contact. The only time there's a noticeable difference is when you only want to work with part of the distribution list. And in those cases, you can just expand the list, then work with the individual contacts as normal. The rest of this section talks about the most common situations you'll encounter when using distribution lists.

Send a Message to a Distribution List

Once you have a distribution list saved in the Contacts folder, you can use it in an e-mail message just like a regular contact. Enter the distribution list in the To field of an e-mail message and Outlook sends the message to everyone in the distribution list. It works the same way with the Cc and Bcc fields.

> **NOTE**   *If you are in a situation where you don't want to automatically give the people on your distribution list access to everyone else on the list, you can send the message to yourself and Bcc the distribution list. That way, everyone on the list will get the message, but only your e-mail address will appear in the message.*

Because distribution lists are expandable, you also have the flexibility to send a message to only part of the distribution list. The next section shows how.

Send a Message to Part of a Distribution List

If you need to send a message to only some of the people on a distribution list, you don't need to type everything in by hand. Instead, you can expand the distribution list and remove the contacts you don't want to receive the message. Because Outlook expands the distribution list in the To, Cc, or Bcc box of the message, adding or removing names affects only the current message and doesn't change the actual distribution list.

When you add a distribution list to the To, Cc, or Bcc box of a message, you'll notice a plus sign (+) to the left of the name of the list. This, by the way, is the easy way to tell if you're looking at a distribution list as opposed to a regular contact within a message.

If you click the plus sign, Outlook expands the distribution list, replacing the single entry for the list with each of the contacts the list contains. But before it does,

Outlook gives you the chance to change your mind by displaying the Expand List message box, where you must click OK to expand the list. You can set the Please Do Not Show Me This Dialog Again check box to prevent this message box from showing up again in the future.

CAUTION   *You cannot collapse a distribution list once you expand it in a message.*

Send a Distribution List to Someone by E-Mail

You may want to share a distribution list with someone else. To e-mail a distribution list, follow these steps:

1. Open and address a new e-mail message.

2. Drag the distribution list from the Contacts folder into the body of the message and send it.

Chapter 7

Stay on Schedule with Calendar

How to…

■ Navigate the Calendar View

■ Use the Calendar

■ Publish and View Calendars

Now it is time to learn about the Outlook Calendar folder. This folder received a pretty significant makeover for Outlook 2007. This work has made the Calendar even more useful than it already was, not to mention more fun to use.

Like a paper calendar, the Outlook Calendar is a place for you to record appointments, track upcoming events and tasks, and figure out how many more days until your big vacation. But the Outlook Calendar is far more versatile than a paper calendar. Not only can it record when activities are going to happen, but also remind you of them. It can help you to schedule meetings and other activities by showing you the schedules of the people who are going to attend these things, sending them invitations, and keep track of who has replied for you. If you have multiple calendars or access to calendars that others have published, you can view them simultaneously, side by side, or overlaid one atop the other.

A new Daily Task List appears at the bottom of the Day and Week views. It shows you the tasks that are due on any given day. It also makes it simple (drag-and-drop simple) to block out a specific time to complete specific tasks so you can be sure to have time to work on them.

If you want to share your calendar with others online, you can do that. You can view someone else's calendar (if they've published it and given you permission to look at it), or subscribe to Internet Calendars published by various organizations so their events will appear on your Calendar view.

As you can tell, there's a lot to learn about the Outlook 2007 Calendar. We should probably get started now.

Navigate the Calendar View

Let's begin by talking about the Calendar view. To open the Calendar, click the Calendar icon in the Navigation pane, or use the CTRL-2 keyboard shortcut. If you do this, you will see something very similar to Figure 7-1.

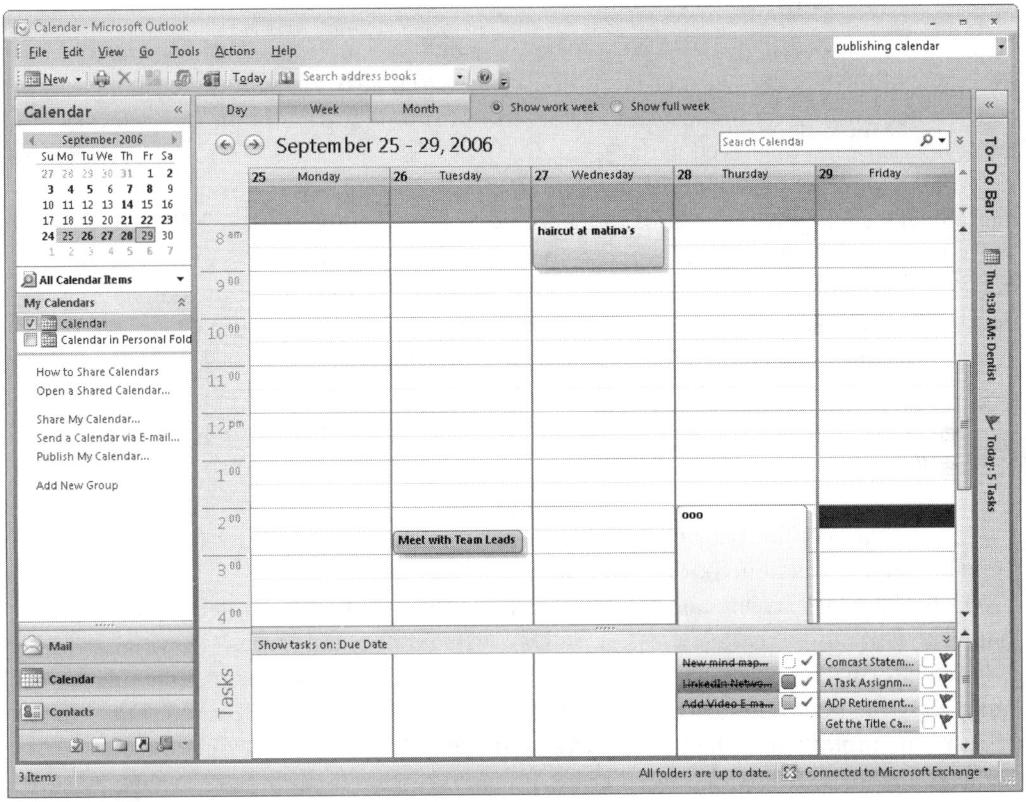

FIGURE 7-1   The Weekly view of the Calendar folder.

NOTE   *Outlook remembers which view of the Calendar you used last, and returns to that view when you return to the Calendar, so what you see may differ. If you do not see the Week view, you can use the View menu to get to the Day/Week/Month view, then click Week at the top of the center pane to get there.*

The view divides into three main panes. On the left is the Navigation pane, with Calendar-specific information in it. On the right (assuming you haven't turned it off or moved it to the bottom of the screen) is the To-Do Bar. In the center is the View pane.

The View Pane

As usual, the real action is in the View pane. The bulk of the View pane is occupied by a view of the week (or day, or month), divided into hourly blocks. At the right edge of the pane is a scroll bar that lets you display different parts of the day, since all 24 hours are not displayed at once.

At the top of the pane you see the date or range of dates that is displayed in the Calendar. In Figure 7-1, that is the work week from September 25–29, 2006. The arrows to the left of the date allow you to scroll through the days, weeks, or months to see what's happening in other time periods. To the right of the date is the ever-useful Instant Search box, which you can use to find a specific Calendar item if you can't remember when it happened or will happen.

> **TIP**   *You can choose whether to display the work week or the entire week using the controls above the date range.*

At the bottom of this pane (unless you turned it off) is the Daily Task List, which we will look at in detail in the next section.

Each of the Day, Week, and Month views has its own unique characteristics that make working in that view easier. In Day view (shown in Figure 7-2), you only see information about the selected day. However, this view does include the handy Previous Appointment and Next Appointment tabs along the left and right edges of the center pane when you are looking at the view for today. Clicking one of these tabs immediately takes you to the previous or next appointment, whatever day it happens to be on, and saves you from having to manually scroll through the days to find out where you need to be next.

The Month view (shown in Figure 7-3) shows an entire month's calendar in a highly compressed form. This view has two special features. First are the Low, Medium, and High detail options at the top of the pane. Select Low details and only all-day items appear. Select Medium, and the view will show you all-day items, plus display colored blocks on days where you have appointments scheduled. Select High details, and the view replaces the colored blocks with blocks containing the names of the first three activities that are scheduled for each day.

The other special feature is the scroll bar on the right side of the pane. In Day or Week view, this scrolls through the hours of the day so you can see all 24 of them. Month view doesn't show the hours of the day anyway, so in this view the scroll bar scrolls you backward and forward through the months, one week at a time. It's really useful for getting a big-picture view of your schedule.

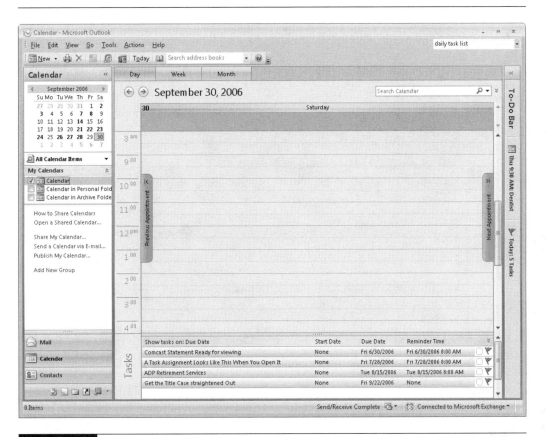

FIGURE 7-2   The Calendar Day view.

The Navigation Pane

The Navigation pane in Calendar views provides Calendar-specific navigation aides. It is divided into several sections, starting at the top:

- **Date Navigator**   A small calendar that you can use to quickly navigate to a specific date without having to scroll through the main calendar view. We will talk more about the Date Navigator shortly.

- **All Calendar Items**   Appears if you have Outlook connected to multiple sources of calendar information. Clicking the down arrow displays a list

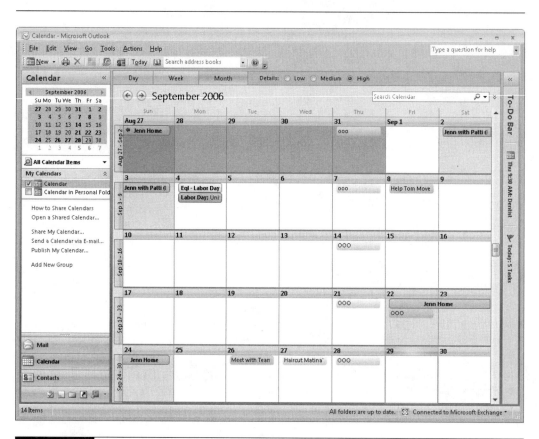

FIGURE 7-3 The Calendar Month view.

of all the places where Outlook will look for calendar information during searches.

- **My Calendars** Gives you access to all your calendars, whether local to your PC, on a SharePoint server, in an Exchange public folder, or shared by another Outlook user. If you select multiple calendars in this section, Outlook will display all of them simultaneously, allowing you to look for conflicts and otherwise get a grip on the totality of your schedules.

- **Current View** Displays a list of the available calendar views and lets you switch between them with a single click.

You will likely find that this option is turned off when you first start working with Outlook 2007. If you want to use it and don't see it, click View | Navigation Pane, and select Current View Pane.

■ **Links** Contains links that allow you to open shared calendars, share your calendar, or customize the current view.

NOTE *The exact links that appear in this section vary, depending on whether Outlook is connected to Exchange, is connected to SharePoint, or is being used standalone.*

■ **Buttons** The buttons at the bottom of the pane work just as they do in Mail view. Click the Mail button to go to the Mail folder, and so on.

7

More on the Date Navigator

When you have Calendar in one of the Day/Week/Month views, the Date Navigator (shown in Figure 7-4) appears at the top of that Calendar pane. Here's what you can do with it. The first thing to note is that it doesn't just show the days of the month. Dates that appear in bold text in the Date Navigator are days with some sort of activity scheduled. Not surprisingly, you can use the Date Navigator to navigate through time. Click a date in the Date Navigator and the View pane switches to show that date.

The Date Navigator becomes particularly handy when you are scheduling activities more than a few days in advance. Click a date in the Date Navigator, and Calendar displays that date in the View pane. Click the right and left arrows in the header of the Date Navigator to see the next or preceding month. With only a few clicks on the Date Navigator, you can quickly get to the date you want to work on, without having to fool around with your view or the buttons on the standard toolbar.

The Daily Task List

As you've already seen, the Daily Task List appears at the bottom of the Day and Week views. Tasks get into the list automatically when you create them using the New Task dialog box. Since Tasks are the subject of Chapter 8, we won't go into this way of getting tasks into the Daily Task List here. Instead, we will look at how

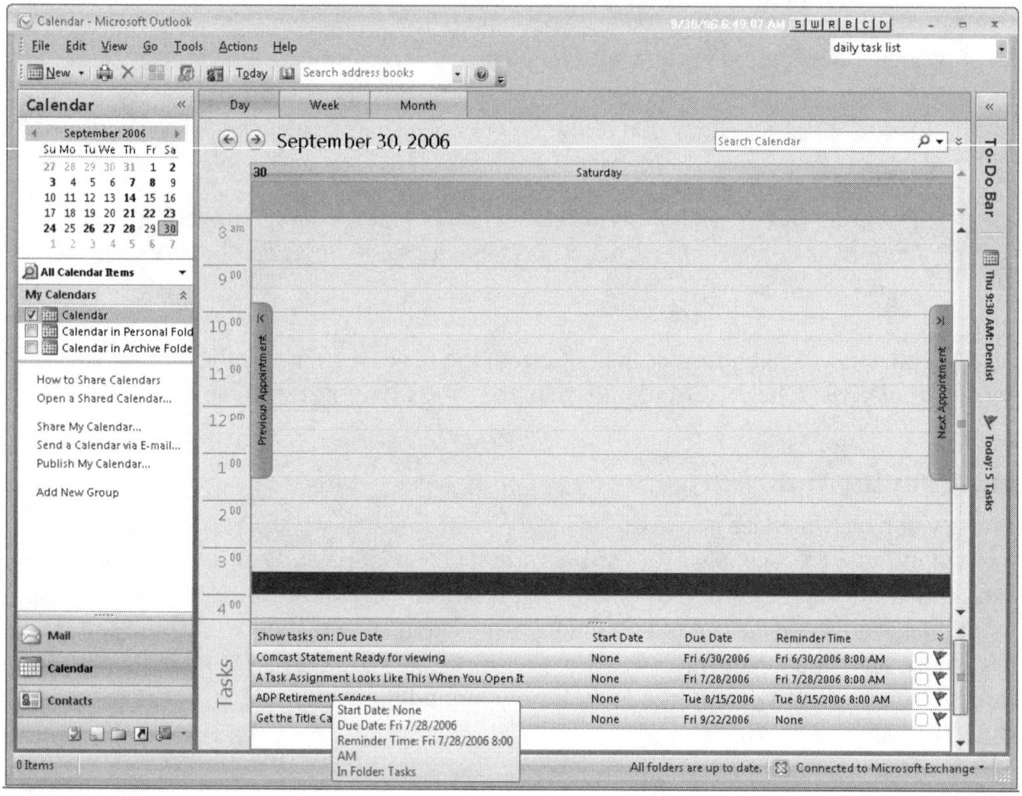

FIGURE 7-4   Use the Date Navigator to get around quickly in Day/Week/Month views.

you use the Daily Task List, and ways that you can manipulate tasks from within the Day and Week views. This intertwining of the two views makes it harder to write about them in an organized manner, but in daily use, makes a lot of sense and is intuitively easy to grasp.

With that said, let's talk about how you navigate the Daily Task List.

Navigate the Daily Task List

The Daily Task List is pretty simple. It has a section for each day that is visible in the Calendar. Those sections contain lists of tasks that are associated with that day. By default, the tasks shown under each day are those tasks that are due on that day.

Tasks that don't have an assigned due date appear under the current day for easy reference.

Because of the size of the available space in the Daily Task List, you can only see some of the information for each task in the list. If you hover the cursor over a task, Outlook displays a bubble containing key information on the task, similar to the one shown here:

Configure the Daily Task List

Because the Daily Task List is so simple, there isn't much you can do to customize it. The three things you can do are:

- Resize it to show more or fewer tasks by dragging the top of the list up or down.

- Change how tasks appear in the list by right-clicking Show Task On and selecting one of the options in the shortcut menu that appears.

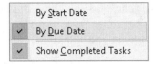

- Control whether the Daily Task List appears in its normal style, appears minimized, or is turned off altogether by clicking View | Daily Task List and then selecting the option you want.

Use the Calendar

It is time to talk about using the Calendar. Most of the time, you will probably work in the Day/Week/Month views. They provide a graphical view of your schedule, allow you to drag items around the calendar with the mouse, and are most reminiscent of the paper calendars we are all used to working with from childhood. Unless otherwise noted, you are assumed to be in a Day/Week/Month view as we go through the rest of this chapter.

Once you understand the different things it can do, Calendar isn't hard to use. Calendar supports three types of items: appointments, meetings, and events.

- **Appointments** An appointment is an activity that doesn't require you to invite other people. Use an appointment to set aside some time to work on a special project. Or use an appointment to set aside time for an upcoming doctor's or dentist's appointment. While other people can be involved in such an appointment, as far as Calendar is concerned, there's only you. You can set a reminder for each appointment, and you can schedule recurring appointments.

NOTE *As you'll see soon, when you drag tasks from the Daily Task List into the Calendar to schedule some time to work on them, they appear in the Calendar as appointments.*

- **Meetings**   Meetings are appointments that involve other people or resources. When you create a meeting item, you specify the people who are invited to the meeting, and select a meeting time. Outlook automatically sends invitations to everyone on the list. In addition to scheduling a meeting and inviting people, you can reschedule meetings, add people to the list of invitees, and even set up recurring meetings.

- **Events**   Events are activities that last for at least 24 hours. They differ from normal appointments and meetings as they don't occupy a particular time slot in the Calendar. Instead, events appear as a banner across the top of your schedule. You can set events to recur. Holidays are good examples of annually recurring events.

> NOTE   *See the "How to Display Holidays in the Calendar" box to see how you can add your favorite sets of holidays to the Calendar without having to manually enter them.*

7

 ## Display Holidays in the Calendar

Do you observe the national holidays of the United States or other countries? Would you like those holidays to appear in Calendar? If so, you've come to the right spot.

> NOTE   *If you upgraded from an earlier version of Outlook, and Calendar already displays holidays for a country or region, you should first remove them before adding the current holiday calendar in Outlook 2007. Instructions on how to do so are at the end of this box.*

To make holidays appear in the Outlook Calendar, follow these steps:

1. In the Outlook main window, click Tools | Options to open the Options dialog box.

2. On the Preferences tabbed page, click Calendar Options to open the Calendar Options dialog box.

Continued

3. In the Calendar Options section of the dialog box, click Add Holidays. This opens the Add Holidays to Calendar dialog box.

4. In the list of countries, select the names of the countries or regions whose national holidays you want to display.

NOTE *Calendar automatically selects your own country or region for you.*

5. Click OK. The Import Holidays dialog box appears and shows progress as Outlook imports the national holiday information.

6. When the download is complete, a message box appears to tell you so. Click OK to finish.

You can also remove holidays from Calendar, but you use a totally different process. To remove holidays from Calendar, open the Calendar view if it isn't already open, then follow these steps:

1. Click View | Current View to open the Current View menu.

2. In the Current View menu, click Events to see a list of all the events (including holidays) in Calendar.

3. Select the holidays you want to delete, then click Delete on the standard toolbar to remove them from the Calendar.

When you look at the Calendar in Day or Week view, any scheduled appointments or meetings block out the section of the day allocated for them (they just show up on the correct day in Month view). Activities won't always be visible, because the time they occur isn't visible. Use the scroll bar on the right side of the view pane to scroll up or down so that you can see the invisible activities.

Use AutoPreview Mode

If you work in Day/Week/Month views and find yourself frequently opening Calendar items to get more information than is otherwise available, you might want to use AutoPreview to preview the items you select without opening them, as shown in Figure 7-5. To get this ability, you need to switch from Day/Week/Month views to Day/Week/Month with AutoPreview views. Use the View menu or select this option directly in the Current View pane (if visible).

7

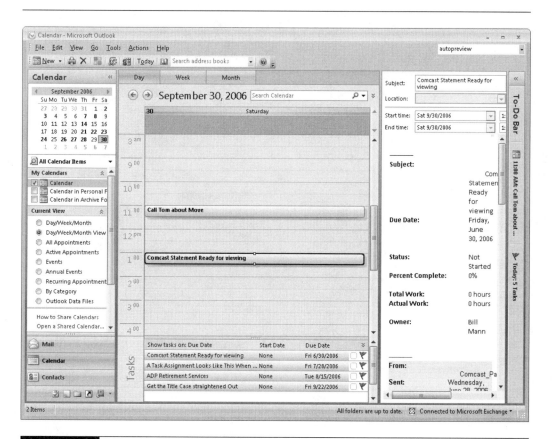

FIGURE 7-5   Using AutoPreview to get more details about the selected Calendar item.

The other thing you need to do to make this work is to turn on the Reading pane in the Calendar. To do this, click View | Reading pane, then select one of the positioning options (Right or Bottom) that appears in the menu. With this set, the Reading pane will appear when you are working in Day/Week/Month with AutoPreview views, and disappear when you are working in regular Day/Week/Month views.

The problem with using AutoPreview is screen real estate. That is, your screen only has so much room on it. Adding the Reading pane to the Calendar makes the screen crowded. If you look closely at Figure 7-5, you will also notice that only a portion of the selected item appears at once in the Reading pane. You need to scroll left and right and up and down to view the whole thing.

Putting the Reading pane below the View pane instead of to the right of it doesn't help much either, as you can see here in Figure 7-6. You get better readability of the

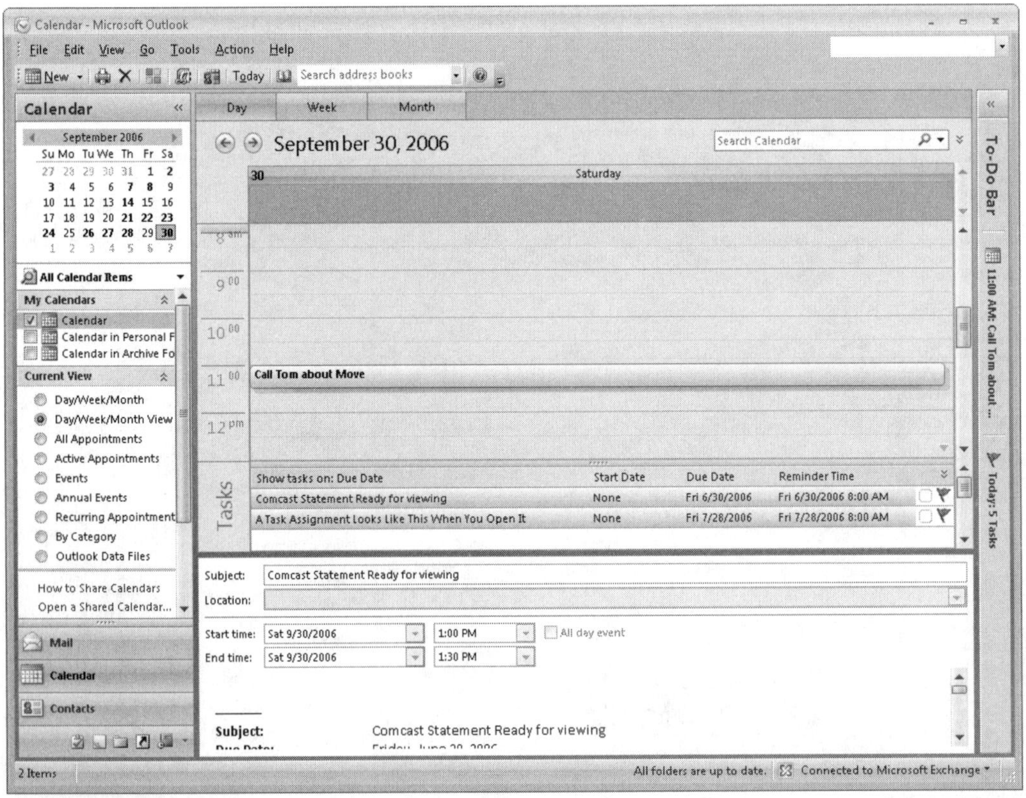

FIGURE 7-6   With the Reading pane below the View pane in the Calendar, things are crowded too.

preview, but lose an awful lot of the hours in the day from the Calendar view.
I suggest you experiment with various permutations to see which works best for you.

> TIP
> *If you are working on a system with a wide-screen display, using AutoPreview with the Reading Pane on the right side becomes much less of a problem.*

Add Stuff to Your Calendar

Finally, we're ready to start adding stuff to the Calendar. Activities get into Calendar in any of five ways:

- If you're using Outlook with Microsoft Exchange server or SharePoint Services, they can add activities to your Calendar.

- You can accept meeting invitations or otherwise receive copies of Calendar items from other people.

- You can add the information and activities manually.

- You can drag tasks from the Daily Task List to create appointments.

- You can synchronize Outlook with a mobile device such as a PDA or smartphone, or with an online service such as Yahoo! (see Chapter 15 for more information on synchronizing Outlook).

Microsoft Exchange and SharePoint Services are the subjects of Chapter 17, so we won't talk more about them here.

Receiving meeting invitations from others is common when you use Outlook for work. If you accept a meeting request, Outlook creates a meeting item and adds it to Calendar. Similarly, someone can drag an event or appointment item into an e-mail message and send it to you.

> TIP
> *You can accept a meeting request with the CTRL-C keyboard shortcut and can decline a meeting request with the CTRL-D keyboard shortcut.*

The most common ways for activities to make it onto your Calendar is for you to put them there yourself, either creating them manually, or dragging them over from the Daily Task List.

Let's take a look at how you can add items to the Calendar yourself.

Schedule an Appointment

To create a new appointment, follow these steps:

1. In the Outlook main window, click File | New, then Appointment. This opens a New Appointment window like the one in Figure 7-7.

TIP *You can also open a new Appointment window with the CTRL-SHIFT-A keyboard shortcut. An even easier way is to double-click the spot on the Calendar where you want the appointment to appear. This opens a New Appointment window with the appropriate starting date and time already filled in.*

2. Enter at least the subject of the meeting, the start time, and the end time.

CAUTION *The last date and time you set for a meeting may appear in the Start Time and End Time fields, so make sure you set the values you want. If you see a message in the Info Bar that reads, "The appointment occurs in the past," the odds are good that the start date is left over from the last appointment you set.*

3. If you want Outlook to remind you of the appointment, use the Reminder field in the Options group on the Appointment Ribbon to schedule it. The Reminder field appears to the right of a ringing bell icon.

7

TIP *You can get to the Reminder field with the ALT, H, Q keyboard shortcut.*

4. If this is an appointment that will recur at regular intervals, click Recurrence in the Options group on the Appointment Ribbon. The Appointment Recurrence dialog box appears (see Figure 7-8).

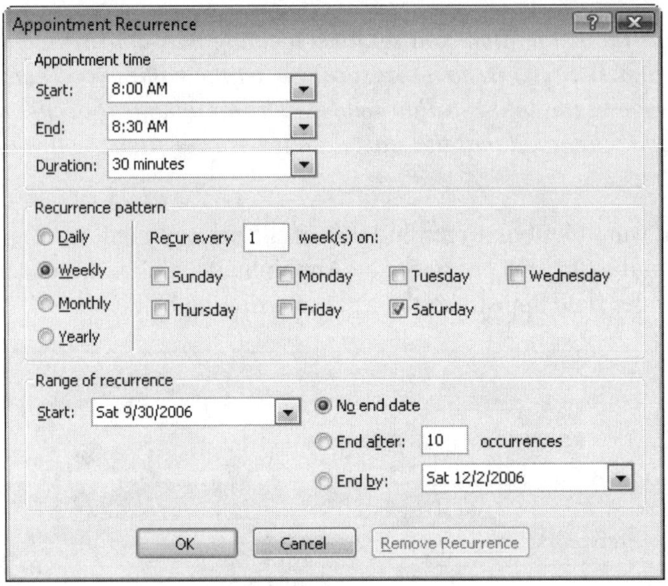

Appointment Recurrence

Appointment time

Start: 8:00 AM

End: 8:30 AM

Duration: 30 minutes

Recurrence pattern

○ Daily   Recur every 1 week(s) on:

● Weekly   ☐ Sunday   ☐ Monday   ☐ Tuesday   ☐ Wednesday

○ Monthly   ☐ Thursday ☐ Friday   ☑ Saturday

○ Yearly

Range of recurrence

Start: Sat 9/30/2006   ● No end date

                        ○ End after: 10   occurrences

                        ○ End by: Sat 12/2/2006

[OK] [Cancel] [Remove Recurrence]

FIGURE 7-8   The Appointment Recurrence dialog box lets you set up repeating appointments.

5. Set the recurrence pattern (when the appointment will recur) and the range of recurrence (how long the recurrence pattern will continue). Click OK when done.

> **NOTE** *For more detailed instructions on creating recurring activities, see the "How to Create a Recurring Activity" box.*

6. Click Save & Close to add the new appointment to your Calendar.

Schedule a Meeting

Scheduling meetings is a little more complicated than scheduling appointments, since meetings involve inviting other people and matching everyone's schedule to find an appropriate date and time.

> **NOTE** *Scheduling meetings assumes that the people involved in the meeting are either on a company network using Microsoft Exchange or SharePoint Services. You can send meeting requests to Outlook users who aren't connected to either of these, but Outlook won't be able to select a time when everyone is free since it won't have access to those people's calendars.*

How to ... Create a Recurring Activity

Recurring activities are activities that repeat on some sort of schedule. That schedule can have the activity repeat at regular intervals, or it can repeat a certain number of days after the date when it was last completed. You can make an activity a recurring activity when you first create it, or you can make a nonrecurring activity that's already in your Calendar into a recurring activity. In all of these cases, you turn the activity into a repeating activity using the Appointment Recurrence dialog box shown in Figure 7-8.

To set the start and end times of an activity, you work in the Appointment Time section of the dialog box. Set the start time and either the end time or the duration. Outlook automatically calculates the duration if you give it start and end times, or the end time if you give it a start time and a duration. Furthermore, if you change the start time, Outlook assumes you want to keep the same duration, and moves the end time automatically.

To set when an activity will repeat, you work in the Recurrence Pattern portion of the Appointment Recurrence dialog box. Start by selecting a Daily, Weekly, Monthly, or Yearly pattern in the left column. The pattern you select in this column determines the options that are available on the right. Set the pattern you want in the right side of the Recurrence Pattern section of the dialog box. Figure 7-8 shows the Weekly pattern, which is the default.

To set the time period (the range of dates, not the time of day) during which the activity will recur, you work in the Range of Recurrence section of the dialog box. Begin by selecting a start date from the available list. Then set an end date, using whichever of the three possibilities makes the most sense for this particular task. Click OK to exit the dialog box.

CAUTION *Don't forget to save and close the activity after you set the recurrence pattern.*

To create a new meeting request, follow these steps:

1. In the Outlook main window, click File | New, then Meeting Request. This opens a blank Meeting window like the one in Figure 7-9.

TIP *You can open a new Meeting request window with the CTRL-SHIFT-Q keyboard shortcut.*

7

A new Meeting dialog box lets you schedule meetings and request attendance
by others.

2. On the Appointment Ribbon, enter a list of the people you want to invite
to the meeting in the To field. You can enter the names or e-mail addresses
directly into the To field, or you can click the To button to select people
from the Address Book.

3. Fill in at least the subject of the meeting, the location, the start time, and
the end time.

4. If you want Outlook to remind you (and all the attendees) of the upcoming meeting, use the Reminder field in the Options group on the Meeting Ribbon to schedule it. The Reminder field appears to the right of a ringing bell icon.

TIP *You can get to the Reminder field with the ALT, H, Q keyboard shortcut.*

5. If this is a meeting that will recur at regular intervals, click Recurrence in the Options group on the Meeting Ribbon. The Appointment Recurrence dialog box appears.

6. Set the recurrence pattern (when the appointment will recur) and the range of recurrence (how long the recurrence pattern will continue). Click OK when done.

NOTE *For more detailed instructions on creating recurring activities, see the "How to Create a Recurring Activity" box.*

7

7. Now this is where things begin to deviate from setting up an appointment. Click Scheduling in the Show group to view the Scheduling page shown in Figure 7-10.

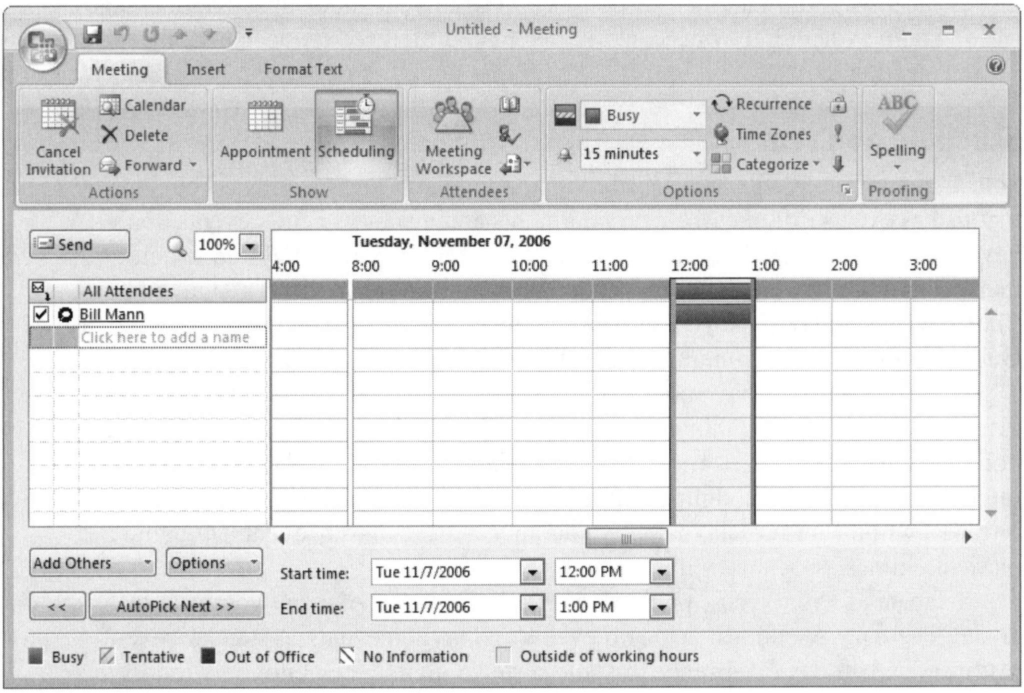

FIGURE 7-10 The Meeting Scheduling page helps you find the right time for a meeting.

TIP   *You can also get to the Scheduling page with the ALT, H, U keyboard shortcut.*

8. The name (or e-mail address) of each person you are inviting appears in a list, followed by a timeline showing the free and busy periods in that person's schedule. Find an open slot in everyone's schedule to hold your meeting, and enter a Meeting Start time and Meeting End time at the bottom of the dialog box. In the example shown in Figure 7-10, the first invitee's schedule is visible, and so his free and busy times appear. The second invitee isn't connected to Exchange or SharePoint Services, so his free and busy times do not appear. Finding an open time in everyone's schedule will require some work outside of Outlook, perhaps even a phone call to see when the second person will be available to meet.

9. Once you have picked a date and time, switch back to the Appointment tabbed page and you'll see that the meeting times you selected are now visible here.

10. Click Save & Close to add the new meeting to your Calendar and send the request to the people you specified. When the people respond to the meeting invitation, their responses appear in your Inbox as e-mail messages stating whether they accepted or declined (or tentatively accepted) the meeting.

Schedule an Event

Scheduling events is a lot like scheduling appointments and meetings. The thing that makes events different from appointments and meetings is that events don't have start or end times. Instead, they run all day for any day or days on which they occur. For example, a two-day meeting might run from, say, 8 A.M. to 5 P.M. Thursday and Friday. Change that two-day meeting into a two-day event, and Outlook will show it as running all day Thursday and all day Friday.

The fact that events have no specific times of day associated with them makes them great for scheduling things such as your birthday or a vacation, which normally don't have particular times associated with them. On your birthday, your Calendar might include a 5:00 P.M. dinner appointment with your spouse to celebrate your birthday, while your birthday itself would appear as an all-day event having no particular times associated with it.

To create an event, you first need to decide what kind of event you want to create. There are two kinds: standard events and invited events. A standard event just marks an all-day occurrence of some sort. An invited event not only marks the occurrence, it lets you invite people to it. I can see invited events being particularly useful for things such as conferences or general get-togethers along the lines of "Why don't you come on over on Saturday?"

To create a standard event, you start by creating a new appointment (use the CTRL-SHIFT-A keyboard shortcut). Now complete the appointment as you would normally, but don't click Save & Close yet.

Set the All Day Event check box to the right of the start time, and watch what happens to your appointment. The title bar of the window now says this is an event, rather than an appointment. The fields where you enter the start time and end time disappear, leaving only the Start and End date fields. Even the Reminder field changes so that the reminder occurs 18 hours before the event. Setting the All Day Event check box converts an appointment into an event. Similarly, clearing the All Day Event check box converts the event back into an appointment.

7

How the Reminder Field Works?

When you convert an appointment into an event, the value in the Reminder field changes to a default value (18 hours) regardless of what you had it set for. If you had set the Reminder field to more than the default value (two days or more), Calendar changes it to the default value anyway.

This isn't a good thing at all. Likewise, when you convert an event to an appointment, Calendar sets the Reminder field to another default value (usually one hour). The way to deal with this is to set the reminder time after you're done switching between appointment and event. That way, you can be sure that you get the reminder when you want it.

To create an invited event, first open a new meeting request (use the CTRL-SHIFT-Q keyboard shortcut). Now fill in the fields of the meeting request as you would normally. On the Appointment tabbed page, set the All Day Event check box, which triggers a transformation similar to the one that occurred when you did this in the Appointment window. Setting or clearing the All Day Event check box switches the activity between a meeting and an invited event.

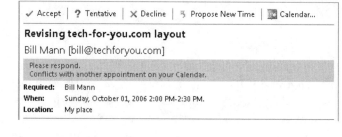

Quickly Respond to Invitations—One Approach

If you get invited to a lot of meetings, you'll like this feature. You don't even need to open a meeting invitation to reply to it. When a meeting invitation is visible in the Reading pane, not only can you see the message, but Outlook displays your options for responding to the invitation at the top of the pane, too. As you can see by looking above the Subject line, you have these options:

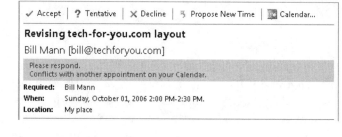

- Accept

- Tentative (tentatively accept the invitation)

- Decline

■ Propose New Time (or date for the meeting)

■ Calendar (open Calendar so that you can check your schedule)

If you click Accept, Tentative, or Decline, Outlook displays a dialog box that gives you three options. Choose one and click OK.

If you clicked Propose New Time in the Reading pane, Outlook opens the Propose New Time dialog box shown in Figure 7-11. Use it to propose another time and date that works for everyone invited to the meeting.

FIGURE 7-11   Use the Propose New Time dialog box to suggest a change of schedule.

NOTE *The attendees in this meeting are using Outlook standalone (as you might when using Outlook at home), so their schedules don't appear in this dialog box.*

Use the tools in the Propose New Time dialog box to come up with a new time for the meeting, then click Propose Time. This causes Outlook to create a New Time Proposed message you can send to the meeting organizer.

Quickly Respond to Invitations—Another Approach

If you are using AutoPreview, there is another way to quickly respond to an invitation. With AutoPreview active, the basic information about a meeting will appear in the Inbox, as shown here. If this is enough information for you to decide about the meeting, you can reply from here.

All you need to do is right-click the meeting invitation to open the shortcut menu. When you do, Outlook includes the five options for responding that you saw in the previous section. Click one, then complete the rest of the steps for responding to the invitation.

Schedule a Task

Outlook has always been good about helping you keep track of the tasks you have to do. Scheduling them for a specific date and popping up reminders that something needs to be done today helps you to get tasks done. If you are like me, however, knowing that a task needs to be done today isn't always enough. Finding the time to get a task done on the right day isn't always easy, so I've resorted to scheduling specific time slots for specific tasks.

In Outlook 2007, scheduling times for specific tasks is easy, thanks to the way the Daily Task List is integrated into the Calendar. All you need to do is drag the task from the Daily Task List and drop it onto the Calendar at the time and date you want to work on it. Outlook creates an appointment for you to do the task. Like a regular appointment, you can open and edit this task appointment, and do anything to it that you would to a regular appointment. It doesn't get much easier than this.

Other aspects of tasks are covered in detail in Chapter 8.

There is one small gotcha to be aware of when you do this. The appointment you create by dragging and dropping onto the Calendar doesn't remain linked to the original task. If you make changes to the task (marking it complete, for example), Outlook doesn't automatically delete the appointment related to the task. On the positive side of this, if you decide to clear the appointment for some reason, Outlook doesn't delete the task. The work still needs to be done, so the task still exists. Only the time slot you scheduled to work on it goes away.

Add Items to the Daily Task List

While working in the Calendar, you can add items directly to the Daily Tasks List if the list is displayed in Normal mode. Follow these steps:

1.   Right-click in the empty space at the bottom of the Daily Task List.

2.   In the shortcut menu that appears, click New Task or New Task Request.

3.   Outlook opens a New Task or New Task Request form for you to fill out as you normally would.

4.   Finish filling out the form, and Outlook adds it to the appropriate day in the Daily Tasks List. The task also appears in the regular Tasks views.

Detailed information on working with tasks and task requests appears in Chapter 8.

Change Your Schedule

While it is best to stick with a schedule once you make it, we all know that's not always possible. Sometimes you just have to make a change. The difficulty of making that change varies depending on the type of event you want to change. There are five cases to consider, in rough order of difficulty of easiest to hardest:

■   Changing a scheduled activity that isn't part of a recurring task

■   Changing a nonrecurring meeting you organized

- Changing a nonrecurring meeting you didn't organize

- Changing someone else's meeting request

- Changing recurring activities

Change a Scheduled Activity That Isn't Part of a Recurring Task

Scheduled activities that aren't part of a recurring series are the easiest to change. To change an appointment or event that isn't part of a recurring series, open it by double-clicking it, then make any necessary changes. Click Save & Close to put the changes into effect.

> NOTE
>
> *You can make some changes to appointments and events without opening them. If an appointment appears in your schedule, you can drag it to a new date and time, edit the subject (click the appointment and type the new subject), or change the length of the appointment by clicking and dragging the beginning or ending.*

Change a Nonrecurring Meeting You Organized

To change a meeting that you organized, open the meeting in question and make any necessary changes. You can change anything, including the list of attendees, simply by editing the values in the window.

When you're done making changes, click Send Update to put the changes into effect. If you have changed the list of attendees for the meeting, Outlook will ask you whether you want to send the update to only the people who were added or deleted, or send it to everyone. You should normally send the update to everyone, since if you don't, the other attendees won't know about the changes you made.

Change a Nonrecurring Meeting You Didn't Organize

If you want to change a meeting you didn't organize, the way you can change it is limited by the fact that it is someone else's meeting. You can make changes to the copy of the meeting that's in your Calendar, but those changes are not sent to anyone else. If you know a meeting is going to change, but the change hasn't been sent out yet (say the person responsible is in another meeting and unable to make the change until later, or you aren't connected and want to make sure the change appears in your Calendar), you can make the change to your copy of the meeting request so that at least your Calendar reflects the latest information.

Change Someone Else's Meeting Request

If you want to make changes to someone else's meeting request, and you want those changes to be published to others involved in the meeting, your options are more limited. All you can do is revoke your acceptance of the meeting request, make your acceptance tentative, or propose a new time for the meeting.

To change a meeting request you didn't organize, open it and look at the top part of the request. Click the down arrow in Propose New Time (in the Respond group of the Meeting Ribbon) to choose between tentatively accepting the current meeting invitation while proposing a new time and declining the current invitation while proposing a new time. You might do the former if you can attend the meeting on the proposed schedule, but another time would be better. The latter comes into play when you can't make it on the scheduled date or time.

Change Recurring Activities

There's only one more thing to consider when you want to change an existing scheduled activity. That's when the activity you want to change is part of a recurring series. If it is, you need to choose between changing the entire series of recurring activities or changing this particular activity in the series, without changing the rest of the series.

To change an activity that is part of a series of recurring activities, double-click the activity you wish to change. Calendar opens a dialog box that asks you if you want to open this particular occurrence of the series or open the entire series. Choose one, then click OK to begin editing the activity as you would normally. If you chose Open the Occurrence, only this particular instance of the activity will be changed. If you chose Open the Series, all future instances will be changed along with the current one.

Change an Item in the Daily Task List

You can make some changes to items in the Daily Task List without opening the task (check Chapter 8 for details on working with open tasks):

- Change the color category by clicking it to apply the Quick Click category, or right-clicking it to see all the color category options.

- Change the follow-up flag by clicking it to mark it complete or add the default follow-up flag, or right-click the flag to see all the follow-up options.

■ Click the name of the item, then without moving the mouse, wait two seconds and click again. This lets you edit the name of the task right in the Daily Task List.

View Multiple Calendars

Since Outlook can display multiple calendars, it only makes sense that you should be able to view them simultaneously. In Outlook 2003, we gained the ability to view calendars side by side. In Outlook 2007, we can do that, and also view calendars overlaid on each other. Figures 7-12 and 7-13 illustrate the difference.

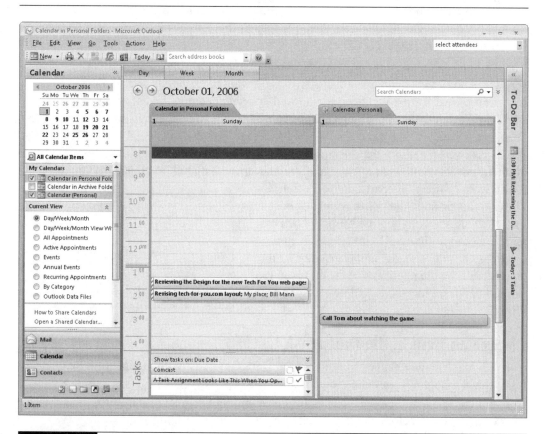

FIGURE 7-12   Two calendars, side by side.

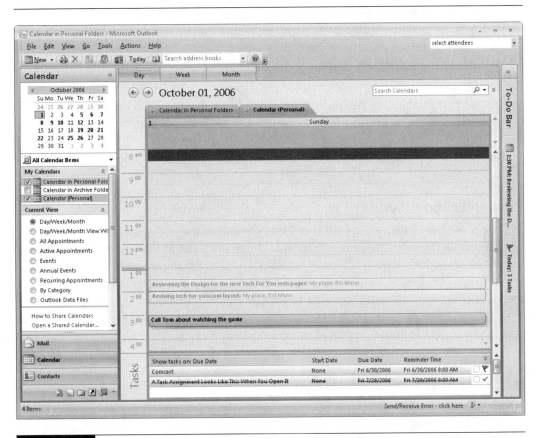

FIGURE 7-13   Two calendars, overlaid with Calendar (Personal) on top.

In Figure 7-12, the two calendars show the same time period, but are otherwise separate. This is useful, but does require you to be careful when you are comparing dates and times between the two, since it would be easy to look at the wrong spot when scanning back and forth.

In Figure 7-13, the two calendars not only show the same time period, they are layered on top of each other, with the information for both visible. Outlook will allow you to overlay up to 30 calendars at once, although I can't imagine how you would make heads or tails out of such a mass of information.

Now that you know the difference between the two ways of displaying simultaneous calendars, here are the instructions for doing it. In both cases, before you start, you need to make sure that the calendars (whether stored in Outlook on your computer, on the Internet, a SharePoint website, Windows Live, whatever) you want to see are listed in the My Calendars section of the Navigation pane.

View Calendars Side by Side

By default, Outlook displays calendars side by side. To see multiple calendars, simply select the calendars you want to view in My Calendars. Each calendar appears with a different color trim to make it easier to distinguish among them. Your primary calendar (Calendar in Personal Folders in Figure 7-12) always appears on the left side, with the other calendars, called *secondary calendars*, arranged to the right.

View Overlaid Calendars

You view overlaid calendars by first selecting the calendars you want to view in My Calendars. They will appear side by side. Next, click the left arrow next to the name of a secondary calendar. This tells Outlook to overlay the secondary calendar on the primary calendar. You can do this for each calendar you are viewing, or you can have some overlaid and some side by side.

   Clicking the right arrow next to the name of a secondary calendar will cause that calendar to switch from overlaid mode to side-by-side mode.

Publish and View Calendars

Being able to see your calendar is of course very useful to you. Calendars can be even more useful when they are shared. Outlook 2007 provides several ways of sharing calendars. To some extent you share your calendar automatically when you are connected to a Microsoft Exchange server or to SharePoint Services, as other users can see your free and busy times when they schedule meetings with you.

   There are other, more direct ways that you can share calendars. These include:

- Sharing with other Exchange users

- Sharing calendars by e-mail

- Sharing calendars published to the Internet

Sharing Calendars by E-Mail

Outlook 2007 gives you the ability to share calendars with other Outlook users by e-mailing them a copy of a calendar. You might consider this a snapshot of the calendar in that it shows the contents of the calendar at a given point in time. If I share my calendar with you today, then make changes to my calendar tomorrow, you won't know about these changes unless I share my calendar with you again. Still, this is an easy and effective way to get my schedule to you when we aren't using more sophisticated tools such as a common Microsoft Exchange server.

> **NOTE** *Outlook uses the iCal standard to share calendars, so you should be able to share your calendar with people who are using other mail and personal information management programs, not just Outlook.*

To share a copy of your calendar with someone else, follow these steps:

1. Open the Calendar you want to share.

2. Right-click the name of the Calendar to open a shortcut menu.

3. In the shortcut menu, click Send via E-mail. This opens the Send a Calendar via E-mail dialog box.

4. Select the options you want to use to create the copy of the calendar. There are a bunch of options here, so you will have to take a moment to think things through. In general, it is a good idea to only share the information the recipient needs.

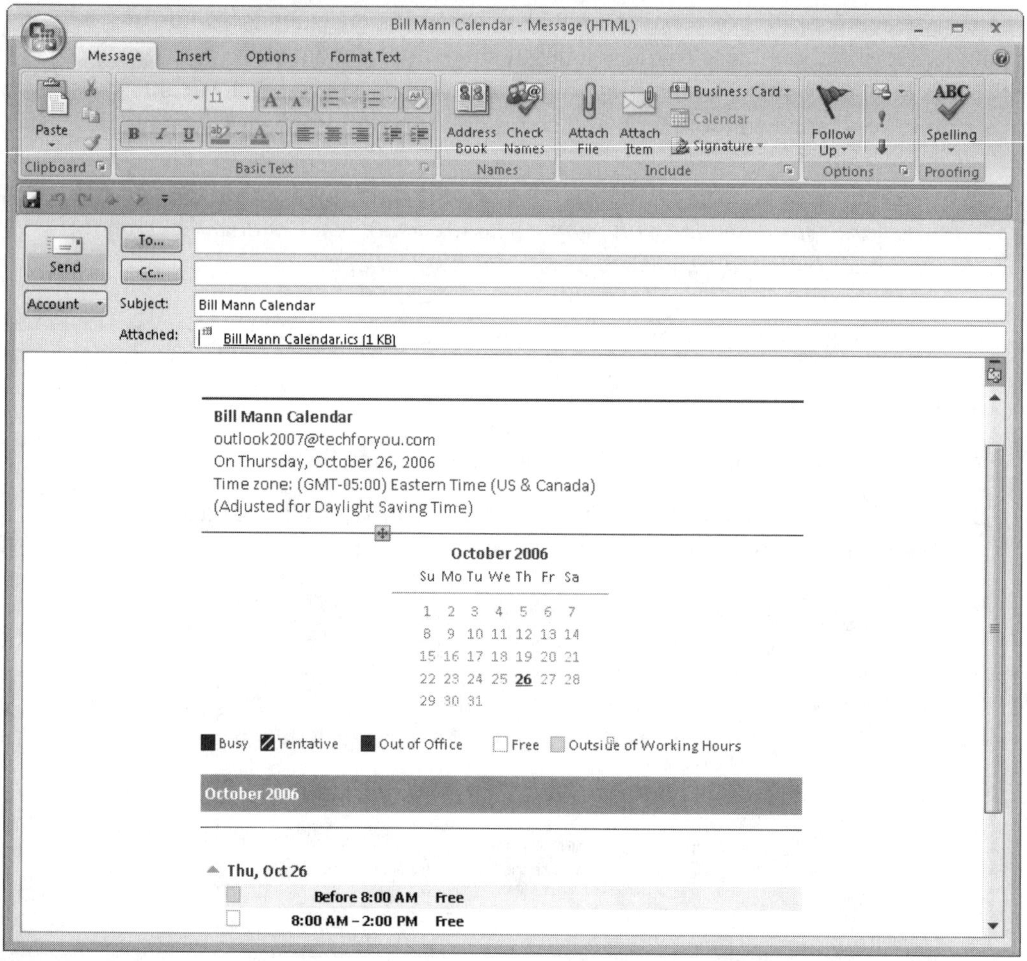

FIGURE 7-14   A message used to share a bit of my calendar.

5. Click OK when you are done selecting options. Outlook takes a few seconds to generate the file containing the calendar information you specified, then creates a message similar to the one in Figure 7-14.

6. Once you see this message, all you need to do is enter the recipients and then send it off.

When someone sends you a copy of a calendar by e-mail, it appears as a message in your Inbox. To view a copy of a calendar that someone shared with you by e-mail, follow these steps:

1. View the message containing the calendar in the Reading pane, or open the message. You will be able to see the contents of the sent calendar in the message.

2. Click Open This Calendar. This option will appear at the top of the message in the Reading pane, or at the far left of the Ribbon if you opened the message. The Add This Internet Calendar to Outlook dialog box appears.

3. Click Yes to open the calendar snapshot in Outlook.

Sharing Calendars Published to the Internet

As noted, when you send a calendar by e-mail, you are really sending a snapshot that does not get automatically updated when the calendar it is based on changes. People can also publish calendars on the Internet in such a way that you can subscribe to them and receive periodic schedule updates. You might encounter this kind of calendar online at a favorite website, or the home page of an organization you belong to.

NOTE *You can create your own calendar that others can subscribe to, but consider the amount of work it will take to update it before doing so. One thing the world doesn't need is any more abandoned online calendars!*

Whatever the source of the content in the calendar, if it has an iCal subscription link, you can tell Outlook to subscribe to it, and check back every so often to get any changes or new information. This might best be illustrated with an example.

For this example, we're going to subscribe to the BBC Foreign Service calendar, with the help of the iCalShare website. You'll not only learn how to set up this kind of calendar subscription, but you'll see that iCalShare has literally thousands of Internet calendars in 40 different categories. Let's get started:

1. Use your web browser to go to the iCalShare website at www.icalshare.com.

2. In the Radio category, navigate through the possibilities until you find the BBC World Service.

3. Click the Subscribe link. You may see a dialog box that starts out with "A website wants to open web content using this program on your computer" (Internet Explorer) or "An external application must be launched to handle webcal: links. Requested link:" (Firefox). Whichever you see, as long as somewhere in the dialog box it mentions Outlook, select "Allow" (Internet Explorer) or "Launch Application" (Firefox). Either one will launch Outlook if it isn't already running. Then the following dialog box is displayed:

4. Click Yes to subscribe with the default settings. You can click Advanced if you want, and adjust the settings, but using the defaults provided is normally the best bet. After a few minutes of work, Outlook downloads the contents of the calendar and displays them alongside your default calendar.

How to ... **Set Calendar Options**

Most people can work just fine with the default Calendar settings. Even so, there are a few options you could well need to adjust to adapt Outlook for your company's work week or your personal schedule and habits. For example, I often start writing at 4:30 or 5:00 A.M. Other people prefer to start their work day at 10:00 A.M. or later. Calendar can be adjusted to match these starting times, as well as many other individual schedule variations.

To set Calendar options, follow these steps:

1. In the main Outlook window, click Tools | Options to open the Options dialog box.

2. In the Calendar section of the dialog box, click Calendar Options. This opens the Calendar Options dialog box.

3. In the Calendar Work Week section of the dialog box, tell Outlook which days are part of your work week by setting the appropriate day check boxes. Set the First Day of Week, First Week of Year, Start Time, and End Time fields appropriately as well.

Now that it is subscribed to the BBC World Service calendar, Outlook will check the calendar for updates every so often, keeping you up to date on changes to the BBC World Service schedule. Apply the same basic steps to any calendar you want to subscribe to, whether one of the ones at iCalShare or any other site.

That's it for this chapter. You now know enough to put the Calendar to work keeping track of your busy schedule. At several places in this chapter, we talked about tasks, while deferring many of the intimate details. It's time to turn to Chapter 8 and learn those details about dealing with tasks, along with their cousins, To-Dos.

Chapter 8

Tasks and To-Do Items

How to...

- Learn About Tasks and To-Do Items

- Learn About the Tasks Folder

- Create Tasks

- Work with Tasks

- Integrate Tasks into the Calendar

- Use the To-Do Bar

Outlook 2007 gives you several ways to keep track of the things you need to do. As we saw when talking about e-mail, with only a click or two, you can create a task that goes with a message and ensures that you don't lose track of what you need to do about it. In this chapter, you will learn what tasks are, how they differ from to-dos, and look at the ways Outlook helps you manage them.

Learn About Tasks and To-Do Items

Outlook 2007 draws a distinction between tasks and to-do items. A *task* is a particular type of Outlook item you track until it is complete. You could create a task to get a haircut, for example. A *to-do item* is any Outlook item that you have flagged for follow up. An e-mail message that you flag as needing action is an example of a to-do item. Outlook automatically flags all tasks for follow up, so every task is a to-do item, whereas not every to-do item is a task.

As you saw in Chapters 4 and 6, respectively, you can easily flag an e-mail message or a contact for follow up. This turns them into to-do items, but not into tasks. While to-do items and tasks show up in many of the same places, what you can do with each differs. You can track the percentage completed and status of a task, as well as assign it to someone else or have it recur over time. You can't do any of those things with e-mail messages or contacts that are also to-do items.

We can attack the subject of tasks and to-do items in several ways. I think the best is to start off with the Tasks folder.

Learn About the Tasks Folder

You reach the Tasks folder by clicking Tasks in the Navigation pane, by clicking Go | Tasks, or by using the CTRL-4 keyboard shortcut. However you get there, your view of the Tasks folder will look something like Figure 8-1. By now, this basic look should be pretty familiar.

The Navigation pane appears on the left, with one or two panes in the center (depending on the view) and the To-Do Bar on the right. We need to look at each of these a little closer, but we'll leave the To-Do Bar until later in the chapter.

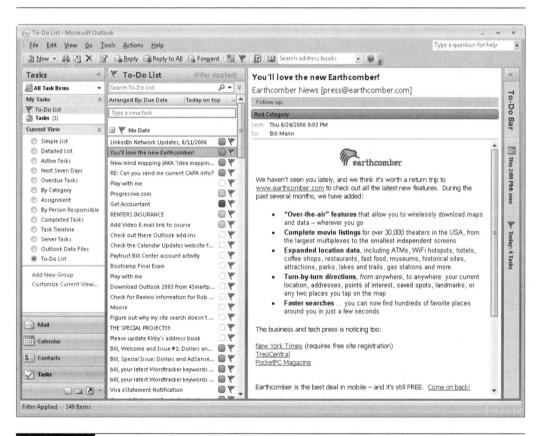

FIGURE 8-1   The Tasks view follows the standard Outlook 2007 layout.

The Navigation Pane

The Navigation pane here looks a little different than it does in other places. At the top is All Task Items, a list that lets you choose which Outlook data files to look in when searching (Chapter 13 talks about Outlook data files). For now, just leave that one alone.

> **NOTE**   *Remember that you can customize the Navigation pane, so if what you see on your computer doesn't exactly match what I describe here, don't fret.*

Next comes the My Tasks pane. Here you can choose to view either your entire To-Do List or only Tasks.

Below that is the Current View pane. This pane lists all the available views you can use with tasks and to-do items. By selecting different views, you can easily sort through the things you need to do in a way that makes the most sense under any circumstances. As with most panes in the Navigation pane, clicking the double up-arrows next to the title closes the pane, and clicking the double down-arrows opens it.

Below the Current View pane are two links. The Add New Group link allows you to create a new group similar to the My Tasks group. Customize Current View lets you change the look of the current view, as well as what information is displayed in it. You are unlikely to ever need to use either of these links, but they are there in case you ever do.

The To-Do List Pane

When you select To-Do List in My Tasks, the center of the Outlook window shows various views of your to-do items. The default view for this is the To-Do List view, which you've already seen in Figure 8-1. In this view, there is a list of to-do items on the left and the Reading pane on the right.

As with the Inbox pane, you can group or change the order of items in the To-Do List with the Arranged By and Today on Top (or Later on Top) buttons at the top of the pane.

The Tasks Pane

When you select Tasks in My Tasks, the center of the Outlook window shows only views of your tasks. The default view for this is Simple List view, which you can see in Figure 8-2. In this view, there is a list of to-do items on the left, and the Reading pane on the right.

In this view, there are no options for grouping tasks other than by date. You can, however, sort the list by clicking the headings for each column. For example, clicking the Due Date heading sorts the tasks by date. A gray arrowhead facing up or down appears in the heading that Outlook is using to sort the list. An up arrowhead means the tasks are sorted in ascending order.

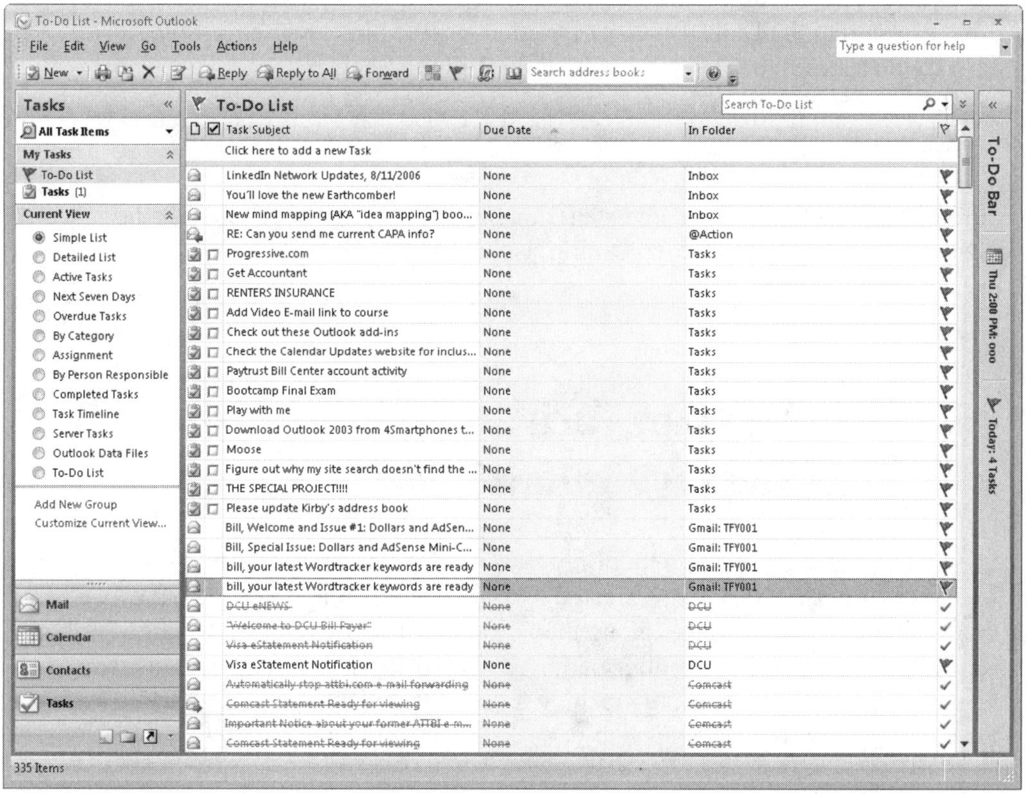

FIGURE 8-2   These tasks are displayed in Simple List view.

Create Tasks

You already know how to create to-do items (flag them for follow up), so now you need to learn how to create tasks. Believe it or not, there are four ways to create a new task in Outlook 2007:

■ Open a new Task window with the New command (on the toolbar or in the File menu).

■ Enter it in the Click Here to Add a New Task box that appears at the top of the Tasks view.

■ Type it into the Daily Task List in Calendar (see "Integrate Tasks into the Calendar with the Daily Tasks List" later in this chapter).

■ Type it into the To-Do Bar (see "Use the To-Do Bar Everywhere" later in this chapter).

Each approach has its own advantages and disadvantages. In general, the last option, typing the task into the To-Do Bar, is the fastest and easiest, but each comes in handy at times.

Did you know?

You Can Turn an E-Mail Message into a Task?

I don't know about you, but a lot of my tasks come to me in the form of e-mail messages. Instead of task items created by someone else and assigned to me, they come as e-mail messages along the lines of, "Bill, can you deal with the Johnson account? Here's the information they need…." I could turn an e-mail message like this into a task by opening a new Task window and retyping (or cutting and pasting) the relevant parts of the e-mail message into the task, but there's a better way.

You can turn virtually any Outlook item into another kind of Outlook item by dropping it on the appropriate navigation button. In this case, all I need to do is drag the e-mail message to the Tasks button in the Navigation pane and drop it there.

When I drop the e-mail message on the Tasks button, Outlook opens a new Task window and copies the content of the e-mail message into the body of the task. Then all I need to do is fill in details, such as the start and end dates, and I'm done.

Using the New Command

Using the New command to create a new task is a standard way to go about it. Click the down arrow next to the New button on the toolbar and then click Task, or in the main menu click File | New | Task to start. Outlook opens a new Task window like the one shown here:

The main advantage of this approach to creating a new task is that you have immediate access to all the task controls here. All the formatting, all the actions, all the options are right here. You have the most power and flexibility when creating tasks.

The main disadvantage of this approach is that it is relatively slow. Outlook has to open the window. You need to type the right information into the right fields. You have to save and close the task when you are done. It takes time and pulls you out of your train of thought.

To create a task this way, at the minimum, you need to enter the subject, then click Save & Close (or use the ALT, H, A, V keyboard shortcut). Beyond that, you can use this window to set start and due dates, reminders, status, priority, the recurrence pattern (we'll talk about this in a bit), and more. If you need to do something beyond the basics, this is probably the approach to use.

8

Using the Click Here to Add a New Task Text Box

This option is a quick way to create a basic task when you are already looking at the Tasks pane. In many task views, the Click Here to Add a New Task text box appears near the top of the pane.

The advantage of this approach is the speed and ease of entering simple tasks. Click in the Click Here to Add a New Task box. Type the title of the task. If you need to finish by a certain date, click in the Due Date box and type in a date or pick it from the calendar that drops down. Want it stored in a particular folder? Click in the In Folder box and type the name of the folder. Press the ENTER key and you're done. You can't get much faster than that.

The disadvantage of this approach is that you are limited in what information you can enter about the task. You trade speed for power.

> TIP
>
> *If you double-click the Click Here to Add a New Task box, Outlook opens a new Task window, as if you had used the New command. It's a fast way to get the full window if you realize that the Click Here to Add a New Task box approach doesn't give you the options you need.*

Work with Tasks

We've talked about some ways to create tasks and to-do items. Now we should talk about how to work with them before we get sidetracked with the Daily Task List and the To-Do Bar. This isn't meant to be an exhaustive study of everything you can possibly do with tasks. That would be exhausting and far more information than anyone needs.

Basic Activities

In your day-to-day work with tasks and to-do items, you will perform a number of basic activities. These include:

- Completing tasks or to-do items

- Working with start dates and due dates

- Setting reminders

- Tracking priority and progress

Let's take a quick look at each of these.

Completing Tasks or To-Do Items

The most basic thing you can do with a task is to finish it. Once you do, you can either mark it as complete or delete it altogether.

In either the To-Do List or the Tasks list, right-click the item and select Delete in the shortcut menu, or select the item in a list and click the Delete button on the toolbar.

To mark a task or a to-do item as complete without deleting it, simply click its follow-up flag in any list. It may disappear from the list (many lists show only active tasks and to-do items, not those that you have completed), but it isn't deleted from Outlook. If you ever need to look at the tasks and to-do items you have completed (perhaps at performance review time), you can use the Completed Tasks view to see what you've accomplished.

Working with Start Dates and Due Dates

Since tasks are defined as things you need to track until completion, they often have real-world start dates and due dates associated with them ("Johnson, if you don't get that report to me by Friday, you're fired!"). You can assign dates to tasks when you create them, or add them later. And you can change them as necessary ("Johnson, I've changed my mind. Get me that report by Thursday noon, or you're history!").

Whether you create the task with the New command or the Click Here to Add a New Task text box, you have the option to enter a due date. You can just type a date into the Due Date box, but what fun is that? Outlook gives you a couple of fun ways to enter dates. First, you can click the down arrow to the right of the Due Date box and Outlook will show you a small calendar you can use to select the due date (this also works for Start Date and any other dates you can enter for tasks).

8

Use the arrows in the calendar header to navigate from month to month, then click the date you want to set. Click Today to enter today's date as the due date, or None to return without setting a date. This approach is easy and fun, but can get tedious when you have to set a date months ahead.

NOTE   *The exact same techniques work if you want to enter the start date for a task.*

Outlook also employs a little intelligence to let you enter dates in natural language. For example, remember the report that Johnson has to have done by noon Thursday? Well, while the big boss is ranting, Johnson can create a new task, and in the Due Date box simply type the word "Thursday." Outlook is smart enough to understand that this means this coming Thursday, and automatically translates that into the proper due date. This also works for entries such as "today," "next month," and "next week." Give this a try and see what you think.

Quickly set or change a task date in the Custom dialog box.

What about changing the start date or due date for a task? That used to require you to open the Task window, make your changes, then save them. Outlook 2007 gives you a better way. In the Tasks list, right-click the task you want to change. When the shortcut menu appears, click Follow Up to see a list of options. If the date you want to set as the due date appears in that list, click it and you're done.

If the date you want doesn't appear in the list, click Custom to open the Custom dialog box. As you can see in Figure 8-3, you can enter start and due dates in this dialog box without having to open the task window. Just make your change, click OK, and you're done.

Setting Reminders

Personal productivity experts such as David Allen suggest scanning your to-do lists whenever you complete a task so you know what to work on next. I'm not disciplined enough to do that consistently, and instead rely on setting reminders to get me to look at the tasks that are most important.

To activate a reminder, you set the Reminder check box, then enter the date and time you want to be reminded. When you are creating the task, you can set up the reminder in the Task window.

Setting and changing reminders has gotten really easy in Outlook 2007. As with changing dates, you can use the Custom dialog box shown in Figure 8-3 to set and change reminders. But if all you want to do is add a reminder, there's an even easier way.

Get Hotmail and Gmail Accounts to Use with Outlook 2007

How to...

- Get a Hotmail Account to Use with Outlook 2007
- Get a Gmail Account to Use with Outlook 2007

If you are using Outlook at work, your company is responsible for providing an e-mail account, usually one connected to a Microsoft Exchange server. But if you want to use Outlook at home, things aren't so clear cut. Even if you have an e-mail account through your Internet Service Provider (ISP), there's no guarantee that it will work with Outlook. And if you are going to travel with Outlook on a notebook computer, things are even worse, since some ISPs only let you send e-mail when you are physically connected to their network (doing this helps prevent spam from being sent through the ISP's network). What's a die-hard Outlook user to do?

How about getting an e-mail account that you can access from anywhere you have an Internet connection—one that isn't tied to your current ISP (so you can keep your e-mail address even if you switch ISPs) and is guaranteed to work with Outlook? How about getting two accounts from two different companies (perhaps so you can use different e-mail addresses for different purposes)? Well, it is possible, I know how to do it, and I'm going to show you exactly how to do it yourself, right now.

We're going to look at two options: Hotmail and Gmail. Hotmail (also called MSN Hotmail) is a mail service from Microsoft. It's probably not surprising that Microsoft's e-mail service can work with Outlook. However, the most popular version of Hotmail, the free one, does *not* work with Outlook. To make Hotmail work with Outlook, you must pay a fee. Fortunately, at this writing, the least-expensive Hotmail account that can work with Outlook is only $19.95 a year, so this isn't a major hardship.

Gmail is Google's free e-mail service. Yes, you can connect a free Gmail account to Outlook. However (there always seems to be some sort of gotcha in stuff like this, doesn't there?) you need to receive an invitation to use Gmail. These aren't too hard to come by, and if you ask around, you can probably find a techie friend who can invite you. If not, you *can* get yourself an invitation without someone else's help, as long as you own a mobile phone that accepts text messages. I know that sounds really weird, but I'll explain when the time comes. For now, let's talk about what the two types of account have to offer and how to choose between the two.

More on Hotmail and Gmail

Hotmail and Gmail, while both Internet-based e-mail services can connect to Outlook, are also quite different. Without going down the technological rat hole of the difference between POP3 and HTTP mail protocols (www.living-with-outlook.com has more details if you're really curious) and differing design philosophies, here are a few points that summarize the differences you will care about between Hotmail and Gmail:

- Hotmail gets its own set of mail folders in Outlook, with its own Inbox, Deleted Items, Sent Items, all of that. Gmail uses the standard Outlook mail folders.

- Changes you make in Outlook's Hotmail folders get reflected in the Hotmail folders on the Web, and vice versa. In other words, the Hotmail folders in Outlook and on the Web remain synchronized. This can be a big bonus if you will sometimes use Outlook to check your mail and sometimes read it online with your web browser.

- Unless you tell it not to, Gmail retains copies of all messages after you download them to Outlook, but changes you make in Outlook don't get reflected to Gmail on the Web, and vice versa. This can be confusing if you sometimes read your e-mail online with your web browser.

- A Gmail account is considered by some to be more prestigious than a Hotmail account, since Gmail accounts are harder to come by.

- A Gmail account that works with Outlook is free; a Hotmail account that works with Outlook isn't.

So the question remains, which type of account should you choose if you are only going to choose one? My suggestions are:

- If you plan to access your e-mail from the Web as well as from Outlook, Hotmail has the advantage.

- If you will use your new account for different purposes than other accounts you currently have connected to Outlook, Hotmail's separate set of folders makes it easy to keep from mixing business with pleasure, as the saying goes.

- If you want all your messages to go into the same Outlook Inbox, Gmail is the only option.

- If you check your mail by looking at what's in the Unread Mail folder, Gmail is the choice unless you will modify the Unread Mail folder to include the Hotmail Inbox.

- If you want a free account, Gmail is the only option.

All this is the long way of saying that there are pros and cons to each and you need to make the final decision.

Get a Hotmail Account That Works with Outlook

There are two ways to go about this, depending on whether you want to upgrade an existing Hotmail account or create a new one from scratch. The next two sections have you covered either way.

Upgrade an Existing Hotmail Account

If you are already using a free Hotmail account, the easiest thing to do is upgrade it to a Hotmail Plus account ($19.95/year) and then connect it to Outlook. Here are the steps you need to follow:

1. Log into your existing Hotmail account on the Web as you would normally.

2. At the top of any Hotmail page, click Options.

3. On the left side of the Options page, click Upgrade.

4. On the Upgrade Options page, click MSN Upgrade Opportunities.

5. Click the button (currently an orange button with a right-pointing arrow) for the Hotmail Plus plan (or Hotmail Premium plan if you like). Make sure you have your credit card handy.

6. Follow the directions that appear on the screen to complete the upgrade process.

Once your account is set up, skip ahead to "Configure Outlook to Work with Hotmail."

Sign Up for a New Hotmail Account

This procedure shows you how to create a new Hotmail Plus account from scratch. Use it if you don't already have a Hotmail account, or don't want to upgrade the one you do have.

1. Using your web browser, go to the Microsoft Online Services sign-up page at http://join.msn.com/.

2. In the E-mail section, click the MSN Hotmail Plus link.

3. Review the features of this account to be sure it suits your needs. Then click Get It Now and follow the instructions that appear on the screen to complete the sign-up process.

Once your account is set up, proceed to "Configure Outlook to Work with Hotmail."

Configure Outlook to Work with Hotmail

Now that you have a Hotmail account that can work with Outlook, you need to configure Outlook to talk to it. There are quite a few steps here, but nothing difficult or tricky. Just work through the steps one by one and you'll have no problems.

1. In the Outlook main menu, click Tools | Account Settings. This opens the Account Settings dialog box you saw in Chapter 4.

2. On the E-mail tab, click New. This launches the Add New E-mail Account Wizard.

3. On the Choose E-mail Service screen, select Microsoft Exchange, POP3, SMTP, or HTTP. Then click Next.

NOTE

You may see a dialog box that asks you to confirm a secure connection. If you do, no worries. Just confirm it and go on to step 4.

4. On the AutoAccount Setup screen, fill in the Your Name field.

5. In the E-mail Address field, enter your full Hotmail mail address (including the "@hotmail.com").

6. Enter your Hotmail password in the Password field. Enter it again in the Retype Password field. (For security, your password appears as asterisks instead of regular characters.)

7. Click Next. The wizard connects to the Hotmail servers somewhere out on the Internet and configures your account for you. Assuming all went well, you will see "Congratulations!" at the top of the screen when the setup is done.

8. Click Finish. This takes you back to the Account Settings dialog box. Your new Hotmail account should appear in the list of accounts on the E-mail tab.

9. Click Close. Then go to a Mail view. You should see a new set of mail folders with the name of your new Hotmail account in the Mail Folders list of the Navigation pane.

Congratulations! You have your new Hotmail account up and running and connected to Outlook.

Get a Gmail Account That Works with Outlook

There are a few ways to go about this. The easiest is to get a friend or acquaintance who already has an account to send you an invitation. Another approach might be to go online and search for a site that gives out invitations. They were fairly common for a while, but seem to have died away. Or…you can whip out your trusty text message–capable (SMS) mobile phone and follow the directions in the next section.

Get a Gmail Account with Your Mobile Phone

What, you ask, do mobile phones and Gmail have to do with each other? It is actually quite an ingenious plan. You can have Gmail send a text message to your phone containing the information you need to get a Gmail account. By sending it as a text message to a phone, Google makes it much harder for spammers and other slimes to get masses of free accounts they can use to cause mischief. So grab your mobile, sit yourself down in front of the computer (you need to visit a web page too), and follow these directions to get your Gmail invitation:

> **NOTE**
>
> Don't have a mobile phone that can receive text messages? Ask your friends to do this for you. Most newer mobile phones have this ability, so it shouldn't be hard to find someone who can help you.

1. Using your web browser, surf over to https://www.google.com/accounts/SmsMailSignup1.

2. Enter your location and mobile phone number into the appropriate fields.

3. Find the oddly shaped text and type it into the field below it. This is another measure to keep creeps from getting lots of accounts. It takes a human to read the weirdly shaped text and enter it into the proper field.

4. Click Send Code. A new web page appears so you can type in your invitation code. Now keep your eye on the mobile phone.

5. When the text message arrives with the invitation code, enter that code on the web page and click Next. This opens the Create a Google Account – Gmail page.

6. Fill this in to finish creating your account.

Once your account is created, you are ready for the next step, which is configuring the Gmail account to talk to Outlook.

Configure Gmail to Talk to Outlook

Technically, what happens here is configuring Gmail for POP3 access, but from our perspective, we're getting Gmail ready to talk to Outlook. Follow these steps:

1. Log onto your Gmail account through your web browser.

2. On any Gmail page, click Settings. The Mail Setting dialog box appears.

3. Click the Forwarding and POP link.

4. In the POP Download section, step 1 sets POP Status. Select an option to enable POP3 and tell Gmail which messages are available by POP3. Since this is a new account, select the option to enable POP for all mail.

5. In step 2, tell Gmail what to do with messages after Outlook downloads a copy of them. If you want to be able to read the messages online, use the "Keep Gmail's copy in the Inbox" option. Otherwise, you can archive or delete Gmail's copy to keep your Gmail Inbox from getting cluttered.

6. Skip step 3 and click Save Changes.

Now that Gmail is ready to talk to Outlook, all we need to do is tell Outlook how to talk to Gmail.

Configure Outlook to Talk to Gmail

This is the last step—or set of steps. We need to tell Outlook how to talk to your Gmail account. These are the steps you need to follow:

1. In the Outlook main menu, click Tools | Account Settings. This opens the Account Settings dialog box you saw in Chapter 4.

2. On the E-mail tab, click New. This launches the Add New E-mail Account Wizard.

3. On the Choose E-mail Service screen, select Microsoft Exchange, POP3, SMTP, or HTTP. Then click Next.

> **NOTE**
>
> You may see a dialog box that asks you to confirm a secure connection. If you do, no worries. Just confirm it and go on to step 4.

4. On the AutoAccount Setup screen, fill in the Your Name field.

5. In the E-mail Address field, enter your full Gmail mail address (including the "@gmail.com").

6. Enter your Gmail password in the Password field. Enter it again in the Retype Password field. (For security, your password appears as asterisks instead of regular characters.)

7. Click Next. The wizard connects to the Gmail servers somewhere out on the Internet and configures your account for you. Assuming all went well, you will see "Congratulations!" at the top of the screen when the setup is done.

8. Click Finish. This takes you back to the Account Settings dialog box. Your new Gmail account should appear in the list of accounts on the E-mail tab.

9. Click Close. Unlike a Hotmail account, you won't see a new set of folders in the Mail Folders pane now. But you can confirm that your Gmail account is active by sending an e-mail message to your Gmail address, and waiting to see that it appears in your Outlook Inbox and Unread Messages folder.

Congratulations! You have your new Gmail account up and running and connected to Outlook.

To add a reminder to an existing task, right-click the task you want to change in the Tasks list. When the shortcut menu appears, click Follow Up, then Add Reminder. The Custom dialog box appears again, but this time it appears with the Reminder check box set, and the last reminder date and time you have set already entered. Make any changes necessary, click OK, and that's it.

Tracking Priority and Progress

You can use tasks as simple reminders of things to do, but by filling in fields such as Status, Priority, and % Complete, and by adding notes to the body of each task, you can use tasks to keep track of your progress in different activities. By filling in the information on the Details page, you can even use your tasks to track billable hours and mileage.

All of the areas described here are on the Task tab of the Ribbon when you are working in the Task page. In the Show group, click Task to enter the status type information.

8

 You can go directly to the Task page with the ALT, H, T keyboard shortcut.

You enter details such as the date the task was completed, the total number of hours, and so on by selecting Details in the Show group and filling in the appropriate fields.

 You can go directly to the Details page with the ALT, H, L keyboard shortcut.

Date completed:	None		
Total work:	0 hours	Mileage:	
Actual work:	0 hours	Billing information:	
Company:			

Once you learn how to assign tasks to people, you can go one step further in using tasks to manage activities and projects. When you assign tasks to people, you can have Outlook automatically track the progress of those tasks and send you status reports on them. See "Keep Track of Assigned Tasks" later in this chapter for details.

Beyond these basic activities are some additional features you may want to use. These include recurring tasks and assigning tasks.

Create and Work with Recurring Tasks

Recurring tasks are tasks that repeat on some sort of schedule. A task can recur at regular intervals, such as once a week or once a month, or recur at regular intervals beginning on the date when it was last completed. You can make a task a recurring task when you first create it, or you can convert a nonrecurring task that's already in your Tasks list into a recurring task. In any case, you turn the task into a repeating task by using the Task Recurrence dialog box shown in Figure 8-4.

To open the Task Recurrence dialog box, open the Task window for the task that will recur, then click the Recurrence button on the Task tab of the Ribbon. You can also get there with the ALT, H, E keyboard shortcut.

To determine when a task will repeat, you work in the Recurrence Pattern portion of the dialog box. Start by selecting a Daily, Weekly, Monthly, or Yearly pattern in the left column. The pattern you select in this column determines the options that are available on the right side of the dialog box. Set the pattern you want in the right side of the Recurrence Pattern section of the dialog box. Figure 8-4 shows the Weekly pattern, which is the default. Figure 8-5 shows the Yearly pattern. Note the way the options change to be appropriate to the recurrence time period.

To set the time period during which the task will recur, work in the Range of Recurrence section of the dialog box. Begin by selecting a start date from the available list. Then choose an end date, using whichever of the three possibilities

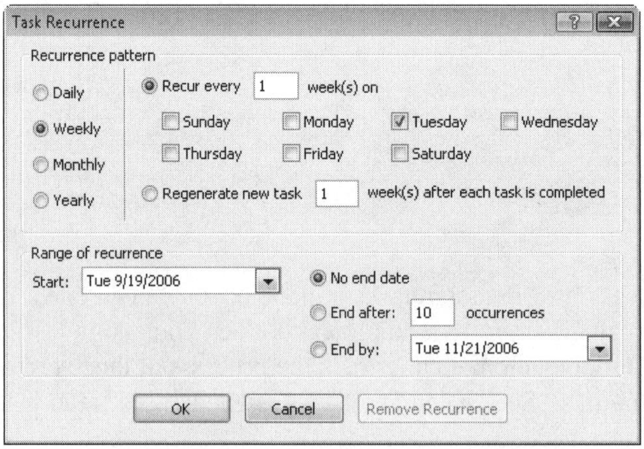

FIGURE 8-4   Use this dialog box to set up the two types of recurring task.

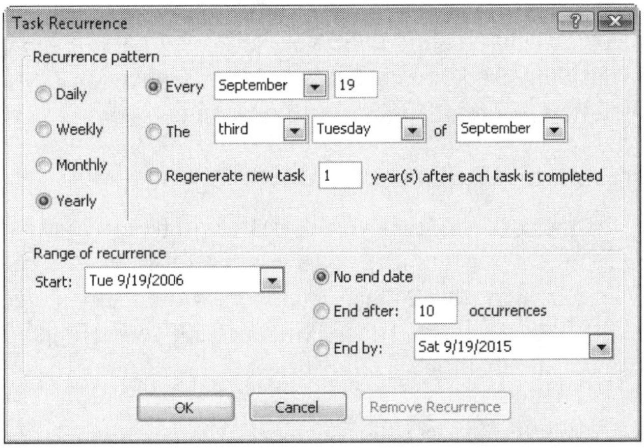

FIGURE 8-5   The yearly recurrence pattern is visible in this figure.

8

makes the most sense for the particular task. Click OK to exit the dialog box and return to the Task window. Don't forget to click Save & Close after you set the recurrence pattern!

> **NOTE** *You can assign recurring tasks to other people as well as create them for yourself.*

Did you know?

Certain Types of Recurring Tasks Can Be Tricky?

Creating tasks that recur at set intervals works the way you would expect them to, but you need to be a little careful when defining tasks that recur a certain amount of time after they are completed.

To make a task recur a certain amount of time after it last occurred, select the Regenerate New Task option button and enter the time interval in the text box. What you need to remember is that the next task will only be regenerated *after* the current instance is marked as complete. If you finish the task and forget to change its status to Completed, Outlook will not generate the next occurrence of the task.

Assign Tasks and Receive Assignments

You can get tasks either by creating them yourself or by having someone else assign them to you. Similarly, you can assign tasks to others or to yourself. This section shows you how to create, assign, and receive tasks.

Assign a Task

While it's likely that most of the tasks you'll create will be for your own use, you can also assign tasks to others. Assigning tasks is very useful when you're managing a team and you want to assign tasks to team members without anyone getting confused about which task belongs to whom. By creating the task yourself and assigning it to someone, you can be sure that the assignment gets relayed properly.

 All team members must be using Outlook for assigning tasks to work properly.

To assign a task to someone, create a task using the Task window, but instead of saving it, follow these instructions:

 You can also assign an existing task to someone by opening the task and then following these same instructions.

1. In the Task tab of the Ribbon, click Assign Task in the Manage Task group (or use the ALT, H, I keyboard shortcut). Outlook adds a To field to the Task window, as shown in Figure 8-6, along with status information in the Info Bar, and a couple of check boxes for tracking the task.

2. Enter the address of the person you are assigning the task to as if you were sending the person an e-mail message.

3. Select or clear the Keep an Updated Copy of This Task on My Task List and the Send Me a Status Report When This Task Is Complete check boxes. You'll learn more about these check boxes in "Keep Track of Assigned Tasks" later in this chapter.

4. Use the body of the task to provide detailed information about the task to the recipient.

5. Click Send to send the task request to the recipient, or click Cancel Assignment to keep the task for yourself.

Receive Task Assignments

Task assignments arrive in your Inbox in the same manner as e-mail messages. However, a task-assignment message icon looks different. It consists of a hand

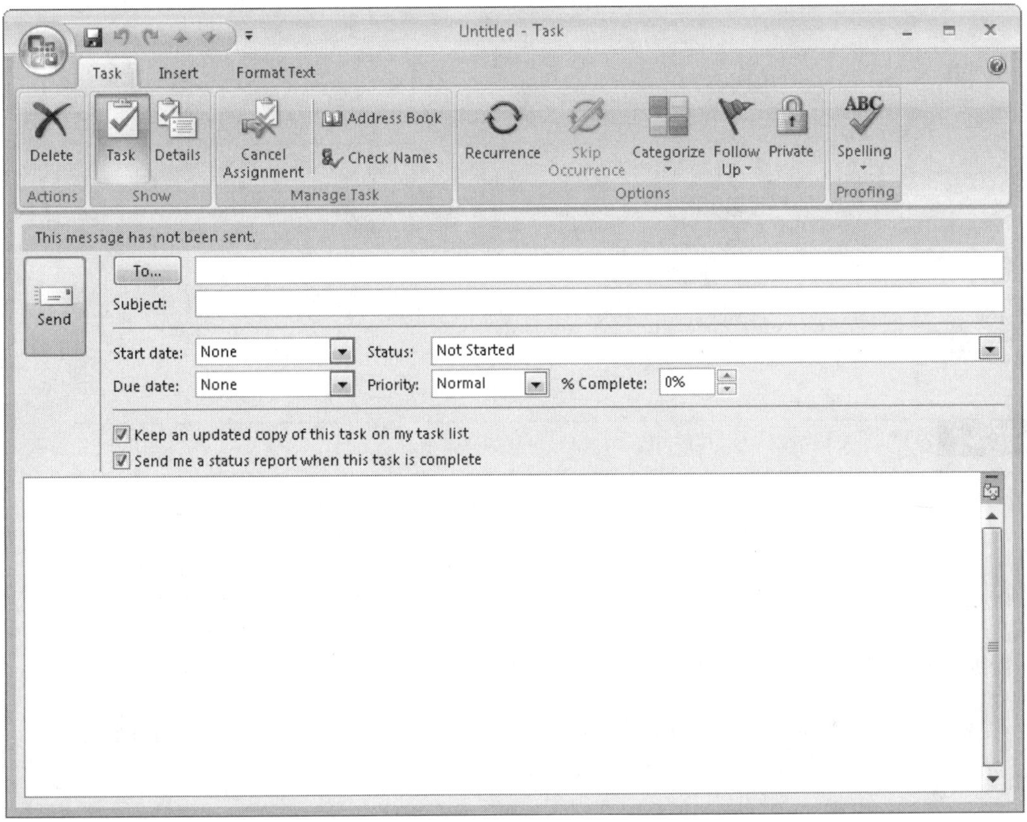

FIGURE 8-6   The Task window picks up some new elements when you assign a task to someone else.

holding a clipboard in front of an envelope. If you have New Item Alerts set up to show them, incoming task messages are labeled as such when they arrive.

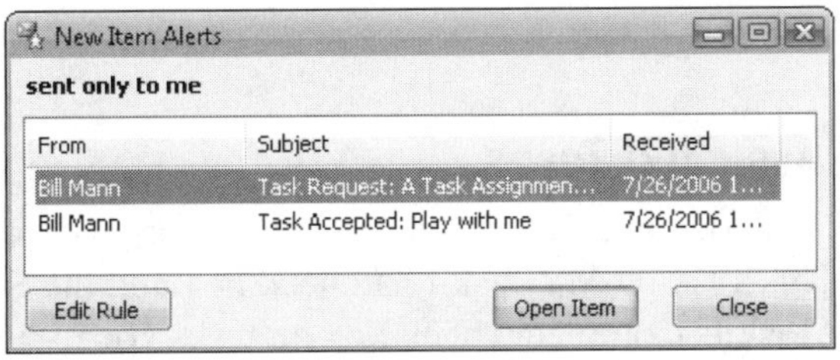

And when you open them in a Task window, assigned tasks look significantly different, as Figure 8-7 clearly shows.

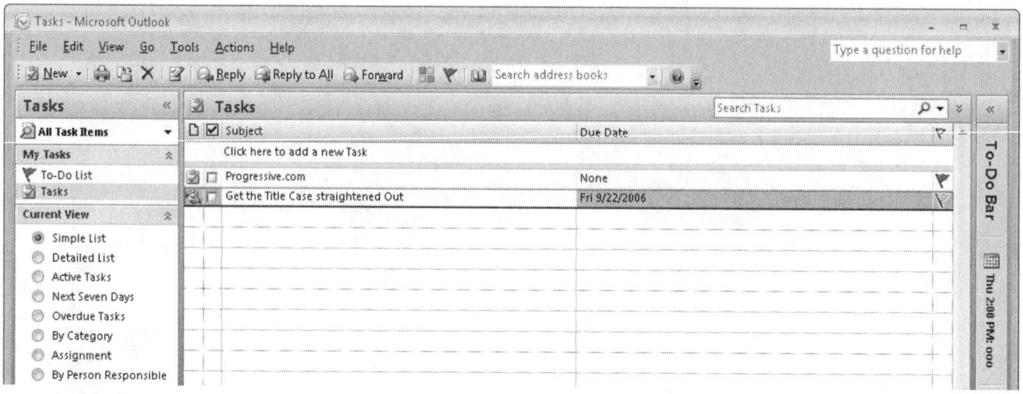

FIGURE 8-7   The Task window showing an assigned task.

Figure 8-8 shows what a typical task assignment looks like. The Task page has basic information about the task, while the Details page contains the kind of information you need to track a task. But the most interesting thing about a task assignment is the Accept and Decline options in the Respond group on the Ribbon.

TIP   *To switch between the Task page and the Details page, click the appropriate button in the Show group on the Ribbon.*

If you click Accept, Outlook creates an Acceptance message and adds the task to your Tasks list. An Accepting Task dialog box pops up so you can add comments to the Acceptance message before sending it or send it as is. Clicking the Decline button produces a message as well, except the task does not get into your Tasks list.

TIP   *You can also press ALT, H, A, C to accept a task or ALT, H, N to decline it.*

Keep Track of Assigned Tasks

Remember that I said, you have the option of selecting or unselecting the Keep an Updated Copy of This Task on My Task List check box and the Send Me a Status Report When This Task Is Complete check box on tasks you assign to people? Setting these check boxes for tasks you assign is the secret to tracking their progress.

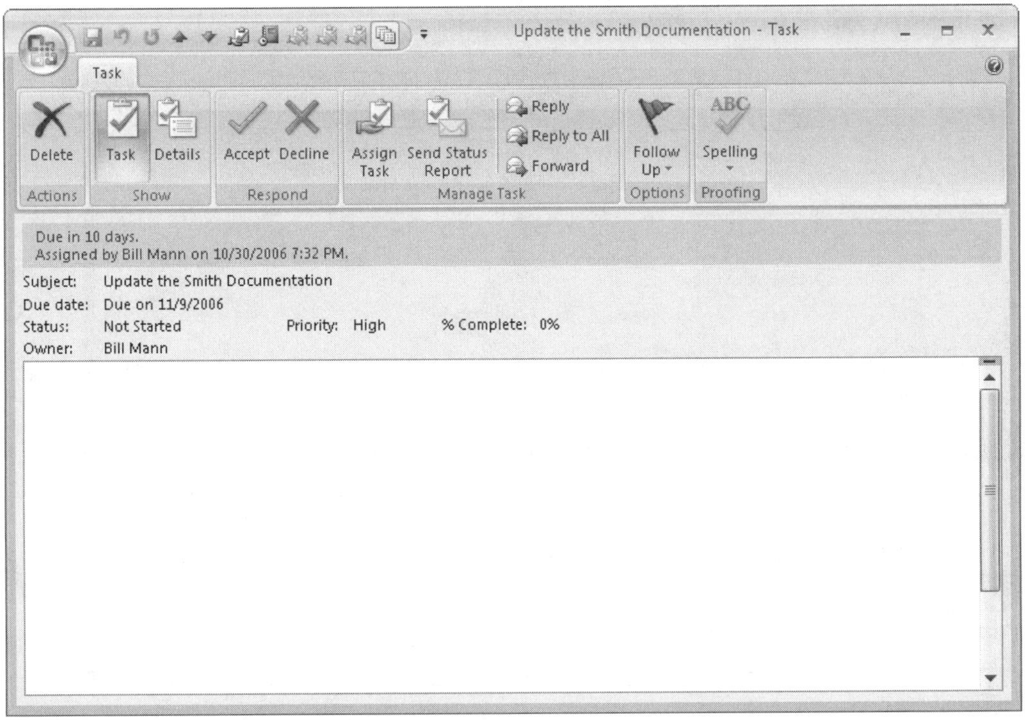

FIGURE 8-8   An open Task Assignment window.

The Keep an Updated Copy of This Task on My Task List check box does exactly that. When you select this option, you can still see the task in your Tasks list. Instead of the usual clipboard with a check mark icon used for regular tasks, tasks that you've assigned to others have a hand holding a check-marked clipboard.

Whenever the person who is working on the task changes its status and saves the task on their machine, their copy of Outlook sends a message to Outlook on your machine that tells it to update the status of the task in your Tasks list. Similarly, when the person working on the task sets its status to Completed,

Outlook sends a message to your machine notifying you that the task is complete. The message will look very much like the one here:

To make keeping track of the tasks you assign to others even easier, you can use Assignment view to sort tasks based on who they are assigned to. To even further sort the tasks you assigned to others, you can click the Checked Out To heading in the Tasks list to sort all the tasks you've assigned by assignee name.

Integrate Tasks into the Calendar with the Daily Tasks List

We already talked about the Daily Tasks list when we talked about the Calendar. As you now know, tasks and to-do items automatically appear in the list on the day they are due. Now we need to talk quickly about how to add a task using the Daily Tasks list.

We're talking quickly because there isn't much to say. To add a new task or task request to the Daily Tasks list, right-click in an empty area of the list (there's always an empty area at the bottom of each day's list) and select New Task or

New Task Request in the shortcut menu that appears. Outlook opens a new Task window and fills in whatever information it can. You need only complete the task, then send it or save and close it.

Like I said, there isn't much to say. This is easy.

Use the To-Do Bar Everywhere

Finally, we're ready to talk about the To-Do Bar. The To-Do Bar appears throughout Outlook 2007. It is meant to help you organize your day and manage your priorities by consolidating key information in one place, including the following:

- A calendar

- Upcoming appointments

- Tasks and to-do items

Pulling all this key information together in one place makes it easy to see and act on the most important stuff. The To-Do Bar replaces the TaskPad from Outlook 2003, and eliminates the need to use the old Outlook Today view. At least the To-Do Bar can appear in every view. Whether or not it does, and exactly how it appears, is customizable from view to view. You can find out all the details about customizing the To-Do Bar in Chapter 11.

You can always get to the To-Do Bar, even if it isn't visible at the moment. If the To-Do Bar isn't visible, or if it is minimized (a narrow bar running down the Outlook window), you can open it to its normal form by clicking View | To-Do Bar and then selecting Normal.

A Quick To-Do Bar Tour

The To-Do Bar has three sections, as you can see in Figure 8-9. The top section is the Date Navigator. Beneath that is the Appointments list. At the bottom is the Task list.

The Date Navigator

The Date Navigator shows the current month and day. If you are a veteran of Outlook 2003, you'll recognize this as the calendar from the TaskPad. Days that

FIGURE 8-9   The To-Do Bar.

have appointments or meetings scheduled appear bold, so you can tell at a glance when you have free days. Things you can do in the Date Navigator are:

- Click a day to go to the Calendar view for that day

- Navigate to the preceding or following month with the arrows in the calendar header

- Jump to nearby months by clicking and holding on the name of the current month, and selecting one of the months that appears in the list

The Appointments List

The Appointments list shows a few of your next appointments (the exact number can be customized). Things you can do in the Appointments list are:

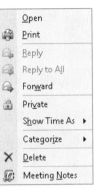

- ■ Double-click an appointment to open it.

- ■ Right-click one to see a menu of options, including printing the appointment, forwarding it to someone, and change some of its characteristics

The Task List

The Task list is a list of tasks and to-do items. It is really just another way to look at the stuff you have to do, scrunched to fit into a much smaller area. Things you can do in the Task list are:

8

- ■ Click the bar at the top of the Task list to change how the items in the list are arranged. Clicking the bar opens this list of options for how to arrange things:

- ■ Open each item. Tasks open in a Task window, whereas other to-do items open in their appropriate window. This means you could be in a mail view, looking at the Task list, and open a Contact to-do item, all without jumping from view to view crazily.

- ■ Right-click an item to see a menu of options. The specific options will vary, depending on the type of to-do item you are working with. Here's what the menu looks like for a task, probably the type of item you will find most frequently in this list:

	O̲pen
🖨	P̲rint
📩	R̲eply
📩	Reply to A̲ll
📩	For̲ward
	Follow U̲p ▶
	Categori̲ze ▶
📩	Mark as U̲nread
	Find A̲ll ▶
✕	D̲elete
🗐	Send to One̲Note

Adding a Task in the To-Do Bar

Now that we've covered the basics of the To-Do Bar, it is time to talk about how we add new tasks using the bar. This is almost anti-climactic. To add a new task using the To-Do Bar, you have two options. In either case you start by going to the Task list section of the To-Do Bar. Then you can:

- Type the subject of the task into the Type a New Task box. When you press ENTER, the task gets added to the list, with default start and end dates of today. This works best for simple tasks that you need to remember to get done right away.

- Double-click in the Type a New Task box to open a new Task window, with start and end dates of today. Because you are now working in a full Task window, you have full control over the details of the task.

That's all it takes to add a task using the To-Do Bar.

TIP *This chapter has given you the information you need to use tasks and the Tasks view effectively, but there are still many more things you can do with tasks. The Outlook 2007 Help system has an extensive section on tasks and task assignments. If you need to do something with tasks that isn't covered in this chapter, chances are good that you can do it with the aid of the Help system.*

Chapter 9

Notes, Shortcuts, and the Journal

How to...

- Navigate the Notes View
- Work with Notes
- Work with the Shortcuts Pane
- Navigate the Journal
- Work with the Journal

The theme of this chapter is keeping track of stuff that doesn't readily fit into other areas of Outlook. While the Mail, Contacts, and Calendar folders are great for tracking and working with messages, contacts, and appointments, you also need to track and work with other kinds of stuff.

Outlook notes are ideal for storing little bits of information that don't otherwise have a home. For example, I have an Outlook note with instructions for updating a friend's website, and another with the model numbers for the toner cartridges for my printer. Notes work perfectly for information like this.

Outlook shortcuts are great when the information you want to track and work with already exists, and you need a way to find it again. For example, I used to keep track of where stuff was on my hard drive and on the network by storing the path to each item in an Outlook note, but I've done away with the notes. Instead, I've created shortcuts directly to these items. It's a much more efficient approach.

Journal is a tool for tracking activities related to a particular contact, as well as tracking when you worked on documents. It displays the information it records in a timeline or a list, and you can open the documents or Outlook items associated with Journal entries.

NOTE *Journal isn't one of the more popular Outlook folders. As a matter of fact, Journal is turned off by default. Even so, if you work on multiple projects and charge clients by the hour, or if you want an easy way to keep track of what you worked on yesterday, last week, or last month, Journal could be the tool for you.*

This chapter walks you through the information you need to put notes, shortcuts, and the Journal to work. After this, you may still misplace your car keys, but it should be a lot easier to keep track of stuff in Outlook.

Navigate the Notes View

The Notes view is a two-panel view, with the Notes pane on the left and notes on the right, as shown in Figure 9-1. To open Notes, click the Notes icon at the bottom of the Navigation pane (it looks like a yellow sticky note with a corner turned up) or click Go | Notes.

> **TIP** *You can go to Notes directly with the CTRL-5 keyboard shortcut.*

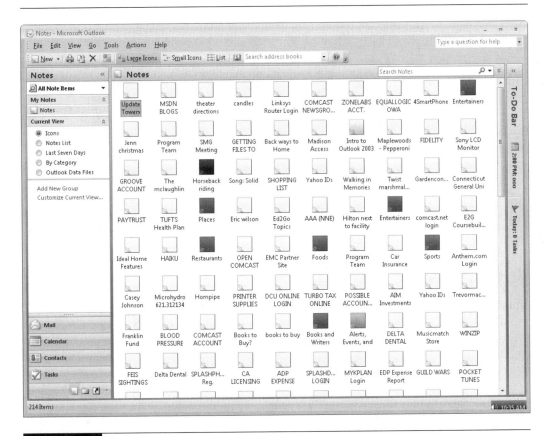

FIGURE 9-1   The Notes view.

The Notes pane has five sections, starting from the top:

- **All Note Items**   Lets you specify which Outlook data files to search for notes. For example, if you have a Hotmail Plus account connected to Outlook, you can display notes from that Hotmail account among the notes stored in Outlook.

> **NOTE**   *The Living With Outlook website has step-by-step instructions on linking Hotmail Plus, Gmail, Yahoo! Mail Plus, AOL Mail, and other e-mail accounts to Outlook. Visit http://www.living-with-outlook.com/outlook-web-mail.html to see the possibilities.*

- **My Notes**   Gives you control over which Notes folders are displayed.

- **Current View**   Lets you easily switch between views of the active Notes folders.

- **Links**   Contains links to Notes view features such as adding new groups for organizing Notes folders and customizing the current view.

> **NOTE**   *The exact links that appear in this section vary, depending on whether Outlook is connected to Exchange, is connected to SharePoint, or is being used standalone.*

- **Buttons**   The buttons on the bottom of the pane work just as they do in every other Navigation pane. Click any button to open its associated folder.

Work with Notes

There really isn't much to working with notes: You can create them, open or close them, sort them, and change their basic appearance. That's it. Aside from being a place to store random bits of information, the cool thing about Outlook notes is that you can leave them open on the desktop. After you create a note, you can just drag it somewhere and drop it. It will stay put until you close the note or close Outlook.

Create a Note

To create a new note, choose File | New | Note. If you're working in Notes view, you can click the New button on the Standard toolbar. A blank new Note window appears. Not much to it, is there?

TIP   *You can also press CTRL-SHIFT-N to open a new Note window.*

After the new Note window appears, type your note into it. The first line of text you type into the note becomes the title that you see on the notes in Figure 9-1. A few characters of the first line are always visible. If you hover the cursor over a particular note, and there's more to the first line that is normally visible, a box appears after a moment showing the rest of that first line.

You can leave the note open on your desktop as long as you want (as long as Outlook is open).

To close the note, click the note icon in the upper-left corner of the Note window, then click Close (or click the Close button in the upper-right corner). Outlook automatically saves a copy of the note in the Notes folder whenever you change it, so you don't have to worry about explicitly saving the note.

View or Edit a Note

To view or edit a note, find it in a Notes view and double-click it to open it. After the note is open, you can view or edit it simply by typing into it. Notes won't hold images or anything fancy, just text. Use the UP and DOWN ARROWS on the keyboard to scroll through a note that's too long to fit in the window. Dragging the lower-right corner of a note lets you resize the note so you can see more information without scrolling.

Basic editing commands are available when you click the note icon in the upper-left corner of the Note window. In addition to editing, you can use this menu to do some interesting tricks, such as forwarding the note to someone or categorizing it.

When you categorize a note, its window changes to the color of the category, as does its icon in the Notes views. Categories come in particularly handy when you are looking at the Notes list, since you can group notes by category. As elsewhere in Outlook 2007, if you get consistent about applying categories to similar items, you'll make your life much easier when it comes time to search for things.

Change the Look of a Note

To help you work with Notes more easily (and perhaps make them a little more fun), Outlook not only changes the color of notes to match their category, it lets you change the fonts in notes as well as the default size of notes on the screen. Let's look at how you manipulate note settings.

9

Change the Default Settings for Notes

You can adjust three default settings for notes: the color, the font, and the size. Follow these simple steps to change notes' default settings:

1. In the Outlook main window, choose Tools | Options.

2. On the Preferences tab of the Options dialog box, click Note Options. This opens the Notes Options dialog box, as shown here. You can set the three main characteristics of notes by using this dialog box.

3. Select the new default color and size you want. These settings will apply to all new notes that you create, but will not change the color or size of existing notes.

4. Click Font to select a new font for your notes.

5. Click OK to put the changes into effect.

CAUTION   *The font you select will apply not only to new notes you create, but to notes you open from this point forward. Suppose that a note open on your desktop is written in Arial font and you go into the Notes Options dialog box and select Times Roman. If you create a new note after you change the font, the new note will use Times New Roman. If you open an existing note that was created with the Arial font, it will appear in Times New Roman. If you close the Arial note that's open on your desktop and then reopen it, it will reappear in Times New Roman.*

Change the Color of the Current Note

You can change the color of an existing note by categorizing it. There are two ways to do so:

- If the note is closed, right-click it, click Categorize on the shortcut menu, and choose one of the options.

- If the note is already open, click the note icon in the upper-left corner of the Note window, select Categorize, and choose one of the available categories, or create a new one.

Show the Time and Date in New and Existing Notes

Notes can show the time and date they were last modified, but they don't do so by default. Follow these steps to make notes display the time and date:

1. Choose Tools | Options to open the Options dialog box.

2. On the Other tab, click Advanced Options. This opens the Advanced Options dialog box.

3. In the Appearance Options section, select the When Viewing Notes, Show Time and Date check box.

That's it for notes. If you're like me, you'll soon find yourself with quite a pile of notes, each containing some random fact or information that you don't want to lose. Somehow I've ended up with around 200 notes—I have no idea how I would keep track of all that stuff if I didn't have someplace like this to store it.

Navigate the Shortcuts Pane

The Mail pane, Calendar pane, Contacts pane, and so on are all specific examples of Outlook's new Navigation pane. Each of them helps you navigate one of the major folders in Outlook. But what about all the folders that aren't "major" folders like Mail or Calendar? What about all the rest of the information you work with? Shouldn't there be a Navigation pane that helps you with all this stuff? There is. It's called the Shortcuts pane.

As shown in Figure 9-2, the Shortcuts pane is a place to store and organize shortcuts to any of your Outlook folders. You might want to consider it a way to create your own custom Navigation pane.

To open the Shortcuts pane, click the Shortcuts button in the Navigation pane. The Shortcuts button is a white box with a diagonal black arrow in it. The Shortcuts

FIGURE 9-2   Gather and group shortcuts to Outlook folders in the Shortcuts pane.

pane is very similar to other versions of the Navigation pane. It is divided into three sections, starting from the top:

TIP *You can open the Shortcuts pane from anywhere in Outlook by pressing CTRL-7.*

- ■ **Shortcuts**   This is the default group for shortcuts you create. This section of the Shortcuts pane can also contain groups that you create for yourself, such as the Gmail groups in Figure 9-2.

- ■ **Links**   The area beneath the shortcuts contains links for adding new shortcuts groups and new shortcuts.

- ■ **Buttons**   The buttons at the bottom of the pane work just as they do in other versions of the Navigation pane.

To use one of the shortcuts, click it in the Shortcuts pane. Outlook automatically takes you to the folder. This is quick and easy when there are a limited number of shortcuts listed.

A Shortcuts pane containing a massive number of shortcuts wouldn't be very useful (might as well just use the Folders pane, which shows them all), and that's where shortcut groups come in. Create groups to organize your shortcuts into logical collections. If you decide to change the organization, you can remove or rename existing groups, as well as move shortcuts between groups, to create an organization that fits your current needs. The rest of this chapter shows how to work with shortcuts and shortcut groups.

Work with Shortcuts and Shortcut Groups

Working with shortcuts and shortcut groups is pretty simple, seeing as there aren't too many things you can do with them. Even so, a few quirks need to be taken into account, and these are covered in the sections that follow.

Create a Shortcut

You can create shortcuts in two ways: with the Add New Shortcut link in the Shortcuts pane, or by clicking File | New | Navigation Pane Shortcut.

To create a shortcut using the Add New Shortcut link, click the link. Whichever way you choose to add a new shortcut, Outlook opens the Add to Navigation Pane dialog box, as shown in Figure 9-3. Click the name of the folder you want to create the shortcut for. If the folder isn't visible in the main list, open the Folder Name list and look for it there.

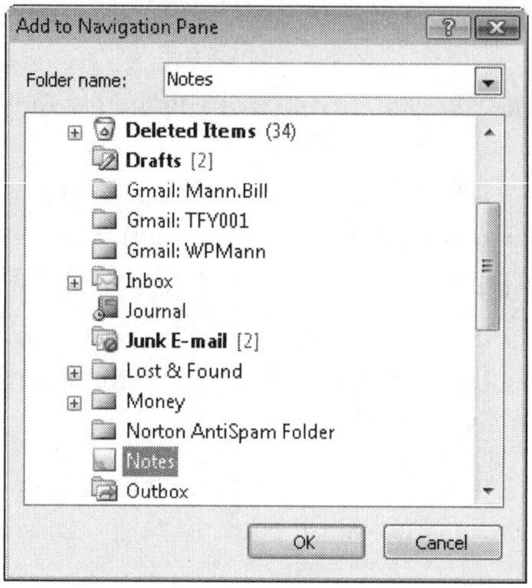

FIGURE 9-3   The Add to Navigation Pane dialog box.

When you add a new shortcut, the shortcut appears in the first shortcut group. If you want to place it in a different group, see "Move a Shortcut to Another Shortcut Group" for instructions.

Remove a Shortcut

To remove a shortcut from the Shortcuts pane, right-click it and click Delete Shortcut. Deleting the shortcut from the Shortcuts pane does not remove the item that the shortcut points to.

Did you know?

The Shortcuts Pane Is Different from Other Panes?

When you click the Mail, Calendar, Contacts, Tasks, or Notes navigation buttons, Outlook displays the associated Navigation pane and opens the relevant folder. When you click the Shortcuts button, on the other hand, the current view stays in place. Only the Navigation pane changes. This way, you can create shortcuts without losing the thread of what you were doing by jumping to a completely different view.

Move a Shortcut to Another Shortcut Group

Moving a shortcut from place to place within the Shortcuts pane is a matter of dragging the shortcut where you want it and dropping it there. To avoid making a mess, you need to drop the shortcut on the name of the group you want to add it to.

Create a Shortcut Group

Create a shortcut group by clicking the Add New Group link. This creates a spot for a new shortcut group in the top section of the Shortcuts pane. Type the name of the new group and press ENTER. Your new group is ready to receive shortcuts.

Rename or Remove a Shortcut Group

To rename a shortcut group, right-click its name, choose Rename Group on the shortcut menu, and then type a new name for the group.

To remove a shortcut group, right-click its name and choose Remove Group on the shortcut menu. Outlook opens a message window asking you to confirm that you really want to remove the group. Click OK to remove the group.

9

CAUTION *When you remove a shortcut group, you also remove all the shortcuts that are in the group. If you want to retain any of the shortcuts, move them to a new group before you remove the group.*

Change the Order of Shortcut Groups

Changing the order of shortcut groups is a clumsy procedure. To do it, you right-click the name of the group you want to move. Then, in the shortcut menu that appears, click Move Up in List or Move Down in List.

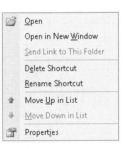

TIP *When you need to do a lot of rearranging of shortcut groups, renaming an existing group and dragging shortcuts between groups is sometimes more efficient than rearranging the existing groups one step at a time.*

That's it for shortcuts. Now it's time to talk about the Journal.

The Journal

Journal is a tool for tracking activities related to a particular contact, as well as tracking when you worked on documents. It displays the information it records in a timeline or a list, and you can open the documents or other Outlook items being tracked from within Journal.

Journal differs from other Outlook folders in more ways than how it displays information. By default, Journal is turned off, and the button to open it isn't even included in the list of buttons at the bottom of the Navigation pane. This clearly isn't one of the most popular aspects of Outlook.

Still, if you need to keep track of when you did things, or you do work on multiple projects and need to keep track of the hours expended on each, the Journal could be useful. We'll take a quick ramble through the Journal, so if you decide to use it, you'll know how.

Activate the Journal

First things first. We can't do anything with the Journal until we turn it on. You can open the Journal view by choosing Go | Journal at any time. However, if you plan to use the Journal, a better choice is to add the Journal button to the set of buttons at the bottom of the Navigation pane. I've provided instructions for doing so later in this chapter.

For now, choose Go | Journal to open the Journal view. If this is the first time you've opened Journal, Outlook displays a dialog box instead of the Journal:

The point of this dialog box is to let you know that you can track e-mail messages associated with contacts without using the Journal. Given this information, you need to decide whether to actually turn on the Journal. The key question is whether you want to track Office documents and other information related to contacts, or just e-mail messages related to contacts. If you just want to track e-mail messages, click No and don't bother reading any more of this chapter. You don't need it.

On the other hand, if you are considering using Journal to track more than just e-mail messages, click Yes and read on.

Work with Journal

Since you're still here, I assume that you decided to give Journal a try. If you clicked Yes in the previous dialog box, you should now be looking at the Journal Options dialog box. This is where you configure Journal to track the information you're interested in.

NOTE   *The list that appears in the Also Record Files From box will vary depending on which Microsoft products you have installed. For example, if you use Visio or Project, you will be able to track those in the Journal too.*

Set Journal Tracking Options

Journal gives you a lot of options, but it doesn't give you real fine-grained control. By that I mean you can specify which Outlook items and Office files you want tracked for which contacts, but you can't specify one set of things to track for one contact, and a different set for a different contact.

To set the Journal options, follow these instructions:

> **TIP** *You can always get to the Journal Options dialog box from the main Outlook window by choosing Tools | Options and, in the Contacts section of the Preferences tab, clicking Journal Options.*

1. In the Automatically Record These Items list, select the check box next to each item type that you want to track.

2. Select the contacts for which you want this information tracked in the For These Contacts list.

3. Select the files you want to track in the Also Record Files From list by selecting the check box next to each file type.

> **TIP** *When Journal tracks a file type, the entries aren't associated with a particular contact.*

4. In the Double-clicking a Journal Entry section of the dialog box, select the appropriate response.

5. Click AutoArchive Journal Entries if you want Outlook to archive the entries that Journal creates. You can get more information on AutoArchiving in Chapter 13.

6. Click OK.

Navigate the Journal View

The two-pane Journal view should look somewhat familiar. On the left side is the Journal pane with the usual sections and features. The right side is where Journal entries appear. Depending on the view you choose, entries appear in lists that are grouped in various ways, or are interspersed on a timeline that reflects when they occurred.

The default view is By Type, which groups all Word documents together, all task requests together, and so on. While this is fine for general use, other views come in particularly handy for specific activities. For example, the By Contact view is great when you are looking for information related to a specific client.

Perhaps even more useful in Outlook 2007 is grouping By Category. You can do things such as applying a specific category to every item related to Project X. Then, in the Journal By Category view, you will be able to easily see a timeline of all the entries related to Project X.

Manually Record Items and Files

You can also record Journal entries manually. You might do this to get finer control over what gets recorded in Journal or to record things such as telephone calls that Journal can't record automatically.

A standard Journal entry is an Outlook item or one of the Microsoft file types that Journal recognizes. To manually record a standard Journal entry, follow these steps:

1. In the Outlook main window, choose File | New, then click Journal Entry. This opens a blank Journal Entry similar to the one shown in Figure 9-4.

> **TIP** *You can also open a new blank Journal entry by pressing CTRL-SHIFT-J, or by clicking the New button in the toolbar if you are already in a Journal view.*

2. Enter a description of the entry in the Subject box.

3. In the Entry Type list, choose the type of entry you want to create.

4. Add any other information as necessary, and then click Save & Close.

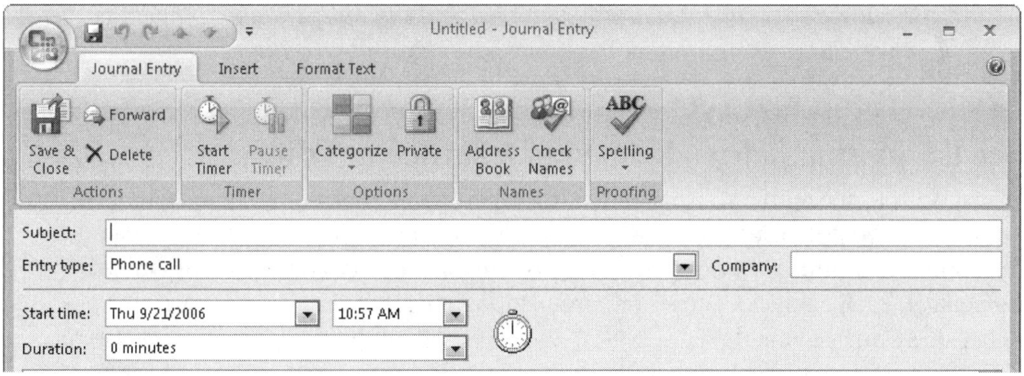

FIGURE 9-4 The Journal Entry dialog box.

A nonstandard Journal entry is *not* an Outlook item or one of the Microsoft file types that Journal recognizes. Follow these steps to manually record a nonstandard Journal entry:

1. Find the file you want to record.

2. Drag the file onto the Journal button of the Navigation pane (the instructions for getting that button in place are coming up) and drop it there. Outlook opens a new Journal entry with Document as the Entry Type setting, and a shortcut to the file in the body.

3. Fill in the Subject field with a descriptive name (Outlook puts the filename here when it creates the entry), and enter any other necessary information.

4. Click Save & Close to record the entry.

Open and Modify Journal Entries

Unless you changed the settings in the Journal Options dialog box, you can open a Journal entry simply by double-clicking it. You can also open a Journal entry by right-clicking it and then clicking Open Journal Entry on the shortcut menu.

After a Journal entry is open, you can modify it in any way you wish. For example, you can change the subject, the entry type, the start time, and the duration.

NOTE   *Because entries in Journal are arranged in a timeline, changing the Start Time fields for a Journal entry moves an entry around within Journal.*

See the Journal Entries Related to a Particular Contact

If you want to see all the Journal entries for a particular contact, there are a few ways to go about it. You can see all your Journal entries in Journal view. You can also organize entries in various ways, one of which is by contact. When organized by contact, each contact's entries are grouped together, but they're still spread across the timeline.

Add the Journal Button to the Navigation Pane

If you're going to use Journal regularly, you might as well follow these steps to add a button for it to the Navigation pane:

1. Click the Configure Buttons button in the lower-right corner of the Navigation pane (it is the down arrow at the far right). A shortcut menu appears.

2. Choose Navigation Pane Options to open the Navigation Pane Options dialog box.

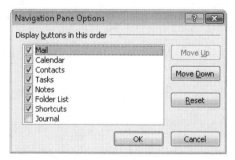

9

3. Select the Journal check box and click OK. The Journal button will now be visible in the Navigation pane.

We've completed our quick tour of notes, shortcuts, and the Journal. With these three tools, you now have a much greater ability to keep track of all sorts of Outlook items.

So far in this book, you've learned how to manage your communications with the world and how to work with your personal information. In the next section, we shift focus to customizing and managing Outlook 2007 itself. The chapters in this section will help you adapt Outlook to your needs in everything from protecting your online security to customizing the way Outlook looks and works. Let's get started.

Part IV

Customize and Manage Outlook 2007

Chapter 10

Take Advantage of Search Folders

How to...

- ◼ Understand Search Folders

- ◼ Use the Default Search Folders

- ◼ Create Your Own Search Folders

- ◼ Turn Searches into Search Folders

- ◼ Customize a Search Folder

Search folders are a powerful feature that arrived in Outlook 2003. Before search folders, you sometimes ran into situations like this one:

You receive an e-mail message from your boss that includes instructions for two different projects. Being the efficient worker that you are, you have separate folders for each of those projects. Where do you store the message? It pertains to two projects, so it belongs in two different folders.

In the bad old days, you might have dealt with the problem by making a copy of the message and putting the original in one folder and the copy in the other. That could work, but the approach had some real problems. Each duplicate message meant another item for Outlook (and you) to manage and a little bit more disk space chewed up. Even worse, with multiple copies of the same message, it was easy to get out of synchronization.

What if you needed to do something with the message after you put multiple copies in different locations? You either needed to let the copies differ, or you needed to remember where each copy of the message was and make the same changes to each one. Did you reply to a message already? You would have to find and check each copy of it, or dig through the Sent Items folder to find out. Even something as simple as deleting an old message became a headache when multiple copies were scattered around different folders.

This is where search folders come in. Search folders are an elegant solution to the problem of what to do with items that need to be in multiple locations. As their name implies, search folders are also a great way to find stuff. This chapter explains what search folders are, how they work, and how you can best take advantage of them.

Understand Search Folders

Search folders look like other folders, but they are not the same. Search folders are actually the results of searches conducted on e-mail messages in some or all of the folders in your Outlook mailbox. As Figure 10-1 shows, the contents of a search folder appear to be e-mail messages. In reality, they are not.

Search folders are actually virtual folders displaying views of links to *mail items* (e-mail messages and RSS feeds) that match certain search criteria. The messages themselves are still in whichever folder you or Outlook stored them in. Neither you nor Outlook has to move them into the search folder. Yet you can work with the messages as if they were located in the search folder.

Look again at Figure 10-1. Although you can't readily tell by looking at them, using rules, I stored those messages in several different Outlook folders. And despite appearing as though they are all in an Unread Mail folder, they are actually still in the folders I assigned them to. The only thing they have in common is that I haven't read them yet. But Outlook's search folder capability gives you access to them based on that commonality, rather than on where the messages are stored.

Here, then, is the solution to the problem of one message that needs to go in two locations. Thanks to search folders, there are many ways to address that particular scenario. Suppose you want to keep all e-mail messages from your boss in a single folder called Boss Messages. You could create a search folder for each project, and after you get things set up properly, Outlook would automatically display all messages dealing with each project in the appropriate search folder. The single message could be stored in the Boss Messages folder, while appearing in two search folders simultaneously.

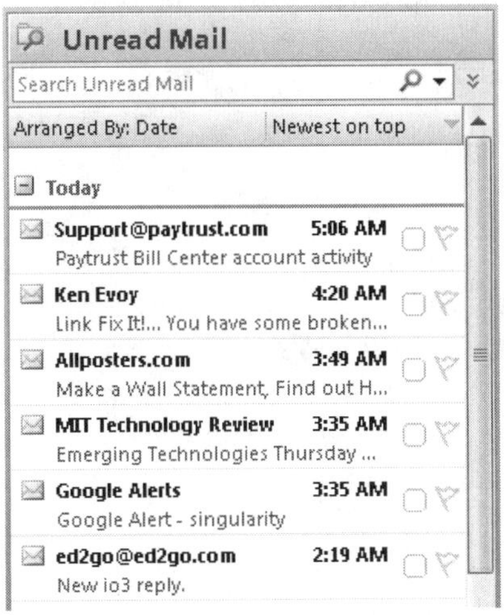

10

FIGURE 10-1   Things are not what they seem when dealing with search folders.

Not only do search folders display the results of a search on the e-mail messages in Outlook, they display *live* search results. Every time you open a search folder, Outlook repeats the search. This makes search folders incredibly powerful. The contents of a search folder are always up to date and, assuming you've set them up properly, show only relevant messages.

Outlook 2007 comes with a set of default search folders, as well as a set of templates for creating your own. You can even create completely custom search folders. Learning to use search folders can make a significant difference in the efficiency of your work in Outlook. We will start things off with the default search folders.

Use the Default Search Folders

Outlook 2007 comes with three default search folders that are set up and operating right out of the box:

- Unread Mail
- Categorized Mail
- Large Mail

In general, you can treat these folders like any other Outlook folder. However, each has some unique characteristics of its own, as described in the next three sections.

Unread Mail shows every message that is marked as Unread, no matter what folder it is in. I find this to be an incredibly useful tool. Figure 10-1 shows what Unread Mail looks like.

TIP   *You can set a message to appear as unread, even after you have read it, by right-clicking it and selecting Mark as Unread in the shortcut menu. Some people use this as a way to keep track of messages they need to deal with. By you marking them Unread, these messages continue to appear in the Unread Mail folder where you will keep seeing them until you do something about them. Not a very sophisticated approach, but it works for some people.*

Categorized Mail shows any messages that have a color category assigned to them. The messages are grouped by color.

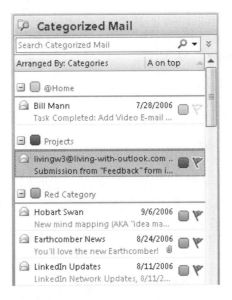

Large Mail shows any messages that are, well, large. That is, messages (plus any attachments) that exceed 100KB in size. The messages are grouped by size.

Use the Unread Mail Folder

The Unread Mail folder is the search folder you will likely use most often. It shows you all the unread mail items anywhere in the Outlook mailbox. By default,

FIGURE 10-2 The Unread Mail folder appears in Favorite Folders and All Mail Items.

the Unread Mail folder appears in the Favorite Folders section of the pane as well as in the All Mail Items section (see Figure 10-2). This gives you quick access to all your unread messages, wherever they happen to be stored in Outlook.

Like other mail folders, you can sort the Unread Mail folder in many ways. Sorting by conversation lets you follow the thread of a discussion regardless of where the relevant mail items are stored. Sorting by folders makes it easy to deal with all the messages in a specific folder at once. If you store messages related to specific projects or subjects in specific folders, you can easily deal with all unread messages related to each project or subject without having to hunt for them.

Use the Categorized Mail Folder

The Categorized Mail folder is like an automatic to-do list, at least when it comes to mail items. Every categorized mail item stored anywhere in your Outlook mailbox automatically appears in the Categorized Mail folder.

As Figure 10-3 shows, the Categorized Mail folder appears in the All Mail Items section of the Navigation pane. By default, Categorized Mail arranges mail items by color. That is, all the items colored blue are grouped together, as are all those with another color. If you use a consistent category scheme with items (everything to do with Project X is red, for example), this grouping scheme gathers together related mail items automatically.

FIGURE 10-3   The Categorized Mail folder is another way to keep track of related mail items.

10

The Categorized Mail folder does some neat tricks that can really help you get your work done quickly. When you're done working on a categorized item, you need only click the little block of color (the one next in the Categorized Mail pane) that indicates the category to clear it and remove the item from the category.

If the item is also flagged as a task (see Chapter 8 for more on flags), you can click the flag to mark the task as complete. The flag is replaced by a check mark that shows the item is complete. The two items here show the possible states of the flag: the first is not yet complete, so it shows a flag. The second is complete, and its flag is replaced by a check mark.

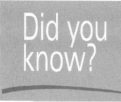

The Difference Between the Categorized Mail and For Follow Up Folders

One of the places where search folders have changed between Outlook 2003 and Outlook 2007 is this folder. Outlook 2003 had the For Follow Up folder, which displayed items that had a flag set. Just as Outlook 2007 categories have superseded Outlook 2003 flags, so has the Categorized Mail folder superseded the For Follow Up folder.

The thing that I've found hardest to adjust to in this change is the behavior of flagged items in Categorized Mail. It used to be that when you clicked a flag to mark an item as complete, it disappeared from the For Follow Up folder. Since the Categorized Mail folder focuses on categories rather than flags, the state of a flag, or even the existence of one, has no effect on whether the item appears in this folder.

It's something to keep in mind if you are used to using the For Follow Up folder to keep track of tasks.

The other neat trick that the Categorized Mail folder can do is quickly convert items from one category to another. You don't need to open an item to change its category. You don't even need to right-click its category and select a new one.

Assuming that the new category is visible in the Categorized Mail pane, you need merely drag the item from its current category into the new one. Drop it there and Outlook automatically changes the category for you. This is quite slick and nicely simplifies life when you realize that you've miscategorized an item. Just drag it where it needs to be and Outlook takes care of the rest.

Use the Large Mail Folder

The Large Mail folder is a search folder that contains, not surprisingly, large mail items. To appear in this folder, an item (along with its attachments) must be at least 100KB (100 kilobytes). Like the Categorized Mail folder, the Large Mail folder does not initially appear in the Favorite Folders section of the Mail pane. To reach it, you need to look in the All Mail Folders section of the Mail pane. As I mentioned earlier, the Large Mail folder normally organizes messages by size, using the groups Large, Very Large, Huge, and Enormous.

The Large Mail folder comes into play in more specialized circumstances. For example, some organizations circulate lots of large documents by e-mail, yet allocate only a small amount of space for Inboxes. In such a situation, the ability to quickly identify large messages and delete them, or strip off their attachments, or just move them off the server and onto the local hard drive can be a lifesaver. For more on deleting messages in search folders, see the "How to Delete Search Folders and the Messages in Them" box.

How to ... **Delete Search Folder and the Messages in Them**

While search folders act in many ways like regular folders, one way in which they differ has to do with deleting messages. Normally when you delete a folder, you also delete all the messages inside it. Not so with search folders. Because a search folder contains only the results of searches, there are no messages in them to be deleted. When you delete a search folder, it goes away, but none of the messages you saw in the search folder are affected in any way.

Here's how to delete the messages in a search folder: Right-click a message and choose Delete on the shortcut menu that appears. You can also open a message and click the Delete button or press CTRL-D. But beware! When you delete a message in a search folder using one of these techniques, you're not just deleting the message in the search folder. You're deleting it from the real folder it is stored in, as well as every search folder it appears in.

If you repeat this process with every message in the search folder, you can delete every message that meets the search criteria for the search folder, wherever the messages are stored in the Outlook mailbox.

If what you really want is a particular message to stop appearing in a particular search folder but still reside in its real folder and any other search folders that show it, you need to do something else. You need to either change the search folder's search criteria (you'll learn how to do this later in this chapter) or change the message so that it no longer matches the search criteria.

Create Your Own Search Folders

The default search folders—Unread Mail, Categorized Mail, and Large Mail—in Outlook give you a good feel for what you can do with search folder technology. But there's a lot more you can do, and Microsoft was thoughtful enough to give normal users like you and me the tools we need to create our own search folders.

You can create your own search folders in two ways. One is to use one of the dozen-plus predefined search folder templates included with Outlook. The other is to create a completely custom folder. The following sections walk you through each approach.

Start from a Predefined Search Folder

Outlook comes with over a dozen predefined search folder templates (including a For Follow Up template for anyone who misses that capability from Outlook 2003), grouped into three broad categories: Reading Mail, Mail from People and Lists, and Organizing Mail. Some templates offer customization options so you can further tweak the behavior of the search folder you create. Follow these steps to create a new search folder based on one of the predefined search folder templates:

1. Starting in Mail view, choose File | New | Search Folder. This opens the New Search Folder dialog box, shown here. You can create a new search folder using predefined folder templates, or strike out on your own and create a custom search folder.

> **TIP** *You can also open the New Search Folder dialog box with the CTRL-SHIFT-P keyboard shortcut.*

2. Select one of the templates from the Select a Search Folder list. Selecting certain templates causes options to appear under the Customize Search Folder heading in the dialog box.

3. Select options to meet your objectives in creating this search folder if any options are visible below the Customize Search Folder heading.

4. The Search Mail In list at the bottom of the New Search Folder dialog box lists all the mailboxes that Outlook has access to. If you wish to have the search folder search a different mailbox than the default mailbox (Personal Folders), select it from this list.

5. Click OK to activate the new search folder.

Create a Custom Search Folder

While Outlook comes with plenty of predefined search folder templates, you may still feel the need to create a search folder from scratch. Follow these steps:

1. Starting in Mail view, choose File | New | Search Folder. This opens the New Search Folder dialog box, shown in the preceding illustration.

> **TIP** *You can also open the New Search Folder dialog box with the CTRL-SHIFT-P keyboard shortcut.*

2. Select Create a Custom Search Folder in the Select a Search Folder list. This causes a text box and a button to appear beneath the Customize Search Folder heading.

3. Click Choose to open the Custom Search Folder dialog box, shown in the following illustration. Use this dialog box to name your custom search folder.

10

4. Click Criteria to open the Search Folder Criteria dialog box, shown in the following illustration. The Search Folder Criteria dialog box lets you create complex and highly targeted searches.

> **NOTE** *Honestly, I've seldom had to create a custom search folder, and don't think most people will ever need to do it. So we aren't spending a lot of time on this dialog box. Instead, I will tell you that the best way to attack this is to start with the Messages tabbed page. Only move on to the More Choices and Advanced pages if absolutely necessary.*

5. The Search Mail In box at the bottom of the New Search Folder dialog box lists all the mailboxes that Outlook has access to. If you wish to have Search Folder search a different mailbox than the default mailbox (Personal Folders), select it from this list.

6. Click OK to activate the new search folder.

Customize an Existing Search Folder

You can customize any existing search folder, including the Unread Mail, Categorized Mail, and Large Mail default search folders (although I strongly advise against customizing those three!). To customize an existing search folder, follow these steps:

1. In the Mail pane, right-click the search folder you want to customize.

2. Choose Customize This Search Folder on the shortcut menu. This opens a Customize Search Folder dialog box.

3. Change the folder name if you wish.

4. If the Criteria button is active, you can click it to change the search criteria using a dialog box.

5. To change the list of folders searched by this search folder, click Browse. This opens the Select Folder(s) dialog box shown in the following illustration. You can get very specific search results by limiting the set of folders that the search folder you create will search. For example, you can create a search folder that only displays items of a specific category for a particular project or a particular subject. You can narrow or expand the range of a search folder's results by selecting the appropriate folders to search in this dialog box.

When to Choose Search Folders or Instant Search

Now that you've learned about search folders, you may be wondering when to use a search and when to use search folders. You may be wondering how to decide which to use when. While there are no hard-and-fast rules, let me suggest some guidelines:

> **NOTE**   *If you are not yet familiar with Outlook's search capabilities, don't worry. You will learn about them in detail in Chapter 13.*

- If you want to search for items other than e-mail messages and RSS feeds, use Instant Search. You can conduct an Instant Search of any type of Outlook item.

- If you are doing a quick, one-time search, use Instant Search. An Instant Search is fast and easy to set up, and doesn't leave the Mail pane cluttered with old searches you no longer care about.

- If you expect to repeat this search in the future, and you are searching only mail items, consider creating a search folder. While this will take longer to set up than an Instant Search, you will be able to do the same search in the future with only a mouse click. You won't have to re-create it each time you want to run the search.

Chapter 11

Customize the User Interface

How to...

- Use and Customize Outlook Today
- Customize Toolbars and Menus
- Customize the Ribbon
- Customize the Navigation Pane
- Customize the To-Do Bar

As we've worked through the different sections of Outlook 2007, we've seen a number of places where you can customize the way the program looks and feels. In this chapter, we will talk about some other ways you can customize how Outlook 2007 looks and feels. What the topics in this chapter have in common is that they are all changes that affect multiple areas of Outlook or otherwise don't fit well into one of the other chapters.

Outlook Today is a consolidated view that combines elements from Mail, Calendar, and Tasks to give you a quick overview of your day. You can make Outlook Today appear whenever you start Outlook, and you can customize the way it presents information. With the advent of the To-Do Bar, Outlook Today may be less useful than it used to be, but it is available if you want to use it, and this chapter shows you how.

Outlook toolbars and menus are designed to help you be productive and efficient. In this chapter, you'll learn a few ways to customize them to even better match the way you work.

The Ribbon is now a major part of Outlook. Given the way it is designed and already adapts itself to show the commands that are most appropriate for whatever you are doing, there is little you can do to customize it. You can, however, control when it is visible, as you will see in a few pages.

Similarly, the Navigation pane, Reading pane, and To-Do Bar all are well designed for their tasks, but can be tweaked a bit. The last part of this chapter shows you how.

Use and Customize Outlook Today

Outlook can contain vast amounts of information, organized by type (e-mail, appointments, and so on). But sometimes, all you may want is to know what's on tap for today. It can be really useful to see all your appointments and tasks for the day gathered in one spot. Likewise, knowing how many unread messages are in your Inbox, and how many drafts you're working on, can really help you get organized for your day.

Outlook Today (see Figure 11-1) is a single view that can show you all these things. You can use it to get a quick preview of your day, and you can set Outlook to automatically open in this view. Even better (and particularly relevant for this chapter), you can customize Outlook Today to make it more fun and more useful for you.

Now that you know a little about Outlook Today, let's see what you can do to customize it.

Switch to Outlook Today View

The first thing you can do is make Outlook Today appear. With just a few clicks, you can switch to the Outlook Today view to get an overview of your day.

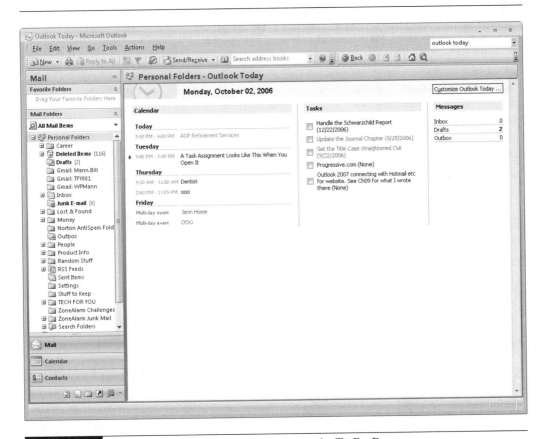

FIGURE 11-1   Outlook Today can be an alternative to the To-Do Bar.

The Differences Between Outlook Today and the To-Do Bar

As you can see if you compare Figure 11-1 and Figure 11-2, Outlook Today and the To-Do Bar have similar, but not identical information. The focus of Outlook Today is on days, more specifically today. The focus of the To-Do Bar is on the things you need to do next, regardless of the day they need to be done.

Outlook Today has the advantage of being its own separate view, leaving a lot more room and less clutter.

The To-Do Bar has the advantage of being integrated into the other Outlook views, making it much more readily accessible. Plus, it fits into the look and feel of the rest of Outlook 2007.

I think that if you try them both, you will eventually find the To-Do Bar to be more useful than Outlook Today. But do try them both and see what you think.

The Outlook Today button appears on the Advanced toolbar, but an even easier way to get to this view is through the Navigation pane. Follow these steps to switch to Outlook Today view:

1. In the Navigation pane, click Mail to open the Mail view.

2. You should see your default mail folder in the Navigation pane. It will probably be named Personal Folders and will have an icon that looks like a tiny house and some other odds and ends.

3. Click your default mail folder to go to the Outlook Today view.

 When you are done working in Outlook Today, click one of the Mail views in Favorite Folders, or switch to another view to leave Outlook Today.

 Later in this chapter, you'll learn how to customize toolbars. If you find Outlook Today useful, you may want to consider adding the Outlook Today button to the Standard toolbar to give you even quicker access. See "How to Add the Outlook Today Button to the Standard Toolbar" for the specific steps.

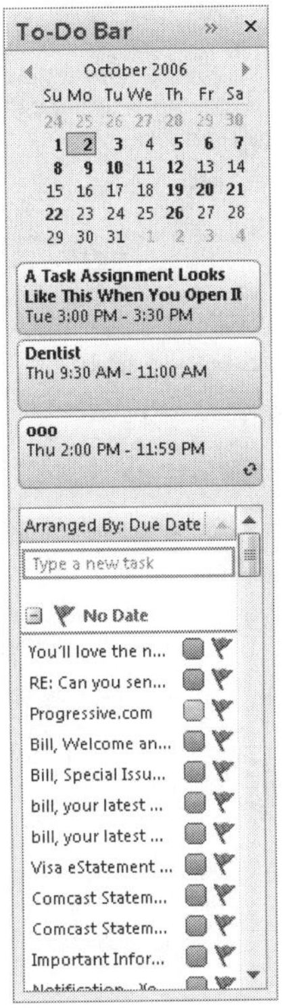

To-Do Bar   »   ×

◄   October 2006   ►
Su Mo Tu We Th Fr Sa
24 25 26 27 28 29 30
1 2 3 4 5 6 7
8 9 10 11 12 13 14
15 16 17 18 19 20 21
22 23 24 25 26 27 28
29 30 31 1 2 3 4

**A Task Assignment Looks
Like This When You Open It**
Tue 3:00 PM - 3:30 PM

Dentist
Thu 9:30 AM - 11:00 AM

ooo
Thu 2:00 PM - 11:59 PM

Arranged By: Due Date

Type a new task

No Date

You'll love the n...
RE: Can you sen...
Progressive.com
Bill, Welcome an...
Bill, Special Issu...
bill, your latest ...
bill, your latest ...
Visa eStatement ...
Comcast Statem...
Comcast Statem...
Important Infor...
Notification   Yo

FIGURE 11-2   The To-Do Bar will probably replace Outlook Today in many users' hearts.

When you are working in the Outlook Today view, you can use a subset of the capabilities of some of the other views without leaving Outlook Today. Click any item to view it. Mark tasks complete by setting the check box to the left of the task name. You can also click the titles of each area (Calendar, Tasks, Messages, and so on) to go to the standard view for that type of information.

Customize Outlook Today

You can customize Outlook Today to display more of the information you want to see, organized in the way you want it organized, in any of several visual styles. The next several topics address customizing Outlook Today. To customize Outlook Today, you work from the Customize Outlook Today view shown in Figure 11-3. To make this pane appear, you first need to open Outlook Today, then click Customize Outlook Today in the Outlook Today view.

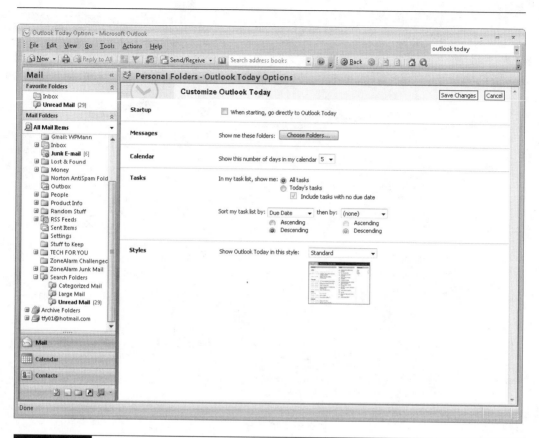

FIGURE 11-3 The Customize Outlook Today view lets you change what the view contains and how it looks.

Make Outlook Today Appear Whenever You Start Outlook

If you turn off your computer at night or close Outlook when you're away from your computer, one of the best ways to use Outlook Today is to set it to appear automatically whenever you start Outlook. This gives you the chance to get an overview of your day, first thing.

To set Outlook Today to appear whenever you start Outlook, follow these steps:

1. Open the Customize Outlook Today view.

2. Select the check box When starting, go directly to Outlook Today.

3. Click Save Changes.

Determine Which Message Folders Outlook Today Will Show You

By default, Outlook Today displays the number of unread messages in the Inbox, along with the total number of messages in the Drafts and Outbox message folders. You can configure Outlook Today to display similar information for any message folders. Just follow these steps:

1. In the Messages section of the Customize Outlook Today view, click Choose Folders. This opens the Select Folder dialog box.

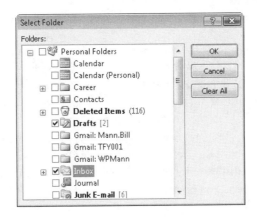

2. In the Folders list of the Select Folder dialog box, choose the folders you would like information on. You aren't limited to choosing folders that contain messages—you can have Outlook Today display information about the Calendar, Contacts, Journal, and even the Deleted Items folders.

3. Click OK and then Save Changes to return to the main Outlook Today view.

Configure the Outlook Today Calendar and Tasks Sections

The Calendar section of the Customize Outlook Today view (refer to Figure 11-3) allows you to specify the number of days of calendar information to be displayed.

The Tasks section of the Customize Outlook Today view (also shown in Figure 11-3) allows you to specify which tasks will appear and the order in which they will be sorted. Select the options you want and click Save Changes to put them into effect.

Set the Outlook Today Style

Outlook Today can display its information using one of the five provided styles. There isn't a lot of variety here, but it's probably worth spending a few minutes trying out each style for yourself.

11

Customize Toolbars and Menus

Many of the controls you'll commonly use for Outlook are accessible through the menu bar or one of the toolbars (others appear on the Ribbon, which we'll talk about soon). You click the button or menu item name to issue the command. Since most menus and toolbars have far more commands than most people use on a regular basis, Microsoft designed them with the capability to automatically alter their contents depending on how you use them. When allowed to do so, Office moves the commands you use most frequently to the top of menus or makes them visible on the toolbar.

CAUTION   *If you use programs that add custom toolbars or menus to Outlook— whether they're Microsoft products, such as Groove, or programs from other vendors, such as Adobe Acrobat—you will almost surely need to acquire an updated version of those programs that is compatible with Outlook 2007. Visit the vendor's website for update information.*

Menu commands that you use infrequently (or not at all) eventually disappear from view. They're still there, but they've been moved out of sight to reduce the clutter on the screen. To see the hidden commands, click the double down arrows at the bottom of the menu, or hover the mouse pointer over the menu for a moment. This opens the full menu.

Change the Way Outlook Reconfigures Its Menus

While some people like the way Outlook menus (and the other Office applications' menus) reconfigure themselves depending on what you do, others dislike that behavior. You can change the default behavior of menus by following these steps:

1. In the main Outlook window, click Tools | Customize to open the Customize dialog box shown in Figure 11-4.

2. On the Options tab, make any changes you wish to the Personalized Menus and Toolbars options. Some of the options may or may not be available depending on which other options are selected.

3. Click the Reset Menu and Toolbar Usage Data button if you want Outlook to start sorting options from scratch depending on how often you use them.

4. Click Close to put the changes into effect.

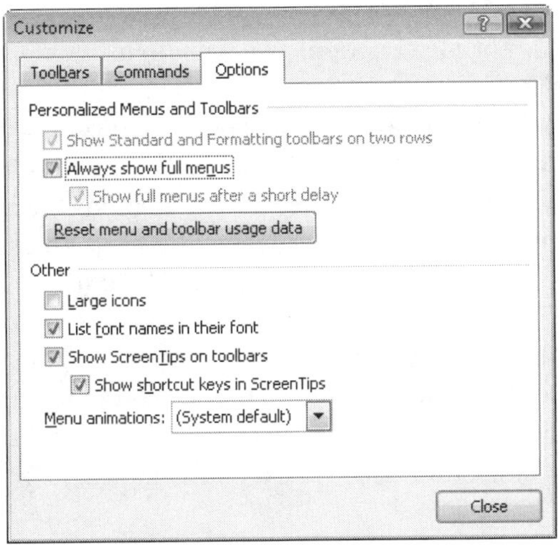

FIGURE 11-4   The Options tab of the Customize dialog box.

Choose Which Toolbars Appear

You can control which toolbars appear. Which toolbars are available varies depending on which applications and Windows features you have installed, but you can select from all the available ones easily. Follow these instructions:

NOTE   *Some applications that work with Outlook add optional toolbars to the Outlook interface.*

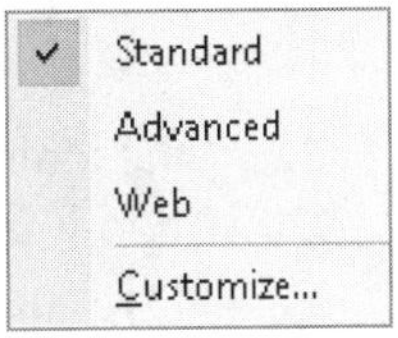

1. Right-click a blank spot adjacent to the menu bar or a visible toolbar. A shortcut menu appears, listing all the available toolbars.

2. On the shortcut menu, click the name of the toolbar you want visible. If a toolbar is already visible, there will be a check mark next to its name. Click it again to make it disappear.

3. As soon as you click the name of the toolbar, the menu disappears, and Outlook displays the toolbar.

4. Repeat as necessary until you have exactly the toolbars you want visible.

Add Items to Menus and Toolbars

Many times, the buttons or menu options you want to use appear on the menu bar or the Standard toolbar. But what if you make frequent use of menus and buttons that are not normally found in these places? One option is to simply make all the toolbars you need visible all the time. But if you use only a few buttons from a toolbar, it seems a waste of screen space to have the entire toolbar visible all the time.

An alternative approach you can take when you need access to only one or two items from a different toolbar or menu is to add the items to the menu bar or the Standard toolbar. That way, they are readily available without wasting a lot of screen space. The following sections show you how to add buttons to toolbars and how to add commands to menus. The procedures here do not apply to the Quick Access toolbar, the tiny toolbar that appears in windows that contain the Ribbon. Specific procedures for customizing the Quick Access toolbar appear a little later in this chapter.

TIP   *For even more options, see the Add a Button, Menu, or Command topic in the Outlook help system.*

Add Buttons to a Toolbar

Adding buttons to the Standard toolbar is one good way to deal with the situation where you need access to only one or two buttons from a toolbar that isn't normally visible. Follow these steps to see how it is done in general, and read the "How to Add the Outlook Today Button to the Standard Toolbar" box for a useful specific example:

NOTE   *This approach will work with any of the toolbars you can display in Outlook.*

1. If the toolbar you want to modify isn't already visible in the Outlook main window, click View | Toolbars and select the toolbar so that it appears in the Outlook window.

2. On the toolbar, click the Toolbar Options arrow. This is the down arrow that appears at the right of the toolbar.

3. In the menu that appears, click Add or Remove Buttons. This opens another menu listing all the toolbars currently visible.

4. Click Customize to open the Customize dialog box shown in Figure 11-5.

FIGURE 11-5   Customize toolbars using this dialog box.

5. In the Categories list on the Commands tab, select the category that contains the button you want. You may need to do a bit of poking around before you find the right category.

6. In the Commands list for the category you selected, find the button you want to add to the toolbar.

7. Drag the button from the Commands list to the exact location where you want it to appear in the toolbar.

8. Click Close when done.

Add a Command to a Menu

Just as you can add buttons to toolbars, you can add commands to menus. This is analogous to adding a button to an always-visible toolbar to save time and screen space. Make sure the menu you want to add a command to is visible, then follow these steps:

1. In the Outlook main window, click View | Toolbars | Customize to open the Customize dialog box.

2. On the Commands tab of the Customize dialog box (refer to Figure 11-5), select the category containing the command you want to add to the menu.

11

3. Drag the command from the Commands list to the menu. Do not release the mouse button. After a moment, the full menu should appear.

4. Point to the spot in the menu where you want to insert the command, then release the mouse button.

5. Click Close in the Customize dialog box.

How to ... Add the Outlook Today Button to the Standard Toolbar

If you like Outlook Today, I recommend that you add the Outlook Today button to the Standard toolbar. That will give you one-click access to Outlook Today, making it a lot easier to integrate into your daily work habits. Follow these steps to do it:

1. If it isn't already visible in the Outlook main window, click View | Toolbars and select the Standard toolbar so that it appears in the Outlook window.

2. On the Standard toolbar, click the Toolbar Options arrow (located at the right side of the toolbar).

3. In the menu that appears, click Add or Remove Buttons. This opens another menu, this one listing all the toolbars that are currently visible, plus a Customize command.

4. Click Customize to open the Customize dialog box.

5. In the Categories list on the Commands tab, select the Advanced category.

6. Scroll through the Commands list of the Advanced category until you find the Outlook Today button.

7. Drag the Outlook Today button right out of this dialog box and onto the Standard toolbar. Drop it wherever you want it to appear in the Standard toolbar.

8. Click Close. Outlook Today should now be visible whenever the Standard toolbar is visible. Click it to go directly to the Outlook Today view.

Customize the Quick Access Toolbar

You can customize the Quick Access toolbar, the little toolbar that appears in windows containing the Ribbon. This toolbar has buttons for several commands that don't change as you switch from tab to tab in the Ribbon. You can customize this toolbar by changing the position where it appears and by adding buttons to it. Here are the procedures you need to follow.

Change Where the Quick Access Toolbar Appears

The Quick Access toolbar can appear in one of two places: in the top left of the window (next to the Microsoft Office button, which is the default position), or directly below the Ribbon. You can choose which position you want it to appear in for each type of window. For example, you can have the Quick Access toolbar appear above the Ribbon when you are editing messages, but below the Ribbon when you are editing Calendar items.

In most cases you will want to leave the Quick Access toolbar in its default location, but if you add a bunch of buttons to it you may want to move it down. In the meantime, here's how you move the toolbar:

> NOTE *We'll talk about adding buttons to the Quick Access toolbar in the next section.*

11

1. In a window where the Quick Access toolbar is visible, click the down arrow at the end of the toolbar (the Customize Quick Access Toolbar button).

2. In the menu that appears, click Show Below the Ribbon to move the toolbar down, or Show Above the Ribbon to move it up.

That's all there is to it. Now, on to adding or removing buttons.

Adding or Removing Quick Access Toolbar Buttons

If you find yourself using the Quick Access toolbar a lot, you may want to add some additional buttons to it so you can use it for even more commands. Like with regular toolbars and menus, there is a whole system for adding or removing commands on the Quick Access toolbar. Let's dig in:

As when moving the toolbar, start by clicking Customize Quick Access Toolbar (the down arrow at the end of the toolbar) to open the menu. The menu that appears includes several commands that you can add to or remove from the Quick Access toolbar without going deeper into customization. Figure 11-6 shows the Customize Quick Access Toolbar menu.

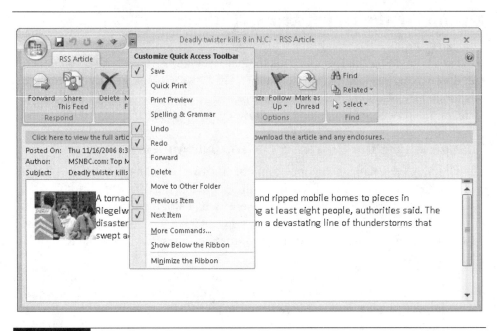

FIGURE 11-6 The Customize Quick Access Toolbar menu lets you choose which commands will appear in the toolbar for this particular window.

The commands that are visible in this menu and that also appear on the toolbar now have check marks next to them. Click a command to set or clear its check box, making it appear or not.

> **TIP** *You can also add commands to the Quick Access toolbar by right-clicking them in the Ribbon and selecting Add to Quick Access Toolbar.*

So far, so good. But did you notice that I said "the commands that are visible in this menu"? That's because there are far more commands that you can add to the Quick Access toolbar than are visible in this menu. To get at them, and to make them visible (or remove them again), you will need to follow this procedure:

1. Open the Quick Access Toolbar menu, and click More Commands. Doing so opens the Customize the Quick Access Toolbar view of the Editor Options dialog box (see Figure 11-7). This dialog box lets you completely customize the Quick Access toolbar. And when you remember that you are customizing the toolbar for a specific type of Outlook window (editing messages, editing Calendar items), you can see how far you can go to customize things.

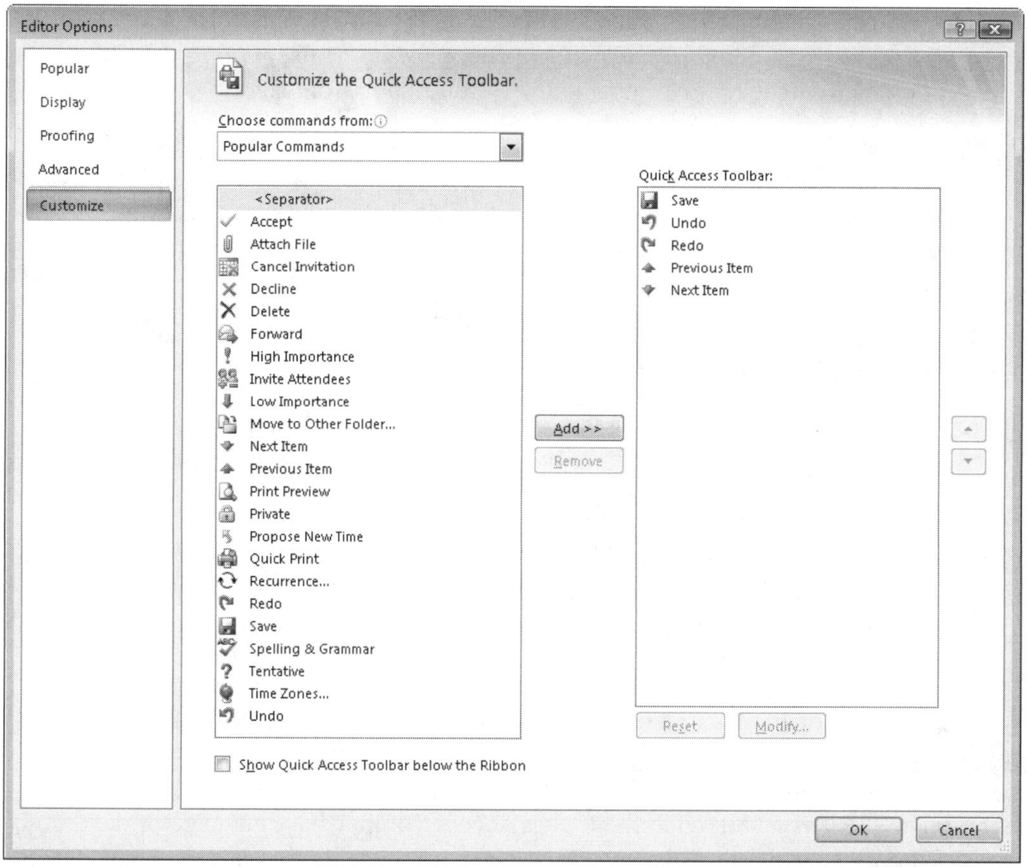

FIGURE 11-7   Control which buttons appear on the Quick Access toolbar from this dialog box.

2. The Choose Commands From list box gives you access to a set of popular commands, or to entire additional groups of commands from the current Ribbon. Looking at all the possibilities is beyond what we can do here. Select Popular Commands in the list box. Just remember that you can find different groups of commands using Choose Commands From.

3. In the list of popular commands on the left, select a command you want to add to the Quick Access toolbar.

NOTE   *One of the possibilities is named "<Separator>." That is a vertical line you can insert between buttons in the toolbar to divide things as you see fit.*

4. With a command selected on the left, click the Add button between the two lists. This copies that command to the list on the Quick Access Toolbar list on the right. Similarly, selecting a command in the list on the right and clicking Remove removes it from the Quick Access Toolbar list.

5. Position the command where you want it to appear in the Quick Access toolbar. The command at the top of the Quick Access Toolbar list appears as the leftmost button in the toolbar, and so on. Select the command you want to move and use the up and down arrows to the right of the Quick Access Toolbar list to move it.

6. Repeat steps 3 through 5 for each command you want to add to, or subtract from, the Quick Access toolbar.

7. When you are done changing the toolbar, click OK to close the Editor Options dialog box and return to the window you were working in. You will see your newly modified Quick Access toolbar.

TIP *If you ever want to restore the Quick Access toolbar to its original state, return to the Editor Options dialog box and click the Reset button below the Quick Access Toolbar list. Doing so resets this particular Quick Access toolbar to its default state.*

With all the commands and options available in Outlook, the possibilities for customizing the Quick Access toolbar are vast. To help you get started, I've developed some sample toolbar layouts for various views, along with the steps to re-create them yourself. Visit the Quick Access Toolbar Layouts page of my website (http://www.living-with-outlook.com/quick-access-toolbar-layouts.html) to try them out.

Animate Outlook Menus

Here's a way to add a bit of fun to your use of Outlook. When you click a menu item on the menu bar, the way the menu itself appears is animated. You can easily change the animation. It won't transform your use of Outlook or anything like that, but it can add a touch of variety to your work. Follow these instructions to change the menu animation:

1. In the Outlook main window, click Tools | Customize. This opens the Customize dialog box.

2. On the Options tab of the Customize dialog box (refer to Figure 11-4), open the Menu Animations list and select an animation to use.

3. Click Close to put the new animation into effect.

Changing the animations doesn't make a major difference in the visuals, but since it only takes a few seconds to do, why not?

Customize the Starting View

Do you like to start your work in Outlook by checking your Calendar? By seeing what's in your Inbox or Unread Mail folders? Looking at your Task list?

You can tell Outlook to start in whichever folder you want it to. The following procedure does the trick:

1. Click Tools | Options to open the Options dialog box, then click the Other tab.

2. In the General section, click Advanced Options to open the Advanced Options dialog box.

11

3. In the General Settings section, click the Browse button to the right of the Startup in This Folder box. This opens the Select Folders dialog box.

4. Select the folder you want Outlook to start in and click OK until you get back to the main window. The next time you start Outlook, it will open in the folder you selected.

Select Folder
Start in this folder:
Personal Folders
Calendar
Calendar (Personal)
Career
Contacts
Deleted Items (117)
Drafts [2]
Gmail
Inbox (1)
Journal
Junk E-mail [11]
Lost & Found
Money
OK
Cancel

TIP *If you want Outlook to open in Unread Mail, you will need to scroll through the list to reach the Search Folders folder. Open that to select Unread Mail.*

Customize the Ribbon

While the Ribbon is a major new element of using Outlook 2007, there isn't a lot you can do to customize it. We've already talked about how to move the Quick Access toolbar, and how to change the buttons that appear on it. As for the Ribbon itself, the only thing we can do with it is to minimize it.

TIP *If you want to temporarily minimize the Ribbon, double-click one of its tabs.*

To minimize or restore the Ribbon, use the CTRL-F1 keyboard shortcut. When minimized, all that is visible of the Ribbon is the set of tabs that go with the Ribbon in the current window, and the Quick Access toolbar. Here's what the Ribbon in a Message window looks like when minimized:

This message has not been sent.

Send	To...	
Cc...	
Account	Subject:	
Attached:	

The four tabs, Message, Insert, Options, and Format Text, are all that is visible. To use the Ribbon, you can either restore it to full size (with the CTRL-F1 keyboard shortcut) or click one of the tabs, or press and release the ALT key to display the Ribbon KeyTips.

Customize the Navigation Pane

Throughout this book, you've learned ways to add folders to the Navigation pane, change views, manipulate the buttons at the bottom of the pane, and otherwise customize it for your work. There are, however, a few additional Navigation pane customizations we haven't talked about yet. In particular, you can add or remove the large buttons (they look like bars) at the bottom of the Navigation pane, as well as change their order. You can also control whether the Current View section appears, or even hide the entire Navigation pane.

Add or Remove Buttons

If you don't ever use one of the major components of Outlook (say you never use Journal), there's little point in having a button for it taking up space in the Navigation pane. It takes only a few clicks to remove Navigation pane buttons (and only a few clicks to restore them too). Follow these steps to see for yourself:

1. In the Navigation pane, click Configure Buttons (the down arrow at the bottom right of the pane) to open the Configure Buttons menu.

2. In the Configure Buttons menu, click Add or Remove Buttons. This opens a menu containing all the Navigation pane buttons. The icons for the buttons that are visible in the Navigation pane are highlighted.

3. Click the icon for a button to add it to or remove it from the Navigation pane. The menu closes and the button appears or disappears.

4. Repeat as necessary to display only the buttons you want to see.

Change the Order of Buttons

The order of the buttons in the Navigation pane is easy to change. Just follow these steps:

1. In the Navigation pane, click Configure Buttons to open the Configure Buttons menu.

2. Click Navigation Pane Options to open the Navigation Pane Options dialog box.

11

3. To change the order of the buttons, select the name of the button you want to move, then click the Move Up or Move Down button appropriately.

4. Click Reset if you want to restore the buttons to the default order.

> NOTE *You can add or remove buttons using this dialog box too. Select or clear the check box next to the name of a button to make it appear or disappear in the Navigation pane.*

Show or Hide Current View

When the Calendar, Contacts, Tasks, Notes, or Journal pane is visible, the pane often includes a Current View section, with a list of the possible views. If you primarily use a single view for one or more of these panes, or you want to eliminate a little bit of visual clutter, you can hide the Current View section. Here's how:

1. With the pane you wish to modify visible, click View | Navigation Pane.

2. In the menu that appears, click Current View Pane. This will hide Current View if it is currently visible, or show it if it is currently hidden.

Show, Minimize, or Hide the Entire Navigation Pane

If you need the maximum amount of room on the screen for the view you're working in, you may want to have the Navigation pane appear minimized, or removed from this view entirely. Showing, minimizing, or hiding the Navigation pane is a two-click process:

1. Click View | Navigation Pane.

2. In the menu that appears, select Normal, Minimized, or Off.

> TIP *You can also show or hide the Navigation pane with the ALT-F1 keyboard shortcut.*

Customize the To-Do Bar

The To-Do Bar is likely to become a big part of the way you work in Outlook 2007. That being the case, it is nice to see that the bar is pretty customizable. The rest of this chapter is dedicated to the ways you can customize the To-Do Bar.

One important thing to remember is that the To-Do Bar works independent of the view you are in. For example, if you minimize the To-Do Bar in one view, you minimize it in all views. This is different from features such as the Quick Access toolbar, which can differ from view to view.

We will look at two broad areas of To-Do Bar customization: what it looks like, and what it contains.

Change What the To-Do Bar Looks Like

Here we look at changing the appearance of the To-Do Bar. These procedures let you control how much screen space the To-Do Bar takes up.

Hide, Minimize, or Show the To-Do Bar

When the To-Do Bar is minimized, it occupies a thin strip along the right side of the Outlook window, but only displays a tiny bit of information. When shown normally, it takes up a good bit of the screen (the next section shows how to change how much of the screen) but displays a lot more information. And when turned off, well, I strongly urge you not to turn off the To-Do Bar. It contains too much good information in such an easy-to-use form that it would be a waste not to use it. Whichever way you choose to go, the procedure is the same:

1. In the Outlook main window, click View | To-Do Bar to see your options.

2. Select Normal, Minimized, or Off to apply that option to the To-Do Bar across all views.

> **TIP**   *If you do decide to hide the To-Do Bar completely, you can make it appear and disappear with the* ALT-F2 *keyboard shortcut.*

Change the Width of the To-Do Bar

When the To-Do Bar is in its normal (open) state, you can change its width by dragging the left margin of the bar with the mouse. If you drag it wide enough, the Date Navigator section at the top of the bar will begin to display two, even three months worth of calendars side by side, but you quickly run out of space for anything else, and Outlook only lets you go so far, as you can see here, where I have made the To-Do Bar as wide as possible:

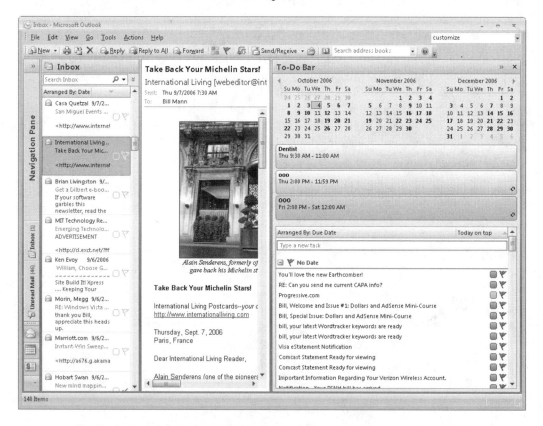

Similarly, you can only make the normal To-Do Bar so narrow before Outlook assumes you want to minimize it and changes it to its minimized state.

Change What the To-Do Bar Contains

Now that you know how to change what the To-Do Bar looks like, it is time to talk about how to change what it contains. There are two things we can do here:

- Control which sections are displayed when the To-Do Bar is open

- Control how many months and appointments are displayed

Doing each of these is quick and easy, although Outlook gives you redundant options for doing so, which can be confusing. As you increase the number of sections displayed, and the number of items in each section, there's less room for the items below. For example, adding more rows of months to the Date Navigator section leaves less room for appointments and tasks below.

Experiment with the possibilities until you come up with the settings that best match the way you work.

> **NOTE**   *This procedure uses the To-Do Bar Options dialog box to control which sections appear and what they contain all from one spot. If you just want to turn sections on and off, you can do so from the View | To-Do Bar menu.*

1. In the main Outlook window, click View | To-Do Bar.

2. In the To-Do Bar menu that appears, click Options to open the To-Do Bar Options dialog box.

3. Set or clear the check box next to each section you want to be visible in the To-Do Bar.

4. For the Date Navigator, enter the number of month rows you want to appear. Don't go crazy here since showing too many rows of months leaves no room for anything else on the bar. I suggest you don't show more than two, unless you have a huge, high-resolution monitor.

5. For the Appointments, enter the number of appointments you want to appear. Again, don't go too crazy, or you won't have room for any tasks to appear. Unless you have an exceptionally busy schedule, the default option of three appointments is probably fine.

6. Click OK to return to the main Outlook window and see what the To-Do Bar looks like with the changes you've made.

7. Repeat steps 1 through 6 until you are happy with what you see.

And with that, we're done talking about ways to customize Outlook. I encourage you to dedicate a little bit of time to experimenting with the many possibilities here. Make one change, then live with it for a while to see how you like it. After that, come back to this chapter and make another change. Keep doing this for a while and you will get Outlook 2007 customized to meet your needs as best it can be. Have fun!

Chapter 12

Create Custom Views and Print Styles

How to...

- Customize Views
- Customize Print Styles
- Use the Calendar Printing Assistant Add-In

One of the nice things about Outlook is its customizability. This chapter looks at two particular areas of customization: views and print styles.

You already know a lot about views. Views are the way Outlook organizes the information it presents to you. Throughout this book, you've seen the default views for the various Outlook folders, and you've tried out some of the other views available in the folders.

When you print an item or a group of items in Outlook, their appearance on the paper is determined by the *print style* Outlook uses to print them. A print style is a combination of paper and page settings that control the format of an item or items you print. Print styles control characteristics such as the font used, the layout of the items on the page, the appearance of the header and footer on each sheet, and so on. Every item and view has one or more print styles associated with it.

Customize Views

You can customize views in a few different ways. Without making any changes to an existing view, you can change the information that appears in the view by applying a filter to it, or by altering the way the items in the view are grouped, sorted, or arranged. Going a step further, you can create custom views based on one of the six view types that Outlook supports. See the "Did You Know What the Six View Types Are?" box for more on the view types.

Change the Information That Appears in an Existing View

Changing the information that appears in an existing view is an easy way to make views more useful. The ability to filter (show only items that meet certain criteria), sort, and group (cause related items to appear together) items makes it much easier to find and work with the items you need. Arrangements (predefined ways of grouping and sorting items) take this one step further, allowing Outlook to do things such as arrange your messages by conversation or importance.

The following sections show you how you can take advantage of filtering, sorting, grouping, and arrangements.

What the Six View Types Are?

Outlook 2007 comes with six basic view types:

- **Table**   Shows items organized by rows and columns. Each row contains the information about one item. Each row can contain a single line of text or multiple lines. This is the most versatile view.

- **Timeline**   Shows items as icons arranged from left to right on a scale that displays time. Primarily useful for viewing Journal items.

- **Day/Week/Month**   Shows items on a calendar, as if in a day planner. Most useful for viewing meetings, appointments, and events.

- **Business Card**   Shows items as graphical representations of business cards. Most useful for viewing contacts. This view, shown here, is new for Outlook 2007.

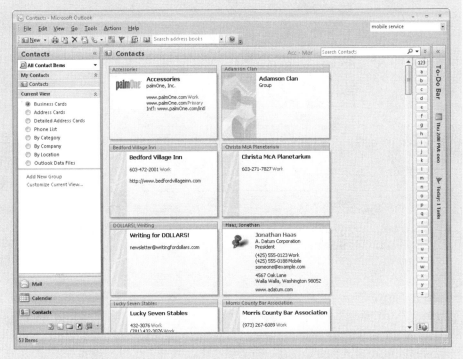

12

Continued

■ **Card**   Shows items as if they were individual file cards, and arranges them in alphabetical order. Most useful for viewing contacts or other items that can sensibly be organized alphabetically. Notice how this view differs from Business Card view. In particular, compare the entries for Jonathan Haas in the two views.

NOTE   *Yes, I do know more people than are shown here. However, to protect their privacy, I've removed their contact information while writing this.*

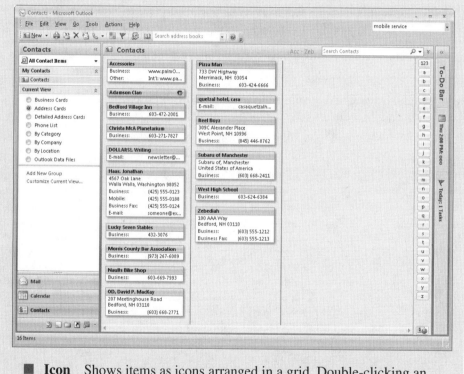

■ **Icon**   Shows items as icons arranged in a grid. Double-clicking an icon opens that item. Most useful for viewing notes.

Filter a View

A *view filter* lets you make Outlook display only the items that match the criteria you specify. You could filter the messages in the Inbox by someone's name, for example. Doing this causes Outlook to display only the messages that have the right name in them. When you apply a filter to a folder, the words "Filter Applied" appear in the left corner of the Outlook status bar (assuming it is visible). When you disable the filter, all the other items in the folder reappear.

To apply a filter to a view (or turn off a filter that's already applied to the view), follow these steps:

1. Select the folder where you want to use a filtered view.

2. On the Outlook toolbar, click View | Arrange By, then click Custom. This opens the Customize View dialog box.

3. Click Filter to open the Filter dialog box, shown in Figure 12-1.

4. Create your filter by entering the appropriate criteria on the tabbed pages of the Filter dialog box.

5. To turn off a filter, click Clear All.

Sort a View

When you sort a view, you tell Outlook to arrange the items in ascending or descending order. You can sort any view other than time-based ones such as the Timeline or Day/Week/Month view. Further, you can sort on any visible field.

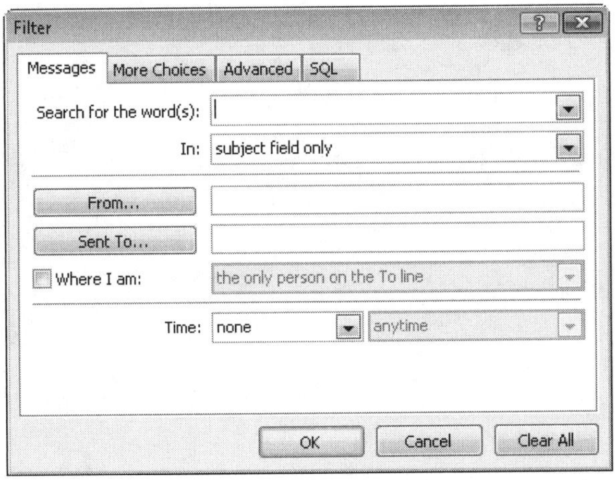

FIGURE 12-1   Use this dialog box to filters the items that appear in a view.

To sort a view, follow these steps:

1. Select the folder you want to sort.

2. On the Outlook toolbar, click View | Arrange By, then click Current View. This opens a menu of the views that are possible for this folder.

3. Select a view that displays items in a table, as icons, as business cards, or as cards.

4. On the Outlook toolbar, click View | Arrange By, then click Custom. This opens a Customize View dialog box.

5. Click Sort to open the Sort dialog box, shown in Figure 12-2.

6. Choose the first field to sort by in the Sort Items By list box. If the field you want to sort by does not appear in the list, select a different field set from the Select Available Fields From list.

7. Click Ascending or Descending to specify the sort order.

8. If you wish to sort by additional fields, follow the same steps in the Then By lists in this dialog box.

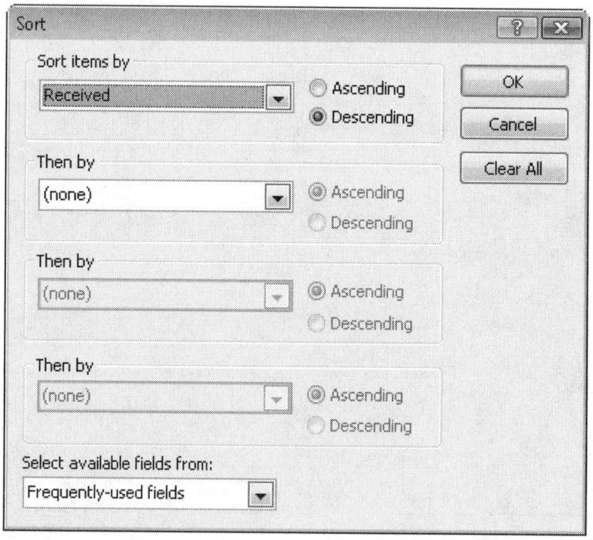

FIGURE 12-2   This dialog box lets you control the way items are sorted in a view.

Group a View

When a set of items has something in common, Outlook can group them for you. By default, many of the views in Outlook automatically group items by preset criteria. You can open or close a group by clicking the plus or minus sign before the group's name. You can also ungroup items, or create your own custom groupings.

A student of mine recently asked a question that was easy to address with groups. She had applied categories to all of her business contacts, which allowed her to tell which were prospects and which were current customers. The question was, "How can I make Outlook show all the prospects, or all the customers?"

She merely clicked the By Category option in the Navigation pane, and let Outlook group her contacts for her. In this case, both categories were visible, but all the prospects would be together as would all the customers. She could easily hide one category or the other by clicking the minus sign in front of the category name. If there was a contact that fell into both groups, it would appear in both groups.

To create your own group, follow these instructions:

1. In the Outlook toolbar, click View | Arrange By, then click Custom.

2. In that Custom dialog box, click Group By. This opens the Group By dialog box, shown in Figure 12-3.

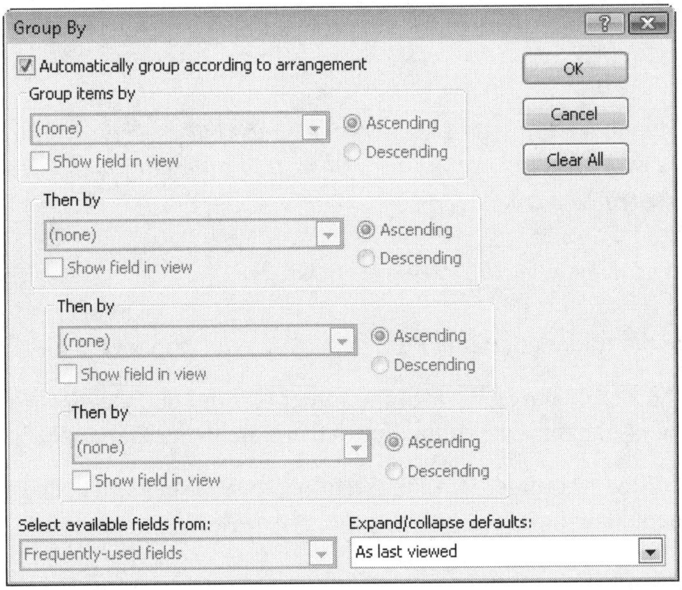

FIGURE 12-3   Specify how the view will group items with this dialog box.

3. If an arrangement is already in place for this view, the Automatically Group According to Arrangement check box will be set and the Group Items By options will be unavailable. Clear the Automatically Group According to Arrangement check box to enable the Group Items By options so you can customize the grouping.

4. Choose the first field to group by in the Group Items By list box. If the field you want to group by does not appear in the list, select a different field set from the Select Available Fields From list.

5. Click Ascending or Descending to specify the grouping order.

6. If you wish to sort by additional fields, follow the same steps in the Then By lists in this dialog box.

If you want to ungroup items instead of creating a new group, navigate to the Group By dialog box (follow steps 1 and 2). Click Clear All to eliminate all groupings in the view.

Use an Arrangement

An *arrangement* is a table view of a folder, with predefined grouping and sorting. Outlook comes with more than a dozen predefined arrangements, which are available in table-based views. By default, each of the groups in an arrangement starts out fully expanded, except for the groups in the Conversation arrangement, which start out collapsed.

NOTE   *You cannot create your own arrangements, but you can create custom views with their own grouping and sorting that will function the same way as an arrangement.*

To use an arrangement, follow these steps:

1. Select the folder containing the items you want to view in an arrangement.

2. Choose a table-based view of the folder by clicking View | Current View and then selecting one of the views from the menu that appears.

3. Click View | Arrange By, then select one of the standard arrangements from the menu that appears.

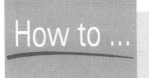

Change Arrangements in Mail Views

When you work in a Mail view, there's a quick way to see what arrangement is active and to change arrangements. The key is in the Inbox pane.

If you look at the top left of the Inbox pane, you can see text that says "Arranged By:" followed by the name of the current arrangement. Click that text and Outlook displays a list of the available arrangements for you to choose from. It couldn't be much simpler.

Arranged By: Date	▾

TIP *See the "How To Change Arrangements in Mail Views" sidebar for an easier way to go when you want to arrange your e-mail.*

Create Custom Views

If you find that you like to set up certain views certain ways, and you find yourself spending time setting up the same combination of view, filters, sorts, and so on, you might want to create your own custom views. You can define one or more custom views for any folder and make them available in the menus as if they were members of the default set of views.

The sections that follow show you how to define custom views for particular folders and make them appear along with the default views. Along the way, I'll show you the dialog box where you'll do the actual creation of custom views. It'll be up to you to create the custom views that do what you need.

Remember that student who had categorized her contacts into prospects and customers and wanted to be able to view each category? A custom view using a filter is a great way to deal with this. On the More Choices tab of the Filter dialog box, you can specify that the view show only items that are in a specific category. All it took was several clicks to define the custom views that showed only members of the two categories. Once she was comfortable that these views worked the way she expected, she created custom views that allowed her to see each category whenever she wanted.

12

You can define your custom views in two ways: from scratch, or by modifying an existing view. Each approach is described here.

Define a New Custom View from Scratch

Defining a custom view from scratch could be your best approach if the view you want differs sharply from any of the available views. Here's how you go about it:

1. Click View | Current View, then click Define Views to open the Custom View Organizer dialog box shown here. Use this dialog box to manage the views associated with a particular folder.

2. In the Custom View Organizer, click New to open the Create a New View dialog box. Set the basic type for your new view as well as where it can be used in this dialog box.

3. In the Create a New View dialog box, enter the name of your new view. In the Type of View list, select one of the available basic types. In the Can Be Used On section of the dialog box, set one of the options to determine how widely available your new view will be. Click OK to open the Customize View dialog box. Use this dialog box to configure your new custom views.

4. The Customize View dialog box is the place where you do the real work of setting up your view the way you want it. Depending on which basic view you selected, any or all of the buttons in this view will be active. Clicking any

of the buttons opens additional dialog boxes where you can make the kinds of changes described next to each button. Since you've probably got some definite ideas about what you want your custom view to look like (or you wouldn't have gone through the work to reach this step), I'll leave it up to you to explore this dialog box and make the changes you want. Click OK in the Customize View dialog box when you're done making changes to the view.

> **TIP** *If you create a multiline view and include several display fields in that view, you may need to increase the number of lines displayed in order to see all of your fields.*

5. When you leave the Customize View dialog box, Outlook takes you back to the Custom View Organizer dialog box. You should see your new custom view in the Views for Folder table, with the Can Be Used On and View Type settings you selected.

6. If you want to put your new view to work right away, click Apply View at the bottom of the Custom View Organizer dialog box. Click Close when you're done with this dialog box.

Define a New Custom View Based on an Existing View

Defining a new custom view based on an existing view is generally faster and easier than defining a new custom view from scratch. Here are the steps to follow:

1. Click View | Current View, then click Define Views to open the Custom View Organizer dialog box shown earlier.

2. Select the view you want to base your new view on, then click Copy. This opens the Copy View dialog box.

3. In the Copy View dialog box, enter the name of your new view. In the Can Be Used On section of the dialog box, set one of the options to determine how widely available your new view will be. Click OK to open the Customize View dialog box shown earlier.

4. In the Customize View dialog box, click the various buttons to open dialog boxes where you can change every aspect of the view you copied. Repeat until you've made all the changes you want. Click OK in the Customize View dialog box when you're done making changes to your copy of the view.

5. When you leave the Customize View dialog box, Outlook takes you back to the Custom View Organizer dialog box. You should see your modified view in the Views for Folder table, with the Can Be Used On and View Type settings you selected.

6. If you want to put your new view to work right away, click Apply View at the bottom of the Custom View Organizer dialog box. Click Close when you're done with this dialog box.

Rename a Custom View

While it is of course always best to give a custom view the perfect name when you create it, that doesn't always happen. If you decide you need to rename a view, here's what you need to do:

1. Click View | Current View, then click Define Views to open the Custom View Organizer dialog box.

2. In the Views for Folder list, select the view you want to rename, then click Rename. This opens the Rename View dialog box.

3. Enter the new name of the view and click OK.

Use a Custom View in Another Place

When you create a custom view, you can specify in which folders it is visible. If you decide you want to use that same view in another place, or make it visible to other people with access to the folder, you can do so by copying the view. These steps show you how:

1. Click View | Current View, then click Define Views to open the Custom View Organizer dialog box.

2. Select the view you want to use in another place, then click Copy. This opens the Copy View dialog box shown earlier.

3. Enter a new name for the copied view, then select one of the options in the Can Be Used On section of the dialog box. The new view becomes available in the folders you selected, and appears on the Current View menu for those folders.

12

Customize Print Styles

While Outlook comes with a set of predefined print styles (see the "Did You Know What the Default Print Styles Are?" box for more information) that are well matched to its items and views, you may find reason to customize print styles by modifying existing ones or creating your own styles. The rest of this chapter gives you the information you need to do exactly that.

> **TIP** *There is another way to customize the printing of Outlook data. That's with the Calendar Printing Assistant for Microsoft Office Outlook 2007. Complete instructions on how to download and install this add-in are available in the Free Stuff section of the Living With Outlook website at http://www.living-with-outlook.com/free-outlook.html.*

Modify an Existing Print Style

The easiest way to customize a print style is to modify an existing one. Here's how you do it:

1. Switch to the Outlook view associated with the print style you want to change. For example, if you want to change the way the Weekly print style looks, you would first get into a Calendar view.

2. Click File | Print to open the Print dialog box. Select the print style you want to modify in the Print dialog box.

Did you know?

What the Default Print Styles Are?

Outlook 2007 comes with several predefined print styles. Which of these styles is available to you at any given time is determined by the type of Outlook item you're working with and the view you're working in. The main print styles are:

- **Memo** Shows each item, one after the other.

- **Table** Shows all items in a list. The fields that are currently visible in the view appear in the table.

- **Daily** Shows one day per page, with Tasks and Notes areas also visible. Each day is displayed from 7 A.M. to 7 P.M.

- **Weekly** Shows one week per page. No Tasks and Notes areas are included.

- **Monthly** Shows one month per page. No Tasks and Notes areas are included.

- **Tri-fold** Shows one day, one month, and the TaskPad. They're evenly spaced to allow you to fold the page into three equal sections.

- **Calendar Details** Shows all selected Calendar items, and also the body of each item.

12

3. In the Print Style section of the dialog box, select the print style you want to use as the basis for your new style, then click Define Styles. This opens the Define Print Styles dialog box. Choose a print style to work with in this dialog box.

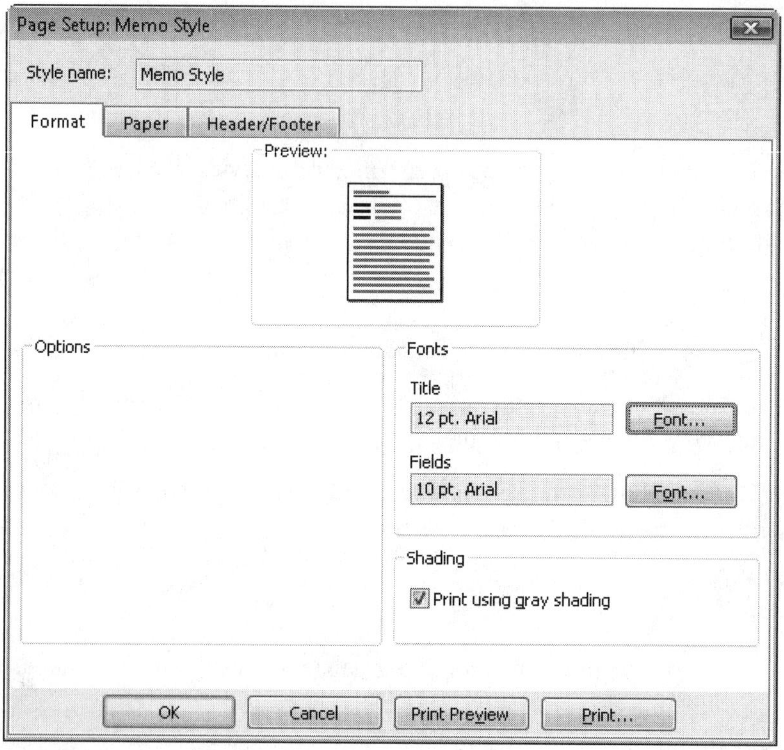

FIGURE 12-4　Use this Page Setup dialog box and its various tabs to modify and preview changes to an existing print style.

4. Click Edit to open the Page Setup dialog box shown in Figure 12-4. The specific options available in this dialog box vary with the print style you selected. For many of the options, you can get a basic idea of the way they affect the page layout by watching the way things change in the small Preview window, as seen here.

Create a New Print Style

If you're looking for a little more adventure, consider creating a new print style instead of just modifying an existing one. These instructions will get you started:

1. Open the view you want to create a print style for.

2. Open the folder containing the items you want to use the print style with.

3. Click File | Print to open the Print dialog box.

4. In the Print Styles list, select the print style you want to use as the basis for your new style, then click Define Styles to open the Define Print Styles dialog box.

5. Click Edit to open the Page Setup dialog box. Enter the name for your new style in the Style Name box, then make your changes to the base style. You can use Preview to get a basic idea of what your new layout looks like, and Print Preview to see exactly what it would look like if you clicked Print right now.

Delete or Reset a Print Style

You can delete any modified print style when you no longer need it. You cannot delete the default print styles. You can, however, reset the default print styles to their original settings if that suits your purposes. The process is mostly the same for doing either; it consists of these steps:

1. Click File | Print to open the Print dialog box.

2. In the Print Styles list, select the print style you want to change, then click Define Styles to open the Define Print Styles dialog box.

3. If you want to delete a modified print style, select it in the Print Styles list and then click Delete.

NOTE   *The Reset button in the dialog box changes to a Delete button when you select a modified print style.*

4. If you want to reset all the default print styles, select any default print style and click Reset. You can't reset default print styles individually.

12

Chapter 13

Find, Manage, and Archive Information

How to...

- Find Items with Instant Search and Advanced Find
- Learn to Manage Items
- Learn to Archive Items
- Design an Item Management and Archiving Strategy

This chapter helps you to find, manage, and archive (save) information stored in Outlook items. These capabilities can work together in Outlook 2007. Outlook's powerful new Instant Search capabilities make it easier than ever to manage information with folders and archives, while still being able to find that information again when you need it.

At the same time, the ability to archive old information makes it easier to work with current information by moving old stuff someplace out of the way. After looking at these capabilities, we end the chapter with a short discussion of the things you need to consider when coming up with a strategy for managing and archiving Outlook items.

Find Items with Instant Search

The longer you use Outlook, the more stuff you accumulate. E-mail messages, contacts, tasks, notes; it all adds up incredibly quickly. I typically have several thousand Outlook items of all sorts stored away. It's great to be able to keep all this information and have it right there when you need it. The trick is finding the right item in that vast pile. Storing related items in the same folder can help, as can Outlook's rules for automatically filtering information, but they're not enough. Sometimes you just have to run a search.

Previous versions of Outlook offered two search tools: Find and Advanced Find. These worked well enough, but were nothing to get too excited about. Besides, these days, when most people think of searching for stuff, they think of Google. When you search for stuff with Google, you can just enter a relevant word or phrase and up pops your information. The search engine does all the work for you.

For Outlook 2007, Microsoft replaced Find with Instant Search. With Instant Search, it is almost as if Microsoft stuffed a web-style search engine into Outlook. Working in the background, Instant Search indexes information, so when you run an instant search, all it has to do is look up the information in the index. Enter a word or phrase in the Instant Search box and Outlook gets you your information almost instantly.

Advanced Find is still available for creating complicated searches not well suited for Instant Search. In the next few sections, we will talk about how to use Instant Search and Advanced Search, and when to use which, along with how to save and restore searches or turn searches into search folders.

Use Instant Search for General Searching

Using Instant Search is quite easy. Find the Instant Search box in whichever view you are using. Look for a text box with a magnifying glass in it, or something similar to this:

Begin your search by starting to type a word or phrase into the Instant Search box. As you type, Outlook displays a list of only those items in the current view that contain the characters you have typed. Within each item, the text that matches the characters you have typed so far is highlighted in yellow, making it easy to pick out. Figure 13-1 shows what a search for the word "new" in my Unread Mail folder might look like.

Of course, there are a few things that have to happen beforehand and in the background for Instant Search to do its thing. Before you can search, Instant Search needs to index your Outlook items. Before that can happen, you may need to download the Windows Desktop Search component that does the indexing. If you need to download it, Outlook will tell you so and walk you through the process.

CAUTION *If you do need to download the Windows Desktop Search component, you will need to restart Outlook, so be sure to close any open items before you do this.*

In the background, Outlook needs to continue to index items to keep up with changes. It does this by waiting until your computer is idle, then performing indexing until something (or someone) else wants to do something with the machine. What this implies is that it is possible that a word or phrase in an item won't appear in the index right away. It will get there, and soon, but it isn't an instantaneous process.

Once all this happens, Instant Search can do its magic.

Now, after my having gone on about how all you need to do in Instant Search is type and your items magically appear, I have to tell you about additional layers

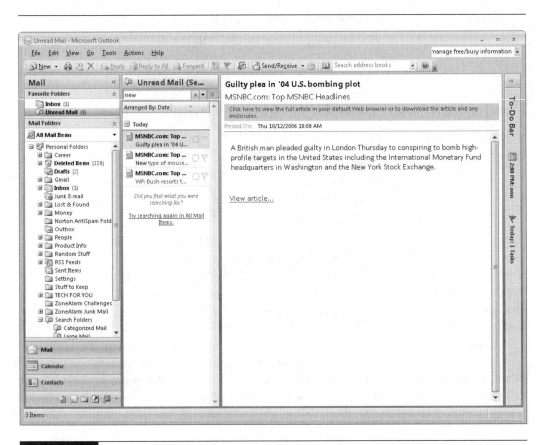

FIGURE 13-1 Finding words or phrases with Instant Search is really easy.

of complexity that are possible in Instant Search. If you look closely at Figure 13-1, you will notice the double down-arrow to the right of the Instant Search box. Click this to expand the Instant Search pane into something like this:

In this expanded Instant Search pane, you can search specific fields of the items in this view by typing your search word or phrase into the appropriate field. You can change the fields that can be searched by clicking the down arrow to the right of each field name, while the Add Criteria option at the bottom of the Instant Search pane lets you add additional fields to the set already included.

You can also constrain the search by selecting a category for the search.

Additional Advanced Search Options

You have one other set of options within the Instant Search pane whether you expand it or not. If you click the down arrow inside the Instant Search box itself, you get yet another menu of options.

Any of several options may appear on this menu. They include:

■ **Recent Searches**   Select this to see a list of the last several searches you have conducted. This is an easy way to repeat a search.

■ **Search All Mail (or Calendar, and so on) Items**   Click this to expand the scope to all of the items covered by this view type, rather than just those in the current view. For example, search all Mail items instead of just those in the Unread Mail view.

■ **Search Desktop**   Tells Instant Search to work with Windows Desktop Search to expand your search outside Outlook.

■ **Indexing Status**   Click this to see if Windows Desktop Search has indexed all available items or if it still has work to do. Check here if you are trying to find a new item that doesn't show up in an Instant Search. Perhaps it hasn't been indexed yet.

13

■ **Search Options**   Click this to see the Search Options dialog box, which provides detailed control over the workings of Instant Search (yes, yet another layer of complexity behind the easy-to-use Instant Search box). This dialog box is covered in the next section.

■ **Help**   Opens a help window displaying the main Instant Search help topic.

Yet More Instant Search Options

Okay, this is really the last level of Instant Search options to deal with. And you don't even have to deal with this one if you don't want to. In the vast majority of cases, the default Instant Search settings will work fine for you and you'll never need to look at this dialog box. But in case you do, let's take a quick look at it. Figure 13-2 shows the Search Options dialog box.

In the Indexing section of the dialog box, you control which locations you want indexed (and therefore included in searches). You also control whether or not you

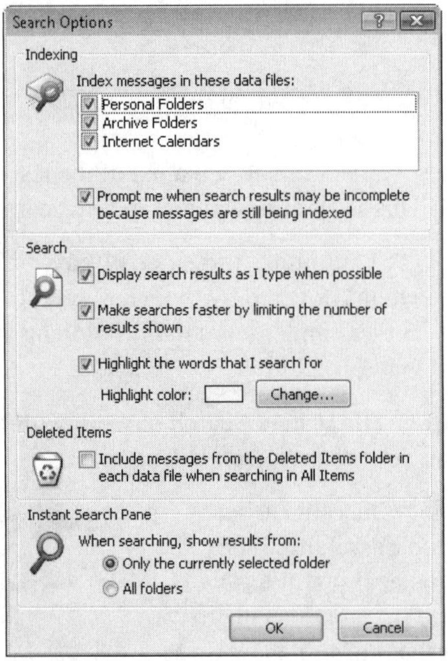

FIGURE 13-2   Use this dialog box to adjust additional Instant Search options.

get prompted when search results might be incomplete because not all items are indexed. I suggest you leave all of the options in this section selected.

In the Search section of the dialog box, you control how searches are conducted. Again, I suggest you leave all these options set. The only thing I would suggest you even consider changing is the Highlight color. The Highlight color is the color Outlook uses to highlight the search text within the body of the item. If you click Change, Outlook presents you with a Color dialog box that lets you choose and use any color that your system is capable of displaying. The default yellow is a good choice, as is any other high-contrast color.

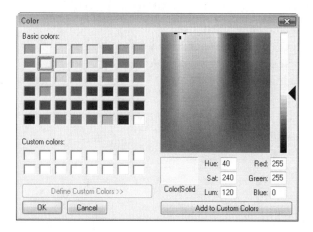

In the Deleted Items section, you tell Outlook whether or not to include items that are in the Deleted Items folder when it conducts searches. By default, this option is not set, and Outlook doesn't include the Deleted Items folder in searches. About the only time I can see anyone setting this option is if they absolutely can't find the item they're looking for and it is possible that they've inadvertently deleted it.

In the Instant Search Pane section, you tell Outlook whether the default search should be only in the currently selected folder or in all folders. For better control of your searches, I recommend you set Outlook to show results only from the currently selected folder.

Use Advanced Find for Serious Searching

If you need to find an item that contains a particular word or phrase, Instant Search will work just fine for you. But if you need to do more sophisticated searches, or need to search on something other than a word or phrase, Advanced Find is the tool for you.

13

Advanced Find lets you search on dates or file sizes, or find tasks with a particular word or phrase in the Subject field. You can search multiple folders simultaneously. The ability to search multiple folders simultaneously is particularly useful once you start actively managing your Outlook items with rules. Once you create some useful searches, you can save them, or even turn them into custom search folders.

In this book, we're going to cover only some of the more commonly used capabilities of Advanced Find, and leave exploring the rest to you. It really is an amazingly powerful tool that you'll find more uses for the more you use it.

Create and Run a Search with Advanced Find

While Instant Search is integrated into Outlook's views, Advanced Find isn't so readily visible. To open the Advanced Find dialog box, go to the main Outlook window and click Tools | Instant Search | Advanced Find. Figure 13-3 shows the Advanced Find dialog box.

You can also open the Advanced Find dialog box with the CTRL-SHIFT-F keyboard shortcut.

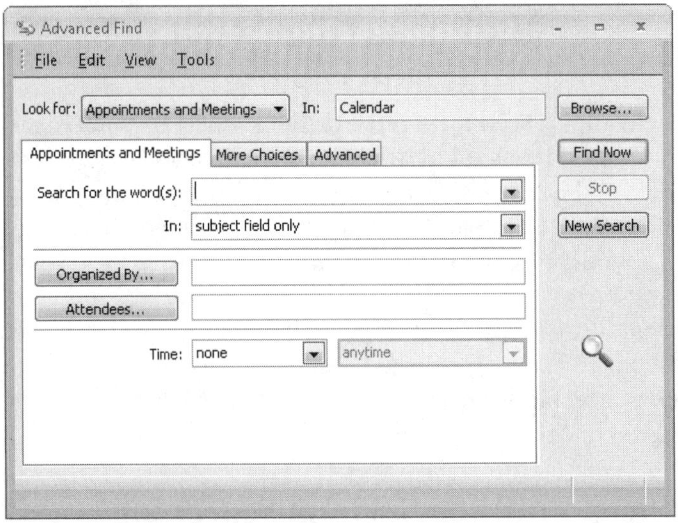

FIGURE 13-3 The Advanced Find dialog box is a busy place.

The following list describes the sections of the Advanced Find dialog box. Figure 13-3 shows the Advanced Find dialog box as it appears when I opened it with the Calendar view visible:

- **Look For list**   The Look For list is where you specify the type of Outlook item you want to search for. By default, the dialog box opens with an object type that is appropriate to the current Outlook folder. You can search for one particular type of item at a time or search all types simultaneously. The type of item you specify in this list also determines the types of search criteria the dialog box presents to you. For example, when the item type in the list is Messages, the first tabbed page in the dialog box shows common search criteria related to e-mail messages. Switch to Contacts, and the name of the first tabbed page presents search criteria that are appropriate for searching for contacts.

- **In list**   The In list is where you specify the folder or folders you want Outlook to search. By default, the In list is set to the current Outlook folder. You can also specify the folder or folders to be searched by clicking the Browse button.

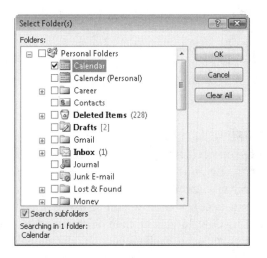

- **Tabbed pages**   The three tabbed pages in the Advanced Find dialog box let you set the search criteria you want to use. As I mentioned a little earlier, the first tabbed page changes to present criteria that are appropriate to the type of item selected in the Look For list. The second and third

13

tabbed pages also change to present criteria relevant to the item type. This makes it pointless to try to describe in detail what you'll find on each page. The best I can tell you is to work your way through the pages from left to right. They're arranged from the most basic criteria to the most complex. Other people may have had different experiences, but I've seldom needed to use the criteria on the More Choices page, and I almost never go to the Advanced page.

- ■ **Find Now button** The Find Now button launches your search.

- ■ **Stop button** The Stop button stops a search that is in progress.

- ■ **New Search button** The New Search button clears all your search criteria, enabling you to start designing a new search with a more-or-less clean slate.

Save Searches

If you create a search that you think you'll want to use again, you can save it. To save a search, click File | Save As in the Advanced Find dialog box. This opens the Save Search dialog box. Use this dialog box to give your saved search a name and select the folder where you'll store it. Saved searches end with an .oss file type.

NOTE   *For help in deciding when to save a search instead of creating a search folder for that search, as well as tips for where to save your searches, see "Design an Item Management and Archiving Strategy" later in this chapter.*

Use Saved Searches

To use a saved search, you need only open it, then run it as if you had just set it up. To open a saved search, click File | Open Search in the Advanced Find dialog box. This opens the Open Saved Search dialog box. This dialog box is the same as the Save Search dialog box, except that now you're using it to find saved searches. Locate the saved search you want to use, then double-click it to load it.

When you load the saved search, all the search criteria that you saved originally are restored. You can either run the search immediately by clicking Find Now, or make any necessary changes to the saved criteria, then run the search.

Delete Saved Searches

The process for deleting a saved search is very similar to that for loading one. You start by clicking File | Open Search in the Advanced Find dialog box to open the

Open Saved Search dialog box. Locate the saved search you want to delete, then right-click it. In the shortcut menu that appears, click Delete.

Turn a Search into a Search Folder

If you find yourself re-creating the same search over and over in Advanced Find, you should seriously consider creating a search folder for that search. The more complex and time-consuming a search is to set up, the more you will benefit from creating a search folder. Follow these steps:

> NOTE *For help in deciding when to create a search folder instead of just saving a search, see "Design an Item Management and Archiving Strategy" later in this chapter.*

1. Run your search using Advanced Find.

2. Make sure that the search results are plausible to you. You need to be careful to create the search properly before you turn it into a search folder. Be sure you have all the right search criteria set before going any further.

3. When you're happy with your search criteria and results, click File | Save Search as Search Folder in the Advanced Find dialog box. This opens the Save Search As Search Folder dialog box.

4. Enter a descriptive name for your new search folder, then click OK. The new search folder will appear in the Navigation pane along with your other search folders.

Decide Which Kind of Search to Use and When

With the speed and flexibility of Instant Search, deciding which kind of search to use and when isn't hard. Use Instant Search first, and only go to Advanced Find if Instant Search doesn't find what you are looking for.

If you find that you are doing the same Advanced Find search over and over, consider turning your search into a search folder.

Learn to Manage Items

While search folders, Instant Search, and Advanced Find make it easier to find what you're looking for in Outlook, they're not a total solution. The real answer to dealing with all the stuff you have stored in Outlook is to come up with a solid system for storing items in folders.

13

Create Folders to Manage Items

In Chapter 4, you learned how to automatically manage e-mail messages by applying rules to them. Perhaps the most common use of those rules is to move e-mail messages into folders. Let's talk about how to create folders for a minute:

 NOTE *For help in deciding what folders to create and what to store in them, see "Design an Item Management and Archiving Strategy" later in this chapter.*

1. In the main menu, click File | New, then Folder. This opens the Create New Folder dialog box shown in Figure 13-4.

TIP *You can also reach this dialog box with the CTRL-SHIFT-E keyboard shortcut.*

2. Enter a name for the folder, making sure to choose a name that will remind you of what is in the folder later on.

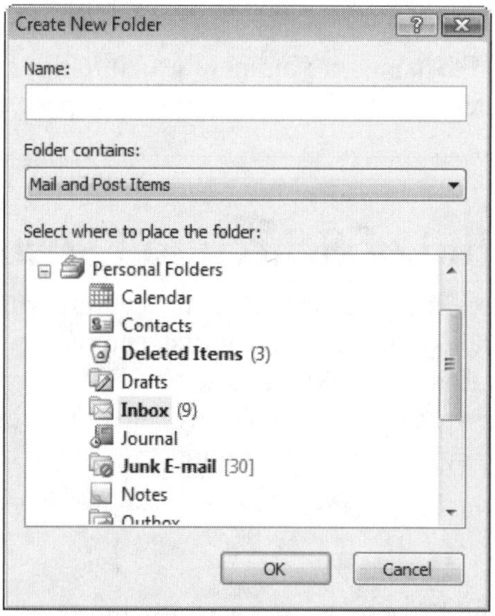

Create New Folder

Name:

Folder contains:

Mail and Post Items

Select where to place the folder:

- Personal Folders
  - Calendar
  - Contacts
  - **Deleted Items** (3)
  - Drafts
  - **Inbox** (9)
  - Journal
  - **Junk E-mail** [30]
  - Notes
  - Outbox

[OK] [Cancel]

FIGURE 13-4   Create new folders to help you manage Outlook items efficiently.

3. In the Folder Contains list, select the type of Outlook items that you plan to store in the folder. If you are creating a folder to hold e-mail messages, use the Mail and Post Items option.

4. In the Select Where to Place the Folder list, select the name of the folder that you want to contain your new folder. For example, select Inbox if you want the new folder to appear as a subfolder of the Inbox.

5. Click OK. Outlook then creates the new folder. It will be visible in the Folder List.

Now you're all set for creating any folders you need. This will come in handy when you are designing your item management and archiving strategy later in this chapter.

Learn to Archive Items

Eventually, you'll need to do something with old Outlook items. When you reach the point where you have hundreds, even thousands of items in individual folders, it just becomes too cumbersome and time-consuming to do anything with them. Or the day of reckoning may come when a System Administrator sends you a message that you are exceeding your Exchange mail quota and won't receive any more e-mail until you make more space. There are several ways to tackle this problem, each with its own advantages and disadvantages.

You can set aside some time every so often to go through folders and delete old items you don't need anymore. The advantage of this approach is that you're in control of every item.

One disadvantage of this approach is that it is very time-consuming and mildly stressful having to decide the fate of dozens or hundreds of items that may or may not be useful someday. And even if you do get rid of only the items you don't need, your folders are likely to keep growing, just a bit more slowly than if you didn't delete old items.

Another approach is to manually delete old items you don't want, and put old items you do want into a different folder for storage. This has the same advantage as the first approach but doesn't eliminate its disadvantages, as moving the old files into yet another folder just shifts the problem to a different spot. Plus, moving the items into some "old stuff" folder makes it harder to find the items when you do need them.

A better approach is to have a file outside of Outlook that can easily store old stuff while still being able to find and retrieve it easily when you do need it. The ideal external storage would compress Outlook items to save disk space and

13

would be accessible from outside Outlook. That way, you could back up this old information on another machine or some long-term storage device.

Of course, Outlook does support exactly this approach. The outside file is an Outlook data file. Data files have a file extension of .pst (which is why people often refer to these files as "PST files"). Data files are flexible, and you can use them at least three different ways.

The simplest way is to drag items into the data file when you want to store them. You can also use the "copy" or "move" command as you normally would in Outlook. This approach lets you store the items (or at least copies of the items) somewhere safe, without having to think about organizing them. You will still have the problem of finding the items you want when you need them, but at least they're not cluttering your regular Outlook folders.

The next way to use a data file is to export entire folders into it. This preserves the organization of the folders you export, but you can export only one folder (and its subfolders) at a time. You also end up backing up all the items in the folder, not just the old ones. Plus, you still have the original items in their original Outlook folders, meaning you still need to clean out the folders manually.

The third approach is the best. You can use AutoArchive to automatically archive items that are over a certain age. Items that get archived are removed from the Outlook folders they were in, so your folders get cleaned up automatically. AutoArchive organizes the contents of the data file the same way your regular Outlook folders are organized, so you can actually find things you store in the data file.

Archive Items Automatically

You need to understand a few things before working with AutoArchive. First, it treats contacts differently than any other items, by ignoring them completely. While it might sound strange at first, it actually makes perfect sense once you think about it. Under any circumstances I can think of, you wouldn't want AutoArchive moving your contacts around on you. It would be sort of like taking cards out of your Rolodex (if you're old enough to remember what those things are) and putting them in a cabinet somewhere. Contacts should always be at your fingertips.

When it comes to the other Outlook items, AutoArchive is interested only in old items and expired items. Old items are items that have been unchanged long enough to be archived. By default, items in the Inbox, Calendar, Tasks, Notes, Journal, and Drafts folders are old after six months without changes.

You can choose to have AutoArchive delete old items or move them to an archive data file. By default, AutoArchive will move old items to the data file instead of deleting them.

Expired items are items (old meeting requests, for example) that are no longer valid after a date you specify. I've found the expired items features of AutoArchive to be of little use. This chapter concentrates on handling old items.

When Outlook runs AutoArchive for the first time, it creates a default archive data file named Archive.pst. This data file appears in the Outlook File List with the name Archive Folders. If you open Archive Folders in the File List, you'll find that AutoArchive moves items into folders with the same names and organization as your regular Outlook folders. As far as you can tell from within Outlook, working with the items in archived folders is the same as working with items in your regular folders.

There are two types of AutoArchive settings: global settings and per-folder settings. Global settings apply to all folders and are the easiest way to set up autoarchiving. Per-folder settings apply to a specific folder. When you set per-folder settings for a folder, they override the global settings. So for example, if your global settings say to archive items every two months, but you want one particular folder to be archived every week, you can accomplish that by changing the per-folder settings in that folder, thereby overriding the global settings.

Configure AutoArchive Global Settings

To configure AutoArchive, you set its global settings. To do this, follow these instructions:

1. Click Tools | Options to open the Options dialog box.

2. On the Other tabbed page of the Options dialog box, click AutoArchive to open the AutoArchive dialog box shown in Figure 13-5.

3. Before you can do anything in the AutoArchive dialog box, you need to set the Run AutoArchive Every X Days check box. This activates all the other AutoArchive controls and options as shown in Figure 13-5.

4. Begin by setting the value in the Run AutoArchive Every X Days field to match the frequency with which you want archiving to occur. By default, Outlook runs AutoArchive every 14 days.

5. Set the Prompt Before AutoArchive Runs check box. This gives you the option to skip archiving if you are busy. AutoArchive can take a while, particularly the first time around. When AutoArchive is running, it definitely slows down your machine. I suggest you watch how long it takes to run on your computer a few times, then decide if you still want Outlook to prompt you before it runs.

13

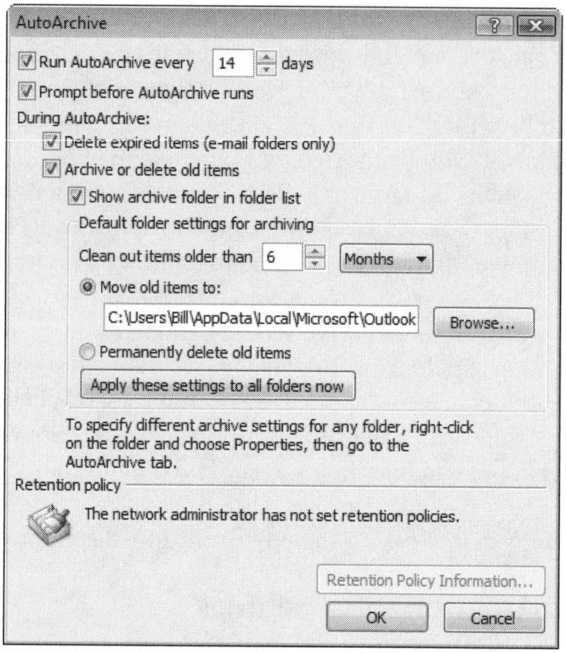

FIGURE 13-5 Use this dialog box to configure AutoArchive global settings.

6. Fill in the rest of the settings as you wish. I recommend setting the Show Archive Folder in Folder List check box, and archiving old messages rather than deleting them (by selecting Move Old Items To and entering a path to the location where the archive will be stored). If this is the first AutoArchive folder you've created, you can use the default settings for the location.

7. When you're done making global settings, click Apply These Items To All Folders Now, then click OK until you are back at the main Outlook window. Your global AutoArchive settings will now be in effect.

Configure AutoArchive Per-Folder Settings

To configure AutoArchive per-folder settings for a particular folder, follow these steps:

1. In the Folder List, right-click the folder you want to work with.

2. In the shortcut menu that appears, click Properties to open the Properties dialog box.

3. Click the AutoArchive tab to open the AutoArchive tabbed page shown in Figure 13-6.

4. On the AutoArchive tabbed page, select the options you want to apply to this folder. One interesting option here is Do Not Archive Items In This Folder. You could use this option for a folder containing information that is useful for a while, but doesn't have any long-term value. You might, for example, use it to keep messages from a friend. While it can be useful to have access to messages about the ball game or whatever for a while, such messages are unlikely to be anything that you want to store for a long time or that will be disastrous to lose if they're not archived.

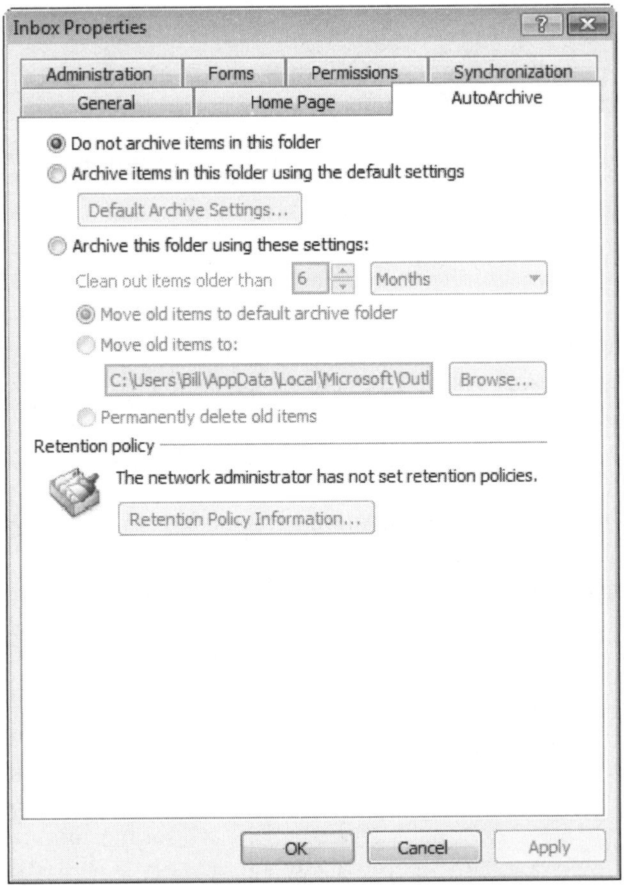

FIGURE 13-6   Use this page to set per-folder AutoArchive settings that override global settings.

Design an Item Management and Archiving Strategy

Coming up with an item management and archiving strategy is a practical and sensible goal. With so much information these days being embodied in e-mail messages and other Outlook items, knowing how to find, manage, and archive items will pay off over time. And coming up with a strategy isn't that hard. The things to consider are:

- How you tend to use Outlook items

- How you organize your daily work

- What your company's policies are with regard to data retention

How you tend to use Outlook items determines how much work you need to put into managing them. If you use e-mails and other items as storage areas for information, you will want to put a lot of effort into making it easy to find things. You will also want to be sure to archive old data so you can find it again if you need it.

If you move important information out of e-mails and items and into some other form of storage like OneNote notebooks or even paper files, you probably don't need to put as much effort into managing and archiving Outlook items. You may even want to set AutoArchive to automatically delete old items instead of archiving them.

The way you organize your daily work primarily determines the folders, rules, searches, and search folders you need to create. The goal is to make your information easy to find when you want it, while minimizing the amount of work you need to do personally to get it arranged that way.

Consider creating folders for each project you are working on and storing relevant items in them. Using search folders for each project might be an even better idea, particularly if you work on a lot of intertwined projects.

For example, I do a lot of work with VMware virtualization software and consequently have lots of Outlook items containing the word "VMware." Some of that work involves writing about VMware, and some of it involves using the product to accomplish other things. A simple rule that moves all items containing the word VMware into a single folder wouldn't work for me, since an item with that word in it might be related to any of several projects. Search folders, with their ability to show an item without actually moving it, work well for this.

Did you know?

Where to Look for Retention Policies?

There's an easy way to tell if your copy of Outlook is subject to data retention policies put in place by the network administrator. You can check for yourself in the AutoArchive dialog box. To get there, click Tools | Options, then the Other tabbed page. On the Other tabbed page, click AutoArchive to open the AutoArchive dialog box. The bottom of this page contains information about any retention policies that might be in place.

With all that said, if you are using Outlook at work, your company's data retention policies override any of these other considerations. These policies, if they exist, may be written down somewhere, or they may be automatically applied to Outlook through the corporate Exchange server. You'll have to rely on your boss, the IT department, or your coworkers for any written policies, but you can find out for yourself if there are any being automatically applied to Outlook. See the "Did You Know Where to Look for Retention Policies?" box for more information.

Decide on an Archiving Strategy

Coming up with an archiving strategy is relatively simple. The strategy really has three parts:

- Do you archive?

- If so, how often do you archive?

- Which folders do you archive, if you archive any at all?

NOTE   *I'm assuming that you will use AutoArchive instead of manually archiving your files. Manual archiving just takes too long and produces too much stress. Unless of course you are getting flogged about the size of your Inbox by the System Administrator, at which point you'll want to do anything possible to free space.*

As we discussed before, deciding whether or not to archive depends on how you tend to use your Outlook items and what your company's data retention policies are, if any.

How often you archive should depend on how much your Outlook items change. If you get five e-mail messages a day, and seldom use notes or tasks, archiving every two weeks is probably more than enough. If you get several hundred e-mail messages a day, archiving more frequently could help eliminate some of the clutter in your Inbox and other folders.

Deciding which folders to archive can take a little thought, although if you stick with the default (archiving everything except contacts), you can hardly go wrong. If you don't want to archive everything, I suggest you concentrate on the Inbox and the folders of your current projects. That should give you a good balance between archiving everything in sight, and risking losing important information.

Chapter 14

Attend to Your Security

How to...

■ Use the Trust Center

■ Deal with Junk Mail

■ Protect Yourself Against Phishing Attacks

It is an unfortunate fact that wherever people go, there are troublemakers. The online world is no different. As the most popular e-mail program in the world, Outlook is a prime target for online troublemakers. Over the years, Microsoft has added a number of features to Outlook to make it more secure against attacks and invasions of privacy. This chapter covers the key security (and privacy protection) features of Outlook 2007.

Did you know?

About IRM?

Information Rights Management (IRM) refers to the ability to control who has the rights to use information, and how they can use it. When it comes to Outlook 2007, IRM technology lets the creator of a message control who can print, forward, fax, copy, or cut and paste the contents of the message. It can even cause a message to expire (become unreadable) after a certain amount of time, or prevent someone running Microsoft Windows from capturing the contents of the message using the Print Screen key.

To set restrictions on what people can do with a message you create, your computer must be running Windows Rights Management Services (RMS), which come preinstalled in Windows Vista. Windows Rights Management Services also requires an RMS licensing server exists and that your copy of Outlook can connect with to acquire a license that allows you to download restricted material. An RMS administrator can also set IRM restrictions that apply company wide.

As you can see, this gets complicated quickly. If your organization uses Windows Rights Management Services (RMS) to implement Information Rights Management (IRM) on your messages, it will be up to the RMS administrator or someone else in the IT department to provide you with the information you need to know and the rules you need to follow to use this technology successfully.

NOTE *Information Rights Management (IRM) is another technology that is related to online security, specifically the online security of your information. It is an optional feature of Office 2007, and requires a special service pack for Office 2007. To learn more about this optional feature, see the Did You Know About IRM? Sidebar.*

Use the Trust Center

One big step Microsoft has taken to make attending to your security easier is the creation of the Trust Center (Figure 14-1).

In this chapter, we look at several of the security areas in the Trust Center, and set options that will greatly increase your online safety. The security areas we cover are:

- E-mail Security

- Attachment Handling

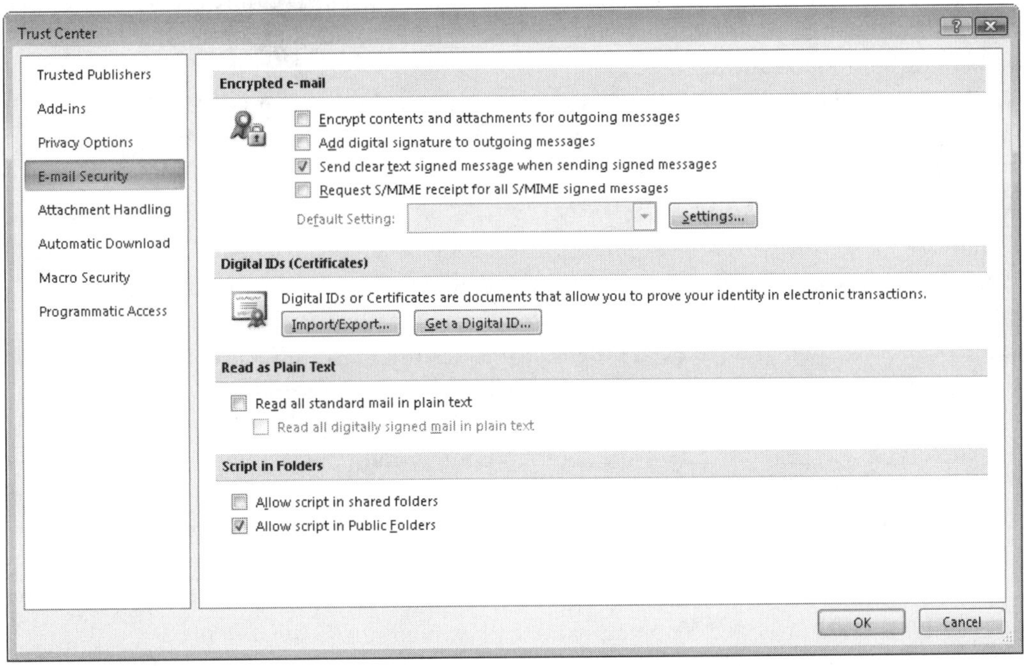

FIGURE 14-1 The Trust Center brings together many of Outlook's security features in one place.

- Automatic Download
- Macro Security
- Programmatic Access

> **TIP** *For more detailed information about any of the security areas in the Trust Center, open that area, then click the Help button in the top-right corner of the Trust Center window (it is a button with a question mark in it) to open a help topic that is specific to the current security area.*

E-Mail Security

As the name implies, this security area (shown in Figure 14-1) is where you set up basic e-mail security. Let's look at some of the sections individually.

Encrypted E-Mail

This section allows you to protect your privacy by encrypting messages you send. The only way to read such messages is through the use of the correct public key. Using public key cryptography to protect your e-mail messages is major overkill for most people. If you have a business requirement to use such heavy-duty security, the IT department at your company will tell you so and provide the appropriate guidelines for you to follow.

As for the rest of us, we'll skip this section and move on to Digital IDs (Digital Certificates). But we may be back, as you'll see shortly.

Digital IDs (Digital Certificates)

Digital IDs (also called *digital certificates*) are files that can be attached to e-mail messages (and other things) to provide security. Outlook can use digital certificates to *digitally sign messages* and to *encrypt messages*. A message that has been digitally signed can be shown to have been created by you (or at least on your computer), thereby protecting against someone impersonating you when sending e-mail messages. A message that has been encrypted has been changed so that only the intended recipient (or someone using their computer) can read it.

> **NOTE** *We're only concerned with digitally signing messages, not encrypting them, as discussed in the last section.*

Digital IDs are provided by organizations known as *certificate authorities (CAs)*. A certificate authority is a known and trusted organization that provides a means to validate each certificate it issues, and presumably will not share your certificate with anyone else. The process for getting a digital ID varies depending on whether or not Outlook is connected to an Exchange server. If your computer is connected to Exchange, your company probably already has a policy on the use of digital IDs. You should contact your network administrator for further information.

To get a digital ID when Microsoft Exchange is not involved, follow these steps:

1. In the Outlook main window, click Tools | Trust Center to open the Trust Center window.

2. Click E-mail Security to go to the E-mail Security area.

3. In the Digital IDs (Certificates) section, click Get a Digital ID. This opens your web browser to a page at the Office Online website. This page provides you with links and instructions for getting a digital certificate.

4. Choose a certificate authority, and follow the instructions to get your digital certificate. You will need to enter some information at the certificate authority's web site, then run the Certificate Import Wizard. If you just stick with the default options that appear on the screen, you should have no problems.

NOTE   *Some certificate authorities offer free certificates for personal use, but most of the available IDs require you to pay a yearly fee for use of the certificate.*

Once you have a digital ID, you need to configure Outlook to use it. You do so by telling Outlook to include your digital signature in messages. To add the digital signature to all future messages, follow these instructions:

NOTE   *A digital ID is one part of a digital signature. A digital signature can include a public key as well as a digital ID, but a public key is not required to create a digital signature.*

1. In the Outlook main window, click Tools | Trust Center to open the Trust Center window.

2. Click E-mail Security to go to the E-mail Security area.

3. In the Encrypted E-mail area, set the Add Digital Signature to Outgoing Messages check box.

14

When you send or receive an e-mail message containing a certificate, Outlook indicates this by adding a red ribbon to the envelope icon used to indicate an e-mail message in the Inbox pane, as well as in the header of the message itself.

If a lot of your communications require digital signatures or encryption, you may want to configure Outlook to always use your digital certificates and automatically attach a copy to each message you send. These steps show you how:

1. In the main Outlook window, click Tools | Options to open the Options dialog box.

2. Click the Security tab to open the Security tabbed page.

3. On the Security tabbed page, click Settings. This opens the Change Security Settings dialog box.

4. In the Certificates and Algorithms section of the dialog box, set the Send These Certificates with Signed Messages check box.

Attachment Handling

For a few years now, one of the primary ways people attack computers has been through e-mail attachments. Many viruses travel disguised as pictures or screensavers, or other types of files attached to innocuous-looking e-mail messages. When the recipient tries to open the attachment, the virus goes to work, wreaking havoc. While it is well known that viruses travel this way, many times every day, someone somewhere tries to open an unexpected e-mail attachment and creates a major headache for themselves, their coworkers, the corporate IT staff, and often every one of their contacts.

How Outlook Protects You Against Bad Attachments

In an attempt to protect you from such threats, Outlook takes a brute-force approach: It prevents you from receiving a wide range of e-mail attachments. It does this by looking at the file extension of each attachment and blocking those that Microsoft (or your IT department) has decided pose a risk.

This approach may be effective, but it may also require you to change the way you do your work. Many people are used to e-mailing various files back and forth in ways that may no longer be possible. Microsoft Office system documents, things such as Word and Excel files, get through just fine. But other commonly used files types, such as batch files (.bat file extension), screensavers (.scr file extension), and help files (.hlp file extension) are blocked. If you sometimes send these kinds of files around, you'll have to change your ways.

Did you know?

Antivirus Software Is Crucial?

While Outlook has several capabilities designed to provide you with better security than previous versions, they're not enough. You need antivirus software too. The manufacturers of antivirus software, companies such as Symantec and McAfee, go to great lengths to keep up with the ever-changing designs of viruses and other harmful programs that are out in the world. If you install antivirus software and keep it up to date, you'll do much to protect the security of your computer.

If your PC is connected to the Internet through a broadband connection, I suggest you investigate products such as McAfee VirusScan online, a subscription service that delivers the latest updates to your PC as soon as they're available.

When you receive a message that contains an attachment Outlook doesn't like, the attachment seems to disappear. You have no access to it at all, and the only way to know it was ever there is to look at the Info Bar in the message. As Figure 14-2 shows, the Info Bar contains a message telling you that Outlook has blocked access to the potentially unsafe attachments, and it lists the names of those attachments.

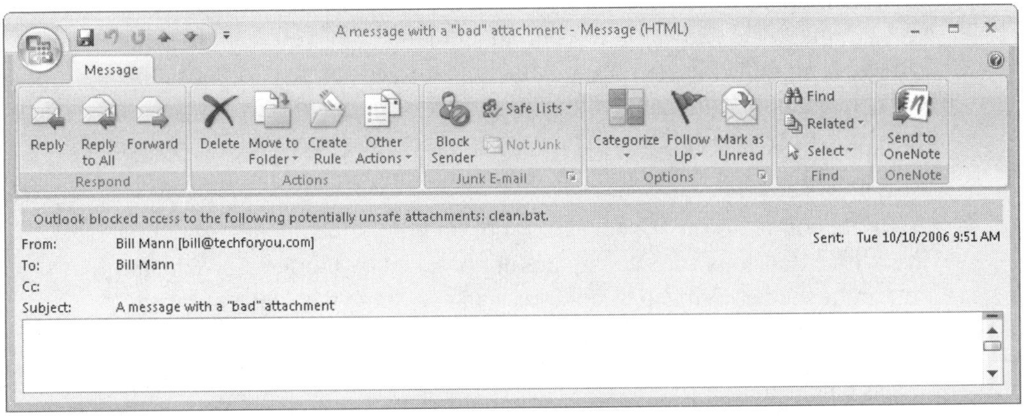

FIGURE 14-2   The Info Bar shows that an attachment has been blocked by Outlook.

Outlook recognizes two kinds of potentially dangerous file attachments: Level 1 and Level 2. Level 1 attachments are file types that could conceivably carry viruses or other dangerous content. Outlook blocks you from even seeing any attachments that are on the Level 1 list. By default, Outlook comes with a list of about 40 file extensions that are treated as Level 1. To see the entire list of extensions that are blocked by default, open the Outlook help system and search for the word "attachments." In the results list that appears, click Attachment File Types Blocked by Outlook to see the appropriate help topic.

The Level 2 list is empty by default. Network administrators can add file extensions to the Level 2 list, as well as convert Level 1 file extensions into Level 2 file extensions. Outlook doesn't completely block Level 2 files, but you cannot open them from within Outlook. Instead, you must save the file to your hard drive before opening it. Doing this gives your antivirus software a chance to scan the file before you open it.

NOTE *If you are connected to Microsoft Exchange, your e-mail administrator can change the security level of file types. Contact the administrator for more information.*

Working Around Attachment Blocking

While Outlook 2007 is set up to prevent you from circumventing its attachment blocking (you could circumvent attachment blocking in the previous version of Outlook), there are still some things you can do to get your attached files through. Either one of the following techniques will get the job done, at the cost of some additional work for both sender and recipient:

- Add a dummy file extension to your attachments. Say you want to send a file with an .hlp extension as an attachment. Outlook would normally block that. But if you change the extension to something like .hlp_dummy, Outlook will let that through. The recipient can then save the file without the _dummy part of the extension, and all will be well.

- Use a file compression or packaging tool on your attachments. Attached files with extensions such as .zip are not blocked by Outlook. If you use a program such as WinZip to compress and package the files you want to send in an attachment, they'll get past the attachment blocking. Then all you need to do is be sure the recipients have the tools and information needed to restore the files to their original forms.

Automatic Download

Many e-mail messages include pictures. Sometimes these pictures are embedded in the message, and sometimes, when the message is in HTML format, it contains a link to a picture that is stored on the Internet somewhere, instead of including the picture in the body of the message. Using links like this reduces the size of the original message.

Unfortunately, the creeps who haunt the seedier side of the Internet have learned to use those picture links to harm you. If you download a picture using the link in the message, it tells the bad guys that the message went to someone with a valid e-mail address. This is important to them for many reasons, including the fact that they can sell your e-mail address for more money if they can show that it is a valid one.

About Web Beacons?

Web beacons, also known as web bugs, pixel tags, and clear GIFs, are usually tiny images, 1 pixel by 1 pixel, that are transparent or the same color as the background of the web page or e-mail message they're part of. We'll concentrate here on how they work when included in HTML e-mail messages.

The idea is to hide one or more web beacons somewhere in the message where they won't be noticed by the recipient. Web beacons typically link to a different web server than the rest of the images in the message. The computer at this destination exists to keep track of which recipients open the message containing a beacon. Prior to Outlook 2003, when you opened a message containing a web beacon, Outlook automatically loaded the image for the web beacon from its web server, the same as any other image. When that happened, the web server was able to gain all sorts of information from your computer.

Spammers use web beacons to determine if someone opens the e-mail message the spammer sent to them. If the spammer's web server detects your computer trying to download the web beacon that was included in the message they sent to you, they know that your e-mail address is an active one. Then the flood of spam really begins, since your address is now known to be a good one.

This is why Outlook 2003, and now Outlook 2007, defaults to blocking HTML content such as images unless it comes from a trustworthy source.

14

There is a lot more to the story than this (see the "Did You Know About Web Beacons?" sidebar), but what it comes down to is the fact that the Automatic Download security area exists to protect you from some of the creeps out there. This is how it works.

When you open the Automatic Downloads security area, you see the options shown in Figure 14-3. By default, Outlook 2007 doesn't automatically download pictures, unless certain conditions apply. You can change Outlook's default behavior by setting or clearing the following options:

■ Permit downloads in e-mail messages from senders and to recipients defined in the Safe Senders and Safe Recipients Lists used by the Junk E-mail filter.

NOTE   *Later in this chapter you will learn how to declare certain senders or domains as Safe Senders or Safe Recipients, thereby allowing Outlook to automatically download pictures and other HTML content from them.*

■ Permit downloads from Web sites in this security zone: Trusted Zone

■ Permit downloads in RSS items

Trust Center

Trusted Publishers
Add-ins
Privacy Options
E-mail Security
Attachment Handling
Automatic Download
Macro Security
Programmatic Access

You can control whether Outlook automatically downloads and displays pictures when you open an HTML e-mail message.

Blocking pictures in e-mail messages can help protect your privacy. Pictures in HTML e-mail can require Outlook to download the pictures from a server. Communicating to an external server in this way can verify to the sender that your e-mail address is valid, possibly making you the target of more junk mailings.

☑ Don't download pictures automatically in HTML e-mail messages or RSS items
    ☑ Permit downloads in e-mail messages from senders and to recipients defined in the Safe Senders and Safe Recipients Lists used by the Junk E-mail filter
    ☑ Permit downloads from Web sites in this security zone: Trusted Zone
    ☑ Permit downloads in RSS items
    ☑ Permit downloads in SharePoint Discussion Boards
    ☑ Warn me before downloading content when editing, forwarding, or replying to e-mail

OK   Cancel

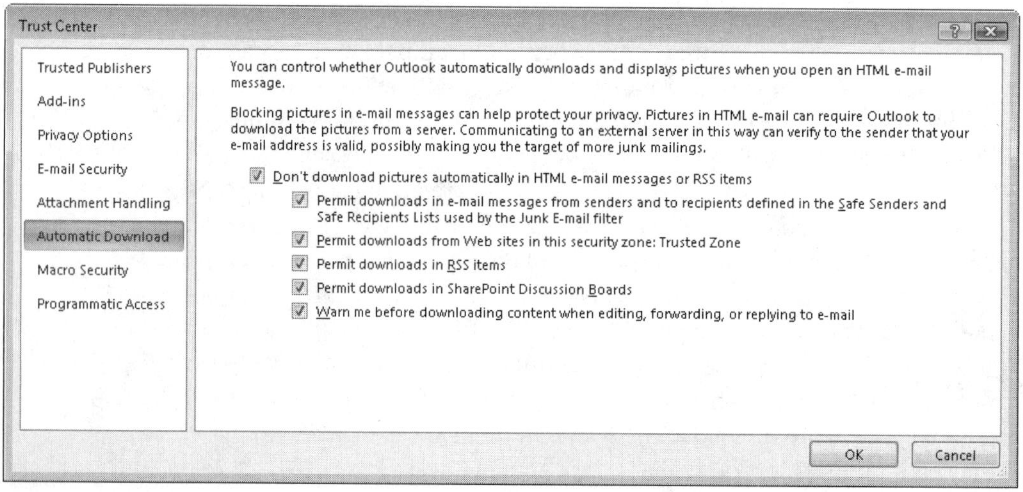

FIGURE 14-3   The Automatic Downloads security area protects you from spammers and other creeps.

- Permit downloads in SharePoint Discussion Boards

- Warn me before downloading content when editing, forwarding, or replying to e-mail

Unless you have a strong reason to do otherwise, your best course of action is to leave all the options selected. Doing so prevents Outlook from downloading pictures, unless the message containing the pictures comes from a trusted source. It is a good compromise between increasing your security and reducing the value of your e-mails.

Macro Security

Outlook can also protect your computer from macro viruses. A computer program such as Microsoft Office Word consists of a set of instructions that are executed by the Windows operating system. Macros are sets of instructions that are executed by programs such as Microsoft Office Word. Macro viruses are harmful macros that can be attached to Microsoft Office Word documents, Microsoft Office Excel spreadsheets, and many other types of files.

Since a macro contains instructions for the program that opens the file containing it, the programs that read the macros can do only certain things with them, which should prevent any problems. However, it's possible to write a macro that defeats the built-in security of the program viewing it, thereby allowing the macro to act like a virus.

Once launched, a macro virus can cause strange behavior on your PC, infect other files, even tell Outlook to mail the infected document to every one of your contacts, thereby spreading the infection. The Melissa virus, which infected millions of computers several years ago, is a well-known example of a macro virus.

To protect you against macro viruses, Outlook takes a defensive posture toward macros. Outlook will not execute the macros in any file unless the developer of the macro is in a list of trusted sources, and the macro itself is digitally signed with the developer's digital ID. Even then, Outlook will warn you before executing a macro.

The only problem with this is that not all of the legitimate macros in use are digitally signed, nor are they in anyone's trusted sources list. If you're in a position where you need to run macros like this within Outlook, you'll need to change macro security settings to accommodate the way you actually work.

14

Change Outlook's Macro Security Level

It takes only a few moments to change the macro security level. But don't do it unless it is really necessary. Microsoft set the security level to High for a reason.

However, if you're running an antivirus program, that should catch macro viruses for you, making it much safer to reduce the security level. Here are the steps to follow:

1. In the Outlook main window, click Tools | Trust Center to open the Trust Center window.

2. Click Macro Security to go to the Macro Security area (see Figure 14-4).

3. Select the security setting you want to use. I suggest you at least let Outlook warn you when it is about to run a macro. While this might be annoying when a macro runs that should run, it will alert you if a macro tries to run in an unexpected location or situation.

NOTE *If you do see a macro warning that makes you suspicious, you should not allow the macro to execute and should instead contact the person who created the message or file that contains the macro, or use your antivirus program to scan your computer.*

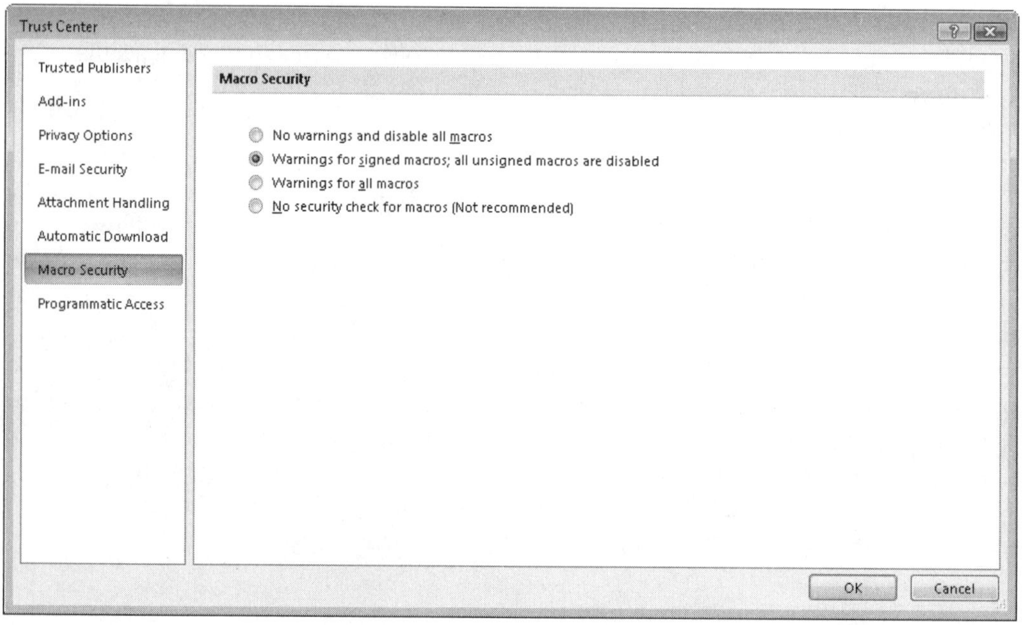

Trust Center

Trusted Publishers	Macro Security
Add-ins	
Privacy Options	⚪ No warnings and disable all macros
E-mail Security	⦿ Warnings for signed macros; all unsigned macros are disabled
Attachment Handling	⚪ Warnings for all macros
Automatic Download	⚪ No security check for macros (Not recommended)
Macro Security	
Programmatic Access	

OK   Cancel

FIGURE 14-4   Set the level of protection against macro viruses in this security area.

Programmatic Access

This less-than-obvious title refers to the situation where some other program attempts to perform one of the following suspicious activities: get Outlook to give it e-mail addresses, or get Outlook to send e-mail messages in your name. While this may be a legitimate activity (HotSync or Active Sync attempting to synchronize your Outlook contacts with your PDA, for example), it may also be some kind of virus or other unauthorized software trying to cause trouble.

The options in the Programmatic Access security area tell Outlook how to react when another program tries to perform a suspicious activity. Your antivirus software plays into this too. (You do have antivirus software installed, don't you?) If Windows detects that your computer has antivirus software installed, and that software is up to date, you can tell Outlook to trust the antivirus software. That is, you can tell Outlook to assume that the antivirus software will prevent any inappropriate programmatic access to Outlook, and stop warning you about it. To do so, follow these steps:

1. In the Outlook main window, click Tools | Trust Center to open the Trust Center window.

2. Click Programmatic Access to go to the security area.

3. Select the security setting you want to use. I suggest you tell Outlook to warn you about suspicious activity only when there is no antivirus software active or it is out of date. That will give you the fewest unnecessary warnings.

Deal with Junk Mail

Junk e-mail (also known as *spam)* has become a major problem for e-mail users the world over. It appears that well over half of all e-mail messages sent in the first half of 2006 were junk e-mail. Despite state and federal laws in the United States and elsewhere, the flood of spam continues to grow.

Outlook 2007 has features designed to reduce the amount of junk e-mail that actually makes it into your Inbox. Specifically, Outlook 2007 provides a sophisticated junk e-mail filter, along with a set of lists that determine whether messages from specific addresses or domains should be blocked by the filter or not. Microsoft regularly publishes updates to the junk mail filter that help it to keep up with the ever-changing tricks of the spammers.

How to ... Keep Spam from Coming in the First Place

While Outlook is good at fighting spam once it arrives, another way to cut down on it is to prevent spammers from sending it to you in the first place. While it's impossible to prevent everyone from sending you junk e-mail, there are steps you can take to reduce the amount that gets sent to you in the first place. Here are some of the best:

- **Never reply to junk e-mail** Some junk e-mail messages arrive complete with instructions on how to opt out of future mailings. While this sounds like a good idea, don't do it. In reality, when you follow the opt-out instructions, you may or may not be removed from that junk mailer's list. But in almost all cases, your e-mail address will be sold to other junk e-mailers. By replying to the message, you've shown that yours is a valid and actively used e-mail address. As we've already discussed, this information is quite valuable to junk e-mailers, and you'll likely get barraged with even more spam than before.

- **Alter your e-mail address when you post it in public** By changing your e-mail address slightly whenever you post it on a website, a newsgroup, or a mailing list, you can thwart some of the software that's used to automatically harvest e-mail addresses for the spam senders. One simple approach is to replace the @ sign in your e-mail address, like this: bill@techforyou.com becomes bill (at) techforyou.com.

- **Create a disposable e-mail address** You can easily create a disposable e-mail address on one of the web e-mail services, such as Hotmail. If you use this disposable address when registering software or filling out forms on websites, most of the spam that you get will go to that address. When the address becomes too much of a target for junk e-mailers, you just stop using it and open a new disposable address. If you use this approach, you can save your main e-mail address for close friends or other people you trust.

Nothing you can do as an individual will protect you from all junk e-mail. But following these suggestions, and using Outlook's junk e-mail handling capabilities, you should be able to greatly reduce the amount of junk e-mail that actually makes it into your Inbox.

While blocking junk mail that arrives at your computer is crucial, this alone won't protect you from the vast flood that pervades the Internet. Making yourself a less-likely target in the first place is important too. The "How to Keep Spam from Coming in the First Place" sidebar has some tips that may help.

Here's some more information on each of the components of the new junk e-mail handling system:

- **The junk e-mail filter**   This filter relies on sophisticated algorithms to identify messages that are likely to be junk. It takes into account factors such as the time of day the message was sent and the actual contents of the message. This approach is more flexible and potentially much more powerful than older approaches, which relied on specific rules.

E-mail postmarks, which we talked about a bit in Chapter 1, also figure into the filtering algorithm. Keep reading this chapter to learn how to use e-mail postmarks.

- **The Safe Senders list**   This list is a place to specify particular senders as people you trust. By doing so, you tell the junk e-mail filter never to block messages from these senders. Note that you don't have to add people to this list to receive mail from them. Instead, add someone to this list if they are accidentally blocked by the junk e-mail filter.

- **The Blocked Senders list**   This list is the place to specify that e-mail from certain senders is always to be treated as junk.

- **The Safe Recipients list**   This list is a little less obvious. You use it to tell Outlook that any e-mail sent to the recipients in this list is not to be treated as junk. You might want to add the addresses of your favorite mailing lists to the Safe Recipients list. That would keep Outlook from blocking any e-mail messages sent to the list and then forwarded to you.

- **The International list**   This list lets you block mail from the domains associated with specific nations, or messages that use different character sets than you want to read.

14

Use the Enhanced Junk E-Mail Filter

By default, the junk e-mail filter is active, and set to the lowest of its three active
security levels. On the Low setting, the filter catches only the most obvious junk
e-mail messages and will likely let some junk messages get through to your Inbox.
The good thing about this setting is that it is unlikely to block messages you should
be receiving. You can adjust the way the junk e-mail filter does its work, and make
changes to the Safe Senders, Safe Recipients, Blocked Senders, and International
lists, using the instructions that follow.

Adjust the Junk E-Mail Filter Settings

To adjust the junk e-mail filter settings, follow these instructions:

1. In the Outlook main window, click Tools | Options. On the Preferences
   tabbed page of the Options dialog box, click Junk E-Mail. This opens the
   Junk E-Mail Options dialog box shown in Figure 14-5.

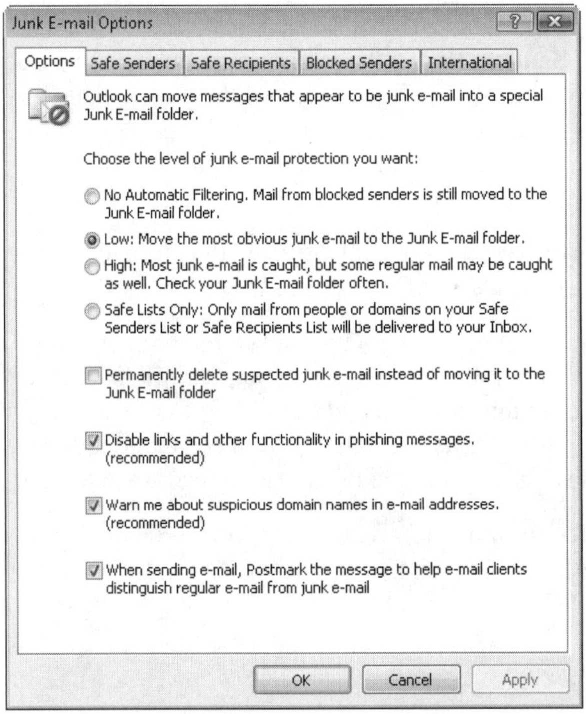

FIGURE 14-5   Fight spam using the Junk E-Mail Options dialog box.

2. On the Options tabbed page of the Junk E-Mail Options dialog box, set the level of junk e-mail protection you want. Choose between Low, High, and Safe Lists Only.

CAUTION   *If you select the No Protection option, you effectively turn off the junk e-mail filter. Don't do this!*

3. Tell Outlook what to do with junk messages. Normally, Outlook puts suspected junk e-mail messages in a Junk E-Mail folder. If you're really comfortable with the way the junk e-mail filter is working, you can tell Outlook to eliminate junk messages instead of storing them in the Junk E-Mail folder by selecting the option Permanently delete suspected junk e-mail instead of moving it to the Junk E-Mail folder.

In addition, this dialog box includes some options related to phishing messages (yes, I did spell that correctly) and postmarking. Both of these topics are covered later in the chapter.

Work with the Lists

All four of the junk e-mail–related lists work the same way. You can follow these basic instructions to work on any of them. In step 2, just choose the appropriate tabbed page for the list you want to work on. For simplicity, these instructions deal with the Safe Senders list:

1. In the Outlook main window, click Tools | Options. On the Preferences tabbed page of the Options dialog box, click Junk E-Mail. This opens the Junk E-Mail Options dialog box.

2. On the Safe Senders tabbed page of the Junk E-Mail Options dialog box (shown in Figure 14-6), use the Add, Edit, and Remove buttons to manage any names in the list.

3. If you have an ASCII text list of senders you want to add to the Safe Senders list, click Import from File and select the appropriate text file. Using the Export to File button, you can similarly export your current list of safe senders to an ASCII text file.

4. To ensure that all your Outlook contacts are automatically trusted (even though they don't appear in the Safe Senders list), make sure that the Also Trust E-Mail from My Contacts check box is set.

14

FIGURE 14-6 Specify addresses and domains that are safe when they send messages to you.

NOTE
The Also Trust E-Mail from My Contacts check box appears only on the Safe Senders tabbed page.

View Blocked External HTML Content

While Outlook automatically blocks external HTML content such as images in many e-mail messages, that doesn't mean you can't see it. You can manually choose the items you want to see. I find the ability to manually choose which external HTML content to view useful when dealing with ads that are sent to me.

When Outlook blocks an external image, it displays a box with a red X where the image would have been. When Outlook blocks external content in this way, a message appears in the Info Bar to explain what happened.

If you shop online, you will likely get an unending stream of e-mails containing ads from those vendors. For some of them, I don't want to stop getting their ads, but I don't want to be distracted by their flashy images or tie up my Internet connection waiting for their fancy HTML content to download. So I let Outlook automatically block their external HTML content. This means I get an ugly message like the one shown here:

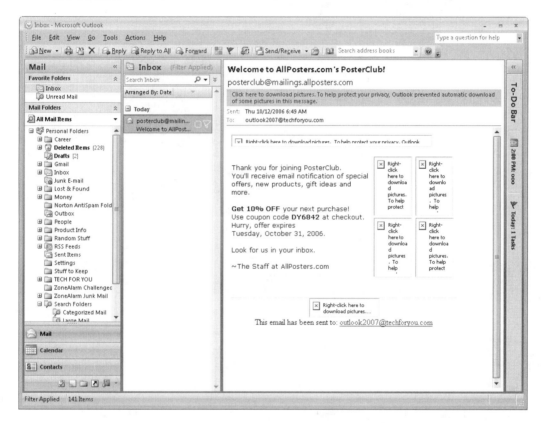

While this isn't attractive, it keeps the images out of my face while letting me know that the vendor has a sale or something going on. If I'm interested, I can easily choose to view the blocked content. There are two ways to see the blocked items. One is to right-click the blocked item, then in the shortcut menu that appears, click View Source or Download Pictures.

The other way to see the blocked content is to right-click the Info Bar. When you do that, a shortcut menu appears with several related options. Click Download Pictures to see the blocked content.

14

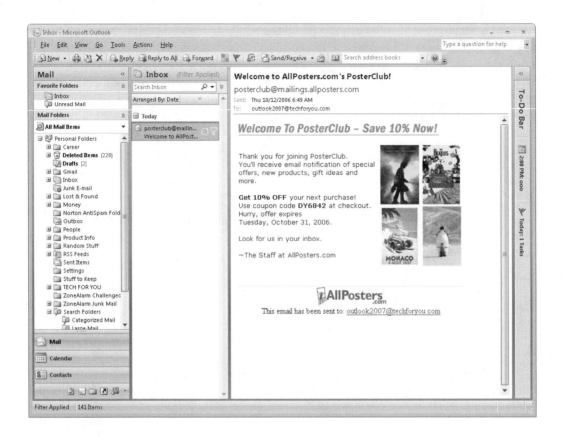

Other options on this shortcut menu allow you to add this sender or the entire domain the message came from to your Safe Senders list.

Use E-Mail Postmarks

E-mail postmarks attack the problem of junk mail from a different angle. While most of Outlook's efforts are to prevent you from receiving junk e-mail, e-mail postmarks are meant to show the recipients of your message that your message isn't junk mail. The idea here is that it takes some computational work to create these special postmarks, which would make it relatively more expensive for spammers, who may send millions of messages a month, to use them.

Recognizing this, when Outlook 2007 receives a message with a valid e-mail postmark, it reduces the odds that the message is junk mail. This knowledge is used by Outlook's junk mail filter when deciding whether to mark the message as junk or not.

NOTE   *Outlook 2007 evaluates each message to see if it looks like junk mail before adding an e-mail postmark to the message. Only messages that might be recognized as junk mail get a postmark.*

It is unclear whether the use of e-mail postmarks will catch on, but they're included in Outlook 2007 and turned on by default. Your only option for dealing with postmarks is to turn postmarking on or off. Here are the steps to do so:

1. In the main Outlook menu, click Tools | Options to open the Options dialog box.

2. On the Preferences tab, click Junk E-mail to open the Junk E-mail Options dialog box (see Figure 14-5).

3. Set or clear the option When sending e-mail, Postmark the message to help e-mail clients distinguish regular e-mail from junk e-mail.

Protect Yourself Against Phishing Attacks

If you've been using e-mail and the Internet for a while, you've probably heard plenty about junk e-mail (spam) and viruses. But what about *phishing?* Phishing is a relatively new tactic that sleazy characters use to take advantage of people online. A phishing attack is designed to get you to disclose personal information that can be used to let the creeps get into your bank accounts, or impersonate you online. Very nasty stuff indeed.

You are a smart person, and you would never knowingly give out personal information to some crook. So how does phishing get that information from you? By impersonating some person or company you trust. A phishing message will typically look like a perfectly legitimate message from your bank or insurance company. They usually describe some problem with your account and ask you to follow a link to their site so you can validate your account. Well-done phishing messages are indistinguishable from something you would expect to get. At least, they are indistinguishable to the naked eye.

Phishing messages look like they come from a legitimate source, but they contain links that point to fake websites. These sites may also look completely legitimate, but instead of being run by your bank, they are run by crooks. The sites themselves push you to enter personal information, or your bank account number and password, or whatever information the creeps think they can sell or use themselves.

14

If you get tricked into complying with a phishing attack, things will likely start to go bad for you pretty quickly. You might find your bank accounts cleaned out, or someone running up big charges on your credit cards, or who knows what.

So now that you know why phishing is so nasty, how does Outlook help protect you from attacks?

The Outlook 2007 junk mail filter guards you against phishing attacks. It does so by scanning incoming messages, and looking for various tell-tale characteristics of phishing attacks. These include things like links in the message that go to places other than the domain that supposedly sent the message.

If Outlook identifies a message as likely being part of a phishing attack, it does several things to the message:

- It sends the message to the Junk E-mail folder.

- It disables all the links in the message.

- It prevents you from using the Reply To or Reply All options with the message.

- It blocks all attachments to the message.

Change Outlook's Approach to Phishing

If you don't like Outlook's fairly aggressive approach to handling phishing messages, you can change it. I don't recommend this, but you can do it if you really want to. For instructions on how to do this, go to the Outlook Help system and search for "phishing protection." One of the topics will tell you how to enable or disable links and other features of messages that Outlook thinks are phishing.

The End of the Beginning

With this chapter, you've finished the main portion of this book. You know how to do all the basic things you need to do in Outlook 2007. But there is a lot more you can do with Outlook. Part V explores topics such as integrating Outlook with other applications and working with Exchange and SharePoint Services.

But before we get to those topics, we hit one that's near and dear to my heart. If you are a mobile professional, or if you just rely on Outlook as your second brain like I do, it is likely that you've run into the problem of figuring out how to get access to your Outlook data when you aren't sitting in front of your computer. Chapter 15 covers techniques and tools for getting access to your Outlook data from anywhere. I think you'll like it.

Part V

Go Even Further

Chapter 15

Access Your Outlook Data from Anywhere

How to...

- Understand the Problem
- Synchronize Between Computers
- Use Outlook Web Access
- Get Data on your Phone with SMS Link
- Is a Hosted Exchange Mailbox the Answer?

This chapter will look at some of the options available for getting access to your Outlook data from anywhere.

Topics include synchronizing one or more PCs through an online service such as Yahoo! Calendar, doing the PDA (or smartphone) Shuttle, using Outlook Web Access (OWA), the new Outlook 2007 Mobile Service, and hosted Exchange accounts.

Understand the Problem

In this age of widespread Internet access and wireless broadband connections, why do we need an entire chapter on getting your Outlook data from anywhere? Your Outlook data lives in one or more .PST files on your computer, or in some Microsoft Exchange server at the corporate data center. Outlook was designed before the world was full of tiny devices with wireless connections and professionals expected to be connected to work, wherever they were.

Besides, you likely have a *lot* of data in Outlook. A quick check on my PC shows that my main Outlook.pst file is approximately 300 megabytes in size. That's a lot of stuff to move back and forth between systems or across the mobile phone network to your phone. And on top of this, you have the problem of keeping everything synchronized. Suppose you somehow have access to your Outlook Calendar while you are out of the office. You decide to schedule a client appointment at 2:00 P.M. While you are doing this, your boss is scheduling a 2:00 P.M. meeting with you back at the office. How can those conflicts be handled?

As you can see, getting access to your Outlook data from anywhere isn't a simple proposition. Consequently, solving this problem isn't simple. But with Outlook being so popular, lots of companies (including Microsoft) have taken shots at addressing the problem. The result is a smorgasbord of products and services that each address different parts of the problem and cater to different needs.

The rest of this chapter looks at the kinds of solutions that are out there, and talks about the pros and cons of each. Because Outlook 2007 is so new, few solutions are available specifically for it, but we can talk about what will likely be available in the months and years ahead. This is an ever-changing area. To help you (and me, since I'm one of those mobile professionals who needs access from anywhere) keep track of what solutions are available and how they work, I've dedicated a section of my Living With Outlook website to this. There, I will be reporting on the solutions that are available, and giving you my first-hand impressions of those that I've used myself.

NOTE *For the latest on getting access to your Outlook data from anywhere, visit the Get Mobile section of my website at http://www.living-with-outlook.com/get-mobile.html.*

Synchronize Between Computers

Here is a problem that vexes people whether or not they need mobile access to their Outlook data: How to get Outlook at work and Outlook at home synchronized. This is a problem that has annoyed me for years. I use Outlook at work. I use Outlook at home. But Outlook at work and Outlook at home contain different items. What I want is to be able to see my entire schedule, or all my e-mail messages in Outlook whether I am at home or at work.

Why do I need to see my home stuff at work, and vice versa? Imagine this situation: We're at the office and trying to schedule an all-day meeting for some time next month. Someone proposes we meet on the 12th. My work calendar is clear that day. But wait! Is that the day of my daughter's big dance recital, or is the competition on the 11th? I can't tell because my personal life is in the copy of Outlook running on my PC at home, and I can't see it from the office.

The same logic goes in the other direction. I'm on the phone at 8:00 P.M. on Wednesday, trying to schedule some urgent repair work on the house, and the supplier wants to know if I can meet her at 10:00 A.M. or 2:00 P.M. tomorrow. I don't know. I think 10:00 A.M. is okay, but I can't see what my work schedule looks like so I don't know whether I'm free then or if 2:00 P.M. is better.

What a pain! I want a solution that lets me synchronize Outlook on my home and office computers.

There are some solutions to this problem, particularly if you can live without synchronizing e-mail between both locations. This probably isn't a big problem, since you probably don't want to be dealing with personal e-mail at work and work e-mail at home anyway (you might even be violating company policy if you try). Let's look at a few of the possibilities.

15

CAUTION *The issue of personal e-mail at work is part of the larger issue of keeping your personal information private. We will be talking about this more as we go along, so for now, please just stick with me.*

Yahoo! Calendar

Let's use Yahoo! Calendar to see how synchronizing Outlook data between two computers with the help of a service on the Internet works. Yahoo! Calendar offers a free utility called Intellisync for Yahoo! (Intellisync) that you install on each computer that you want to synchronize with Yahoo! Intellisync handles the actual transfer of data between the computer and Yahoo!, determining what needs to be changed and spotting any conflicts that need your intervention. Conceptually, the way this works is pretty simple, as shown in Figure 15-1.

NOTE *While I am using the phrase Yahoo! Calendar here, the synchronization process we are talking about can actually synchronize your Outlook Contacts, Calendar, Notes, and Tasks to their Yahoo! counterparts.*

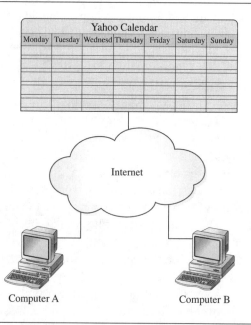

FIGURE 15-1   Synchronizing two computers with the help of Yahoo! Calendar.

> **TIP**   *If all you want is synchronization of your Calendar items, Google Calendar is another tool you can use to synchronize to a service on the Internet. With the help of applications such as CompanionLink for Google Calendar (www.companionlink.com), you can synchronize Outlook and your mobile device to Google Calendar. For more on products like CompanionLink, visit the Get Mobile section of my website at http://www.living-with-outlook.com/get-mobile.html.*

1. I make a change to my Outlook Calendar on Computer A.

2. A copy of Intellisync on Computer A detects the change and makes the appropriate changes to the data on Yahoo! Calendar, leaving it synchronized with Computer A.

3. At the same time, Intellisync receives any changes from Yahoo! Calendar and makes appropriate changes to the data on Computer A, leaving it synchronized with Yahoo! Calendar. The Yahoo! Calendar changes can be changes that you made directly to Yahoo! Calendar, or they could be the result of synchronization between Yahoo! Calendar and Computer B.

4. Some time later, the copy of Intellisync on Computer B performs the equivalent of steps 2 and 3, leaving Yahoo! Calendar and Computer B synchronized.

The result is that your Yahoo! Calendar, Computer A, and Computer B all have the same information. At least they have the same information as of the last synchronization by the copy of Intellisync on each computer.

> **TIP**   *You can use this technique to synchronize your PDA with your PC too. More on synchronizing PDAs later.*

15

But what happens if someone changes a Calendar item on Computer A and someone else changes the same item on Computer B before the change made on Computer A gets synchronized to Computer B? That would be a disaster if it were allowed to happen, so Intellisync checks for exactly that kind of thing.

Without going into the gory details (trust me, I used to work at the company that created Intellisync for Yahoo!, and there are lots of gory details that it handles), Intellisync checks for this kind of problem and gives you some options on how to deal with it. So this could be a viable solution for synchronizing your Outlook Calendar (and Contacts too) between two computers. Even better, synchronizing through the Yahoo! Calendar is free.

There are, however, a couple of disadvantages to this solution. The biggest one is that you need to manually synchronize each computer to Yahoo! Calendar. This isn't inherently a problem, but it means you have to remember to do it. This also means that your data doesn't get synchronized when you are away from your computer.

An example will make this clearer. For a while I used Yahoo! Calendar to synchronize between my home and office computers. At the time, I worked for a boss who was on the West Coast, while I was on the East Coast. As a result, sometimes she would schedule meetings for the next morning, but do so long after I had gone home for the day. Because I wasn't there to manually synchronize my work computer to Yahoo! Calendar, those requests didn't get synchronized to my home computer, regardless of how many times I synchronized my home computer with Yahoo! Calendar. A solution that continually synchronized my work computer to Yahoo! Calendar so I could see it on my home computer would have alleviated this problem.

Mind you, no information was ever lost, because the next time I synchronized my work computer to Yahoo! Calendar, everything got synchronized just fine. Even so, it defeated the purpose of synchronizing my work computer with my home computer if I still didn't find out about a meeting until I reached the office.

Another, smaller drawback is that you need to install the synchronization software on each of the computers that you want to keep synchronized. Yet another drawback is that the Intellisync for Yahoo! help system cannot (at the time of this writing) be viewed on computers running Windows Vista. Hopefully this will have been updated by the time you read this chapter.

A third possible drawback has to do with the way your computer is configured. Many companies restrict the applications users can install on their work computers in some way. You might not be allowed to install a program such as Intellisync for Yahoo! at work, or perhaps your computer is set up so that only an administrator can install any software on your computer. Check with the IT department before installing Intellisync for Yahoo! at work.

If you are interested in trying out this approach, the following section walks you through setting up the software on a PC and synchronizing with Yahoo! Calendar. The first step is to get a Yahoo! account if you don't already have one you want to use for this.

Getting a Yahoo! Account

A Yahoo! account that you can use for this project is free. To get one, follow these steps:

1. Browse to http://www.yahoo.com.

2. On the Yahoo! home page, click the My Yahoo! button or link. This takes you to the My Yahoo! home page.

3. Click the "Sign Up Now – It's FREE!" link in the Sign in section of the page.

4. Yahoo! walks you through one or more pages where you can specify your interests for the My Yahoo! page that is created as part of the sign-up process. Eventually, you will get to a page where you find another Sign Up link.

5. Click the Sign Up link. A form appears.

6. Fill in the fields on the form and click the Submit This Form Securely button to create your Yahoo! ID and password. When you are successful, the Registration Completed page will appear. Follow the directions on this page to go to your My Yahoo! home page.

7. The Registration Completed page mentions a confirmation message. That message is sent to the Yahoo! mail address you created during registration.

15

This address has the form of YahooID@yahoo.com. When you arrive at your My Yahoo! home page, find and click a Mail link to go to your Yahoo! Mail Inbox. Review this message to see if there's anything you want or need to do. Once you are done with this message, click the Calendar tab at the top of the page. This takes you to your Yahoo! Calendar, which will be pretty empty since you just created the account.

Installing Intellisync for Yahoo!

As mentioned earlier, the software you install on your computer to enable it to synchronize with Yahoo! Calendar is called Intellisync for Yahoo! (Intellisync for short). You get Intellisync free from Yahoo! if you have a Yahoo! account. The following steps show you how to acquire and install Intellisync for Yahoo!:

1. On your Yahoo! Calendar page, click the Sync link near the top right of the page. This takes you to the Intellisync for Yahoo! page shown here.

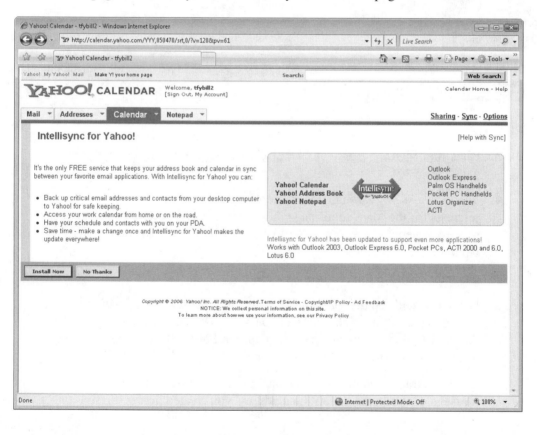

2. Read the information about Intellisync for Yahoo!, then click Install Now.

Even though it doesn't say so on this page, Intellisync for Yahoo! works fine with Outlook 2007 since both Outlook 2003 (which it already supported) and Outlook 2007 use the same format for their .PST files.

3. Follow the instructions on the pages that appear, then download and run intellisync.exe (the Intellisync for Yahoo! program).

Windows may display a security warning when you do this, stating that it cannot verify the publisher of intellisync.exe. Ignore that warning and run the program anyway.

Internet Explorer - Security Warning	[X]
The publisher could not be verified. Are you sure you want to run this software?	
Name: intellisync.exe	
Publisher: **Unknown Publisher**	
	[Run] [Don't Run]
⊗ This file does not have a valid digital signature that verifies its publisher. You should only run software from publishers you trust. How can I decide what software to run?	

4. Work through the steps of the Intellisync Setup Wizard. You can accept all the default options.

5. When you see the InstallShield Wizard Complete screen, click Finish. Don't set the Launch Intellisync for Yahoo! check box.

Look at your Windows desktop. You will see the Intellisync icon on the desktop.

You will use this icon to launch the program whenever you want to configure Intellisync or synchronize this computer with your Yahoo! Calendar.

Configure Intellisync for Yahoo!

Configuring Intellisync involves telling it how to connect to your Yahoo! account, entering any proxy server settings that might apply to your Internet connection,

15

and telling it which Outlook folders to synchronize to Yahoo! Calendar. Follow these steps to configure Intellisync:

1. Launch Intellisync for Yahoo! using the desktop icon. This opens the Settings & Configuration window, which looks like the one in Figure 15-2.

2. Enter your Yahoo! ID and password. If you would like to avoid reentering this information every time you synchronize this PC with Yahoo! Calendar, set the Remember My Password check box as well.

3. If your computer uses a proxy server to connect to the Internet, click the Proxy Server Settings button and enter the appropriate information in the dialog box that appears.

4. It's time to tell Intellisync what information you want it to synchronize with Yahoo! Calendar. Click Application Settings. This opens the application configuration dialog box shown in Figure 15-3. Look at the Yahoo! Applications window in the figure. It lists the Yahoo! applications that you can synchronize with Outlook. The naming conventions in Yahoo! are different from those in Outlook, so just be aware that Address Book in this dialog box corresponds to Outlook Contacts, Notepad to Outlook Notes, and To Do List to Outlook Tasks.

FIGURE 15-2   The Intellisync for Yahoo! Settings & Configuration window.

Use this dialog box to control which information gets synchronized.

5. If you want to synchronize your Outlook Contacts, set the Address Book
    check box. This opens the Choose Application dialog box.

6. In the Available Applications list, select MS Outlook. When you do, the
    Operation section of the dialog box become active. Assuming you want to
    synchronize your main Contacts folder, make sure that Operation is set to
    Synchronize and then click OK.

15

CAUTION   *You can make synchronization very complicated by setting all sorts of options and synchronizing folders other than the default ones. For most of us, there is no need to do any of that, and synchronizing the default folders with the default options is all we are really interested in. Mess with that other stuff at your own risk!*

7. Repeat steps 5 and 6 for each of the other Yahoo! applications. Once you have configured Intellisync for Yahoo! to synchronize everything you want, click OK. This returns you to the Settings & Configuration window shown in Figure 15-2.

8. Click Save to go to the main Intellisync for Yahoo! window shown in Figure 15-4. Now that you have configured Intellisync for Yahoo!, this is the window that will appear when you launch the program.

You now have Intellisync for Yahoo! configured to synchronize this computer with Yahoo! Calendar. All that remains is to do your first synchronization.

Synchronize a PC with Intellisync for Yahoo!

When you are ready to synchronize a PC using Intellisync, follow these steps:

1. If it is not already running, start Intellisync.

2. Click the Sync button. A Synchronization progress dialog box pops up to show you what's happening.

FIGURE 15-4   The main Intellisync for Yahoo! window.

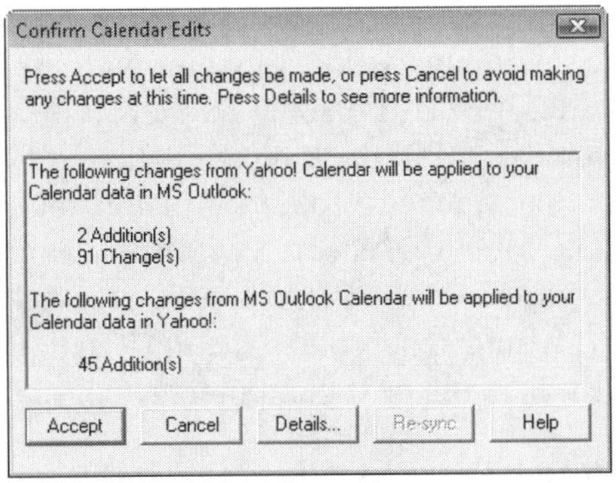

FIGURE 15-5   Intellisync shows you the potential changes so you can decide what to do next.

3. Once it analyzes the differences between an Outlook folder on your PC and the corresponding data on Yahoo!, Intellisync displays a dialog box like the one in Figure 15-5, showing the changes it suggests for a particular folder.

4. Click Accept to allow Intellisync to make the changes it suggests. If you want a detailed description of each change it suggest, click Details. Click Cancel to abort all changes for this folder.

5. Steps 3 and 4 repeat for each folder that Intellisync is configured to synchronize.

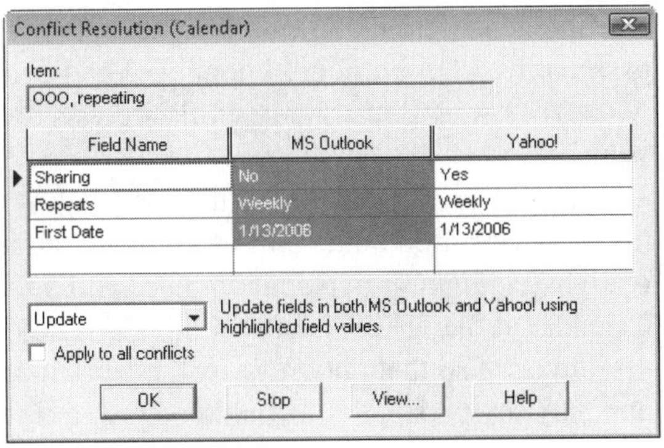

When there is a conflict between the data on Yahoo! Calendar and the data on a computer, Intellisync displays a Conflict Resolution dialog box similar to the following one. In it, Intellisync displays the conflicting data side by side so you can choose how to deal with the conflict. You have to use your own judgment here, basing it on your knowledge of the situation. I can't give you more specific guidance beyond that. Sorry.

Let's look at some other ways to get your Outlook data to be available wherever you need it.

15

The PDA Shuttle

My next stab at synchronizing my work computer with my home computer involved the PDA Shuttle. A *PDA* (Personal Digital Assistant) is a handheld device that can store some or all of the kinds of data that Outlook contains in its *PIM* (Personal Information Manager) folders—that is, the Calendar, Contacts, Tasks, and Notes folders. Most PDAs come with software that allows them to synchronize with Outlook. To do the PDA Shuttle, all I did was replace Yahoo! Calendar with a PDA. I would synchronize the PDA with Outlook on one computer, then when I was at the next computer, synchronize the PDA with Outlook on that one.

CAUTION   *Just as some companies will prevent you from installing a product such as Intellisync for Yahoo! on your work computer, some companies will prevent you from installing PDA synchronization software on your work computer. As before, check with the IT department before trying to synchronize with your work computer.*

You may be wondering what the heck I accomplished by this. Wasn't it easier to let the computers synchronize through Yahoo! Calendar? Wasn't I even more likely to miss a meeting notice or other Outlook change if the only time my computers were synchronized was when I physically carried my PDA between them? Yes, it was easier to let the computers synchronize through Yahoo! Calendar. Yes, I was more likely to miss a change this way.

There was, however, one overwhelming advantage to this approach: I could see my Calendar, Tasks, and Contacts when I was away from either computer. As long as I had my PDA with me, I could see and even change much of my Outlook data wherever I was. Because my work life was becoming more mobile, this was very valuable.

Another big advantage of this approach was that I could set things up so all my data wasn't on both computers. Think about this for a minute: Would you really want *all* your personal contacts and appointments to appear on your Outlook Calendar at the office? I know I didn't. With the PDA Shuttle approach, I could set things up so that only my work information appeared in Outlook at the office, and only my personal information showed up in Outlook at home, but *all* my information appeared on my PDA, and all of it was accessible wherever I was.

Most PDAs are designed to synchronize data with Outlook. They typically come with a program that you install on your computer to handle the synchronization chores. When you connect your PDA to the computer (using a cable or some kind of docking cradle), you can manually or automatically synchronize the data stored in the PDA with the data in Outlook. By synchronizing the PDA with each of your computers, you can shuttle data between them all to keep them synchronized.

In Windows Vista, the Windows Mobile Device Center handles the synchronization chores (for PDAs running Windows Mobile 2003 or Windows Mobile 5.0 software). You can configure it to synchronize not only e-mail, calendar, task, and contact information from Outlook, but Mobile Favorites (links to websites), multimedia files (videos and music), and Microsoft Office OneNote as well.

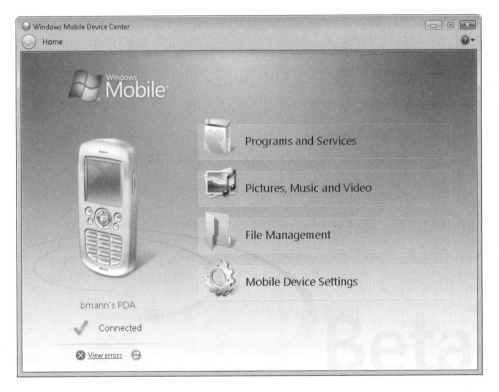

As of this writing, Windows Mobile Device Center was still a beta product. Visit Living With Outlook (http://www.living-with-outlook.com) for a detailed look at the released version of Windows Mobile Device Center once it is available.

NOTE

15

We've already covered some of the pros and cons of this approach. The biggest benefit of this approach is that it lets you bring a copy of your Outlook data with you wherever you go. Drawbacks include the hassle of manually connecting your

PDA to each computer to synchronize it, and the fact that the data for a given computer is only as current as the last time you synchronized the PDA to that computer.

Another issue here is that plain-old PDAs are themselves dying out. Over the last few years, PDAs and mobile phones have merged into smartphones, single devices that serve as both phone and PDA. The logic of this is hard to refute: Why carry two electronic gizmos wherever you go when you can carry one that replaces both? We will talk more about smartphones later in the chapter. For now, I want to tell you about Outlook Web Access.

Mobilize Outlook

PDAs, smartphones, Outlook Web Access. Technologies like these are becoming more and more important because we are becoming more and more mobile. The rest of this chapter looks at some ways to get your Outlook data to travel with you wherever you are. I'm not even talking about synchronizing your PDA with Outlook, then carrying around a copy of your data. I'm talking about having full-time, live access to your latest Outlook data, wherever you are, thanks to wireless technology and some smart software.

One thing all of these technologies have in common is that they require some sort of wireless Internet connection. If you have a laptop or some kind of PDA with Wi-Fi wireless networking capabilities, you can get a wireless Internet connection at thousands of wireless hotspots around the world. Places such as Panera Bread provide free access to customers, with the goal of getting people in the store and eating the food. Some wireless hotspots are provided by individuals or groups as a public service. Some towns provide service to their entire downtown area, treating wireless Internet access like any other municipal service.

The other form of wireless Internet access is through the pager or cell phone networks. People with smartphones (or notebook computers with the appropriate add-in card) can tap into these wide-area wireless networks to get their connection without regard to the location of hotspots, although they still have to deal with dead coverage areas.

In either case, the availability of a wireless connection makes it possible to have live access to your Outlook data. There are lots of different ways for this to happen. Instead of trying to break down the various solutions into different categories or anything like that, I'm using the rest of this chapter to describe some of the types of solutions that are out there. If you decide to go for wireless access to your Outlook data, you will need to investigate the specific solutions that are available for the device you are using and the wireless carrier you choose.

Desktop Solutions

A desktop solution is a synchronization program that runs on your (desktop) computer as opposed to running on a mail server such as Microsoft Exchange. These kinds of solutions will watch for changes to your Outlook data, and synchronize the changed information whenever it changes, or on a set schedule.

The Wireless Sync software that came with my Motorola Q smartphone is a good example. Once installed and configured on my desktop computer, it can send synchronization messages across the cell phone network (Verizon Wireless in this case) to and from my phone, automatically keeping the information on the phone and desktop computer up to date. This includes my Outlook Inbox, so I can work with my e-mail as well as my Calendar, Contacts, and other personal information.

At first blush, this sounds like the perfect solution, at least for having live access to my Outlook data on my phone. As always, there is a drawback. This kind of solution relies on Outlook to download the information being pushed out to the phone. But this can only happen when the desktop push software is running and so is Outlook. If your computer and these two programs aren't running, your phone doesn't get updated. So either you leave your computer, Outlook, and the desktop push software running at all times, or you accept that synchronization won't occur when any of those aren't running for any reason.

A desktop solution can be particularly effective when you have multiple e-mail accounts from different services. Imagine that you have an Exchange e-mail account, a Yahoo! Mail account, and a Gmail account. Those all come through different services. The only place messages from all three services appear together is in the Outlook Inbox on your desktop. A desktop solution can see the messages from all three services and pass them along to your phone. A server-based solution, the subject of the next section, sees only the messages that go through that particular server.

> NOTE *While this kind of solution is usually used for synchronizing between Outlook and a phone, you can now get mobile data cards that fit into a notebook computer and connect it to a cell phone network. It is possible that you will be able to find software that works with one of these cards to synchronize Outlook data between desktop computer and notebook computer.*

15

Use Outlook Web Access

Outlook Web Access is a way to work with your Outlook data using a secure connection on a web browser. Outlook Web Access creates a reasonable facsimile of the Outlook window in your web browser (Internet Explorer works best for this), where you have most of the capabilities you would have if you were sitting at your regular PC working in Outlook. The following illustration shows Outlook Web Access for Exchange Server 2003. Note how much it looks like Outlook. The version for Exchange 2007 will look even more like Outlook 2007, including such features as Unified Messaging (see Chapter 17 for more on Unified Messaging) and automatic e-mail updates (no more clicking Check Message to see if you have new mail).

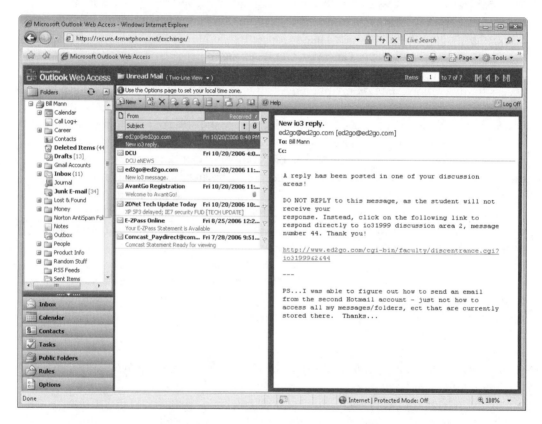

NOTE   *Outlook Web Access is only available if your Outlook data is stored on a Microsoft Exchange server.*

Using Outlook Web Access is a different approach than the synchronization approaches we've talked about so far. Here you don't try to get the copy of Outlook at home to contain the same data as you see in Outlook at the office. Instead, you are working with your Outlook data without regard for the computer you are working at. Within the bounds of any company policies regarding data access, you can use Outlook Web Access to work with the data stored on Exchange from anywhere in the world that has an Internet connection. Oftentimes, just being able to check your Calendar, or see if that message from the Tokyo office has arrived, is enough, and total integration of all your business and personal data isn't necessary.

If you want to try Outlook Web Access, and your Outlook data is stored on an Exchange server, contact the IT department or the E-mail Administrator in charge of Microsoft Exchange, and ask about getting access. They will provide you with the URL to use to connect to Outlook Web Access, along with any policies or procedures associated with using this capability.

> TIP   *While Outlook Web Access is normally a way to get at your work data, there are some solutions for personal data too. I'll tell you more at the end of this chapter.*

Get Data on Your Phone with SMS Link

SMS Link for Microsoft Office Outlook 2007 (SMS Link) is a service that lets you send and receive text messages between Outlook and any mobile phone that supports SMS messaging (texting). With SMS Link, you can receive e-mails and reminders as text messages, even view a copy of your calendar for the day. You can also send messages from your phone through SMS Link.

SMS Link is designed to keep you in the loop when it comes to vital, time-sensitive information. It doesn't allow you to browse through your Inbox or work with old items. It is a limited interface to Outlook for dealing with real-time events. To use SMS Link, you must have an SMS-compatible mobile phone (most are), a text messaging plan for that phone, and must sign up with a mobile service provider.

At the time of this writing, SMS Link for Microsoft Office Outlook 2007 was just coming online. You can find the latest information on SMS Link for Microsoft Office Outlook 2007 on the SMS Link page at the Living With Outlook website (http://www.living-with-outlook.com/sms-link.html).

Is a Hosted Exchange Mailbox the Answer?

We've looked at a few different solutions for taking your Outlook data with you. But when it comes right down to it, Outlook is designed from the ground up to work with a Microsoft Exchange server. If you use Outlook at work, it is probably connected to an Exchange server. If your company has Outlook Web Access set up,

15

and you have a PDA, smartphone, or notebook computer with wireless Internet access, you can probably get at your office Outlook data from anywhere.

But what about your personal Outlook data? Wouldn't it be cool if you could have your personal Outlook data on an Exchange server? Then you would have all the benefits for both work and home.

As the title of this session has already tipped off, you can get an Exchange mailbox for your personal e-mail. And you can do it without even having to change your e-mail address. It'll cost you a few bucks a month, but you can get something called a hosted Exchange mailbox that may be the closest thing possible to a perfect way to access your Outlook data from anywhere.

Several companies run Microsoft Exchange servers that are accessible across the Internet. For a fee, they will host one or more mailboxes for you on their Exchange servers. When you sign up, you provide them with the information they need to log onto your existing e-mail account. With this, their servers connect to your existing e-mail account and download your messages into your new Exchange mailbox. You reconfigure Outlook to connect to the new Exchange mailbox, and everything is set. You send and receive e-mail normally, except that it is now going through the hosted Exchange mailbox.

TIP *Hosted Exchange services like this can also be a great way for small businesses to get the benefits of Outlook and Exchange without installing and supporting their own Exchange server. See the "Did You Know Small Businesses Can Outsource Their E-Mail" box for more information.*

Did you know?

Small Businesses Can Outsource Their E-Mail

If you are a small business owner, hosted Exchange services such as 4SmartPhone could be very useful to you. Instead of installing and maintaining your own Exchange server, and handling all the technical issues necessary to give your employees mobile access to their e-mail and other data, let a third party do it for you.

For a reasonable monthly fee, you can get multiple Exchange accounts with shared access to folders and all the other benefits of Microsoft Exchange, all accessible through your existing Internet connections. In many cases, you can even get free copies of Outlook for each user, sparing you the expense and hassle of purchasing a new copy of Outlook every time you add an employee.

Why do all this? Because having your mail on an Exchange server gives you several big advantages. You can have several copies of Outlook all pointing to the same Exchange mailbox, with all of them synchronized to it, without worries about programs running on the desktop or remembering to click the Sync button before leaving the office or anything like that.

As you've probably guessed by now, I like this approach, and am using it myself. The particular service I use is from a company called 4SmartPhone (http://www.4smartphone.net). As the name implies, this service caters to smartphone users—in particular, to users with smartphones running one of the Windows mobile operating systems—but it works with "most data-enabled phones, smartphones, and wireless PDAs."

Not only 4SmartPhone can synchronize your Exchange mailbox with the kinds of devices described here, but a subscription to the service includes a free copy of Outlook 2003 (it is highly likely that you will be able to get a free copy of Outlook 2007 instead of 2003 once 2007 ships). Although 4SmartPhone hadn't said anything officially about Outlook 2007 support as of mid-October 2006, the Outlook Web

15

Access version that they provide (yes, you get Outlook Web Access as part of the monthly fee) already includes an RSS Feeds folder as you can see in Figure 15-6.

To give you some idea of how useful this service can be, let me tell you how I use it. I have a Professional membership to 4SmartPhone, which gives me (among other things) a free copy of Outlook 2003, and the ability to synchronize between my Exchange mailbox and Outlook (synchronization with a smartphone is included in all levels of subscription).

I have set up 4SmartPhone so their server takes mail from my main personal e-mail account and some of my secondary accounts and makes it available in my Exchange mailbox. 4SmartPhone provides pretty solid instructions on how to configure your smartphone to work with their service, and can create a configuration file that you can download and transfer to the phone so you don't have to do the work manually. Similarly, they provide instructions and a downloadable profile for synchronizing Outlook to the Exchange mailbox.

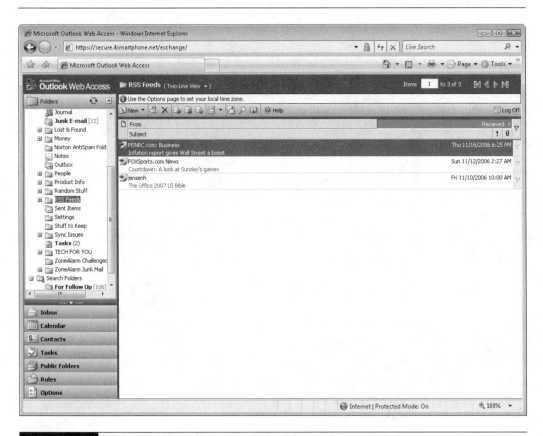

FIGURE 15-6   Outlook Web Access to my hosted Exchange account.

I used these tools to configure the copies of Outlook on my desktop computer, my notebook, and my smartphone to get their data from the Exchange mailbox. Now my phone and all my copies of Outlook are always in synch with each other. I can read a copy of a message or make a change to my schedule on the phone, and the changes automatically get synchronized to Outlook on my PCs. Similarly, changes I make on either PC find their way to the other two. Remember, too, that because you connect to this kind of account across the Internet, you aren't tied down. I sometimes work at the local Panera Bread shop while grabbing lunch. They have a wireless access point I can connect to, so I have my mail right there. This is exactly what I needed on the home front.

There are only two snags in this approach that I can see. One is that setting up a hosted Exchange mailbox account can be a little more difficult than setting up a regular e-mail account. There are a few extra steps required, and a few more options to think about when it comes to how the Exchange server interacts with the server that hosts your original e-mail account.

The other snag is that you can only have Outlook talk to one Exchange account in any user profile. I still need to use Outlook Web Access or one of the solutions we discussed earlier if I want to see my corporate Outlook data at home, or my personal Outlook data at work. But perhaps that's for the best in the end. All my information is accessible at any location now, even if it isn't intermingled. I have the option to manually copy items between work and home Exchange accounts when it is appropriate, while my personal privacy and my company's corporate information are both otherwise protected. Not a bad solution for a few bucks a month.

> **TIP** *The 4SmartPhone section of my Living With Outlook website (http://www .living-with-outlook.com/4smartphone.html) provides detailed step-by-step instructions on how to connect a 4SmartPhone-hosted account to your current POP3 e-mail account, and from there to Outlook and your smartphone. You will also find a discussion of the pros and cons of each particular option you need to select when you set up the account, and a link to a 15-day free trial of the service.*

15

As you've seen in this chapter, getting access to your Outlook data from anywhere can be complicated. There is no one perfect solution for every situation. There are, however, lots of different options available. With a little work and some compromises, getting access to your Outlook data from anywhere is possible.

Chapter 16

Integration with Office 2007

How to...

- Share Information Between Outlook and Other Office 2007 system Applications
- Work with OneNote, Groove, and InfoPath 2007
- Use Smart Tags to Interact with Other Applications

As part of the 2007 Microsoft Office system, Outlook is designed to interact smoothly with basic applications such as Word, Excel, Access, and PowerPoint. You've seen examples of this throughout the book, such as using Word as your Outlook e-mail editor and linking documents to an Outlook contact.

Outlook also works well with relative newcomers InfoPath, OneNote, and Groove. We talk about each of them separately, so you can get a real feel for what's possible. We won't go into too much depth though—this is *How to Do Everything with Microsoft Office Outlook 2007*, after all, so we do have to stay focused on the Outlook side of things.

This chapter covers some more general ways that Outlook can interact with the other applications in the Office system. The most basic ways involve copying and pasting information between Outlook items and documents created with other applications. These are followed by ways to link documents to Outlook items or embed them within Outlook items.

Smart Tags provide a more sophisticated way for Office system applications to interact. Smart Tags help you work with various types of information in documents, and can activate Outlook to do things such as schedule a meeting on a date that appears in a Word document.

Share Information Between Outlook and Other Office 2007 System Applications

You can share information between Outlook and other Office system applications in several ways. You can:

- Cut and paste information between documents in different applications.
- Drag and drop information between documents in different applications.
- Collect and paste multiple items of information into multiple Office system applications.
- Link or embed files in an Outlook item.

Copy, Cut, and Paste Information

This is a basic way to share information between Outlook and other Office system applications. When doing this, you really want to have memorized these three simple keyboard shortcuts:

- ■ CTRL-X is the keyboard shortcut for Cut. This cuts the selected content out of the document it is in now and puts it on the Clipboard.

- ■ CTRL-C is the keyboard shortcut for Copy. This copies the selected content from the document it is in now (without removing it from that document) and puts it on the Clipboard.

- ■ CTRL-V is the keyboard shortcut for Paste. This pastes the last content you cut or copied at the location of the cursor.

You've probably cut, copied, and pasted in Office documents such as Word before, even if you didn't use the keyboard shortcuts. There are two huge advantages of learning and using these shortcuts. One is that they are just more efficient than clicking menu options or Ribbon commands.

The second advantage is that you can use them (at least you can use CTRL-C) in places where you don't have menu options or Ribbon commands available. This means that you can copy content from a message or item that you can't otherwise edit. A good example of this would be when a buddy e-mails you a cool quotation or interesting bit of text. You can select it and copy it right from the e-mail message and use it in another document with a minimum of fuss.

Drag and Drop Information

Dragging and dropping is the mouse equivalent of cutting, copying, and pasting. Here you select the information you want to share, then drag it (point at the information with the mouse cursor, press and hold the left mouse button, then drag the information) to a new location in the new document. If you drag by holding down the right mouse button, a shortcut menu appears that lets you choose to copy or paste the information, as appropriate.

16

Collect Information to Paste into Office System Applications

If you have only one or two chunks of information you want to move between Outlook and other Office system applications, you can use the standard Windows cut-and-paste or drag-and-drop operation to get the job done. But if you have a lot of stuff to move, you should consider using the Clipboard, which allows you to collect up to 24 items and paste them into any Office system application. In Figure 16-1, the Clipboard is the pane at the far right of the Outlook window. As you can see from the figure, with the Clipboard open, things can get kind of crowded on the screen. Even so, when you are moving masses of content from one Office application to another, it comes in mighty handy.

TIP *See the "How to Collect and Paste Between Applications" sidebar for detailed instructions on working with the Clipboard.*

When you are done moving the current chunks of content through the Clipboard, you can make room for a fresh batch by clicking Clear All.

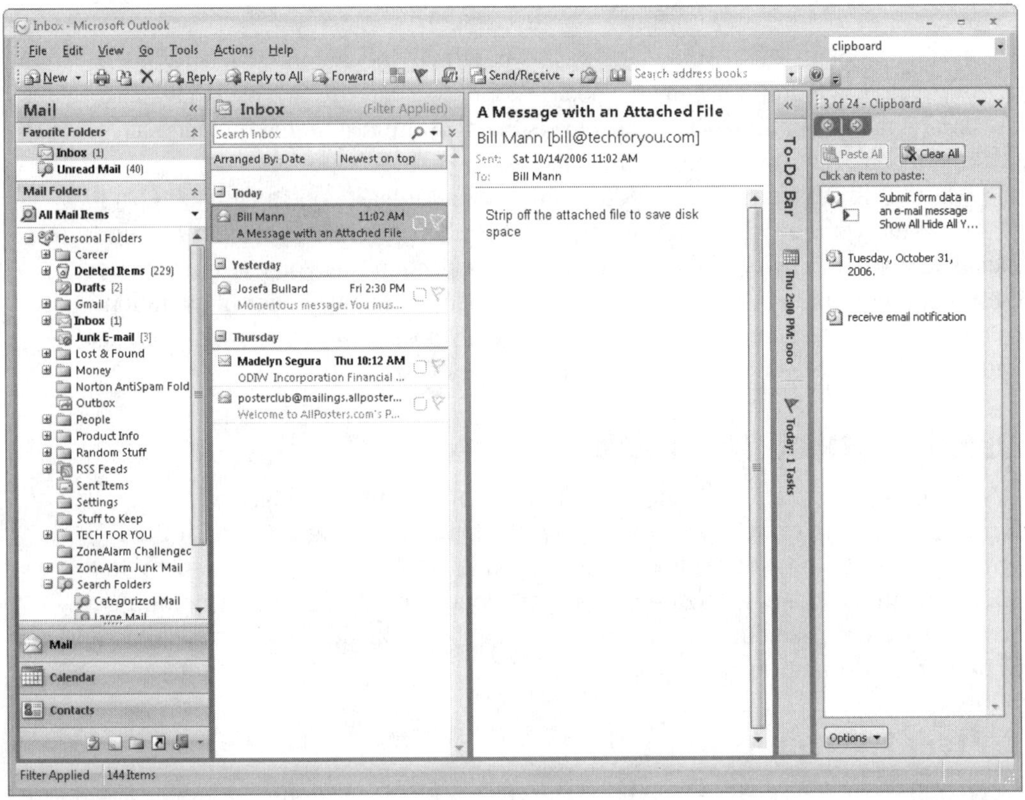

FIGURE 16-1 Gather multiple chunks of information in the Clipboard.

How to ...   Collect and Paste Between Applications

Follow these steps to collect items that you want to paste into Outlook or copy from Outlook into another application:

1. If the Clipboard isn't visible, click Edit | Office Clipboard from the main menu in any open Office system application to open the Clipboard.

2. Select one of the items you want to copy into another application, then click Copy on the Standard toolbar. This adds the item to the Clipboard, where it appears as an icon along with the first bit of the text you copied.

3. Repeat steps 1 and 2 for each item you want to add to the Clipboard. You can collect up to 24 items in the Clipboard.

To paste items from the Clipboard into Outlook or another Office system application, follow these steps:

1. If the Clipboard isn't visible, click File | Office Clipboard in any open Office system application to open the Clipboard.

   NOTE   *The Clipboard may not be available in some Outlook views. In this case, you must use drag and drop or some other technique to paste the item into the view.*

2. Click the spot in Outlook or any other Office system application where you want to paste an item from the Clipboard.

3. Click the item (or items) you want to paste into this location.

4. Repeat as necessary.

   TIP   *If you want to paste all the items in the Clipboard to the same location, click Paste All in the Clipboard pane.*

16

Link or Embed Office System Documents in Outlook Items

The ways of sharing information that we've covered so far in this section have one flaw: They put a copy of the information in a new location, instead of maintaining a direct link to the original file the information comes from. This is important when the information you're interested in can change. If you just copy (or collect) and paste information between documents and the original document changes, the documents you copied the information into won't get changed. That's where linking or embedding documents comes into play.

In Chapter 6, you learned about linking Office system documents to an Outlook contact. You can similarly link part or all of an Office system document to an Outlook item. When you create a link like this, there is a connection between the linked document and the Outlook item. If the original document changes, that change is reflected in the Outlook item that is linked to it.

Complications arise when you plan to share or e-mail Outlook items containing linked documents. Making the link to the original document accessible to people using different computers, different parts of the corporate network, or even different networks altogether requires special steps. See the Link or Embed Files topic in the Outlook help system for more information on how to create linked documents and what you must do to make those links work in various circumstances.

Did you know?

How Easily You Can E-Mail Documents?

The integration between Outlook and other Microsoft Office 2007 system applications such as Word and Excel makes it easy to e-mail copies of documents you are working on. If the application is displaying a menu bar, click Tools, then Send E-mail. If it is displaying the Ribbon, click the Office button, then E-mail, or Send.

In either case, an Outlook new message window appears, with the document included as an attachment. All you need to do is fill in the rest of the information needed to send the message, and click Send. Sending a copy of a document couldn't get any faster than this.

You can also embed a copy of an Office system document into an Outlook item. In this case, the embedded document becomes part of the Outlook item. If you make changes to the embedded document, those changes appear in the Outlook item, but there is no link back to the original document. Again, see the Link or Embed Files topic in the Outlook help system for more information.

TIP

Office 2007 makes it easy to send copies of documents using Outlook. See "Did You Know How Easily You Can E-mail Documents?" for more information.

Work with OneNote, Groove, and InfoPath 2007

These three applications are newer additions to the Microsoft Office system, and each of them can interact well with Outlook. As I mentioned at the top of the chapter, we need to stay focused on the Outlook side of things, so I won't go into the details of how these other applications work beyond giving you the information you need to understand how Outlook can interact with them. Ready?

Outlook and OneNote

OneNote 2007 is a tool for gathering, organizing, searching, and sharing information of all sorts. You might envision it as an electronic form of a paper notebook. That's the metaphor Microsoft uses for the product, organizing its content into individual notebooks, colored tabs, and pages.

OneNote 2007 can interact with Outlook 2007 in several ways. With the two applications installed on your computer, you can:

■ Create Outlook tasks in OneNote

■ Link OneNote notes to Outlook meetings and contacts

■ Send e-mail messages from Outlook to OneNote

■ Send e-mail message from within OneNote

16

Of these four activities, two of them require you to do things in Outlook. Here are instructions for linking OneNote notes to Outlook meetings and contacts, and sending e-mail messages from Outlook to OneNote.

Link OneNote Notes to Outlook Meetings and Contacts

If you have OneNote installed on your computer, linking OneNote notes to Outlook meetings or contacts is really simple. Take a look at Figure 16-2. Notice the Contact Notes button in the OneNote group at the right end of the Ribbon. If you were to open a meeting request, you would see the same group. This is the visible part of the connection between Outlook and OneNote notes.

When you are ready to add a OneNote note to a contact, just click this button and a new OneNote page (like the one in Figure 16-3) appears in the Unfiled Notes area of OneNote.

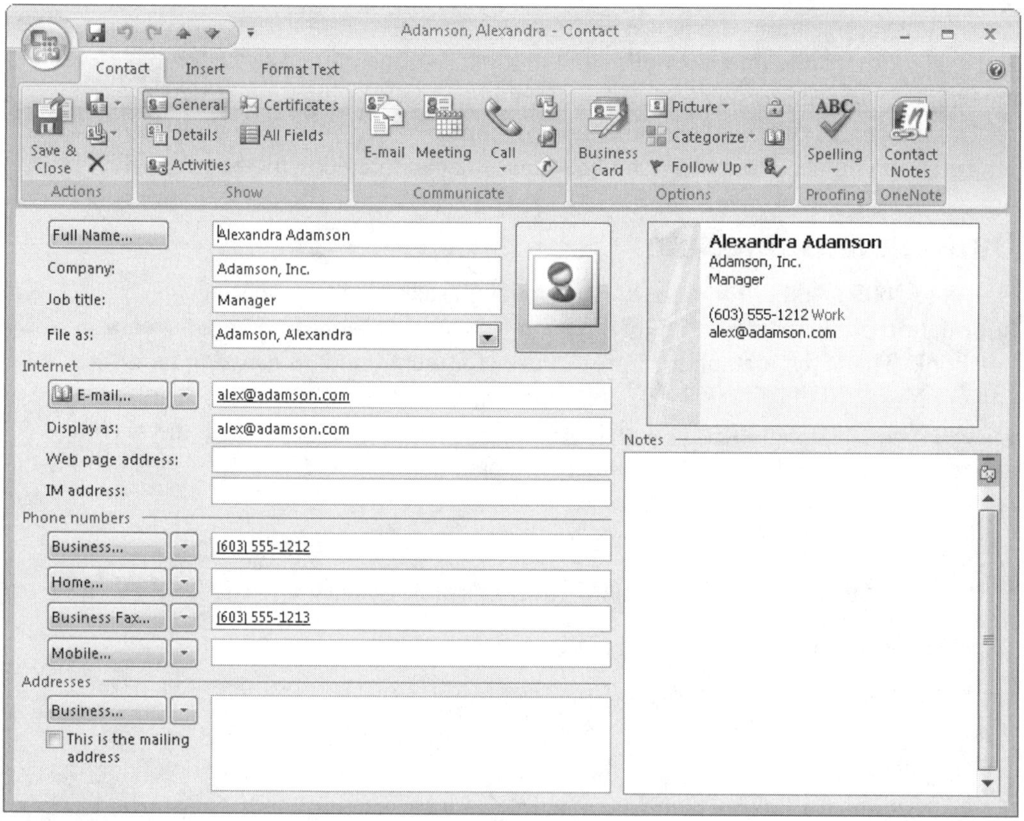

FIGURE 16-2 Adding OneNote notes to Outlook contacts or meetings takes only a few clicks.

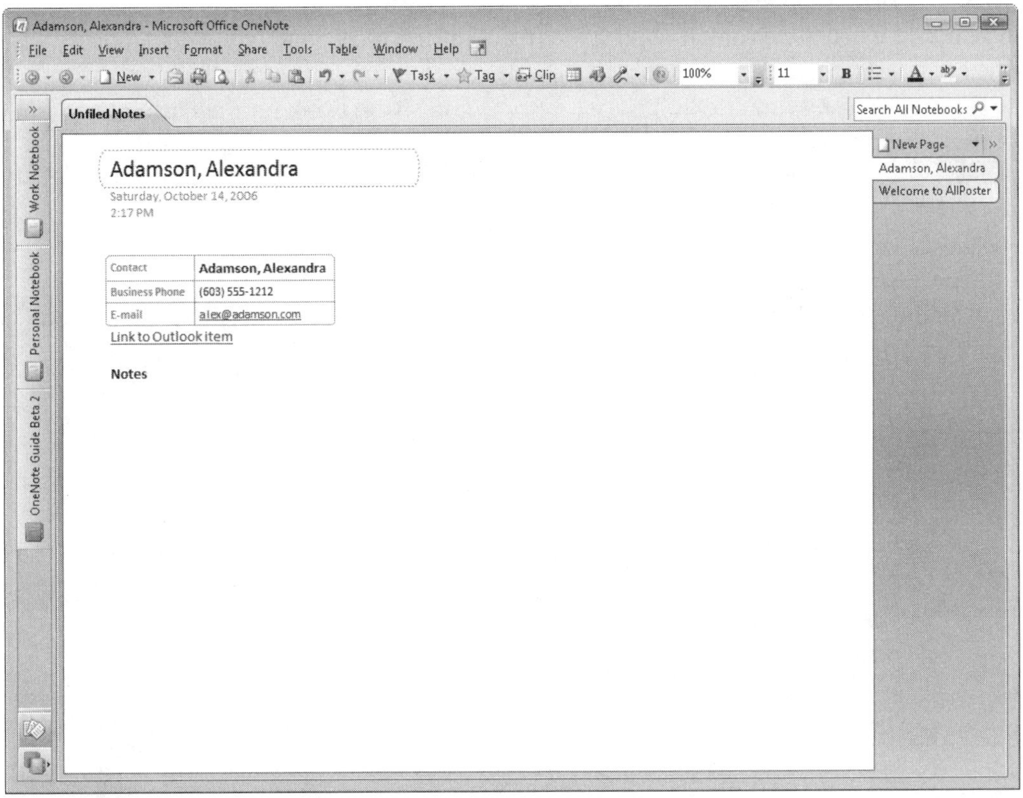

FIGURE 16-3   A OneNote note that is linked to an Outlook contact.

Once the note exists, you can use all of OneNote's capabilities to enter information into the note. This can include text, images, sound or video clips, chunks of web pages, all sorts of goodies.

NOTE   *Look at Figure 16-3 again. Do you see the Link to Outlook Item link? This is the way to go from the OneNote note to the linked Outlook item (the Alexandra Adamson contact in this example).*

Once you create a linked OneNote note for a particular contact or meeting, clicking the OneNote button in that Outlook item opens that note instead of creating another new one.

16

Send E-Mail Messages from Outlook to OneNote

If you start to use OneNote as a place to collect information, you will eventually want to get information from Outlook e-mail messages into OneNote. This, too, is a matter of just a few clicks. Take a look at Figure 16-4. Look for the OneNote button directly to the left of Send/Receive.

When you click this button, Outlook sends a copy of the selected e-mail message to OneNote, where it appears in the Unfiled Notes area, just like the contact and meeting notes we created in the previous section.

The difference between this process and the one in the last section is that the copy of the e-mail that appears in OneNote is not linked to the message in Outlook. Editing the message in OneNote does not affect what you see in Outlook in any way.

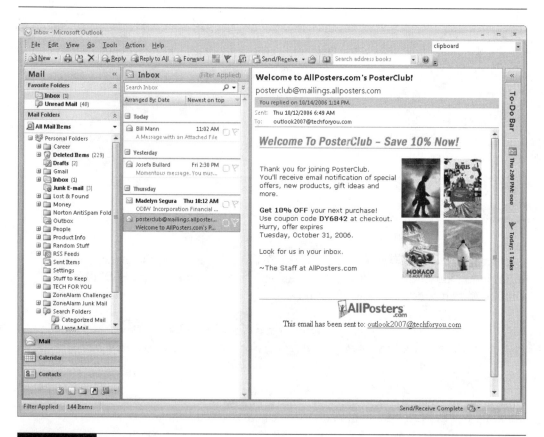

FIGURE 16-4   A couple of clicks sends a copy of an e-mail from Outlook to OneNote.

Still, this is a great way to get content out of e-mail messages and into OneNote. It's certainly easier than the copy-and-paste techniques we talked about before.

Outlook and Groove

Groove 2007 is an electronic collaboration tool that allows teams to create virtual shared workspaces that are accessible from anywhere member's computers can get Internet access. Groove keeps an encrypted copy of the virtual workspace on each member's computer, and synchronizes any changes as they occur. Even when a computer doesn't have Internet access, you can still work in your copy of the virtual workspace, and Groove will automatically synchronize any changes with other members as soon as a connection is restored.

TIP   *You can learn more about Groove by visiting www.groove.net.*

Groove 2007 can use Outlook to send invitations to new workgroup members. There's nothing you really need to do to make this happen. It all goes on automatically in the background.

Outlook and InfoPath

InfoPath is an electronic forms application. With InfoPath, users can design electronic forms and use them to gather information that can then be analyzed in Excel or other applications. Where Outlook fits into this equation is in the distribution and collection of those electronic forms. InfoPath 2007 can create forms that can be distributed as e-mail messages through Outlook 2007. Recipients of these messages need only click Reply, fill out the form, and send it. Outlook and InfoPath work together to get the form into the original e-mail message and get the information out of the reply.

As with Groove, there isn't really anything you need to do on the Outlook side of the fence for this to work. Outlook simply provides the means for moving the InfoPath forms back and forth.

Smart Tags Mean Smart Interactions Between Applications

16

Smart Tags are a feature of Microsoft Office system that first appeared in Office XP. Smart Tags can help you complete common Office system tasks, as well as provide additional control over various automatic features of Office. Of particular interest to us in this book, Smart Tags can cause other Office system applications to interact with Outlook. For example, one Smart Tag option in Word helps you create an Outlook appointment starting with a date in a Word document.

Smart Tags are indicated by a series of purple dots under text in documents, or by a little purple triangle in the lower-right corner of Excel spreadsheet cells. When you place the cursor over a Smart Tag, a small button appears on the screen above the tagged text or cell. When you point to this button with the mouse, a small down arrow appears next to it. Clicking this down arrow opens a menu containing the actions provided by the Smart Tag.

The Smart Tag button of most interest when it comes to making Outlook work with other Office system applications is the Smart Tag Actions button. This button, which appears as an *i* inside a circle, inside a square (see the following illustration), offers a range of options that varies with the tagged text or cell. Many of these options involve Outlook.

The action that helps create an Outlook appointment from a date in a Word document is a perfect example of Outlook working with another Office system application. Let's walk through that one.

Assuming that your copy of Word 2007 is configured with Smart Tags activated (more on this in the next section), whenever you type a date into a document, Word associates a Smart Tag with that date. If you point at the date with the mouse, the Smart Tag Actions button appears. If you then point to the icon and click the down arrow that appears, you will see a menu similar to the one in the illustration. If you look at the second and third options in that menu, you can see two ways that the Smart Tag Actions button causes Word to interact with Outlook.

The Schedule a Meeting option opens a Meeting window, with the start and end dates automatically filled in with the dates associated with the Smart Tag. While you still have to fill in all the rest of the information yourself, using the Smart Tag to get the meeting request started is certainly easier than doing it manually.

The Show My Calendar option opens Outlook in Calendar view and displays your calendar for the particular date associated with the Smart Tag. This is a nice convenience if you want to check your calendar for the day you're writing about.

Activate Smart Tags in an Office System Application

Smart Tags can help you use other Office system applications with Outlook, but they may not be activated for each of the Office system applications you use. The way you activate Smart Tags varies from one Office system application to another. The one commonality is that you configure Smart Tags from the AutoCorrect Options dialog box of any application. If you want to activate the Smart Tags for a particular application, here's how I suggest you go about it:

1. Open the help system of the application for which you want to activate Smart Tags.

2. Search for the term AutoCorrect.

3. Follow the directions in the help system to get to the AutoCorrect options dialog box, shown here.

16

4. In the AutoCorrect options dialog box, click the Smart Tags tab.

5. Set the Label Text with Smart Tags option.

6. Under Recognizers, select the types of things you want the application to apply Smart Tags to.

7. Make sure the Show Smart Tags Actions Buttons option is set.

8. Click OK until you get back to the application's main window.

Once you complete this process, Smart Tags should appear in this application, enabling interactions between this and other Office system applications, including Outlook.

Chapter 17

Work with Microsoft Exchange and Windows SharePoint Services

How to…

- Use Outlook with Microsoft Exchange
- Use Outlook with Windows SharePoint Services

Throughout this book, we've looked at Outlook primarily as a standalone application tapping external services such as mail servers, RSS feeds, and instant messaging programs. But especially in a corporate environment, Outlook becomes even more powerful when coupled with Microsoft Exchange and Windows SharePoint Services.

Microsoft Exchange is a corporate messaging and collaboration server. It helps businesses communicate more efficiently by providing consolidated, reliable, manageable, and secure e-mail services as well as hosting public folders and Outlook private folders.

Collaboration and information sharing are a big part of the future of the Microsoft Office system. Windows SharePoint Services provide a central place to access, store, manage, and share information. With Windows SharePoint Services, you can create team websites that serve as the central storage and collaboration area for team resources. With the appropriate permissions, team members can create additional pages within the team site, such as document and picture libraries, lists for contacts and tasks, even discussion boards, online surveys, and web pages. With these tools, the team can build a site that is customized for its needs, providing access to and storage for only the resources the team needs.

Use Outlook with Microsoft Exchange

Using Outlook with Microsoft Exchange is in most ways the same as using it as a standalone application. Here are some of the differences you'll notice:

- Setting up an e-mail account looks different and requires the help of your corporate e-mail administrator. In the vast majority of cases, your e-mail account will be set up for you and all you will need to do is change the password on it.

CAUTION   *Most e-mail administrators take a very dim view of employees making any changes or additions to their e-mail accounts and settings. I strongly recommend that you contact your e-mail administrator before trying to set up an e-mail account on an Microsoft Exchange.*

■ You may have access to a set of *Exchange public folders*. These folders are like your personal folders in Outlook, but the public folders reside on the Exchange server and are meant to be shared among many people.

■ You may be able to use Cached Exchange Mode to facilitate working in Outlook when you're not connected to the Microsoft Exchange server or you have a slow or unreliable connection.

■ You may choose to store some of your Outlook information on your PC or notebook, rather than on the Exchange server.

■ You may have access to an additional address book, the Global Address List (GAL).

■ You can create rules that run on the Exchange server or your PC or notebook.

■ You can use Exchange Unified Messaging.

Setting Up an Exchange E-Mail Account

As mentioned at the beginning of this chapter, the chances are very low that you will need to set up your own corporate Exchange e-mail account. If you are required to do so, the Exchange administrator or IT department will surely provide you with detailed instructions for doing it.

If you are required to set up your own account, be aware that the procedures for doing so in Outlook 2007 differ from those for previous versions. Be sure to use the appropriate instructions.

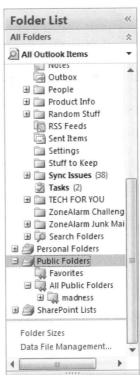

About Exchange Public Folders

Exchange public folders are folders that are accessible to multiple people. Organizations typically set up public folders to share information between members of a project team. If you have been granted permission, you can view or post items in public folders.

If your organization has created a set of public folders, they will be available in the Folders list under the heading Public Folders. If your work requires the use of public folders, the project lead or whoever is responsible for managing the folders will be able to give you more information.

17

NOTE   *I think that the role of Exchange public folders in supporting project teams is being supplanted by Windows SharePoint Services. The new release of SharePoint in particular does most anything public folders can do, plus a whole lot more.*

Use Cached Exchange Mode

Cached Exchange Mode is a feature that requires Outlook to be connected to an Exchange server that is itself configured for this mode of operation. In Cached Exchange Mode, Outlook stores a copy of your Exchange mailbox on your computer. Outlook frequently updates the information in this copy with information taken from the mailbox on the Exchange server so that you have current information to work with.

While Cached Exchange Mode isn't a big benefit if your computer is always connected to Exchange through a standard network connection, it can be extremely useful if you use a laptop or other mobile computer, or if your connection to the Microsoft Exchange server is slow or intermittent (perhaps you use a dial-up modem to connect from home or are connecting through a crowded wireless access point). See the "Did You Know How Cached Exchange Mode Can Improve Your Outlook?" box for more information on how Cached Exchange Mode improves your connection to Outlook under various conditions.

Your e-mail administrator will need to set up your account to work in Cached Exchange Mode. If this was not done before you created your Exchange e-mail account, you'll need to turn on Cached Exchange Mode yourself. Once Cached Exchange Mode is set up, the next time you have a connection to the Exchange server, Outlook will download a copy of your Exchange mailbox to your computer.

TIP   *The next section tells you how to turn on Cached Exchange Mode. You can also follow the procedure to find out whether or not Outlook is running in Cached Exchange Mode. Complete steps 1 through 3 and see whether Use Cached Exchange Mode is set, then click Cancel to exit without making any changes.*

Once Cached Exchange Mode is set up properly, it should be totally transparent to you when you're connected to the same network as the Microsoft Exchange server. When you're using a slow connection to the Exchange server, you should find that Outlook works better than it did before you activated Cached Exchange Mode.

Did you know?

How Cached Exchange Mode Can Improve Your Outlook?

Cached Exchange Mode can greatly improve your Outlook experience if you ever work offline, or if you do not have a solid, fast connection to Microsoft Exchange at all times. Previous versions of Outlook stored all your Exchange data in your Exchange mailbox on the Exchange server. If you lost your connection to Exchange, you were out of luck. You couldn't get to any of your data that was stored on the server, and Outlook often crashed in the attempt to reach it.

As you read earlier in this chapter, Cached Exchange Mode involves storing a copy of your Exchange mailbox on your computer, and frequently updating that mailbox to ensure that you have the latest data to work on. Outlook works with the data in the cache, instead of getting it directly from the Exchange server. This way, if you lose your connection to the Exchange server when you're using Cached Exchange Mode, you see little difference. You won't be able to send e-mail until you have a connection again, and you won't receive any messages or meeting notices or anything else, but at least you'll be able to work with the Outlook items that were available at the instant you lost the connection.

But Cached Exchange Mode does more than that to improve Outlook performance. Outlook can automatically determine the speed of its connection to the Exchange server. It uses that information to decide what information to update in the local copy of your mailbox and the copy on the Exchange server. If you have a fast connection to the server, Outlook updates entire items. If you have a slow connection to the server, Outlook may update only headers. If you open an item that consists only of the header, Outlook can then download the rest of the item from the Exchange server (assuming you have a connection at the time). This kind of optimization allows Outlook to make efficient use of the available connection to the Exchange server, while still providing you with access to your Outlook items.

If you have no connection to the Exchange Server, you can still read and reply to messages, create new items, delete old ones, and so on. What happens when you have a connection again is that Outlook synchronizes the data in your computer's copy of the mailbox with the data in Exchange's copy of the mailbox. This resolves any discrepancies between the two mailboxes. Outlook does this synchronization in the background, and you can continue working while synchronization is taking place.

17

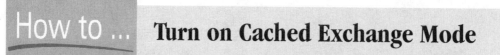

How to ... Turn on Cached Exchange Mode

Once your administrator sets up your Exchange e-mail account to work in Cached Exchange Mode, you may need to turn on Cached Exchange Mode in Outlook. If so, follow these steps:

1. In the Outlook main window, click Tools | Account Settings to open the E-mail Accounts dialog box shown in Figure 17-1.

2. On the E-Mail tab, select your Exchange e-mail account and click Change.

3. In the Microsoft Exchange Server section of the Change E-Mail Account dialog box, set the Use Cached Exchange Mode check box.

Change E-mail Account

Microsoft Exchange Settings
You can enter the required information to connect to Microsoft Exchange.

Type the name of your Microsoft Exchange server. For information, see your system administrator.

Microsoft Exchange server: snshbea100.4smartphone.snx

☑ Use Cached Exchange Mode

Type the name of the mailbox set up for you by your administrator. The mailbox name is usually your user name.

User Name: Bill Mann   Check Name

More Settings ...

< Back   Next >   Cancel

4. Click Next and then Finish to complete the change.

5. Exit Outlook and restart it for the change to take effect.

The E-mail Accounts dialog box is where you manage all your accounts.

And if you're using Outlook without any connection to the Microsoft Exchange server, the fact that you're able to work almost as well as if you were still connected should be a great improvement.

Store Information Locally

As we've just discussed, when you use Cached Exchange Mode, Outlook stores a copy of all your data on your hard drive. But that's just so you have it accessible to work on, regardless of the state of your connection to the Exchange server. What I want to talk about here is different.

17

Most organizations put some sort of limits on the amount of Outlook data each user can store on the Exchange server. Given the price of disk storage these days, the amount of information you can store on the server is typically large, but it isn't infinite. So what do you do when you have more Outlook data than you are allowed to store on the Exchange server? You could go through all your stuff, print old messages you want to keep, delete the least important items, fun things like that. Or you could archive old data to get it out of the way but still have it accessible.

NOTE   *Chapter 13 talks about archiving your data.*

As another alternative, you can create a Personal Folders file that sits on your hard drive, and store some of your stuff there. By moving items from the folders on the Exchange server into the Personal Folders file, you can avoid hitting the limits while still keeping your stuff in Outlook and accessible.

NOTE   *You can store Personal Folders files wherever you want to on your hard drive, and back them up the same way you would any other file, so you don't have to worry about losing the data stored in them.*

Personal Folders files appear in a separate set of folders in the Folders list. You can work with them as if they were any other folder, run searches that find information stored in them, and so on.

When you create a Personal Folders file, Outlook creates a duplicate of the file structure you have in your Outlook Mailbox, but doesn't put anything in the folders. You move items into (or out of) the folders the same ways you would move them between the folders of the Mailbox. Drag and drop works, and so does right-clicking an item or folder and selecting the Move option in the shortcut menu that appears.

To create a new Personal Folders file you can use to store information locally, follow these instructions:

1. In the Outlook main menu, click File, then Data File Management to open the Data Files tab of the Account Settings dialog box, as shown in Figure 17-2.

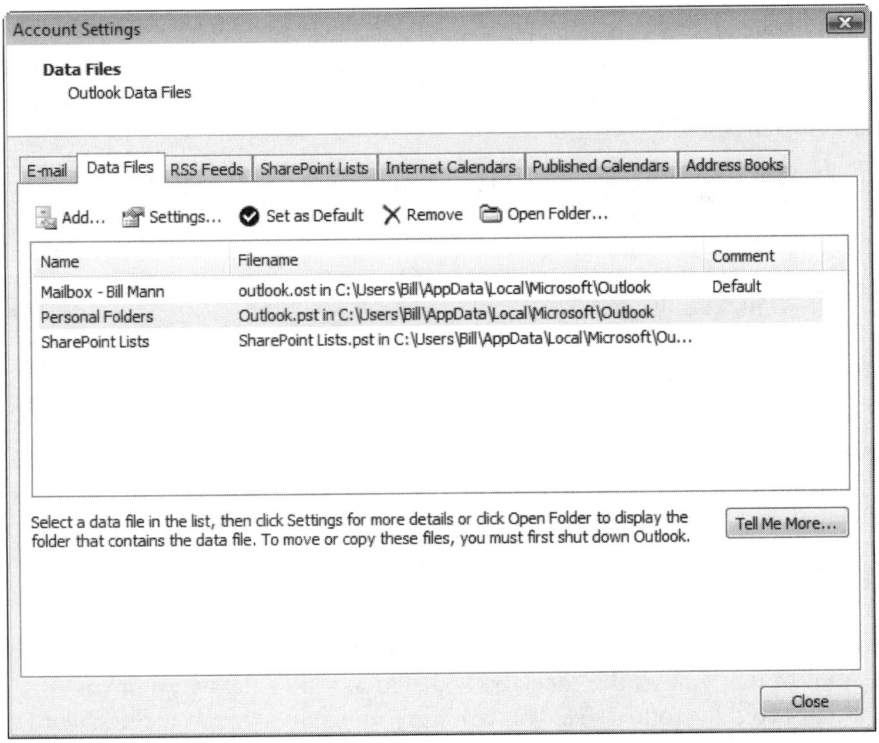

FIGURE 17-2 Manage Personal Folders files and other data files from this tab.

2. Click Add to open the New Outlook Data File dialog box. Under Types of Storage, select Office Outlook Personal Folders File (.pst) to create a standard Outlook 2007 Personal Folders file, then click OK.

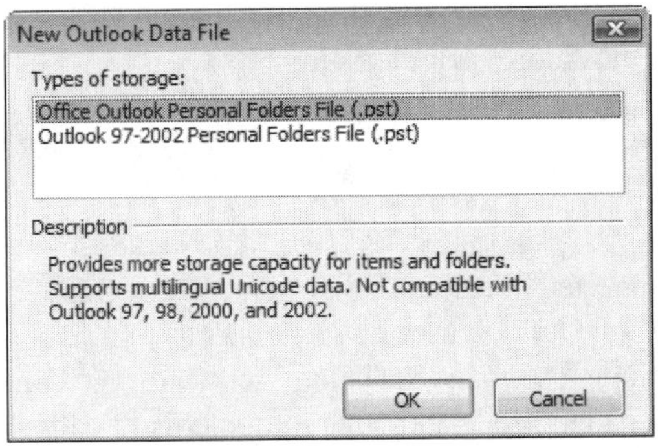

17

3. In the Create or Open Outlook Data File dialog box that appears, enter a file name to use for the new Personal Folders file. Unless you plan on storing it somewhere else as part of a backup strategy or have some other reason to do so, you can leave the rest of the default options for creating the file. Click OK.

4. In the Create Microsoft Personal Folders dialog box that appears, enter a name for the file. This name will be the one you see in the Outlook Files list once the file is created.

5. Optionally, enter a password for this file. If you enter a password, that password is used to keep people from reading the contents of the Personal Folders file from outside your copy of Outlook. If you do enter a password, make sure you set the check box labeled Save this password in your password list; otherwise, you will have to manually enter the password every time Outlook tries to look in the Personal Folders file. Click OK.

6. Outlook creates the new Personal Folders file. It becomes visible on the Data Files tab of the Account Settings dialog box, as well as in Outlook's Folders list.

Access to the Global Address List (GAL)

A *Global Address List* (GAL) is an address book that is shared among all employees connected to Exchange. If your organization uses one, it will appear in Outlook as one of the options in the Address Book dialog box.

TIP   *Use the CTRL-SHIFT-B keyboard shortcut to open the Address Book dialog box.*

When you are connected to the Exchange server through the corporate network, the GAL is available and Outlook uses it when it needs to find address information for someone you are sending a message to. Things get a bit more complicated when you are using Cached Exchange Mode and your computer isn't connected to the network.

In this case, Outlook can use something called an *offline address book,* which is a snapshot of the basic information in the GAL. The offline address book makes it possible for you to work with contacts that are stored in the GAL without having direct access to the Exchange server.

Use the Offline Address Book in Cached Exchange Mode

You get to choose whether Outlook uses an offline address book when it is running in Cached Exchange Mode. I strongly recommend you do so, as having the ability to address messages when Outlook doesn't have a full connection to Exchange is very helpful.

Follow these steps to have Outlook download the offline address book so you can use it in Cached Exchange Mode:

1. In the main Outlook menu, click Tools, then Send/Receive.

2. In the Send/Receive menu that appears, click Send/Receive Settings.

3. In the menu that appears next, click Define Send/Receive Groups to open the Send/Receive Groups dialog box.

4. Select the Send/Receive group that contains your Exchange account. In most cases this is the All Accounts group. Click Edit to open the Send/Receive Settings dialog box for that group. It will look something like the following illustration:

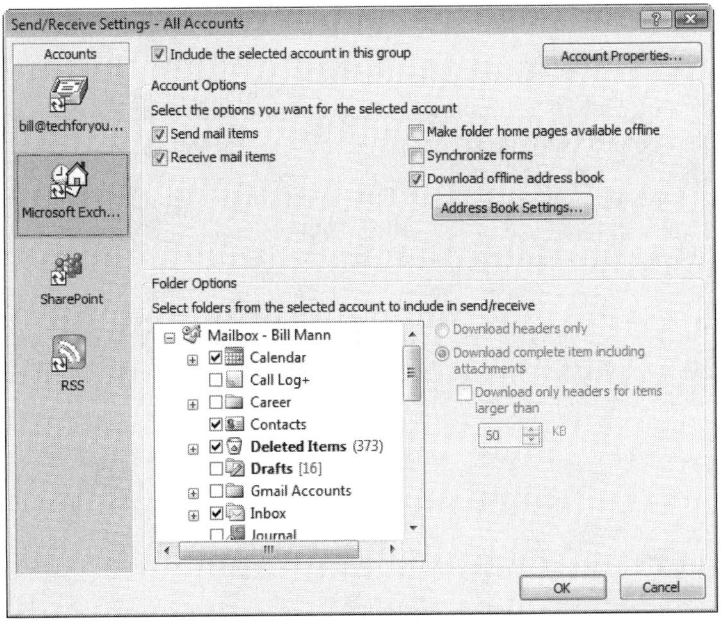

17

FIGURE 17-3   Control whether or not the offline address book gets downloaded in Cached Exchange Mode

5. Select your Exchange account in the Accounts list on the left side of the dialog box.

6. Set the Download Offline Address Book check box.

7. Click Address Book Settings to open the Offline Address Book dialog box shown in Figure 17-3.

8. Select Full Details to minimize the amount of time Outlook is unresponsive while it connects to the server to get more information.

9. Click OK, then OK, and then Close to return to the main Outlook window. Outlook will have use of the offline address book in Cached Exchange Mode from now on.

NOTE   *If Outlook is continuously connected to Exchange while in Cached Exchange Mode, it will update the offline address book once a day or so to keep the information in it current.*

Local and Server Rules

When you are connected to Exchange and you create rules, some of them will run on your local copy of Outlook, and some will run on the Exchange server. One advantage of *server-based rules* is that they will run whether Outlook is running or not. Another is that you don't need to recreate them on every one of your computers if you have, say, a desktop machine and a notebook both connected to the same Exchange account.

When you create a rule for an account that uses an Exchange Mailbox, Outlook automatically creates the rule as a server-based rule if possible. To run on the server, a rule must be applied when a message arrives in the Inbox, and it must be possible to execute it totally on the server. For example, a rule that moves a message to a folder in a Personal Folders file on your desktop computer cannot run when your desktop computer is turned off, so it can't be a server-based rule. Similarly, rules that involve making a sound when a message arrives, or printing the message can't be server-based rules since they require access to resources that aren't part of Exchange.

If you create a rule that cannot run on the Exchange server, Outlook displays a dialog box similar to the following one that lets you know the rule is client-based. The dialog box also gives you the option to run the rule now on the messages that are in the Inbox.

NOTE   *If you want to use a client-only rule on each of your computers, you will have to manually create it on each of those computers.*

Take Advantage of Exchange Unified Messaging

17

Exchange Unified Messaging is a feature of Microsoft Exchange 2007 that allows you to receive voice mail from your corporate phone system in your Outlook Inbox. If your corporation is using this capability, Outlook will have some additional controls that work with it. In particular, the Options dialog box will include a Voice Mail tab, where you can configure this feature.

Voice mail messages look much like regular e-mail, but they include controls that allow you to listen to your voice mail directly on your computer, or to play the voice message on a telephone.

If your organization is using Exchange Unified Messaging, you will receive more detailed instructions for its use from your IT department or your Exchange administrator.

Use Outlook with Windows SharePoint Services 3.0

Using Outlook with Windows SharePoint Services depends on the availability of team websites. These are typically set up by an administrator who then invites team members to join the team sites. SharePoint team sites can also include subsites that hold information related to specific meetings.

TIP

See the "Did You Know How to Get SharePoint Services for Your Organization" box for information on how you can get SharePoint Services for your organization.

Did you know?

How to Get SharePoint Services for Your Organization

To get the benefits of Windows SharePoint Services, your organization can install Microsoft Office SharePoint Server 2007. The SharePoint Server makes it possible to create and manage Windows SharePoint Services throughout the enterprise, making them available on your corporate intranet or the Web.

You can also license the Windows SharePoint Services through Microsoft Certified Application Service Providers (ASPs) such as eInfoSystems.net and Apptix.net.

In other words, a team site is a place where team members can share SharePoint features (also called *SharePoint lists*) such as announcements and event notifications, documents, contacts, tasks, discussions, RSS feeds, and more. Figure 17-4 shows a SharePoint Services team site I set up for this book. You can manage and work in a team site with nothing more than your web browser.

All this SharePoint stuff is cool and clearly has value for teams that must collaborate online, and you are probably wondering what it has to do with Outlook.

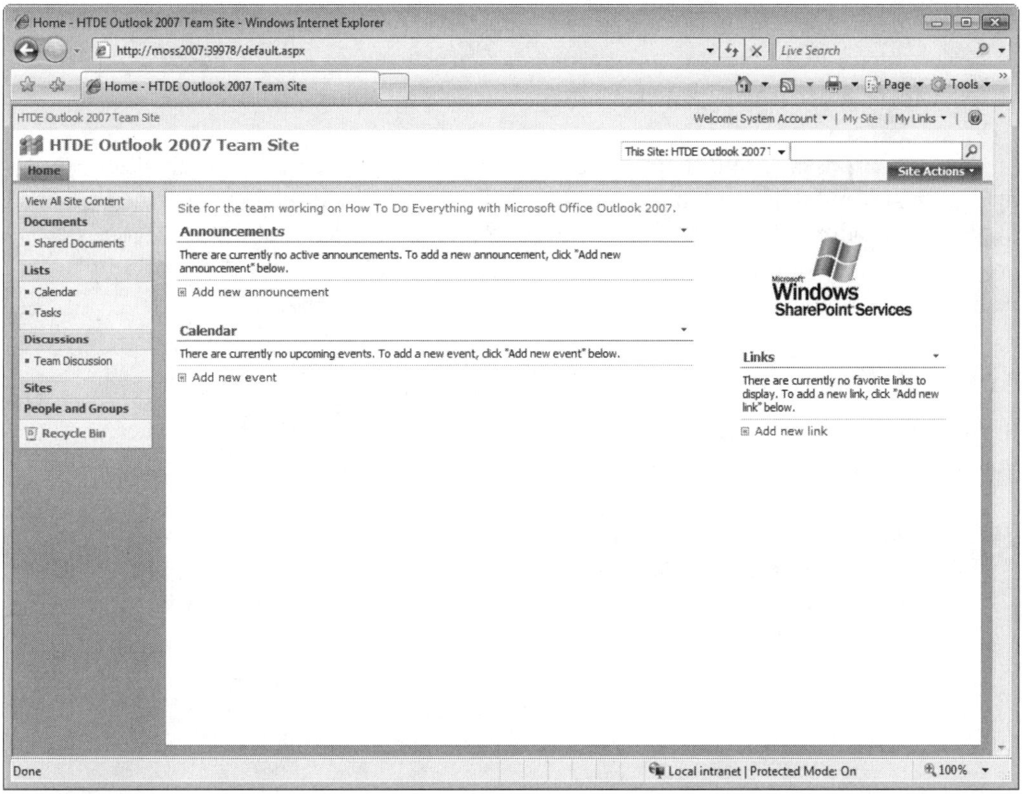

FIGURE 17-4   A SharePoint Services team site created for this book.

17

Outlook 2007 is well integrated with Windows SharePoint Services. That integration means you synchronize these SharePoint features with Outlook:

- SharePoint calendars with Outlook calendars
- SharePoint contact lists with Outlook contacts
- SharePoint task lists with Outlook tasks
- SharePoint discussion boards with Outlook folders
- SharePoint document libraries with Outlook folders

TIP *When a SharePoint feature is synchronized (or shared) with Outlook, changes to the feature on either end get synchronized when Outlook does the next Send/Receive operation.*

For the purposes of this chapter, we will assume that someone has already set up a team site and that you have joined the site by following directions provided to you by the administrator. Once you have the preliminaries out of the way, you are ready to start connecting Outlook to the team site. Let's see how this works by walking through the process with a calendar.

Share a Team Site Calendar with Outlook

If you have access to a team calendar, you can make it visible in Outlook, where you can treat it like any other calendar. To set this up, follow these steps:

NOTE *What you can do with a team calendar is governed by the permissions you have been granted on the team site. Sharing like this is a different way to work with the team calendar. It doesn't give you new or different permissions for that calendar.*

1. On the computer that contains the copy of Outlook you want to link to the team calendar, use Internet Explorer to open the team site.

2. Navigate to the page for the calendar you want to work with.

3. Click Actions. On the menu that appears, click Connect to Outlook.

4. A security dialog box may appear, warning you that the website wants to open web content on your computer using Outlook. This is exactly what you are trying to make happen, so click Allow.

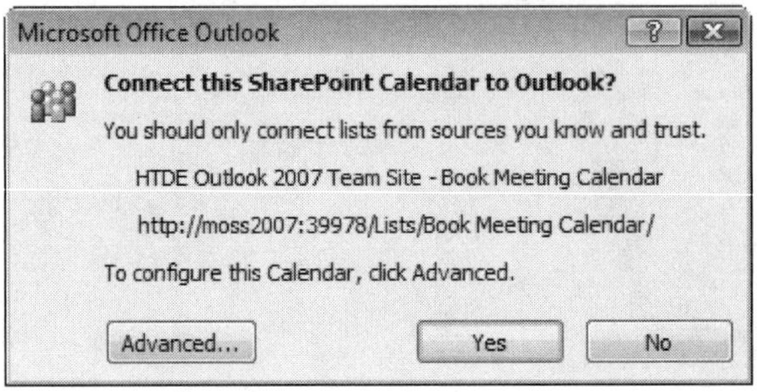

FIGURE 17-5 Connect SharePoint to Outlook, and tweak the setting if necessary.

5. The dialog box shown in Figure 17-5 appears, asking if you want to connect this SharePoint calendar to Outlook. To create the connection using default settings, click Yes. To adjust the connection settings first, click Advanced to open the SharePoint List Options dialog box, make any changes necessary, click OK in this dialog box, and then click Yes in the dialog box from Figure 17-5.

6. Once the connection is complete and SharePoint and Outlook begin sharing the calendar, it appears in the Outlook Calendar pane under the Other Calendars heading like any other calendar Outlook can see. Figure 17-6 shows a local Outlook calendar (on the left) side by side with a team site calendar (on the right).

Work with Shared Calendars

Once you have access to a calendar on the team site, you can work with it as if it were one of your own calendars (within the limits of the access permissions assigned to you). You can create new items in the team calendar, or share items between the various calendars.

If you are going to share items between calendars, the easiest way is to view them side by side and simply drag items back and forth between the two. Whenever you move an item from Outlook to the team site in this manner, you will see a dialog box describing what happens if the item you are copying from

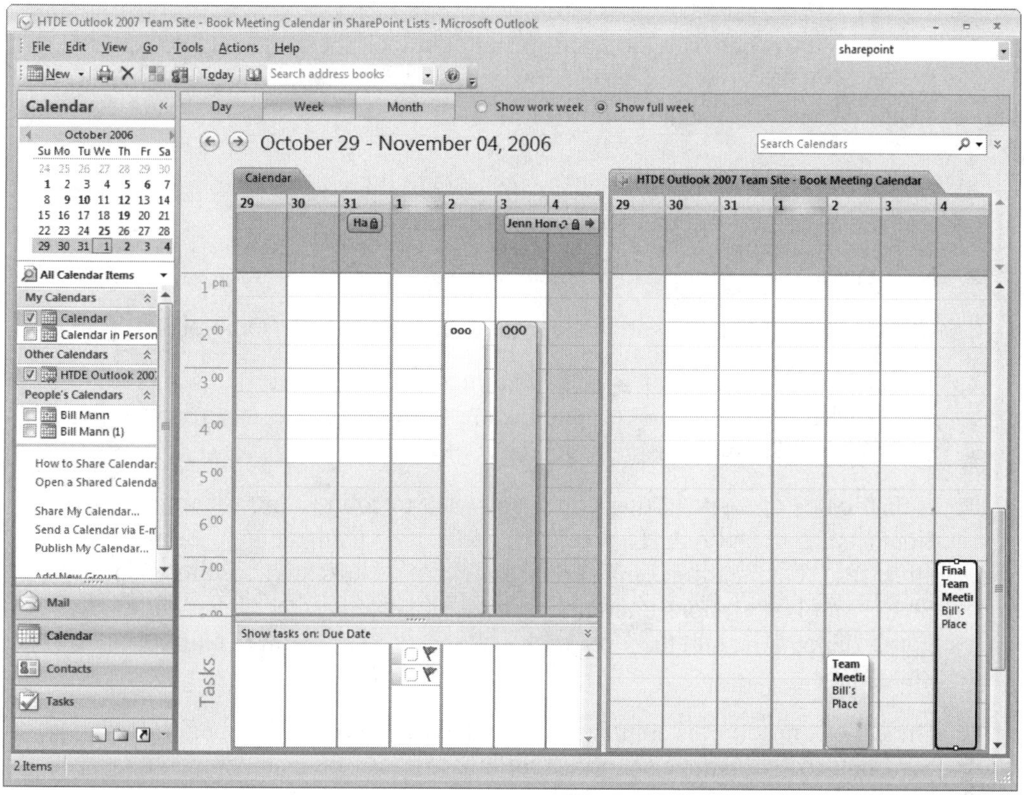

FIGURE 17-6   Viewing both a local Outlook calendar and a team site calendar in Outlook.

Outlook contains content that is incompatible with the SharePoint list (the team calendar in this case) you are adding the content to. It is nothing to worry about.

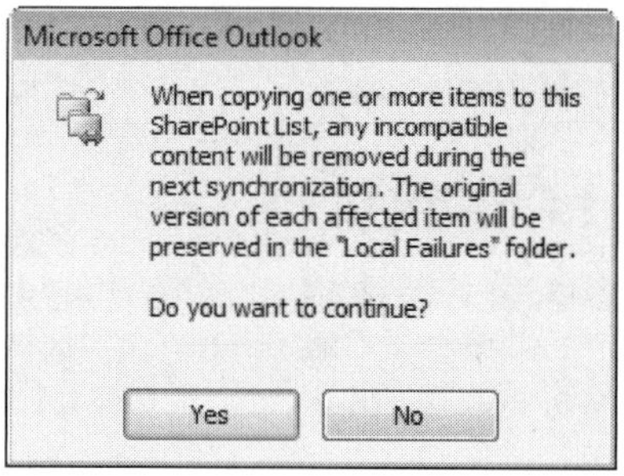

Share Contacts Between a Team Site and Outlook

You can share contacts between the team site and Outlook the same way you share a calendar, and you can copy and paste between the two as well. To share contacts between Outlook and a team site, follow these steps:

1. On the computer that contains the copy of Outlook you want to link to the team contacts, use Internet Explorer to open the team site.

2. Navigate to the page for the contacts you want to work with.

3. Click Actions. On the menu that appears, click Connect to Outlook.

4. A security dialog box may appear, warning you that the website wants to open web content on your computer using Outlook. This is exactly what you are trying to make happen, so click Allow.

5. A dialog box appears, asking you if you want to connect this SharePoint Contacts list to Outlook. To create the connection using default settings, click Yes. To adjust the connection settings first, click Advanced to open the SharePoint List Options dialog box, make any changes necessary, click OK in this dialog box, and then Yes in the "Connect SharePoint to Outlook" dialog box.

6. Once the connection is complete and SharePoint and Outlook begin sharing the Contacts list, it appears in the Outlook Contacts pane under the Other Contacts heading, like any other contacts folder Outlook can see.

NOTE   *As you've seen if you've followed along with the calendar and contacts examples, there is a recurring pattern to working with Outlook and SharePoint team sites and the lists they contain. At the beginning, you go onto the team site using your browser and set up the connection. Once you set things up, the lists function much the same as their Outlook counterparts and you can work with them as if they were local folders instead of lists on the team site.*

Work with Shared Contacts

Working with shared contacts is like working with shared calendars. Within the limits of your permission to change the team site Contacts list, you can copy and paste items between the two, edit them, delete them, and so on.

The one thing you need to remember is that the synchronization between Outlook and the team site occurs when Outlook does a Send/Receive, so it isn't instantaneous. Also, the SharePoint server may need a few minutes to digest any changes and get them posted to the team site, so if your changes don't appear online right away, check back in a little while.

Sharing and Working with Other Team Site Lists

Now that you've seen how shared calendars and contacts work, you will have no trouble working with shared tasks. They work just like calendars and contacts.

Once we get past the terminology, working with discussion boards and document libraries is also simple. When you share a team site discussion board with Outlook, that board appears in Outlook's Mail pane and Folder Lists as a *Mail and Post Items* folder. This kind of folder allows people to post short documents directly into it. Figure 17-7 shows what this looks like in Outlook.

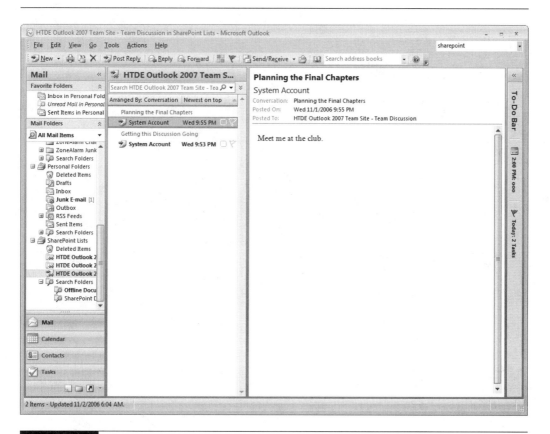

FIGURE 17-7   A team site discussion board as it appears in Outlook.

As you can see in the figure, you can view the contents of an item posted to the discussion board in the Reading pane as if it were a mail message or an RSS item. You can also double-click a posted item to open it in a new window, like the one shown here.

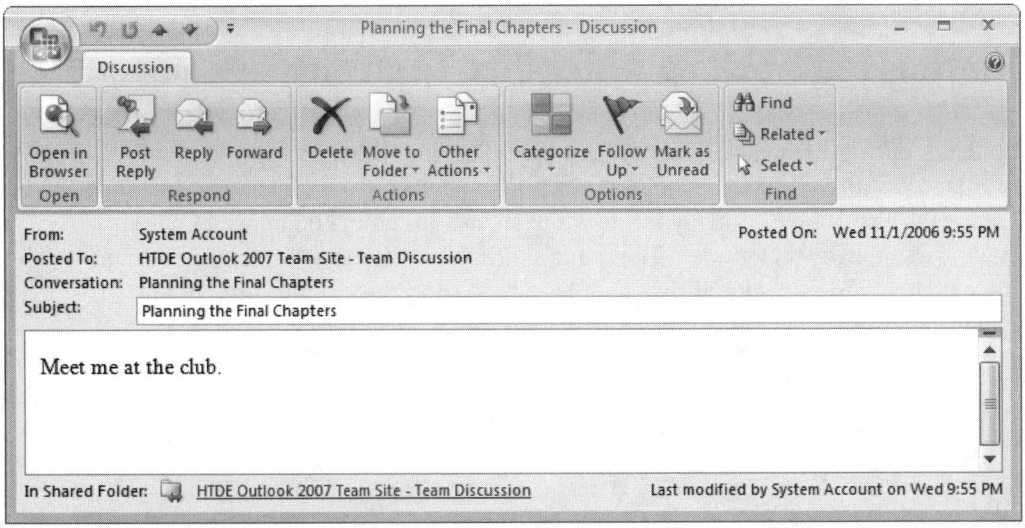

You can make your own posts to the discussion by clicking New, which opens a new Discussion window.

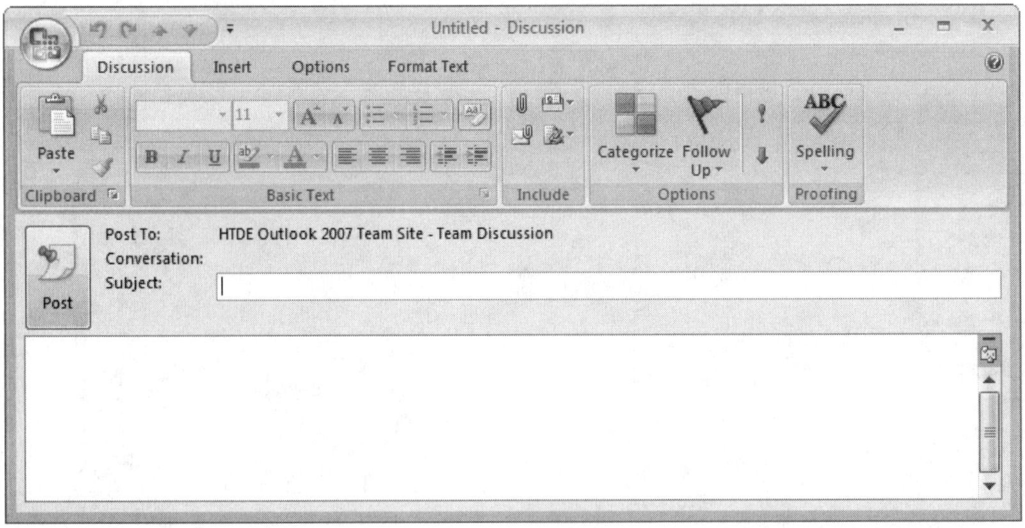

Shared document libraries also use Outlook Mail and Post folders. But libraries are places to store content from the team site. They will typically be read-only folders from Outlook's perspective. That means you can't add content to them from within Outlook. You can open them and view what's in them, you just can't add stuff yourself.

Finding Stuff in Shared Lists

Outlook's Instant Search and Advanced Find can both find items that are shared with a team site. All you need to do is make sure that the search includes the shared folders. Instant Search will automatically index any SharePoint lists that you are sharing so that's taken care of for you. Remember these few simple rules and you will have no problems:

- Search All Calendar Items to find items in shared team site calendars.

- Search All Contact Folders to find contacts in shared team site contact lists.

- Include the SharePoint Lists folder in searches for any other shared team site items.

The End

We've done it! We've reached the end of the book (well, aside from assorted appendixes and the like). We've been exploring Outlook 2007 together now for 17 chapters and hundreds of pages. We've covered everything you need to know to get up and running with Outlook 2007. I hope you've found this book to be full of useful information and at least a little bit of fun to read.

So what happens next? I have some ideas for you:

1. I suggest your next step is to check out the appendixes to this book for some useful information that didn't fit well into the main body.

2. Put the information in this book to use. Keep it next to your computer and refer to it whenever you aren't sure how to do something, or whenever you have a few minutes free to try out a new feature, or learn a new keyboard shortcut to become a little faster and more efficient in your everyday tasks.

17

3. Visit my Living With Outlook website (http://www.living-with-outlook
.com). The site is full of fun and useful stuff that didn't make it into this
book, from tips and tricks, to free add-ons, to what's new and changed in
the world of Outlook. In my years working with Outlook I've learned that
there are always changes, always new ways to do things, always a work-
around to some problem, and always something to talk about that couldn't,
wouldn't, shouldn't be in a book, but that people should know about. That's
what Living With Outlook is all about. Please come and visit the site,
browse around a bit, and sign up for the RSS feed to keep informed about
the latest changes. I think you will be glad you did.

Part VI

Appendixes

Appendix A

Outlook 2007 Keyboard Shortcuts

How to...

- Use Ribbon-style Keyboard Shortcuts
- Use Old-style Keyboard Shortcuts

While using the mouse to navigate and control Outlook is the easiest way to go, it isn't the fastest. Many of the functions and commands in Outlook have associated keyboard shortcuts, or combinations of keystrokes that replace pointing and clicking. Using keyboard shortcuts is faster than pointing and clicking, assuming there's a shortcut for what you want to do, and you remember it.

If you are an old-time Outlook user, you've probably already memorized a number of the keyboard shortcuts that have been used in the last few versions of Outlook. Early in the development of Outlook 2007, we learned that in places where the Ribbon appeared, the old keyboard shortcuts would be replaced with the new Ribbon-style shortcuts (I'll explain the difference in a bit). That caused quite a bit of upset among those of us who have used Outlook for a while.

Apparently, Microsoft felt our pain. The old-style keyboard shortcuts are back! You can still use the Ribbon shortcuts when the Ribbon is visible, but you can also use the old shortcuts. Within the body of this book, I've mentioned a number of shortcuts. As an additional aid, I've gathered a pretty comprehensive list of keyboard shortcuts in this appendix. Use it as a reference guide and as a tool to help you learn commonly used shortcuts. Be aware that this is not close to a comprehensive list of all the keyboard shortcuts in Outlook 2007. For a comprehensive list, search the help system for the topic Keyboard Shortcut.

NOTE *Many of the keyboard shortcuts described here are common across Office System 2007 applications.*

Ribbon-style Keyboard Shortcuts

With the continuing availability of the old-style keyboard shortcuts, and the addition of the Ribbon, many commands have two keyboard shortcuts associated with them. This can be confusing. On the other hand, every command that appears on the Ribbon has a keyboard shortcut, while not every command has an old-style shortcut.

So, where does this leave us? I think it leaves us with some experimentation to do to find the right balance of old and new shortcuts to use to get the most

FIGURE A-1   The Ribbon in a new Message window.

productivity for ourselves. To support that, in this part of the chapter, we will talk more about how to use the Ribbon-style keyboard shortcuts. After that, I've listed some particularly useful Ribbon-style shortcuts.

How Ribbon-style Keyboard Shortcuts Work

You start to enter a Ribbon-style keyboard shortcut by pressing and releasing the ALT key in any window where the Ribbon appears. When you do this, a set of Key Tip badges appear. These are letters or numbers that appear in boxes on top of specific Ribbon commands. To illustrate, let's walk through an example. Figures A-1 through A-2 walk you through using a Ribbon-style keyboard shortcut to get to the dialog box where you can insert a file in a message.

Pressing and releasing the ALT key triggers the appearance of Key Tip badges. The first set of badges to appear lets you select the tab you want to use on the Ribbon. In this example, we want to attach a file to the message, so I press N to go to the Insert tab on the Ribbon.

Now the badges appear on the commands that are available from the Insert tab. As you can see in Figure A-2, some of the badges here have a single letter in them, while others have two letters. To attach a file, we need to press the letter (or letters) in the badge associated with this command, so we press A, then F.

> NOTE
> *If you are following along with this example on your computer, you will notice that when you press the A key, the badges that don't start with the letter A disappear.*

FIGURE A-2   Pressing N brings us to the Insert tab, where a new set of Key Tip badges appears.

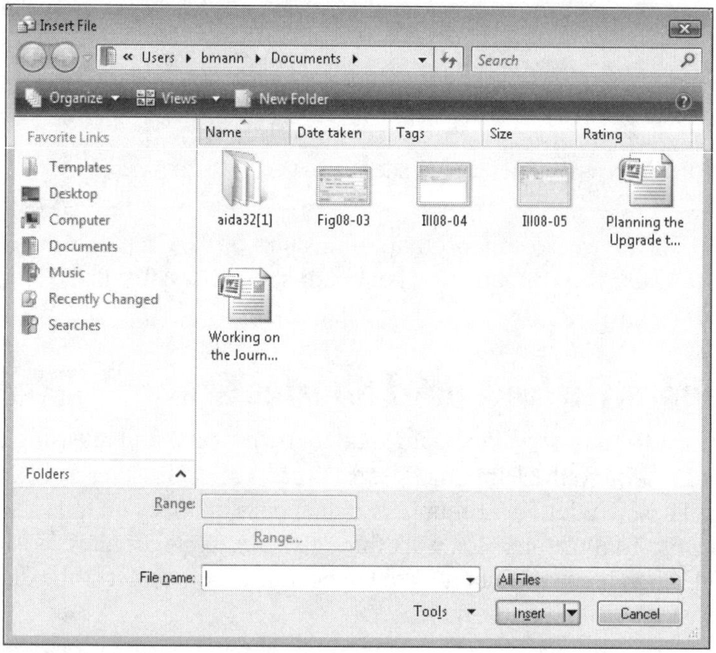

FIGURE A-3   The Insert File dialog box opens when we finish pressing the keys in the shortcut.

As soon as we press the last key in the badge, the associated command starts. In this case, that means opening the Insert File dialog box shown in Figure A-3.

Some Particularly Useful Ribbon-style Shortcuts

While I generally stick to the old-style keyboard shortcuts (they're often shorter than the Ribbon-style equivalents, and many of us have them ingrained into our muscle memory from years of use), there are some Ribbon-style shortcuts that I think you'll definitely want to learn.

Ribbon-style Shortcuts for Editing Text

When you are editing text in messages or Calendar items, or even the Notes field of a contact, the shortcuts in Table A-1 can be very useful.

Action	Keyboard Shortcut
Open Quick Styles	ALT, O, L
Open the Zoom dialog box to zoom in or out on the contents of the text editing area	ALT, O, Q
Increase or decrease the indent level of the selected text	ALT, O, AO (increase) ALT, O, AI (decrease)

TABLE A-1   Ribbon-style Text-editing Shortcuts

Ribbon-style Shortcuts for Working with Messages

When you are working with an open message window, the shortcuts in Table A-2 can be very useful.

Action	Keyboard Shortcut
Insert a business card into the message	ALT, H, AA
Insert a signature into the message	ALT, H, G
Display a menu of Follow Up flags you can apply to the message	ALT, H, W
Choose the format of the message (Plain Text, HTML, or Rich Text)	ALT, P, L (Plain Text) ALT, P, H (HTML) ALT, P, R (Rich Text)

TABLE A-2   Ribbon-style Shortcuts for Messages

Ribbon-style Shortcuts for Working with Contacts

When you are working with an open Contact window, the shortcuts in Table A-3 can be very useful.

Action	Keyboard Shortcut
Request a meeting with a contact	ALT, H, E
Add or edit a contact's business card	ALT, H, B
Show a map of the contact's location	ALT, H, F

TABLE A-3   Contact-specific Ribbon-style Shortcuts

Ribbon-style Shortcuts for Working with Calendar Items

When you are working with an open Calendar item, the shortcuts in Table A-4 can be very useful.

Action	Keyboard Shortcut
Open a menu to set the status of this item (Free, Tentative, Busy, Out of Office)	ALT, H, B
Set the time for a reminder of this item	ALT, H, Q
Open a menu that allows you to categorize the item	ALT, H, G

TABLE A-4   Calendar Item–specific Ribbon-style Shortcuts

Old-style Keyboard Shortcuts

These keyboard shortcuts will be familiar to you if you learned to use shortcuts in previous versions of Outlook.

Help System Keyboard Shortcuts

Help system keyboard shortcuts work across all the applications in Office System 2007. Some of them are specific to the Help window, while others work in the Help window. The keyboard shortcuts in Table A-5 are effective when you are working in the Help window.

Action	Keyboard Shortcut
Select the next item in the Help window	TAB
Select the preceding item in the Help window	SHIFT-TAB
Perform the action for the selected item	ENTER
Scroll forward through the Help window	DOWN ARROW
Scroll backward through the Help window	UP ARROW
Go to the previous page	ALT-LEFT ARROW
Go to the next page	ALT-RIGHT ARROW
Scroll ahead one full window	CTRL-SPACE

TABLE A-5   Help Window Keyboard Shortcuts

General Menu and Toolbar Keyboard Shortcuts

The keyboard shortcuts in Table A-6 apply across the applications in Microsoft Office System 2007. That is, they should work in Word, Excel, and other Office System applications as well as in Outlook.

Action	Keyboard Shortcut
Select or deselect the menu bar or Ribbon	F10
Move to the next item in the selected toolbar or Ribbon	TAB
Move to the preceding item in the selected toolbar	SHIFT-TAB
Select the next toolbar (does not apply to the Ribbon)	CTRL-TAB
Select the preceding toolbar (does not apply to the Ribbon)	CTRL-SHIFT-TAB
Open the selected menu or perform the selected action	ENTER
Display a shortcut menu for the selected item	SHIFT-F10
Display the window shortcut menu	ALT-SPACE
Select the first item in a menu (does not apply to the Ribbon)	HOME
Select the last item in a menu (does not apply to the Ribbon)	END
Close an open menu	ESC
Display all the commands in a menu when some are hidden	CTRL-DOWN ARROW
Display the Windows Start menu	CTRL-ESC

TABLE A-6   General Office System Keyboard Shortcuts

Basic Outlook Navigation Keyboard Shortcuts

The keyboard shortcuts in Table A-7 help you quickly navigate between the sections of Outlook.

Action	Keyboard Shortcut
Switch to the Mail pane	CTRL-1
Switch to the Calendar pane	CTRL-2
Switch to the Contacts pane	CTRL-3
Switch to the Tasks pane	CTRL-4
Switch to the Notes pane	CTRL-5
Switch to the Navigation pane's Folder list	CTRL-6
Switch to the Navigation pane's Shortcuts list	CTRL-7
Switch between panes	F6
Select the next item in the pane	TAB
Open the Go to Folder dialog box	CTRL-Y

TABLE A-7   General Outlook Navigation Keyboard Shortcuts

Item and File Keyboard Shortcuts

These shortcuts speed your work with items and files. Many of them are Outlook-specific, while some will also work in other applications.

Item and File Creation Keyboard Shortcuts

The keyboard shortcuts in Table A-8 let you create new Outlook items or files instantly.

Action	Keyboard Shortcut
Create a new appointment	CTRL-SHIFT-A
Create a new contact	CTRL-SHIFT-C
Create a new distribution list	CTRL-SHIFT-L
Create a new fax	CTRL-SHIFT-X
Create a new folder (within Outlook)	CTRL-SHIFT-E
Create a new journal entry	CTRL-SHIFT-J
Create a new meeting request	CTRL-SHIFT-Q
Create a new message	CTRL-SHIFT-M
Create a new note	CTRL-SHIFT-N
Create a new Office document	CTRL-SHIFT-H
Post an item to the selected folder	CTRL-SHIFT-S
Create a new task	CTRL-SHIFT-K
Create a new task request	CTRL-SHIFT-U

TABLE A-8   Shortcuts for Creating Items and Files in a Flash

Other Item and File Keyboard Shortcuts

The keyboard shortcuts in Table A-9 perform functions on items and files other than creating them.

Action	Keyboard Shortcut
Save the open item	CTRL-S
Save (or Send) and Close	ALT-S
Save As	F12
Undo the last action	CTRL-Z
Delete the selected item	CTRL-D
Print the selected item	CTRL-P
Copy the selected item	CTRL-SHIFT-Y
Move the selected item	CTRL-SHIFT-V
Open the Search toolbar to find particular items	F3
Create a new Search folder	CTRL-SHIFT-P

TABLE A-9   Other Item and File Keyboard Shortcuts

Keyboard Shortcuts for Working with E-Mail

The keyboard shortcuts in Table A-10 can be quite useful and efficient when you're working in a Mail view.

Action	Keyboard Shortcut
Check for valid names in the recipients fields when Word is your e-mail editor	ALT-K
Check the spelling of the message body (cursor must be in the message body for this to work)	F7
Open the Custom dialog box to flag a message	CTRL-SHIFT-G
Add a Quick Flag to the selected message	INSERT
Forward a message	CTRL-F
Send a message	ALT-S
Switch to the Inbox	CTRL-SHIFT-I
Switch to the Outbox	CTRL-SHIFT-O
Reply to a message	CTRL-R
Reply to all recipients of a message	CTRL-SHIFT-R
Post to the selected folder	CTRL-SHIFT-S
Check for new mail	F9
Scroll down through a list of messages	DOWN ARROW
Scroll up through a list of messages	UP ARROW
Mark a message as having been read	CTRL-Q

TABLE A-10   Shortcuts Related to E-Mail

Keyboard Shortcuts for Working with Appointments and Tasks

The keyboard shortcuts in Table A-11 will improve your efficiency when you are working with appointments (including meeting requests) and tasks.

Action	Keyboard Shortcut
Accept a meeting or task request	ALT-C
Decline a meeting or task request	ALT-D
Set the recurrence pattern for an appointment or task	CTRL-G
Go to the next appointment in the Calendar	CTRL-. (PERIOD)
Go to the previous appointment in the Calendar	CTRL-, (COMMA)

TABLE A-11   Shortcuts for Working with Appointments or Tasks

Keyboard Shortcuts for Working with Contacts

The keyboard shortcuts in Table A-12 are useful when working with contacts.

Action	Keyboard Shortcut
Search for a contact	F11
Dial the phone number of the selected contact	CTRL-SHIFT-D
When in an open Contact window, go to the next contact	CTRL-SHIFT-. (PERIOD)
Display e-mail address 1 in an open contact's Internet section	ALT-SHIFT-1
Display e-mail address 2 in an open contact's Internet section	ALT-SHIFT-2
Display e-mail address 3 in an open contact's Internet section	ALT-SHIFT-3

TABLE A-12   Shortcuts to Use when Working with Contacts

Keyboard Shortcuts for Formatting Text

The keyboard shortcuts in Table A-13 are useful for formatting text in Outlook items and also work in other Office system 2007 applications.

Action	Keyboard Shortcut
Open the Format menu or Ribbon	ALT-O
Change the case of selected text	SHIFT-F3
Make the selected text bold	CTRL-B
Turn the selected line of text into a bullet item	CTRL-SHIFT-L
Italicize the selected text	CTRL-I
Increase the indentation of the current line	CTRL-T
Decrease the indentation of the current line	CTRL-SHIFT-T
Left-align the selected text	CTRL-L
Center the selected text	CTRL-E
Right-align the selected text	CTRL-R
Underline the selected text	CTRL-U
Cut the selected text	CTRL-X
Copy the selected text	CTRL-C
Paste the selected text	CTRL-V
Remove all formatting from the selected text	CTRL-SHIFT-Z

TABLE A-13   Keyboard Shortcuts for Formatting Text in Outlook Items

Keyboard Shortcuts for Working with Views

There are quite a few keyboard shortcuts that affect views. In some cases, the same shortcut has different effects, depending on the type of view that's active and whether or not a group is selected.

Keyboard Shortcuts for Working in a Table View

The keyboard shortcuts in Table A-14 work when you are in a Table view.

Action	Keyboard Shortcut
Open the selected item	ENTER
Select all the items in the view	CTRL-A
Select the item at the bottom of the View pane (not necessarily the last item in the view)	PAGE DOWN
Select the item at the top of the View pane (not necessarily the first item in the view)	PAGE UP
Extend the group of selected items by one	SHIFT-DOWN ARROW
Shorten the group of selected items by one	SHIFT-UP ARROW
Go to the next item without extending the list of selected items	CTRL-DOWN ARROW
Go to the preceding item without shortening the list of selected items	CTRL-UP ARROW
Select or deselect the active item	CTRL-SPACE
Open or expand the items in a selected group	ENTER

TABLE A-14   Shortcuts for Working in Table Views

Keyboard Shortcuts for Working in the Day/Week/Month Views

The keyboard shortcuts in Table A-15 are useful when you are working in the Day, Week, and Month views.

Action	Keyboard Shortcut
View multiple days, starting with the selected day	ALT-1 through 9
View 10 days, starting with the selected day	ALT-0
Switch to Week view	ALT-HYPHEN
Switch to Month view	ALT-EQUALS
In Day view, select the time slot that corresponds to the start of your work day	HOME
In Day view, select the time slot that corresponds to the end of your work day	END
In Day view, select the next time block	DOWN ARROW
In Day view, select the preceding time block	UP ARROW
Extend the selected block of time	SHIFT-DOWN ARROW
Shorten the selected block of time	SHIFT-UP ARROW

TABLE A-15   Shortcuts for Working in Day/Week/Month Views

Keyboard Shortcuts for Card Views

The keyboard shortcuts in Table A-16 are helpful for working in Address Card and Business Card views.

Action	Keyboard Shortcut
Select the preceding card	UP ARROW
Select the next card	DOWN ARROW
Select the first card in the list	HOME
Select the last card in the list	END
Go to the preceding page worth of cards	PAGE UP
Go to the following page worth of cards	PAGE DOWN

TABLE A-16   Shortcuts for working with Card views.

Appendix B

Maintain Outlook for Best Performance

How to…

■ Maintain Your Data Files

■ Do Some General Housekeeping

■ Use AutoSave

■ Use Microsoft Office Diagnostics

This appendix describes some maintenance activities you can do to help ensure that Outlook runs quickly and efficiently while consuming a minimum of disk space. Maintaining your data files, repairing them, compacting them, and backing them up is one area where you can do some significant maintenance on your own. But if all your personal folders are stored on the corporate Microsoft Exchange server, you won't have to worry about even these aspects of maintenance.

General housekeeping activities are things that any Outlook user can do, regardless of whether you store your Personal Folders file on your own computer or on the corporate server. None of them will make a major improvement in Outlook performance, but they take only a few minutes and can certainly help. Feel free to pick and choose among the activities.

Maintain Your Data Files

If you are using Outlook in the office and it is connected to a Microsoft Exchange server, your personal folders and items are likely stored on the Exchange server and are nothing you need to worry about. If, however, you're not using Exchange, all the information in your personal folders is likely stored on your hard drive, in a data file called Outlook.pst.

> **NOTE**　*See Chapter 13 for more information on Outlook.pst.*

In this case, you should consider doing some basic maintenance on the Outlook. pst data file. Doing so will ensure that Outlook works as efficiently as possible, and will help protect you against the catastrophic loss of the items stored in your personal folders. I suggest three activities to keep your Personal Folders file in top shape: repairing it when it gets corrupted, compacting it so that Outlook runs more efficiently and uses less disk space, and backing it up so that you can recover from a disaster.

Repair Your Personal Folders File

While it doesn't happen often, it is possible for Outlook.pst to become corrupted. If that happens, you can use the Inbox Repair tool to try and correct the problem. The Inbox Repair tool (Scanpst.exe) can examine Outlook.pst and make repairs to it.

The Inbox Repair tool is automatically installed along with Outlook. To run the Inbox Repair tool, follow these instructions. The procedure is a little bit complicated, but it certainly beats losing all the items in Outlook.pst.

1. Shut down Outlook. You cannot run the Inbox Repair tool successfully if Outlook is running.

2. Run Scanpst.exe by double-clicking its icon. You can normally find Scanpst.exe at C:\Program Files\Microsoft Office\Office12.

3. In the Inbox Repair Tool dialog box (shown next), enter the path to Outlook.pst. See "How to Find Your .PST Files" for tips on finding this.

4. Click Start to begin scanning your data file. Scanpst will run through several phases of checks on the selected file. If problems appear during the scan, the Inbox Repair tool displays a dialog box like the one in the following illustration and prompts you for permission to fix the problems. If you see this dialog box, click Repair.

5. Once the Inbox Repair tool finishes fixing errors, it displays a message box that tells you when the repairs are complete. Click OK to complete the process.

6. Start Outlook using the e-mail profile associated with the data file you're trying to repair. If you haven't created additional e-mail profiles, just start Outlook normally.

7. If the Folder list isn't already visible, click Go | Folder List to open the Folder list (or just use the CTRL-6 keyboard shortcut).

8. Look in the Folder list. You may see a Recovered Personal Folders folder, or a Lost And Found folder. The Recovered Personal Folders folder, if visible, contains default Outlook folders that have been recovered. The Lost And Found folder, if visible, contains any other folders or items that the Inbox Repair tool was able to recover.

9. Move any recovered folders or items to the appropriate locations in the Folder list.

10. Once you have retrieved all the recovered items from them, you can delete the Lost And Found folder and the Recovered Personal Folders folder.

This .PST file is now done. Repeat this process for any other .PST files you have to ensure that they are all cleaned up properly.

> **TIP** *You can have the Inbox Repair tool create a log of its activities by clicking Options and then selecting the options you want in the dialog box that appears. The log file appears in the same location as Outlook.pst.*

Compact Your Personal Folders File

One surprising thing about the way Outlook stores information in data files is that the files don't automatically get smaller when you remove items from them. Without some sort of intervention on your part, your data files will only get bigger and bigger. To squeeze out the unused space in data files, you must manually compact them.

How to ...   **Find Your .PST Files**

Perhaps because Outlook's .PST files are so important and so fundamental to the proper function of the program, Microsoft doesn't leave them sitting out in the open where they are easy to find. They are hidden files, stashed in an out-of-the-way location. Once you make hidden files and folders visible, however, it is much easier to track down your .PST files. The process is a bit weird, but it works. Here's how you find your .PST files to repair them or back them up.

> NOTE *This procedure assumes you are using Windows Vista. If you are using Windows XP, you'll need to modify some of the steps for the way Windows XP searches.*

First, you need to make hidden files and folders visible. You only need to do this once, as running through this procedure makes all hidden files and folders throughout Windows visible until you come back here and make them hidden again. Let's begin:

1. Click the Windows Start button. In the Start menu, click Control Panel.

2. In the left pane of the Control Panel, click Control Panel Home.

3. In the Search box on the Control Panel Home, enter the word **Folder**. This displays several items, including a set of folder options.

4. Under Folder Options, click Show Hidden Files and Folders. This opens a Folder Options dialog box.

5. In the Folder Options dialog box, click the View tab.

6. In the Advanced Settings list, set the Show Hidden Files and Folders option and then click OK.

Now that you can see hidden files and folders, we can easily search for .PST files. Here are the steps to find these elusive files:

1. Click the Windows Start button, then select Search. This opens the Search dialog box.

2. Start by entering ***.pst** into the search box. This tells Windows that you want to find anything that ends in ".pst". Windows will automatically start finding items that match the search term. It will *not* find your .PST files yet.

3. Click the down arrow next to Advanced Search to see advanced search options. Set the Include Non-indexed, Hidden, and System Files (Might Be Slow) check box, and click Search. Windows now expands its search and returns several more files.

4. Look for files with the Type of "Microsoft Office Outlook Personal Folders." Those are your .PST files.

5. Make note of the names of the .PST files and the folders in which those files are located. One gotcha here for users of previous versions of Windows is the way Windows Vista displays the location of the folder. If the search returns a location (in the Folder field) that looks like "Office12 (C:\Program Files\Microsoft Office)" for the file Outlook.pst, the actual path is "C:\Program Files\Microsoft Office\Outlook12\Outlook.pst." I usually need to write all this down before moving to the next step.

> TIP
> *Don't forget that the full name of the .PST file ends in .pst, whether or not the Search dialog box shows that ending. In other words, if this particular search shows that there is a file named Outlook, the full name of the file is actually Outlook.pst.*

6. Close the Search dialog box. You have the information you need to find your .PST files.

How to ...   **Password-Protect Your Data Files**

For additional security, you can apply password protection to your data files. You might want to do this to ensure that people with physical access to your computer can't get at your e-mail just by starting Outlook. When you password-protect Outlook.pst, you need to enter that password before Outlook will display any information. Partway through its startup process, Outlook displays the Personal Folders Password dialog box, where you need to enter the correct password for Outlook.pst to complete the startup.

Follow these instructions to set or change password protection on your data files:

1. Click File | Data File Management. This opens the Outlook Data Files dialog box.

2. In the Data Files list, select the data file you want to password-protect. Select the one named Personal Folders to protect your active Outlook items.

3. Click Settings to open the data file's General Settings dialog box.

4. Click Change Password to open the Change Password dialog box.

5. If the data file is already password-protected, enter the old password as well as the new one. If the data file is not password-protected yet, leave the Old Password field blank.

NOTE   *You can tell your computer to remember your data file passwords by setting the Save This Password In Your Password List check box. But do this only if you have your computer user account password-protected and you log out whenever you're going to be away from your machine.*

While you are working with your .PST files, you might want to password-protect them for additional security. If this sounds interesting to you, read the "How to Password-Protect Your Data Files" sidebar.

Compacting a data file reorganizes the information in it, allowing it to shrink to occupy only the amount of space actually needed for the items it contains. Compacting a data file can take several minutes but can free a lot of disk space and perhaps improve Outlook's performance.

To compact a data file, follow these steps:

1. Click File | Data File Management to open the Outlook Data Files dialog box in Figure B-1. You should see one or more data file names in the list. You can manage all your Outlook data files from this dialog box.

Account Settings

Data Files
Outlook Data Files

E-mail | Data Files | RSS Feeds | SharePoint Lists | Internet Calendars | Published Calendars | Address Books

Add... | Settings... | Set as Default | X Remove | Open Folder...

Name	Filename	Comment
Archive Folders	archive.pst in C:\Users\bmann\AppData\Local\Microsoft\Outlook	
Internet Calendars	Internet Calendar Subscriptions.pst in C:\Users\bmann\AppData...	
Personal Folders	Outlook.pst in C:\Users\bmann\AppData\Local\Microsoft\Outlook	Default
tfy01@hotmail.com	Outltfy01@hotmail.com-00000004.pst in C:\Users\bmann\AppD...	

Select a data file in the list, then click Settings for more details or click Open Folder to display the folder that contains the data file. To move or copy these files, you must first shut down Outlook.

Tell Me More...

Close

FIGURE B-1 Compact and manage Outlook data files using this dialog box.

2. Select the data file you want to compact (Outlook.pst should appear in the list with a name of Personal Folders), then click Settings to open a settings dialog box for that data file.

3. Click Compact Now, and Outlook will squeeze out the wasted space in your data file.

TIP   *I suggest compacting your data files a few times a year, more frequently if your PC is low on disk space.*

Back Up Your Personal Folders File

Backing up your Personal Folders file once in a while is a sensible precaution. While the Inbox Repair tool can fix many problems with Outlook.pst, it isn't foolproof. Considering how much information you're likely to have stored away in your Personal Folders file after a while. Backing it up seems only prudent. Here's how you do it:

1. Figure out where Outlook.pst is stored on your computer. Some of the folders you need to navigate through may be hidden. See the "How to Find Your .PST Files" sidebar for instructions on how to make hidden files and folders visible; then find your .PST files.

2. Once you know where Outlook.pst is stored, navigate to that folder and then shut down Outlook.

3. Using the backup method of your choice, store a copy of Outlook.pst in a safe place. As long as Outlook is closed, you can copy and paste Outlook. pst just like any other file. But you need to pay attention to the size of the file. Outlook.pst can grow to occupy hundreds of megabytes of disk space, making it impractical to back up on floppy disks or other low-capacity storage media.

4. If Outlook.pst is just a bit too big for any of your available backup options, consider compacting it, then trying to back it up again. Depending on a variety of factors, compacting Outlook.pst can significantly reduce its size.

5. Restart Outlook and resume your work.

For more information on backing up your .PST files, and managing your Outlook data in general, visit my Living With Outlook website at http:// www.living-with-outlook.com and check out the Manage Data section of the site.

Do Some General Housekeeping

Throughout this appendix, you've seen various ways to maintain Outlook for best performance. This last section contains a grab bag of additional things you can do to eke out a little more performance and use a little less disk space with Outlook. There's nothing earthshaking here, just a few tips you might want to investigate. The general housekeeping actions are:

- Retrieve deleted items
- Empty the Deleted Items folder
- Empty the Sent Items folder
- Consider removing attachments

Retrieve Deleted Items

Outlook provides two ways to retrieve deleted files, one of which is available for any Outlook user, and one of which works only when you're connected to an Exchange server and the feature has been enabled by the e-mail administrator. I cover the first way here. For more on retrieving deleted items when you're connected to an Exchange server, turn back to Chapter 17.

You can retrieve deleted items from the Outlook Deleted Items folder. This folder will either hold deleted items until you manually empty the Deleted Items folder, or delete them every time you exit Outlook, depending on the options you choose.

> **TIP**
> *See the "Empty the Deleted Items Folder" topic in the next section for instructions on emptying the folder and on configuring Outlook to automatically empty it for you.*

Retrieve a Deleted Item from the Deleted Items Folder

To retrieve one or more items from the Deleted Items folder, follow these steps:

1. In the main Outlook window, click Go | Folder List to open the Folder list (or just use the CTRL-6 keyboard shortcut).

2. In the Navigation pane, click Deleted Items to open the Deleted Items folder. Files that are deleted but can still be retrieved will appear in the folder as shown here. You can instantly retrieve any of these items.

3. Drag the item or items you want to retrieve to the folder you want them in, and you're done.

> **NOTE**
> *You can retrieve deleted tasks that were assigned to someone else, or for which you were receiving status reports, but they will no longer be assigned to the other person and you will no longer receive status reports on them.*

Empty the Deleted Items Folder

Emptying the Deleted Items folder is an easy way to reclaim some disk space. You can do this manually every so often if you like, or you can tell Outlook to empty it for you automatically.

NOTE
Since the contents of the Deleted Items folder are readily accessible from within Outlook, simply deleting a message from your Inbox doesn't do much to prevent others from seeing it. Anyone with access to your computer for even a moment or two can look into your Deleted Items folder and see what's there. If you want to keep casual snoops from seeing your deleted messages, set Outlook to automatically empty the Deleted Items folder and then manually empty it after deleting any particularly interesting messages.

Automatically Empty the Outlook Deleted Items Folder

To set Outlook to empty its Deleted Items folder automatically, follow these steps:

1. In the main Outlook window, click Tools | Options to open the Options dialog box.

2. On the Other tabbed page of the Options dialog box (see the following illustration), set the Empty the Deleted Items Folder Upon Exiting check box. Use this page to tell Outlook to automatically empty its Deleted Items folder whenever you exit the program.

3. Normally, Outlook will notify you before emptying the Deleted Items folder. If you want to eliminate this notification message, click Advanced Options to open the Advanced Options dialog box shown in the following illustration. Clear the Warn Before Permanently Deleting Items check box to eliminate the warning. You can use the Advanced Options dialog box to eliminate the warning that appears before emptying the Deleted Items folder.

Manually Empty the Outlook Deleted Items Folder

To empty the Deleted Items folder yourself, follow these steps:

1. In the main Outlook window, click Go | Folder List to open the Folder list (or use the CTRL-6 keyboard shortcut).

2. In the Folder list, right-click the Deleted Items folder icon, then click Empty "Deleted Items" Folder in the menu that appears.

Empty the Sent Items Folder

By default, Outlook saves a copy of every e-mail message you send, including all those you copy or forward to someone. These copies go in the Sent Items folder. If you send a lot of e-mail, this folder can quickly accumulate hundreds or thousands of copies of old messages. This uses up disk space, makes your old e-mail readily accessible to anyone with physical access to your computer, makes your Personal Folders file bigger and harder to back up, and generally creates unneeded clutter. It makes sense to occasionally clean out your Sent Items folder.

Remove Items from the Sent Items Folder

You can delete all the messages from the Sent Items folder, or pick and choose the ones you want to keep. Sometimes I find it helpful to retain copies of messages I've sent, particularly if they deal with important or controversial topics. But in general, it's easiest just to delete all the messages in the folder every so often.

CAUTION   *Messages you delete from the Sent Items folder do not go into the Deleted Items folder. Instead they are deleted immediately and permanently. So make sure you don't delete a message you may need again.*

Follow these steps to remove items from the Sent Items folder:

1. In the main Outlook window, click Go | Folder List to open the Folder list (or just use the CTRL-6 keyboard shortcut).

2. In the Folder list, click Sent Items to open the Sent Items folder. Copies of the messages you've sent since the last time you emptied the Sent Item folder appear here.

3. Select the messages you want to delete from the Sent Items folder. To delete all the files in the Sent Items folder, click Edit | Select All.

4. Click Delete on the Standard toolbar, or use the CTRL-D keyboard shortcut.

Consider Removing Attachments

When you receive files as attachments, what do you do with them? If there are ones you don't expect, you probably delete them and the message they came in with. But what if they're attachments you do expect? Do you save the attached file and then use it? If so, you end up with multiple copies of the file. One of them is still attached to the e-mail message it arrived on, and the other is wherever you stored it before you started working with it.

If you want to conserve disk space and lessen the chance of confusion between different versions of the attached file, you should remove the attachment after you've saved a copy of it elsewhere on your hard drive. If you want to try this, it's easy. Here's how you do it:

1. Double-click the message containing the attachment you want to remove so that it opens in a separate window.

2. In the message window, right-click the attachment. This opens the shortcut menu shown in the illustration.

3. Click Remove to remove the attachment from the message.

NOTE   *You have one last chance to recover the attachment if you realize you don't want to remove it. Since you opened the message in its own window, that window remains open after you remove the attachment. When you try to close the message Window, Outlook asks you if you want to save the changes (the changes in this case being the removal of the attachment). If you click No, Outlook restores the attachment and closes the window, so you don't lose anything.*

Glossary

Aggregator   A program that reads RSS feeds. Another name for an RSS reader.

Arrangement   A table view of a folder, with the grouping and sorting of the items in the view already defined as part of the arrangement.

Attachment Preview   A feature that gives you a safe, limited view of the contents of a file attached to a message. Attachment Preview only works with certain file types.

Auto Account Setup   A wizard that attempts to connect to existing e-mail accounts and configure Outlook to work with them. When the wizard is able to do its work, this is much faster and easier than configuring an account manually.

AutoPreview   An option that displays the contents of an Outlook item without your having to open the item in a new window.

Cached Exchange Mode   A method for connecting Outlook to an Exchange server that involves keeping a copy of Exchange information on the local computer so Outlook can continue to function when the connection to Exchange is slow or nonexistent.

Certificate Authority   An organization that validates digital IDs (digital certificates).

Client/Server   A system where one computer (the client) gets its information from another computer (the server). When connected to a Microsoft Exchange server, Outlook acts as a client, and the Exchange server is the server.

Color Categories   A way to group items into categories and indicate those groupings by applying colors to items.

Conversation   A group of messages on the same subject is a conversation. It takes the form of an initial message, with replies to that message, and replies to the replies, and so on.

Date Navigator   A small calendar that appears in the To-Do Bar. It displays views of one or more months, with the date bolded for each day that contains a scheduled item. Arrows in the Date Navigator let you change which month (or months) are visible.

Dial-Up   A way of connecting to the Internet using regular phone lines. This method is becoming less and less common as broadband connections such as cable and DSL become widespread.

Digital ID   A security file that can be attached to a message to prove who sent the message (to digitally sign the message) or to scramble it so only the intended recipient can read it (to encrypt the message). Also known as a digital certificate.

Discussion Thread   A series of messages on a particular topic.

Electronic Business Card   Electronic versions of the classic paper business card. Outlook 2007 can display contacts in this form, making them appear like a regular business card on the screen. Electronic business cards can be attached to messages with the information they contain displayed on the screen and added to the appropriate fields in Contacts.

E-mail Postmark   A new technology from Microsoft meant to indicate that a message is unlikely to be spam, while also being difficult for junk e-mailers to apply to the messages they send.

Embedded File   A file that is made a part of an Outlook item. Changes to the original file do not affect the embedded file.

GAL   See Global Address List.

Global Address List   An address book that is available to all the users on an Exchange server. Also known as the GAL.

Hosted Exchange Account   A mailbox on a Microsoft Exchange server that is run and maintained (hosted) by an organization that provides accounts to subscribers.

iCal   A widely supported standard for sharing calendars between programs.

IM   See Instant Messaging.

Info Bar   A bar that appears at the top of the Reading pane or an open message window. Various messages can appear in the Info Bar.

Information Rights Management   Technology that controls how information is used and distributed in Microsoft Office applications.

Instant Messaging (IM)   An instant communication method using typed messages.

Instant Search   A new, fast, indexed search tool that replaces the Find tool from Outlook 2003.

Item   A single chunk of information in Outlook. Messages, contacts, appointments, and notes are items.

Linked File   A file that is connected to an Outlook item, but not part of it. Information from a linked file is visible in the Outlook item, and if the original file changes, those changes are visible in the item linked to the file.

List   When referring to SharePoint Services, a list is comparable to an Outlook folder.

Macro   A set of instructions that can be executed by a program to perform various tasks. Troublemakers sometimes create macros that do harmful things, then try to spread them to innocent people's computers.

Mail and Post Items Folder   A folder that can hold e-mail messages or other documents.

Mail Items   Items that can appear when Outlook is displaying a Mail view.

Microsoft Exchange   An e-mail server that Outlook can work with. When Outlook is connected to Microsoft Exchange, Exchange handles sending and receiving messages for multiple users. Outlook is the client program, acting as your interface to Exchange.

Navigation Pane   The standard location for navigation links and buttons, along with links to additional shared resources. When visible, it is the leftmost pane in most Outlook views.

NetMeeting   A tool for conducting online meetings. Outlook 2007 does not support NetMeeting, whereas previous versions of Outlook did.

Newsgroup   An Internet equivalent of a bulletin board.

Newsreader   A program that lets you read and write newsgroup messages.

News Server   A computer that stores and distributes newsgroup messages.

NNTP   Network News Transport Protocol. A set of rules for sending and receiving newsgroup messages.

Offline   When Outlook is not connected to an e-mail server or not actively communicating, it is offline.

Offline Address Book   A snapshot of the Global Address List that can be stored on the local computer when it is running in Cached Exchange Mode.

Online   When Outlook is connected to an e-mail server and actively communicating, it is online.

PDA   Personal Digital Assistant. An electronic calendar, appointment, note-taking device. There are many types of these available, including smartphones, and most can synchronize data with Outlook.

Personal Digital Assistant   See PDA.

Personal Folders File   A file stored on the local computer, containing a set of Outlook folders corresponding to those in the user's Mailbox. Personal Folders Files have a file extension .pst and can be used as alternate locations to store Outlook items.

Phishing   An attempt to get someone to disclose personal information that can be used for identity theft or other illegitimate purposes.

Presence   An indication of whether someone is available online, or at least whether their IM program is online.

Primary Store   The main file containing your Outlook data.

Print Style   The way Outlook presents information on paper.

PST File   The main type of file Outlook uses to store data. So called because the extension on these files is .pst.

Public Folders   A set of folders on an Exchange server that are available to multiple Outlook users. They are public in that multiple users can have access to them, but they are still only accessible to authorized Exchange users, and not the general public.

Quick Access Toolbar   A small toolbar with common commands that appears on or below the Ribbon.

Reading Pane   A vertically oriented section of the screen where you can read messages like you were reading a column of text from a newspaper or magazine, without having to open a message in a new window. You can control where the Reading pane appears in the Outlook window.

Ribbon   A new user interface element that replaces menus and toolbars in Outlook windows that deal with editing text.

RSS   Really Simple Syndication. A technology for publishing information on the Internet. RSS is quickly replacing older technologies such as Usenet newsgroups.

RSS Feed   A source for articles delivered using RSS. Outlook 2007 has a built-in RSS feed viewer.

RSS Reader   A program used to read RSS feeds. Also known as an aggregator.

Secondary Calendar   Any calendar that Outlook can view that is not the main calendar in the Mailbox.

Send/Receive Group   A group of accounts that all behave the same when it comes to how frequently they check for new mail and how they behave when Outlook is online or offline.

SharePoint Services   A technology that Outlook can work with to gain access to team websites and the resources they contain.

Smartphone   A mobile phone that has computer-like capabilities, usually including the ability to manage personal information such as contacts and a calendar.

Smart Tag   An icon that can appear in items and when clicked, opens special context-sensitive menus and options.

Spam   Junk e-mail.

Synchronize   In the context of this book, to synchronize is to ensure that Outlook and some other program have the same information. Synchronization gets the most current information from Outlook and whatever it is synchronized with, and resolves any conflicts that might exist between them.

Task   A task is a type of Outlook item you track until it is complete.

TaskPad   A small view of your tasks that could be displayed in the Day, Week, and Month views in the Outlook 2003 Calendar. TaskPad has been replaced by the To-Do Bar in Outlook 2007.

To-Do Bar   A single collapsible pane that appears in most views and can display upcoming appointments and tasks. Also includes the Date Navigator for rapid movement between dates.

To-Do Item   Any Outlook item you have marked for follow-up.

Trust Center   A common location for many of the privacy and security features of Outlook and Microsoft Office 2007.

vCard   A widely supported standard for sharing business card information between programs.

View Filter   The way that Outlook causes only certain items to appear.

Web Beacon   A tiny image file included in messages and used by junk mail senders to detect when someone has read a message.

Index

3/07